The
COAST OF MAINE
Book

A Complete Guide

Wading in water off Thomas Point Beach, Brunswick.

THE COAST OF MAINE BOOK

A Complete Guide

Fifth Edition

Nancy English

The Countryman Press
Woodstock, Vermont

On the cover:
Front Cover: *Lobster lines, buoys, traps, and boats; Corea, Maine, July 2000.*
 Photo © Paul Rezendes.
Back cover: Author's photo by Emma English.

THE COAST OF MAINE BOOK: A COMPLETE GUIDE
FIFTH EDITION

ISBN: 1-58157- 058-9
ISSN: 1056-7968 (series)

Editor: Susan Minnich. Managing Editor: Philip Rich. Design and composition: Dianne Pinkowitz. Cover design and composition: Jane McWhorter. Index: Diane Brenner.

Published by Berkshire House, an imprint of The Countryman Press, P.O. Box 748,
 Woodstock, Vermont 05091
Distributed by W.W. Norton & Company Inc., 500 Fifth Avenue, New York, NY 10110

Manufactured in the United States of America

10 9 8 7 6 5 4 3 2

No complimentary meals or lodgings were accepted by the author and reviewers in gathering information for this work.

Berkshire House Publishers'
Great Destinations™ travel guidebook series

Recommended by NATIONAL GEOGRAPHIC TRAVELER and TRAVEL & LEISURE magazines.

. . . a crisp and critical approach, for travelers who want to live like locals.

USA TODAY

Great Destinations™ guidebooks are known for their comprehensive, critical coverage of regions of extraordinary cultural interest and natural beauty. The authors in this series are professional travel writers who have lived for many years in the regions they describe. Each title in this series is continuously updated with each printing, in order to insure accurate and timely information. All of the books contain over 100 photographs and maps.

Neither the publisher, the authors, the reviewers, nor other contributors accept complimentary lodgings, meals, or any other consideration (such as advertising) while gathering information for any book in this series.

Current titles available:

The Adirondack Book
The Berkshire Book
The Charleston, Savannah & Coastal Islands Book
The Chesapeake Bay Book
The Coast of Maine Book
The Finger Lakes Book
The Hamptons Book
The Monterey Bay, Big Sur & Gold Coast Wine Country Book
The Nantucket Book
The Napa & Sonoma Book
The Santa Fe & Taos Book
The Sarasota, Sanibel Island & Naples Book
The Texas Hill Country Book
Touring East Coast Wine Country

If you are traveling to, moving to, residing in, or just interested in any (or all!) of these enchanting regions, a **Great Destinations**™ guidebook is a superior companion. Honest and painstakingly critical, full of information only a local can provide, **Great Destinations**™ guidebooks provide you with all the practical knowledge you need to enjoy the best of each region. Why not own them all?

Acknowledgments

The first four editions of this book were written by Kathryn Buxton and Rick Ackermann. Their research and humor and diligence remains inside this fifth edition the way the earth carries evidence of all its inhabitants. They were ready with new recommendations as well. I want to thank them for breaking ground and list-making and all the many details of their good work.

Elizabeth Edwardsen, whose nature-focused book *The Longstreet Highroad Guide to the Maine Coast* can be found in the bibliography, shared her knowledge of the coastline with generosity and encouragement. She always helped me, whether with names of restaurants, rumors of closings, or the consolation of sturdy friendship, and I am so grateful.

Curtis Rindlaub, whose cruising guides for people lucky enough to visit Maine in their boats are also listed in the bibliography, did a lot of research from his sailboat for this book, and provided many details and some pictures. His wife Carol Cartier assisted in those evaluations and insists you all try XYZ (see the index). His aunt, Anne Dow, aided this book with her own highly qualified restaurant recommendations. I thank the whole adventurous, gourmand family for their help.

Many others had restaurants to extol, and the people who love to eat out are the people who know. Nancy Button, Evelyn Boxley, Marion Baker, Lauri Lundy, Wayne Curtis, and other friends and friends of friends offered recommendations that found their way inside this book, and I remember you, for The Frogwater Café, for The Seaweed Café, and for many wonderful meals. Thank you again, and I wish you all many more good dinners.

I give thanks to my sturdy daughter, Emma, whose restaurant experience is now so broad for someone so young. She grew adept at noting details and was ever eager to try new things, especially dessert.

Susan Minnich did the work of an editor with such calm authority and steady pulse, never showing stress despite the strange convolutions of sentences she had to grapple with. She improved the sense of things in here, and she smoothed out the reorganization of details that required so much attention. Thank you, Susan.

Philip Rich had a skilled hand to guide me through the chapters, as managing editor, and made the enterprise sail smoothly. His gentle voice often assured me that all would be well, and indeed it was. I thank him for his encouragement, and his openness to changes and all the work they involve. He supervised the mapmaking, a wonderful addition.

Contents

INTRODUCTION
Some Essentials Before You Begin
COASTAL GEOGRAPHY & THE BASICS
1

CHAPTER ONE
The Nature of the Coast
HISTORY
13

CHAPTER TWO
How to Get Here and Get Around
TRANSPORTATION
30

CHAPTER THREE
Endless Beaches
KITTERY TO KENNEBUNK
40

CHAPTER FOUR
Our City on the Sea
THE PORTLAND REGION
Biddeford to Freeport
71

CHAPTER FIVE
A Long Reach Into the Sea
BRUNSWICK, BATH
The Harpswells, the Phippsburg & Georgetown Peninsulas
115

CHAPTER SIX
From Crowds to Tranquil Shores
WISCASSET, DAMARISCOTTA
The Boothbay & Pemaquid Peninsulas
134

CHAPTER SEVEN
The Great Bay
WESTERN PENOBSCOT BAY
Waldoboro to Bucksport
155

CHAPTER EIGHT
Studios Among the Granite Hills
THE BLUE HILL PENINSULA & DEER ISLE
195

CHAPTER NINE
Where the Mountains Meet the Sea
**ELLSWORTH TO HANCOCK &
MOUNT DESERT ISLAND**
213

CHAPTER TEN
Blueberry Barrens and the First Sunrise
SCHOODIC & NORTH
245

CHAPTER ELEVEN
Practical Matters
INFORMATION
270

Principal Towns and Communities along the Maine Coast

(SEE REGIONAL MAPS FOR FURTHER DETAIL)

Kittery to Kennebunk
Cape Arundal
Cape Neddick
Cape Porpoise
Kennebunk
Kennebunkport
Kittery
Kittery Point
Ogunquit
Wells
York Beach
York Harbor
York Village

Portland Region
Biddeford
Cape Elizabeth
Chebeague Island
Freeport
Old Orchard Beach
Portland
Saco
Scarborough
South Freeport

Brunswick to Bath
Arrowsic
Bailey Island
Bath
Brunswick
Cundy's Harbor
Five Islands
Georgetown Island
Harpswells
Marrtown

Orrs Island
Phippsburg peninsula
Robinhood
Sebasco Estates
Sebascodegen Island
Westport Island

Wiscasset to Pemaquid
Boothbay Harbor
Bristol
Camden
Christmas Cove
Damariscotta
Damariscove Island
East Boothbay
New Harbor
Newagen
Newcastle
Ocean Point
Pemaquid Point/Pemaquid Light
Rockland
Round Pond
Southport Island

Western Penobscot Bay
Belfast
Cushing
Friendship
Hatchet Cove
Islesboro
Lincolnville Beach
Matinicus
Monhegan Island
North Haven
North Haven Island

Port Clyde
Pulpit Harbor
Rockland
Rockport
Searsport
Tenant's Harbor
Thomaston
Vinalhaven
Waldoboro

**Blue Hill Peninsula & Deer
   Island**
Blue Hill
Brooklin
Brooksville
Cape Rosier
Castine
Deer Isle
East Orland
Isle au Haut
Little Deer Isle
Stonington
Sunset

Ellsworth to Acadia
Acadia National Park
Bar Harbor

Bass Harbor
Hancock
Hancock Point
Hulls Cove
Isleford
Little Cranberry Island
Manset
Mount Desert Island
Northeast Harbor
Otter Creek
Southwest Harbor
Swans Island

Schoodic & North
Columbia
Corea
Dennysville
Eastport
Jonesport
Lubec
Machias
Machiasport
Prospect Harbor
Steuben
West Gouldsboro
Winter Harbor

The
COAST OF MAINE
Book
A Complete Guide

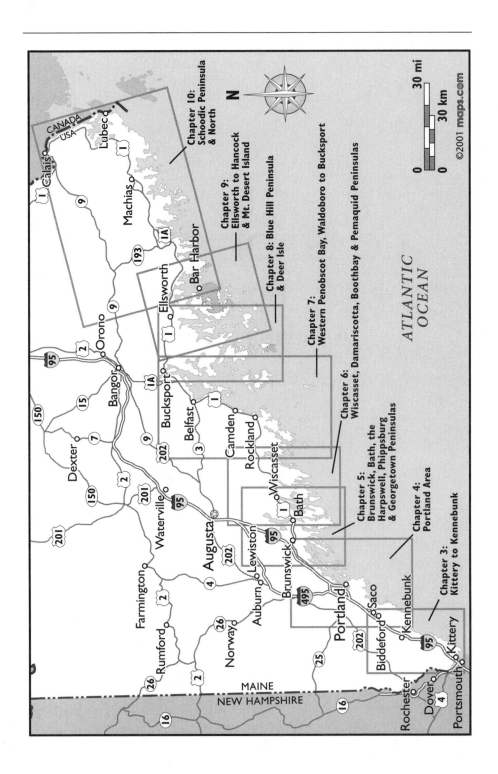

Chapter 10:
Schoodic Peninsula
& North

Chapter 9:
Ellsworth to Hancock
& Mt. Desert Island

Chapter 8: Blue Hill Peninsula
& Deer Isle

Chapter 7:
Western Penobscot Bay, Waldoboro to Bucksport

Chapter 6:
Wiscasset, Damariscotta, Boothbay & Pemaquid Peninsulas

Chapter 5:
Brunswick, Bath, the
Harpswell, Phippsburg
& Georgetown Peninsulas

Chapter 4:
Portland Area

Chapter 3:
Kittery to Kennebunk

ATLANTIC
OCEAN

N

30 mi

0   30 km

©2001 maps.com

CANADA
USA

Calais
Lubec
Machias
Orono
Bangor
Bucksport
Belfast
Camden
Rockland
Wiscasset
Bath
Brunswick
Lewiston
Auburn
Augusta
Waterville
Farmington
Dexter
Rumford
Norway
Saco
Biddeford
Kennebunk
Portland
Kittery
Rochester
Dover
Portsmouth
Ellsworth
Bar Harbor

MAINE
NEW HAMPSHIRE

1
9
193
1A
1
95
2
150
15
7
9
202
3
1
95
201
150
2
201
4
26
2
495
25
202
95
16
4
26
2
16

INTRODUCTION
Some Essentials Before You Begin
COASTAL GEOGRAPHY & THE BASICS

Herb Swanson

A view of Camden Harbor from Mount Battie.

The first thing to understand is the lay of this land. Imagine a necklace: at each end the chain stretches out bare of ornament, but through the long middle length of it, jewels hang like pendants from little chains attached to the main necklace. The coast of Maine is roughly like this, with Route 1 running the length of it, and many long peninsulas stretching south of the highway with jewels like Deer Isle and Mount Desert at their end. It is distressing to drive south on one of these narrow fingers of land for an hour and then learn the place you wanted to go, while visible across a channel a 15-minute boat ride away, can't be reached in your car without driving back to Route 1 and back south again down a different peninsula.

But if this makes a risk for a road trip, it also leads to delight. There are so many of these little peninsulas that you can adventure south and discover wonderful, quiet harbors, like Corea Point, where Maine writer Louise Dickenson Rich spent time and wrote, or find yourself in the middle of a blueberry field and the top of a trail in a wildlife refuge called Petit Manan, in Steuben, that you might have all to yourself even in the beginning of August.

THE WAY THIS BOOK WORKS

Chapters One, Two, and Eleven (*History, Transportation,* and *Information*) offer information that will be useful to you wherever you are planning to travel. The areas covered in Chapters Three to Ten are organized around the necklace metaphor: by the peninsulas and islands and around the bays that make up the coast; each chapter covers one region. Be sure to look at the map facing page one to help understand the geographic relationships between the different areas. Many join along the chain of the necklace, Rte. 1.

Chapters Three through Ten are divided into five sections: **Lodging, Dining, Culture, Recreation,** and **Shopping**. Specific venues are listed under each of those sections, grouped by area. Yet, much overlaps along the coast. To avoid repeating ourselves in every chapter, some information that can be generalized follows. Whatever other questions you may have, the best sources for year-round tourist information are the Maine Tourism Association (207-623-00363 or 800-633-9395; www.visitmaine.com; metainfo@mainetourism.com) and the various chambers of commerce listed in Chapter Eleven, *Information.* Note that Maine has only one area code: 207.

LODGING

Lodging Rates: Everywhere in coastal Maine, rates can vary widely between off-season and in-season, generally increasing close to Memorial Day and peaking from July through the leaf season in mid- to late October. Special packages are often available for two or more nights' stay, and frequently there are even better values during the off-season. If breakfast and/or dinner are included with the price of a room, we do not alter the rate category; we just note that the room rate includes one or more meals.

Inexpensive—Up to $65   Expensive—$125 to $180
Moderate—$65 to $125   Very Expensive—$180 and up

These rates exclude Maine State lodging tax or individual hotel service charges that may be added to your bill.

Credit Cards: Several lodging places we recommend in this book do not take plastic. If they do not, they almost always take personal or travelers' checks. Following are credit card abbreviations:

AE—American Express   DC—Diner's Card
CB—Carte Blanche   MC—MasterCard
D—Discover Card   V—Visa

Minimum Stay: Many inns and B&Bs require a minimum stay of two or more nights during the summer season. We have noted minimum stays when possible, but it's best to check when making room reservations. Many also have policies excluding children of various ages, which are noted in the descriptions here.

Deposit/Cancellation: To reserve a room on the Maine coast, it is generally necessary to make a deposit to cover the first night of your stay—and some places may require up to 50 percent of the cost of the intended stay. Cancellations often must be made at least seven to ten days in advance. Ask about the inn's policy when you make reservations.

Handicap Access: Many of the inns and B&Bs in this book have yet to comply with federal regulations regarding handicap access. We have noted handicap access as available in inns, B&Bs, and hotels where the owners can guarantee at least one room with access.

Other Options: For information on camping see below under **Recreation.**

For alternative listings, you can contact the **Maine Tourism Association** (P.O. Box 2300, Hallowell, ME 04347; 207-623-0363 in Maine; 800-533-9595 out-of-state and Canada; metainfo@mainetourism.com). Every year they publish the *Guide to Inns & Bed & Breakfasts*, a list of inns and B&Bs by region. All of the listings are written and paid for by the owners, so you should take their content with a grain of salt. The Maine Innkeepers Association Food & Lodging Guide, with advertising from hotels, motels and inns throughout the state, is available at most tourist information centers, or from the association (305 Commercial St., Portland, ME 04101; 207-773-7670; www.maineinns.com; info @maineinns.com)

DINING

Dining **Rates**: We've noted the restaurants' serving times and seasons as they were when we made the final survey for this guide. As with all things, times, phone numbers, and sometimes addresses are subject to change according to the changing seasons and demands of the economy. Call first. If you can, make reservations. Things can get busy at all the coastal restaurants, especially during July and August. Many restaurants, even white tablecloth ones, don't take reservations, though. So if you're really hungry, plan to arrive early enough to stake a good place in line.

The price range we list is meant to reflect the cost of a single meal, usually dinner, unless the review talks about breakfast or lunch. What we've tried to represent as a typical meal is an appetizer, entree, dessert, and coffee, although several of the places we review are not appetizer places. We do not include the price of alcohol or other drinks in the estimated cost.

Dining Price Code

Inexpensive—Up to $10	Expensive—$20–30
Moderate—$10–20	Very Expensive—$30 or more

After the restaurant listings, we have included a list of **food purveyors** as well. Some are delicatessens that will sell almost anything to go, others are bakeries or gourmet shops, ethnic food, and beer and wine stores.

CULTURE

It has not been possible to list every historic site or arts organization. There are more than 115 registered museums alone in Maine, and it is estimated there would be more than 300 if you count all the small private collections of painting, sculpture, memorabilia, ephemera, and historical bric-a-brac that are put on display here. The arts thrive in the summer, especially, with crafts fairs, music festivals, and schools. Whatever your interests are—gardening, theater, music, museums, old buildings—be sure to contact the chamber of commerce for the area you will be visiting. See Chapter Eleven, *Information*, for a complete listing.

Wherever you are visiting, if you are a serious history buff and want to do some additional research, check in with the *Maine Historical Society* (207-774-1822; 485 Congress St., Portland 04101; www.mainehistory.org; ncoming@ mainehistory.org); the *Maine Historic Preservation Commission* (207-287-2132; 55 Capital St., 69 State House Station, Augusta 04333-0065; kirk. mohney@state .me.us); or the *Society for the Preservation of New England Antiquities* (603-436-3205; Piscataqua Maine Region, 143 Pleasant St., Portsmouth, NH 03801; www. spnea.org). The last will provide you with a free visitors' guide to their historic homes in Maine if you send a self-addressed, postage paid envelope (you'll need two first-class stamps).

An excellent guide for those embarking on driving survey of coastal architecture is *Maine: A Guide 'Downeast* published in 1970 by the *Maine League of Historical Societies and Museums*. Although the book is out of print, it is available in the Maine collections of most local libraries.

All along the Maine coast there are many **historic buildings**—homes and other sites that date from Maine's earliest days as part of the Massachusetts Bay Colony and are open to the public; many of them are the product of the boom times the maritime industry experienced in the late 18th and early 19th centuries. Be aware that seasons, hours, and admission policies frequently change.

For information on the restoration and preservation of **lighthouses**—symbols of our maritime heritage, contact the *United States Lighthouse Society* (415-362-7255; 244 Kearny St., Fifth Floor, San Francisco, CA 94108; uslthseso@aol.com).

RECREATION

Fun on the coast used to be a one-season affair. Nineteenth-century tourists came here to enjoy cool breezes when cities to the south—Boston, New York, and Philadelphia—sweltered in the summer sun. Today the Maine coast holds plenty of opportunities for pleasure year round. Although most people choose to hike and camp here in the summer, many know to take advantage of the off seasons and avoid the crowds.

Whatever season you visit, remember the weather. The outlook often changes quickly, and the combination of ocean wind and water can make 40 degrees Fahrenheit seem much colder. Bring along a good selection of warm clothes and rain gear. (See **Climate and What to Wear** in Chapter Eleven, *Information*).

Bicycling

First, here's what The Law says:
- You need to have brakes so you can stop within a reasonable distance. (Seems fair.)
- You need a headlamp if you're riding at night; night being that time when cars by law should have their headlights on.
- The headlamp has to produce a white light that someone in front of you can see from at least 200 feet.
- You need a rear red reflector visible from at least 200 feet and reflector strips on your bike pedals and handlebars.
- Helmets are not the law for adult cyclists in Maine (they are for kids). However, we strongly suggest them. Coastal paved roads, dirt roads, and trails open to cyclists are often narrow and winding as they follow the terrain. Traffic at the height of summer can make those byways even more dangerous. Wearing a helmet will help protect you from injury should you hit a bad piece of road or path. It also could save your life should you encounter a car wanting more than its share of the road. We'd also like you to consider that biking — and any other outdoor activity in Maine — requires paying careful attention to weather conditions. Be sure to dress properly. Even if it promised to be a warm day, take along a windbreaker that will help you ward off a sudden damp fog.

Now, here's a roundup of biking on the coast.

There are three highways closed to cyclists: the Maine Turnpike, the interstate highway system, and Rte. 1 between Brunswick and Bath.

Otherwise, go crazy. Great areas to pedal include: the stretch of U.S. Rte. 1 between Belfast and Bucksport which is littered with old sea captains' homes; the perimeter of Megunticook Lake and on to Lincolnville.

Several chambers of commerce offer bike tour maps of their areas; if you want to make your own way, the state publishes excellent, inexpensive highway maps. Write for information from the Maine Department of Transportation, State House Station 16, Augusta, 04333-0016.

DeLorme Mapping Company offers an inexpensive pamphlet titled *Bicycling*. It can be found at bookstores and large supermarkets in the magazine/map/recreation areas. Another excellent guide for cyclers is *25 Bicycle Tours in Maine* by Howard Stone (Back Country Publications, P.O. Box 175, Woodstock, VT 05091). Both books offer excellent maps and directions for touring cyclists.

Maine's **beaches** are the crown jewels of the coast. Almost all are flanked by the rugged terrain that gives the coast its distinct beauty and character—jagged outcroppings of metamorphic rock, sheer cliffs, and exhilarating

Atlantic surf. More than 40 percent of the visitors to the coast make the south coast their destination. Many of these beaches have lovely sandy bottoms perfect for swimming. Non-residents often find the water a little cool.

Wild **berries**, whether blueberries, red or black raspberries, or berries of the cultivated kind, including strawberries, somehow taste better in Maine. Maybe it's because spring here is usually a long, cold, and damp affair. Maybe it's because you get to pick them yourself, sneaking a taste now and then to determine whether the big ones or smaller ones are sweeter this year. Whatever the reason, berry season in Maine is heavenly, beginning with strawberries in late June to early July, and with wild blueberries in late July.

Keeping track of the birds near the lighthouse on Petit Manan, one of the best places in the country to view the European whimbrel.

Tom Hindman

Bird life in the woods, bogs, ponds, open lands, rocks, and beaches of the Maine coast is amazingly rich. Maine is a favored stop for many migrants, both from the north in winter and from the south in summer. If you want to know the latest action on the wing call the Maine Audubon bird alert hotline at 207-781-2332. The hotline operates 24 hours every day.

If you've never watched birds, Maine raises your awareness of them. As your car crosses an inlet or shallow river, your eye is suddenly caught by a four-foot-tall great blue heron—still as a post, ankle deep in running water, coiled to spear his lunch on a six-inch yellow beak. Or on a beach you see a flock of sandpipers do their tiny quickstep all together, slow down to stoop and feed together along the curl of a retreating wave, soar away together with a flash of white along each wing. It's hard to imagine that these tiny creatures may have spent the winter in Palm Beach and have Arctic plans for the summer. Among them may be one with longer legs—a yellowlegs— or higher up the beach, a plumper bird with a reddish back looking under seaweedy pebbles—a ruddy turnstone.

Any birder north of Portland will look for bald eagles nesting. All will want to visit the extraordinary flocks of ocean birds that breed in early summer among the more than 2,000 sheltering islands and the plankton-rich waters fed by the icy Labrador Current. The puffin is the most famous; other notable breeds include buffleheads, grebes, mergansers, loons, black headed gulls, razorbills, black guillemots, arctic terns, and Leach's petrels, hard to spot because they fly at night.

During the 19th century, puffin feathers graced so many heads of fashionable women that these colorful sea birds were almost plucked from the species list. Their eggs were also a favorite meal of gourmands. Also known as sea parrots because of their colorful curled beaks, their population is on the increase with help from their friends at the Audubon Society, which launched a major campaign in 1973 called Project Puffin. The project has been successful to date, although puffins may never reach their pre-1800 population. The society relies on private donations to fund the repopulation. To make one, write to **Project Puffin, National Audubon Society**, HC 60, Box 102-P, Medomak, ME 04551.

The struggle to repopulate puffin colonies off the coast is understandable. Puffins prefer to nest on the remote islands stretching from mid-Maine to Canada. They don't reproduce until after their fifth year, and each mating pair produces only one egg each year. Today puffins flourish to the north in Newfoundland, Iceland, and Britain. In Maine, colonies of the birds nest on Matinicus Island, Machias Seal Island, Eastern Egg Rock in Muscongus Bay, and Seal Island in Penobscot Bay. Early summer is the best time to see them. Some tour boat operators split ticket sales with the National Audubon Society, which watches over these puffin sanctuaries.

For anyone interested in **boating** the coast is a paradise. Excellent guides for pleasure boaters in Maine are *A Cruising Guide to the Maine Coast* by Hank and Jan Taft and Curtis Rindlaub (Diamond Pass Publishing, Inc., Peaks Island, Maine), and *The Maine Coast Guide for Small Boats*, by Curtis Rindlaub (same publisher). Both are packed with charts, tips, and history for those viewing the coast from the water.

Boating on Maine's shore was once exclusively the activity of members of the Abenaki tribe cruising the coast in well-made birch bark canoes. Today few people venture on saltwater in modern fiberglass and aluminum canoes, let alone birch bark. Most recreational boating is now done in sailboats, motor boats, and kayaks. Some will argue that **ferries**—a way of life for many Mainers—are also a form of recreational boating. Windjammers and sightseeing cruises to have their own listings.

The Maine coast is a boater's paradise. These fishing vessels line the Kennebunk River.

Canoeists reign on the small inland waterways, fresh and saltwater ponds, and salt marshes. Extended solo sea kayak trips are not the stuff for amateurs. It's not so much the kayak as the elements that can cause problems. Weather changes quickly, currents and tides can be dangerous and tricky. Knowing how to handle your kayak properly will give you an edge out on the water. You can learn the basics in a couple of hours on a few weekends. You begin with wide, stable kayaks, then you learn how to flip. After a while, it won't feel too tippy. A great reference for kayakers is *Sea Kayaking Along the New England Coast* (AMC Books, $14.95). It contains an excellent roundup of information on everything about coastal kayaking conditions throughout New England, including the *Maine Island Trail*. (See sidebar, in **Boating**, Chapter Six.)

For the sailboat or motorboat cruiser, there are hundreds of deepwater anchorages, beautiful fishing villages, and quaint, albeit sophisticated, towns. Islands make for great side trips. The smallest are great places to anchor and enjoy a swim on a warm summer day and eat lobster on the rocks; the largest offer almost all the amenities of the mainland.

If your visit takes you **camping,** there are hundreds of private and public campgrounds along the coast. Many offer priceless views of the water at campers' prices. Some are no bigger than a modest parking lot. Others are mammoth. If you plan to camp with an RV, be sure to make reservations well in advance. If you plan on tent camping, most of the national and state parks and national forests campgrounds are available on a first-come, first-serve basis, although some advance reservations may be made for National Parks during the summer season.

Because the summer camping season is short in Maine, we recommend calling well ahead for reservations. For a complete list of private campgrounds, contact the *Maine Campground Owners Association* (207-782-5874; www. campmaine.com; info@campmaine.com; 655 Main St., Lewiston 04240). The *Maine Tourism Association* also publishes a statewide travel information planner. Call or write for one (207-623-0363 or 800-533-9595 out-of-state; www. mainetourism.com; metainfo@mainetourism.com; P.O. Box 2300, Hallowell 04347).

If you want to go **fishing** or **clamming** while you're visiting, freshwater fishing licenses may be bought at the *Kittery Trading Post* in Kittery, *L.L. Bean*, and *Peregrine Outfitters* in Freeport, as well as many other Maine sporting goods stores (no licenses are required for saltwater sport fishing). The rate for a one-day license is about the price of a movie. The longer you plan to fish, the cheaper it gets. Junior licenses are available for those ages 12 to 16. For more information call or write the *Department of Inland Fisheries and Wildlife* (207-287-8000; 284 State St., 41 State House Station, Augusta 04333). They also can give you dates for the freshwater fishing season and send maps showing waters open and restricted to fishing. People have fished in Maine's waters since before recorded history. Tribes of the Algonquin nation used to erect weirs—traps of net and wood that fish swim into, but can't get out of—in the bays and inlets of the coast. The Portuguese are believed to have fished here long before the coast of Maine was first "discovered" by the British and French. The cold waters off the coast were famous for their abundant supply of bluefish, striped bass, mackerel, and tuna. Today, the waters are not as populated as they once were. Commercial fisheries during this and the last century have depleted much of the natural supply of saltwater fish. While large schools of fish are now rare on the coast, there are many opportunities both for salt and freshwater fishing. Fishing tackle master Bob Boilard, one of the most knowledgeable sports fishermen in the Saco Bay area, suggests bottom fishing for cod, pollock, and mackerel. Well-known spots for saltwater fishing are Boothbay Harbor, the waters off Rockland, and Passamaquoddy Bay near Eastport. If your taste runs more to trout and bass, try the rivers near the coast. Late spring and early summer are traditionally good seasons for freshwater fishermen, when hungry fish come to the surface to feed on insects and their larvae.

Clamming regulations can be more confusing; certainly they are hard to generalize. The rules vary from town to town, so first, you must call the town clerk of the town you are in and comply with their requirements. Some towns do not allow non-residents to harvest any clams, or have only a few day licenses available. Also, call the *Shellfish Hotline* to find out if a red tide closure is in effect, at 800-232-4733, or see the same message in print on the web, at www.state.me.us/dmr/. Red tide, a kind of algae, can cause paralysis or death if eaten in contaminated clams. Town clerk offices will know about the closures as well.

Going hiking? *DeLorme Mapping Company* offers an inexpensive booklet titled *Hiking: Volume 1 Coastal & Eastern Region*. It is available in most bookstores and larger supermarkets and has several routes mapped with experience levels clearly marked.

Maine's **Nature Preserves** offer great birding, hiking, and many kinds of exploring, as well as protecting some of Maine's all-too-often-threatened

Fall Foliage in Maine

Leaf peeping is relatively new to Maine. For years, devoted foliage aficionados have chosen New England neighbors to the south and west of Maine. That wasn't for any lack of color, say state tourism officials, but merely because the state had failed to promote the fall season. The truth is the coast does have a lovely foliage season, and is often less crowded than New Hampshire or Vermont.

The change begins almost immediately after Labor Day, when night temperatures begin to drop. The big change comes about a month later, when warm days and cool nights cause trees to begin storing energy to get them through the winter. Trees extract sugars, starches, and other nutrients from their leaves, causing leaves to turn from green to red, yellow, and orange. First trees inland change, then those on the coast.

Down East from Acadia to Washington County is the first region on the coast to turn—generally around the end of September or early October. The western coast stretching from Kittery to Bucksport usually turns about a week later. Peak foliage usually lasts for about three to four weeks. This can all change from year to year, depending on the prevailing temperatures, the rainfall and other weather factors. For an inside tip on color conditions, call the Foliage Hotline (207-582-9300; out-of-state 800-533-9595) after September 15. The state publishes a leaf peepers' guide with several coastal driving tours between 100 and 250 miles long; ask for it at any of the state information centers listed in Chapter Eleven, *Information*.

If you want to find your own way, here are some tips on colorful routes. St. George's Peninsula near Port Clyde usually has great color. So does the Blue Hill Peninsula. Acadia is a favorite spot, particularly if you drive the park loop road or hike up Cadillac or the other Mount Desert hills.

The Camden Hills are another excellent site for autumn foliage. The Saco River near Biddeford and the Royal River in Yarmouth are two great canoe trips for viewing the foliage. One of our favorite sights is the blueberry barrens that cover the hillsides way Down East. As the weather cools, they turn a brilliant scarlet. We also think the shortcut (See "Shortcuts" in Chapter Two, *Transportation*) on Rte. 182 between Ellsworth and Cherryfield is one of the prettiest autumn drives in New England.

ecosystems. The state may seem vast and unpopulated to visitors from the north and south, but the fact is that less than four percent of Maine's lands are publicly held. That makes Maine 47th in the union in the preservation of public access lands. Three groups are actively trying to increase the supply of lands protected from commercial development.

The Maine chapter of the **Nature Conservancy** (207-729-5181; www.tnc.org; Fort Andross, 14 Maine St., Suite 401, Brunswick 04011) has been able to convert more than 103,000 acres of Maine wilderness to protected preserves since it was founded in 1956 at the urging of naturalist Rachel Carson. The group's recent projects included a close study of the saltwater ecosystem of Cobscook Bay, one of the most biologically diverse ecosystems on the East Coast—the group's first research and preservation efforts focused below the tidal waterline. The Nature Conservancy owns and manages more than 20,000 acres of nature preserves, including 50 Maine islands and several coastal preserves.

Day use of the Conservancy's lands are welcome, including the string of nature preserves called the Rachel Carson Sea Coast. *The Maine Audubon Society* (207-781-2330; P.O. Box 6009, Falmouth 04105) operates several nature centers on the coast as well as inland. Founded in the early 1970s by Peggy Rockefeller and Tom Cabot, the *Maine Coast Heritage Trust* (207-729-7366; 169 Park Row, Brunswick 04011) has worked to preserve and protect more than 66,000 acres through conservation easements, and includes 173 entire islands and 250 miles of shoreline.

While there is very little downhill **skiing** on the coast, **cross-country** is another story. Many of Maine's parks and nature preserves convert summer hiking or bicycling trails to cross-country ski trails with the first snowfall. Almost every town along the coast has a park and trails that cross-country skiers take over in the wintertime. We've listed some of the better-known areas, but you can find out more by contacting the local chamber of commerce where you plan to visit.

Wherever you ski, remember that it can be unsafe to ski alone. Stay on the trails, and be prepared for Maine's mercurial weather. Also, don't forget to carry out your trash. Call beforehand for snow and trail conditions.

SHOPPING

The earliest trade, both with Europe and their fellow colonists, was in furs and lumber, then ships and granite. Later, coastal residents began selling manufactured goods to the rest of the world: fabric woven in textile mills to the south; shoes from leather tanned and handsewn at factories inland; paper made at pulp mills on many of the state's rivers; and herring and sardines canned at factories Down East. Not all the commerce was one-sided. Mainers were world-class shoppers, and during the 18th and 19th centuries world travelers—ship captains and merchants filled their homes with riches from Europe, the Far East, and ports to the south. Mainers have been commercially adept since the early 1600s. The Pilgrims of Plymouth Colony sent their most industrious members north to establish a fur trade out of Bagaduce (now known as Castine) on the Blue Hill peninsula. They paid off the debts for their voyage in just a few years, evidence of the resources they found there.

Maine these days is known for its outlets as well as its inlets. The outlet trail stretches north and eastward from Kittery all the way to Ellsworth, near Bar Harbor. Maine's outlets may be traced back in history to the first L.L. Bean store in Freeport, a shopping mecca for hunters, fishermen, and outdoors people. The descendants of L.L. Bean, the man who invented the Maine Hunting Boot, still keep shop in Freeport on Casco Bay and in two "factory stores," one in Ellsworth and another in Freeport.

Shopping for **antiques** on the coast is almost as popular as outlet hopping, but slower paced. To really know who has what and what it's selling for, pick up a copy of the Maine *Antique Digest*, the bible for coastal and inland antique

*Arts and crafts flourish in
Maine; this gallery in Warren
is one of many to be found.*

Herb Swanson

shoppers. It's published in Waldoboro and can be found at most newsstands in the state.

Friends who visit Maine love them, and we still enjoy many independent **bookstores.** Several are known for their specialties—like women's studies or local history or fine old volumes only a bibliophile could love. Others you can count on for having a good translation of Homer as well as the top ten from *The New York Times Book Review.* Perhaps it's the long winter and the fact that people here really do curl up by the fireplace with a good book. Maine's pre-eminent weekly, *The Maine Times,* has surveyed its readers and found they read, on average, 50 books a year. If you're into old books, you may request a directory of dealers by contacting the *Maine Antiquarian Booksellers Association* (207-443-1510).

WELCOME CANADIANS/BIENVENUE AUX CANADIENS

We hope this book will give Canadians an idea of all the good things there are to do on the Maine coast. We have kept our northern neighbors in mind and have tried to provide pertinent information.

Nous voulons que ce livre donne aux Canadiens une idée de tous les endroits où on peut s'amuser sur la côte du Maine. Nous apprécions la visite de nos voisins du nord, et nous essayons de leur fournir des renseignements pertinents sur cette partie du Maine. Il y a beaucoup d'aubergistes et de restaurateurs sur la côte du Maine qui parlent français. Si vous êtes en train de planifier un séjour sur la côte du Maine et vous aimeriez consulter quelqu'un qui peut vous renseigner en français, communiquez avec le Maine Tourism Association (P.O. Box 2300, Hallowell, ME 04347; 207-623-0363 au Maine; 800-633-9595 au Canada; www.visit maine.com; metainfo@mainetourism.com). Ce service publie plusieurs brochures en français.

CHAPTER ONE
The Nature of the Coast
HISTORY

Roy Zalesky

Cadillac Mountain in Acadia National Park. At 1,530 feet, it is the tallest coastal mountain in the eastern United States and one of the most visited.

Nothing is still where land meets water. In the course of a minute, grains of sand swirl, snails creep, a clam digs out of sight. In the course of an eon the whole landscape goes through revolutions. We struggle to foresee the changes, to replace the sand winter storms eat away. Perhaps we will not be able to save what we know and love from nature's and our own depredations.

But maybe we can. We have restored parts of the land, resettled birds, augmented the cod, already.

Everywhere on the Maine coast people work to care for the sea and themselves. We understand the need to help the beach grasses grow, to protect and keep intact the dunes that in turn protect the area further inland. Threatened populations of nesting piping plovers and least terns are protected on some beaches with fenced-off areas next to the beach grass, helping to reestablish these rare birds. The piping plovers were counted at over a hundred in 2001, after nearly vanishing in southern Maine.

Elsewhere, on the long flat stretches of mudflat at low tide, local clam diggers can make a living again reaping a harvest, just below the pocked sand, of soft-shell clams. They are in luck because of the Clean Water Act, and federally mandated sewage treatment plants that now line the coast that have stopped the flow of pollution into much of the coastal water. Portlanders can swim off East End Beach these days for the same reason. And the water near the city is also beholden to The Friends of Casco Bay, who have run a pumping service for small boats, and who have become the guardians of the bay, ready to assist at any emergency, and endlessly teaching how to care for the water. There are more seals now swimming in Portland Harbor than remembered years past. The coastal waters grow more and more lovely.

At the northern end of the coast is a bay called Passamaquoddy, which is also the name of the nation of some of the Native Americans who live on it, in Sipayik, the Wabanaki name, or Pleasant Point. The word Passamaquoddy refers to the sight of huge schools of pollock, flashing in the sun as they dove into massive schools of herring in a feeding orgy. This vision is a memory in the language only, although a man overheard in an Eastport restaurant recollected seeing a huge cloud of pink in the water of the bay, when the shrimp were running. "You don't see that anymore," he said.

Fishing restrictions, so painful for the lives of coastal fishermen and women and their families, seem to have produced an increase in the cod, which had seemed nearly gone just recently. All the while the lobster catch has been huge, a record for several years past, and some people think that is the consequence of so few cod, which would otherwise be swallowing up the spawn of lobsters. Others are sure a collapse in the lobster population will come soon, as a consequence of overharvesting.

Whatever we prove able to preserve or reestablish, we never lose our fascination with the sea, and its power and mystery. The sea that licks the coast of Maine is cold and formidable in winter, and sweet and cool or cold in summer, a backdrop or a main stage, a place for endless contemplation. "Vacationland," the Maine license plates proclaim, insistently. But we like to see the sea when we work here, or drive to the grocery store, or take the bus to school, because it is always beautiful.

NATURAL HISTORY

Three hundred ninety million years ago, the coast of Maine was shoved into another body of land called Avalonia, and the intervening ocean, predecessor of the Atlantic, was squeezed shut. The earth at the junction of these huge landmasses was tortured over millions of years and under enormous force into folds and mountains, while some of it was sucked down, under the edges of long fault lines, into the super-heated magma below the earth's crust. Some rock metamorphosed, at lower temperatures, into slate, marble, quartz, and schist. Other sedimentary rock melted and rose back to the surface through cracks and faults, cooled, crystallized, and became granite. Stripes of black

NATURAL HISTORY

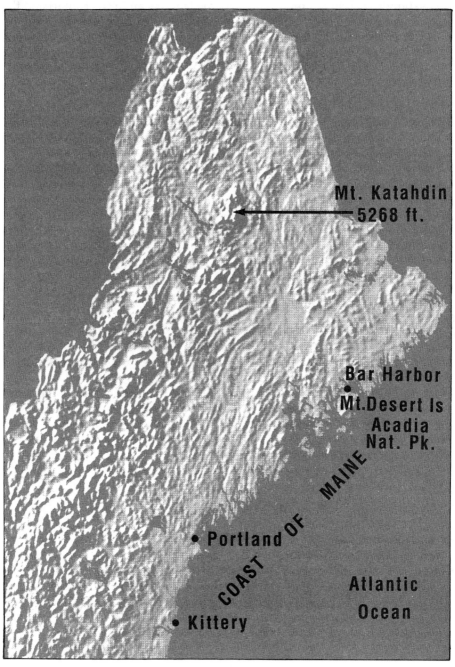

Mt. Katahdin
5268 ft.

Bar Harbor
Mt.Desert Is
Acadia
Nat. Pk.

COAST OF MAINE

Portland

Atlantic
Ocean

Kittery

TOPOGRAPHY OF MAINE

basalt from later in this ancient time cut clear bands called dikes through the red granite; you can see them on Schoodic Peninsula beaches. Every rock has a story we can read.

One hundred eighty million years ago, the land began to crack apart and the modern continents slowly took shape. Fossils of animals of European origin, found in Thomaston, Maine, reveal this old connection and date its end. Maine and the rest of North America slowly rotated northward and west, splitting apart from Europe and Asia at about the rate that a fingernail grows, according to David Kendall, author of *Glaciers and Granite*. We are still drifting west, at the rate of two centimeters a year, and the Atlantic continues to grow. But the fault lines under the land in Maine are quiet now, and the volcanoes long gone. We have occasional earth movements, but none that have caused damage in the recent past.

THE DROWNED COAST

Looking down in front of your feet when you stand on Cadillac Mountain, in Acadia National Park, you can see grooves and indentations in the rock. A mile-thick layer of ice dragged itself, with its load of stone and sand, across this granite, heading south, until a shift in the climate melted it away. Less than ten thousand years ago, glaciers that had come and gone before made their final retreat, leaving behind enough sand and gravel to build Interstate 95 and thousands of other roads and buildings. They also dropped "erratic" boulders, stray giant rocks that you can see all over the coast, along Route 1 north of Machias, along hiking trails in the woods of Camden Hills, and on the side of South Bubble Rock, where a famous one is named Balancing Rock.

Rivers created under and in front of the retreating glaciers cut valleys out of the softer rock and sorted the glacial till, carrying the fine sand down to the edge of the sea and sending the silt further. Georges Bank, historically one of the finest fishing grounds in the world, sits on a bed of glacial silt and clay, and was itself once the extreme limit of the glacier over New England. The deep and enormous load of ice pushed the surface of the earth down underneath it, and as the ice melted, the sea rose deep into the land. For a while the sea was 400 feet higher than it is today, and the coast was underwater. Then the earth moved upward, lifting itself out of the sea; old deltas are now far from water, leaving curiosities like the Desert of Maine, in Freeport, where overgrazing exposed an old sea shore, or the 25 square miles of flat land of Pineo Ridge, north of Machias, where blueberries love to grow.

The earth is now sinking slightly, in southern and northern tips of Maine; and the sea has been rising, six feet in the last 3,000 years. The coastline changes all the time, under the relentless action of the sea.

Major Bays of Maine

Casco	Dyer
Merrymeeting	Narraguagus
Sheepscot	Pleasant
Muscongus	Western
Penobscot (by far the largest)	Chandler
Isle au Haut	Englishman
Blue Hill	Machias
Union River	Cobscook
Frenchman	Passamaquoddy

THE LABRADOR CURRENT

The water off the Maine coast refrigerates the air in the summer and warms the air in the winter. A current that flows down from Canada cools the ocean here and tempers the summer heat, making a swim too cold for many of us, but leaving a breeze and a refreshing climate that attracts people from far away. The cold current mixes with the southern, warmer Gulf Stream off of Cape Cod, engendering the perfect circumstances for microscopic sea animals that are fed on by larger fish and crustaceans.

A hundred years ago it was believed a kind of climactic wall separated the southern sea from the northern or cold-temperate sea off Maine, but creatures other than human have migrated up the coast, or vanished and reappeared elsewhere, disproving any barrier. The green crab is now established in the tide pools on Maine's beaches, but it was not welcome as it moved in during the first 50 years of this century and began to dine on the young soft-shell clams. Bluefish arrived in 1971, if I may believe the handwritten note in the margin of my library copy of Rachel Carson's *Edge of the Sea*.

The Asian shore crab hitchhiked to the Atlantic Coast on the belly of a tanker, perhaps; it has definitely migrated up the coast and was first identified in Maine in the summer of 2001, by children searching tide pools at Fish Camp in South Portland.

The tides shift from high to low every 12 hours and 25 minutes, and are highest and lowest at the full and the new moons. They are also much higher in the northern end of the state than the southern; 20 feet in Eastport, compared to 9 at Kittery. Various narrow tidal rivers up the coast offer the spectacle of reversing falls, as the tide comes in or out. When warm air crosses the hot land and moves over the cold ocean, it can make a fog that can persist over the coastline for days, though a drive a few miles inland would put you under a sunny sky. The ferryboats now have radar that usually warns them before they hit any obstacles as they cross in the fog; and they sound their horns repeatedly during the crossing, to alert other ships.

The foghorns along the coast mingle, or singly mourn the weather, and make anyone slow down and wonder, where are we?

The Inn at Canoe Point sits on Frenchman Bay, near the rising and falling tides and their crops of weed.

Inn at Canoe Point

The pollock that used to leap in Passamaquoddy Bay are still part of a fishing boat's catch, and often used in the manufacture of fish sticks. The local salmon readily available is raised on farms near Vinalhaven or up around Eastport, while the wild Atlantic salmon is ever more rare; the relationship between aquaculture techniques and declining wild salmon populations is always the subject of controversy between environmentalists and aquaculture and business people. Cod is still caught offshore, and Atlantic sturgeon, the alewife and striped bass, yellowtail flounder and halibut and haddock. These will all come into stardom in this guide in the restaurant sections, where they have been broiled and sauced to perfection. And everywhere are the delicious and wonderful soft-shell clams and hard-shell lobsters. Every ferryboat spends its summer trying to dodge the lobster trap buoys, that can wind around a propeller and stall the engine, while the lobster boats lay ever more traps to lure the inland-summering lobster in for a nice piece of old fish head. Bait is not a delicacy.

The best of a beach, for most children and many adults, is the tide pools. On less popular shorelines you might find a sand dollar or a northern sea star, but everywhere are the periwinkles, the tiny green and Atlantic rock crabs, and hermit crabs that have stolen off with someone else's exoskeleton or shell. Whelks are also easily discovered in the tide pools, where they manage to drill into periwinkles and mussels with "teeth," sandpaper-like bumps on the creature's tongue. They then excrete an acid that eats a hole through which they can suck a mussel out for their dinner. If you lean over and look at the opened barnacles that are under the water in a tide pool, you can see their feet waving around, somehow lapping up the passing tiny bits of food. The seagulls flying nearby, if they are not stealing your child's graham crackers — and every year

Tidal Zones

As day after day these great tides ebb and flow over the rocky rim of New England, their progress across the shore is marked in stripes of color parallel to the sea's edge. The bands, or zones, are composed of living things and reflect the stages of the tide, for the length of time that a particular level of shore is uncovered determines, in large measure, what can live there. The hardiest species live in the upper zones. Some of the earth's most ancient plants — the blue-green algae — though originating eons ago in the sea, have emerged from it to form dark tracings on the rocks above the high-tide line, a black zone visible on the rocky shores in all parts of the world. Below the black zone, snails that are evolving toward a land existence browse on the film of vegetation or hide in seams and crevices in the rocks. But the most conspicuous zone begins at the upper line of the tides. On an open shore with moderately heavy surf, the rocks are whitened by the crowded millions of the barnacles just below the high-tide line. Here and there the white is interrupted by mussels growing in patches of darkest blue. Below them the seaweeds come in — the brown fields of the rockweeds. Toward the low-tide line the Irish moss spreads its low, cushiony growth — a wide band of rich color that is not fully exposed by the sluggish movement of the neap tides, but appears on all the greater tides. Sometimes the reddish brown of the moss is splashed with the bright green tangles of another seaweed, a hairlike growth of wiry texture. The lowest spring tides reveal still another zone during the last hour of their fall — that sub-tide world where all the rock is painted a deep rose hue by the lime-secreting seaweeds that encrust it, and where the gleaming brown ribbons of the large kelp lie exposed on the rocks.

—From *The Edge of the Sea* by Rachel Carson

they are more bold — might be dropping a mussel shell on the nearby rocks, to split it open for their lunch.

THE WEALTH OF THE LAND

One of the first things seen in Maine by the eyes of Europeans was also one of the first things exploited by them here. The enormously tall white pine trees, unbroken by years of coastal wind and storms, made magnificent masts for generations of sailing ships. The Maine State Seal centers on a pine tree, and it still supports many people here, where second growth pine is harvested for pulp and lumber mills, and can be seen laid flat on the bed of lumber trucks on stretches of Route 1, Down East.

A 33-acre stand of century-old white pine graces the campus of Bowdoin College in Brunswick and allows a modern visitor a sense of the majesty and peace of an old forest.

White and red spruce are common near the water, where they can manage to grow on the thin bit of soil over the bedrock and granite of the mid- and northern coast. Birch trees grow along the rivers and in the north, making graceful groves just as they did when ancestors of today's Wabanaki harvested their bark for their canoes, a craft that is still practiced.

Birds find a good living in the various forests and along the coast shorebirds migrate according to their seasons. Warblers, chickadees, cardinals, starlings, and crows love the busy south coast, and to the north thrush, vireo, boreal chickadee, and gray jay can be seen, with luck. Along the ocean the great blue heron can rise from a salt march anywhere from Peaks Island off of Portland to Machias. Kingfishers dive for fish by Tenants Harbor, bald eagles coast serene as the air itself over Bagaduce River, osprey bring dinner back to their nest off the docks at Robinhood Marina.

Hundreds of birds visit Maine, many stay here a season, and some have made a return after years of absence. The bald eagles and osprey have been able to return as their numbers have grown after DDT was banned (the chemical fatally weakened the birds' eggs, after the birds had eaten prey full of it). Other birds have reestablished themselves with human protection, helped by the 1918 Migratory Bird Treaty Act, which made killing wild birds against the law. Puffins, perhaps Maine's most adorable birds, with bright bands of colors on their beaks at mating season, have been reintroduced to two Maine islands by the work of Audubon Society scientists and workers, fulfilling the vision of Stephen Kress. Ten-week-old puffin chicks were flown south to Eastern Egg Rock off Rockland from Newfoundland's giant puffin colony on protected Great Island, starting in 1973. Years of persistence and patience led, in 1981, to a breeding pair on an island that had not harbored breeding puffins for over a hundred years. Audubon tours and boat trips, with no landing allowed, can now bring you out to see puffins on this island during the summer from Rockland and New Harbor, as well as further north on Machias Seal Island, considered a Canadian island, where terns have also established themselves.

Puffins

By 1901, after centuries of hunting, there remained only one pair of puffins south of the Canadian border. That pair lived on Matinicus Rock, a lonely outpost twenty-two miles from the Maine shoreline, in Penobscot Bay. All the other puffins had been killed. But in that same year, a group of scientists and concerned people hired the Matinicus Rock lighthouse keeper to keep the gunners away. He was one of America's first wildlife wardens.

With Matinicus Rock under protection from hunting, puffins began to come back.

—From *Project Puffin: How We Brought Puffins Back to Egg Rock*, by Stephen W. Kress as told to Pete Salmansohn

SOCIAL HISTORY

THE PEOPLE OF THE DAWN

The coast has been inhabited for thousands of years. After the retreat of the last glaciers, hunters of now extinct animals like the wooly mammoth and bison (now repopulating in the Plains States) moved across the newly exposed lands, trailing their prey. Perhaps it was the coastal beauty that persuaded some to settle, for graves dusted with red ochre (powdered hematite) have been excavated; they are evidence of settlement here 7,000 years ago.

The Red Paint People, as these ancient people are called, became the subject of romantic history. They were imagined to be a race now vanished and connected with another myth, of a fabulous, rich city called Norumbega, rich in gold and jewels, the confabulation of a European explorer in the 1600s. But they are now believed to be the ancestors of the Wabanki of Maine.

The heavy woodworking tools buried with these people were evidence of dugout canoes; perhaps the dead were considered in need of the tools to make a canoe to reach the Land of the Dead. There are also plummets that show they were fishing. Their settlements along inland rivers are continually being investigated and our ideas about their lives reexamined.

Settlements at the coast prior to 5,000 years past have been damaged or entirely submerged by a slow increase in the sea level. Scallopers now and then drag artifacts up from underwater, like stone knives or an axe, which may be 6,000–7,000 years old.

But there are a number of sites that have been carefully investigated by archeologists, many in recent years working with the Abbe Museum in Acadia National Park. The Red Paint culture itself is understood to have been sophisticated exploiters of coastal life and traders with widespread contacts. Although they ate the little creatures at hand, like clams and oysters, the most striking harvesting they did was in their sea journeys, when they hunted swordfish. They had barbed harpoons, and seaworthy boats, and would haul enormous swordfish back to shore, as recovered "swords" attest.

About 3,800 years ago, stone points began to be crafted with a technique called flaking that created sharper, smaller, more lethal points. And 2,800 years ago, the technique of molding and baking clay ushered in the Ceramic Period, which has left clear traces. According to Dr. Steven Cox, co-writer of the Abbe Museum's *The Indian Shell Heap: Archeology of the Ruth Moore Site*, this may have been the time the birch bark canoe was developed. The people who made that agile canoe traded with natives of Nova Scotia and Labrador, as well as people inland as far away as the Great Lakes, as witnessed in the cherts, a nonnative stone, and hammered copper.

According to the same book, the clam shells and sea mink teeth found on Gotts Island (just south of Southwest Harbor on Mount Desert) prove by their habit of growth that people lived on the coast through the winter, and spent some of the summer away, possibly to follow the salmon migration up the rivers. Later bones and shells show more year-round residence. During the cold season the cod fishing was excellent, but other things eaten included wolffish, haddock, sculpin, seals, sea mink (now extinct), beaver, whale, ducks, geese, and the great auk (also extinct). Sculpin and flounder could have been caught by making walls of brush in the water at high tide, which would have trapped these bottom feeders as the tide went out and left them trying to hide in the silt, ready to be picked up.

One of the curious mysteries of Native American habitation is that, apparently, they never ate any of the many, many lobsters.

EUROPEANS

By the 1500s fishing ships from Europe were already harvesting cod from the incredibly abundant water of Georges Bank. At that time the wave of European explorers began to make visits to a coast that would end its centuries of Native habitation. In the 19th century, Penobscot people recounted a story told of the first encounter, when an elder on a hunt with young men saw strange footprints, of hard-soled shoes:

"Upon seeing the strange tracks, all the warnings which have been giving us, how that a time is coming when we must look for the coming of the white man from the direction of the rising sun. . . I could not withhold the tears that rushed on my brow. Knowing that a great change must follow his coming it made me weak and the weakness overcame me, because his coming will put a bar to our happiness, and our destiny will be at the mercy of the events." (From *The Life and Traditions of the Red Man*, by Joseph Nicolar)

Indeed, though at first French explorers and Jesuit missionaries seemed willing to trade and work with the Native Americans, less moral English and Dutch explorers saw nothing wrong in stealing stacks of hides out of an unattended wigwam, or in stealing the Native Americans themselves, and bringing them to England as a kind of trophy. An initial period of trading, in which members of the Micmacs became the oceangoing entrepreneurs of fur trading, ended in battles that pitted Micmacs against ancestors of the Passamaquoddy, and in failed European colonies in Popham, in Port Royal, then at Mount Desert where the French were routed by the English. Henry Hudson, eponymous discoverer of the Hudson River, first stopped in the Gulf of Maine in Penobscot, trading and then stealing whatever he wanted. But worse than anything was the sickness carried into the Native communities that they could not withstand, of smallpox and plague. Perhaps 75 percent of the native population died, by the year 1616. After that time, the Europeans had only to settle the fight among themselves, and go to their king, to declare themselves owners of the forested land along the rivers and coast of Maine.

The "bar to our happiness" had been raised.

DREAMS FOR "THE MAIN"

The first permanent European settlements in Maine were at Monhegan in 1622, Saco in 1623 and Agamenticus (later York) in 1624. In 1629 the Pilgrims of the Plymouth Colony in Massachusetts established a trading post at Bagaduce, on the Penobscot or Blue Hill peninsula. From there they sent their English sponsors furs and other goods to pay off the debt for their New World voyage. The French didn't like the English being in what they considered their territory. Forty years later Baron de St. Castin took it by force.

Archeological dig done in the late 19th century under the direction of antiquarian John Henry Cartland uncovered British officers' quarters at Fort William Henry, Pemaquid Point, first built in 1692.

R.L. Bradley. Courtesy, Maine Historic
Preservation Committee

In 1635 King Charles I of England, assuming it was his to give, gave Maine to Sir Ferdinando Gorge and named him "Lord of New England." Sir Gorge chose Agamenticus, which had grown into a small village, as the center of his empire. Five years later, he named it after himself, Gorgeana. Sir Gorge's hopes to develop "the main" — or the mainland and later "Maine" — were never realized. His heirs sold out his dream in 1677, and Gorgeana was reorganized as the town of York.

PRELUDE TO THE FRENCH AND INDIAN WARS

Uneasy relations between the French and English continued for years before formal war was declared. The coastal lands of Maine, particularly those east of the Penobscot River, were in a fairly constant state of dispute.

Although the French controlled most of the area east of the Penobscot, the English had managed to establish two trading centers there — one at Machias and one at Penobscot village. The French raided the posts in 1634 and 1635, and the English retook them in 1654. In 1664, the Duke of York was granted the lands between Pemaquid Point and the St. Croix River. In 1667, the English King Charles II surrendered his claim on lands including Nova Scotia, Acadia, and Penobscot to the French under the Treaty of Breda. At that time, Baron de

St. Castin established himself in Penobscot and proceeded to protect France's interest while trading with both the English and the Native Americans, who had good reason to prefer cooperating with the French. He remained there until Sir Edmund Andros, the governor of New York and Massachusetts, forcibly took the town for the English.

Official hostilities between the two countries lasted from 1675 to 1763. In the British colonies it was known as the Indian War. Saco, Scarborough, and Casco were the first towns to be attacked in September 1675. The Native Americans perhaps were still angry with Waymouth's kidnapping of their five kinsmen 70 years earlier. Certainly they were threatened by the English colonials' encroachment on their land. They sided with the French, who largely had left them and their ancestral claim to the land alone. The acrimonious 88-year struggle preoccupied the small native and colonial populations of Maine and was the reason why colonization nearly halted during that time. Following the defeat of the French at Quebec in 1759, English colonists began to settle on the coast in larger numbers.

THE REVOLUTIONARY WAR

In the mid-18th century, Maine was still very much a part of Massachusetts. Whereas Bostonians threw tea into the harbor, a Falmouth (now known as Portland) mob seized the Imperial tax stamps in 1765. Still, many residents along the coast of northern Massachusetts were actively doing business with the British. Although Boston was the capital of Maine, Mainers valued above all their independence from London and Boston.

Once the Revolutionary War started, Mainers refused to ship their highly prized masts to the British fleet. The Royal Navy bombarded the city then called Falmouth and burned much of it to the ground. Before that, zealous Maine patriots claimed the first naval victory of the war when in 1775 colonists captured the British cutter *Margaretta* in Machias Bay, a battle James Fenimore Cooper called the "Lexington of the seas."

Another Machias battle gave some glory to its near neighbors, the Passamaquoddy and their chief, Francis Joseph Neptune. He had been consulted and asked for allegiance by a man named John Allen, who was made a colonel by George Washington after persuading him of the danger that the remaining Maine Native Americans, collectively known as the Wabanaki or People of the Dawn, could be enlisted by the British.

When a British cutter tried to run up the Machias river, full of British soldiers intent on attacking the town, Chief Neptune managed to surprise them with a couple of musket shots from the bank, the second of which brought down an officer standing on the deck. The large group of armed Passamaquoddy with him "burst into a blood-curdling war chant," according to writer Bill Williamson of Kennebunkport, and the British cutter turned around and made away. The musket fire and flaming arrows that followed them down the river almost set the ship on fire.

The first colonial warship, *Ranger*, was built at Kittery in 1777. Two years later the colonies suffered a disastrous setback when 19 armed ships and 24 transports with more than 1,300 soldiers and marines were lost to the British at Castine. At the war's end in 1783 the Treaty of Paris established Maine's most easterly border at the St. Croix River.

POSTWAR PROSPERITY AND THE WAR OF 1812

After the Revolutionary War, Maine prospered and grew. The era of logging began. Maine became a center for production of lumber for houses, barrels for trade, masts for ships, and wood for fuel. Ships from safe harbors all along the coast established trade routes around the world. Maine began to think about breaking away from Massachusetts.

Then France declared war on England in 1793. Short of men, England's navy began boarding American ships and impressing sailors with naval duty under pretense they were still subjects. For this reason President Jefferson finally ordered an embargo in 1807 disallowing trade with any foreign country. The embargo was particularly tough on the people and ports of Maine.

Many of the region's maritime businesses turned to smuggling. Eastport, just south of Canada, became the busiest port in the country. When the United States went to war against England in 1812, Mainers at first offered little resistance to the British, who were their best customers. People along the coast also continued trading with their own government. Worse, for the British, they continued building ships used by the American navy. The British set up a blockade and captured Castine and the surrounding towns.

With the Treaty of Ghent in 1814, the war ended as did England's blockade. The people of Maine started thinking again about breaking off from Massachusetts. In 1820, Maine was granted statehood as part of the Missouri Compromise. The separation papers were signed at the Jamestown Tavern in Freeport (the tavern still operates today down the street from L.L. Bean). The 23rd state to join the union established its current-day capital inland at Augusta 12 years later.

WOODEN SHIPS

"There are still any number of working lobster boats, plenty of yacht yards, and even a few deep-sea fishermen. . . . These are inadequate compensations, though, for anyone brought up in the knowledge of Maine's deepwater supremacy, those great times when Maine skippers were admired from the Elbe to the Amazon, and Maine-built ships were the world's criteria of seaworthiness. In those days, local prodigies like the stupendous six-masted schooner *Wyoming* were legends of the sea," wrote Jan Morris in *New England Monthly* magazine.

By 1850, Maine was considered the preeminent shipbuilding capital of America. By 1860, one fifth of the state's population were mariners, 759 of them masters of ships. Ten percent of the nation's deepwater shipmasters lived in Searsport at the top of Penobscot Bay. Bath, midway up the coast, was the United States' fifth busiest port. A little farther up the coast, Wiscasset was the busiest international port north of Boston.

Maine's romantic era of wooden shipbuilding ended with a complex set of economic events that came just before the Civil War. The invention of ironclad ships didn't help. Foreign trade moved to other ports. Maine businessmen began looking for other industries to bank on; they didn't have to look far. Forests that once supplied timbers for masts and lithe hulls now are devoted almost entirely to the production of paper.

Fisheries were among the industries that flourished, with fishermen reaping a bounty from the cold waters off northern New England, including the fish-rich Georges Bank. At its peak in 1902, the state landed and processed 242 million pounds of cod, cusk, hake, haddock, ocean perch, mackerel, halibut, pollock, crabs, clam, shrimp, mussels, lobster, herring, and sardines. Canneries built during the height of this fishing boom, now abandoned, are still in evidence from Yarmouth to Eastport. The canning industry fell on hard times. The nation's hunger for canned herring and sardines slaked with the advent of refrigeration and the easy transport of fresh fish at the turn of the century. Other popular whitefish species, such as cod, halibut, haddock, and pollock, have become scarcer as fishermen have overfished the waters off Maine's coast.

ARTISTS "DISCOVER" MAINE'S COAST

Painting the landscape near Somesville on Mount Desert Island.

Herb Swanson

In 1844, Thomas Cole, founder of the Hudson River School of painting, visited Bar Harbor, loved what he saw, and spread the word around the art community. He also told his wealthy patrons. More than 200 lavish summer "cottages" were built. Grand hotels appeared. Developers were quick to claim Mount Desert Island's thick fogs were "as healthy for the body as basking in the sun." Bar Harbor became as well known as Newport, Rhode Island.

The Maine Almanac, compiled by the *Maine Times*, reports that in 1870 "Tourists begin arriving in Maine." Not only did they come to see Maine's rocky coast, they came to see and be near the rich people who lived on the coast. In 1912 Leon Leonwood Bean invented the Maine Hunting Shoe, an ugly duckling of a shoe, half-leather, half-rubber that nevertheless has made many a hunter happy. "L.L.," as Freeport residents and shop clerks still call him, might as well have invented shopping. The shoe, and the store that grew up around it, eventually turned the little village of Freeport into the second most popular place in Maine.

THE BIRTH OF ACADIA

Somesville on Mount Desert Island.

Herb Swanson

The most visited place in Maine was being established at about the same time. A group of wealthy Mount Desert "rusticators" decided to donate large parcels of land to be used for a national park. Today Acadia is a public toehold on a coast that is mostly privately owned, although up and down the coast land trusts and preserves are increasing their acreage. In 1947 much of Bar Harbor was destroyed in a forest fire. The French paper *Le Figaro* mistakenly reported the peasants of Maine had struck a blow against feudalism. The town's year-round residents did not like being called peasants.

The fact is there are no aristocrats in Maine. It is a place where millionaires and lobstermen — Yankees who above all value self-reliance — talk about politics, the weather, and their boats over pie and coffee in homespun diners. The beauty of the coast and the ocean is considered more important to the people who live and visit here than what is being worn on the streets of Boston or New York, or even on themselves. "We are hardly fashionable," wrote Frances Fitzgerald, whose family members have been longtime summer residents of Northeast Harbor, in the August 1989 *Vogue*. "You might say we are consistent to the point of atavism."

THE MODERN ERA FOR THE WABANAKI

By 1790 the few Native Americans who had survived the French and Indian Wars were made wards of the Commonwealth and confined to two reservations — one at Old Town, near Bangor, and the second at Perry, near Eastport. Massachusetts came to an agreement with representatives of the Wabanaki, in 1818, agreeing to pay, in exchange for all the rest of Maine, one six-pound cannon, one swivel, 50 knives, 200 yards of calico, two drums, four rifles, one box of pipes, and 300 yards of ribbon, as well as a yearly supply of 500 bushels of corn, 15 barrels of wheat, seven barrels of clear pork, one hogshead of molasses, 100 yards of double width broadcloth (to be red and blue on alternate years), 50 good blankets, 100 pounds of gunpowder, six boxes of chocolate, 150 pounds of tobacco and 50 dollars in cash. A year later, when Massachusetts ceded its control of Maine, and Maine became a state of the Union, Maine took over this agreement. The book, *Maine, A Guide Downeast*, first published in 1937, that details this list, states, "It has been a long time since these goods could be regarded as adequate compensation."

Members of the Micmac Tribe in Bar Harbor at the turn of the century.

After four years, according to Susan Steven's *Brief History of the Passamaquoddy Indians*, Maine began to renege on its agreement, selling and leasing for 999 years land meant to provide for the Native Americans, and using interest for the state budget from a trust fund set up by Massachusetts, among other abuses of trust.

In 1957, Native Americans in Maine were allowed to vote in national elections, and not until 1967 were they allowed to vote in state elections. These dates are both many years subsequent to the 1928 bill that made all Native Americans in the United States citizens, and they reflect badly on the state of Maine. In 1977 the Penobscot, Passamaquoddy, and Maleseet Indians sued the state claiming that all treaties granting land to Maine were null and void, because Congress never ratified them. They asked for $25 billion and 12.5 million acres of land. In 1980 they received a settlement of $81.5 million, but no land.

CHAPTER TWO
How to Get Here and Get Around
TRANSPORTATION

The high Waldo–Hancock County Suspension Bridge, built in 1931, takes you downeast.

Herb Swanson

Sections of coastal U.S. Rte. 1 in Maine, which today runs from Kittery to Fort Kent by way of Rockland, Ellsworth, and Machias, follow ancient Native American trails. Settlers marked the trails during the 1600s and named the resulting road the King's Highway. The route first was used by mail couriers traveling from Boston to Machias; later, as settlements grew up along the coast, the public highway was traversed by horse-drawn vehicles.

The first stagecoach began operating between Portland and Portsmouth in 1787. The 90-mile journey took three days. Keep that slow crawl in mind as you're creeping through Wiscasset, where the traffic lights create a backup almost every summer day.

Despite the early full-fledged "highway," most of the coast was serviced by roads that were muddy and impassable during much of the year. The preferred method of travel then was by sea; ships and shipping were the industries that made Maine.

By the 1850s, 246 sailing vessels and 12 steamships called regularly on the port of Portland while 31 different railway lines carrying lumber and passengers criss-crossed the state. At the turn of the century electric trolleys carried tourists from Boston up the coast to Kennebunkport and Bar Harbor.

With the creation of the Interstate Highway System during the 1950s, suddenly half the populations of the United States and Canada were within a day's drive of the Maine coast. Today, most visitors come by highway.

The Widening, a Five-Year Project on Interstate 95

Between 2001 and 2005 the 30 miles of I-95 that start in York and end in Scarborough will be widened to three lanes in both directions. By rerouting traffic the project usually causes only slight delays, but occasionally traffic does get backed up. The Maine Department of Transportation hosts a website, www.widening.maineturnpike.com that lets you know the schedule. The huge project, subject to successive referendums before being approved in 2000, includes 18 reconstructed bridges, as well as new lanes, improved guardrails, and wider outside shoulders for those inevitable stops. The work has involved a massive recycling effort, saving the topsoil moved from each border area, and the gravel, for use in the next phases of construction.

TRANSPORTATION TODAY

Airports at Boston, Portland, and Bangor service domestic and international airlines with direct flights from Canada and Europe. Smaller airports, including Rockland and Bar Harbor, serve as connecting points for air travelers. Passenger train service to Maine ended during the 1950s, but has, after years of delays, begun once again between Boston and Portland, Maine. Car ferries run regularly between the maritime provinces of Canada and Bar Harbor and Portland, including the new high speed *Cat* out of Bar Harbor.

GETTING TO THE COAST

BY CAR

From Connecticut, New York, New Jersey, and South: I-95 goes right across the Piscataqua River separating New Hampshire and Maine and into Kittery, the first and oldest town on the coast.

From New York City: I-95 runs along the coast of Connecticut, up through Providence, Boston, and Portsmouth. For a more direct route take I-95 to New Haven, I-91 north to Hartford, I-84 northeast until you get on the Mass. Pike at the Sturbridge entrance. Take the Westborough exit and follow I-495 northeast to where it joins I-95, just south of the New Hampshire border.

MAINE ACCESS

The chart below gives miles and approximate driving times from the following cities to Portland:

City	Time	Miles
Albany	5.5 hours	237
Boston	2.5 hours	109
Hartford	4 hours	200
Montreal	6 hours	255
New York	7 hours	317
Philadelphia	9.5 hours	424
Quebec	6.5 hours	278
St. John	7 hours	309
Toronto	14 hours	621
Washington, D.C.	12.5 hours	557

The chart below gives you miles and approximate driving times from the following cities to Bangor.

City	Time	Miles
Boston	5.5 hours	249
Montreal	7.25 hours	306
New York	9 hours	452
Quebec	5.75 hours	236
St. John	3 .5 hours	163
Toronto	13.25 hours	609
Yarmouth	19 hours	850

From Boston: Although this route adds a few more miles, it is faster than fighting your way up Rte. 1. Take I-93 north to Rte. 128 east until it rejoins I-95. On the way home there's also the added benefit of saving the Tobin Bridge toll—and avoiding traffic.

From Montreal: AAA recommends you take Rte. 10 to Magog; Rte. 55 south to the international border just north of Derby Line, Vermont. Pick up I-91 at the border and follow to Rte. 2 in St. Johnsbury. Continue east on Rte. 2 through Gorham, New Hampshire, and on to Bethel, Maine.

If your destination is the south coast region, pick up Rte. 26 in Bethel and follow to Portland.

For the central region, continue on Rte. 2 from Bethel to I-95 near Newport, Maine, and follow to Bangor. From there you can take Alternate Rte. 1 to Stockton Springs and Belfast. Or you can take Rte. 1 south to Ellsworth and points east.

From Quebec City: Take Rte. 73 to Rte. 173 and the border, about 10 miles south of Armstrong. Pick up Rte. 201 at the border and follow all the way to Skowhegan, Maine. To access the south and midcoast regions, continue on Rte. 201 to Waterville where you pick up I-95 south. If you're headed to the central coast or Down East, pick up Rte. 2 east of Skowhegan. It connects with I-95 near Newport, Maine, and goes to Bangor. From there you can take Alternate Rte. 1 to Stockton Springs and Belfast. Or you can take Rte. 1 south to Ellsworth and points east.

From Saint John or Fredericton: Take Rte. 1 from St. John to the international border at St. Stephen, then south to Calais, Maine. Continue on Rte. 1 toward Machias and points south. Rte. 190 in Perry veers off toward Eastport. An alternate route to the midcoast and south coast regions is to follow Rte. 1 to Rte. 9 near Calais. Follow Rte. 9 to Bangor.

From Toronto: You have the choice of traveling north or south of Lake Ontario. Both routes take approximately the same amount of time. The southern route is super highways—and tolls—most of the way. The northern route is smaller roads and no tolls.

Traveling north around the lake, take Rte. 401 east to Cornwall, just north of the international border. Pick up Rte. 37 in Rooseveltown, New York, and follow that east to Malone. Take Rte. 11 East to Swanton, Vermont, where you get onto I-89 south. Take this highway to Montpelier. Pick up Rte. 2 east and follow all the way through St. Johnsbury on to Bethel, Maine.

If your destination is in the Portland region, pick up Rte. 26 in Bethel and follow to Portland.

For central coast and Down East regions, continue on Rte. 2 from Bethel to I-95 near Newport, Maine, and follow to Bangor. From there you can take Alternate Rte. 1 to Stockton Springs and Belfast. Or you can take Rte. 1 south to Ellsworth and points east.

Traveling south around Lake Ontario, take the QEW to the international border. Take I-190 through Niagara Falls, New York, to I-90. Follow I-90 to the connection with the Mass. Pike. Take the Mass. Pike to the Westborough exit and follow I-495 northeast to where it joins I-95, just south of the New Hampshire border.

```
Maine Turnpike
```

Maine Turnpike

To find out what the weather or traffic is like on the turnpike, call 800-675-PIKE. Following is a list of Maine Turnpike interchanges and their numbers.

Exit No.	Location
1	Kittery, York
2	Ogunquit/Wells
3	Kennebunk
4	Biddeford
5	Old Orchard, Saco
6	Scarborough
6A	Portland/I-295
7	South Portland
8	Portland/Westbrook
9	Falmouth Spur, Freeport, Yarmouth
10	Portland North
11	Gray
12	Auburn
13	Lewiston
14	Gardiner
End	Augusta

BY BUS

Along the coast, *Concord Trailways* (207-828-1151 or 800-639-3317; www.concordtrailways.com) leaves from Boston for Portland, Brunswick, Bath, Wiscasset, Damariscotta, Waldoboro, Rockland, Camden, Rockport, Lincolnville, Belfast, Searsport, and Bangor. Concord also offers an express bus from Boston to Bangor with one stop in Portland, and a free movie. There is no direct bus link to points in Canada.

Greyhound (800-231-2222; www.greyhound.com) will take you as far as Boston, but from there *Vermont Transit* (207-772-6587 or 800-451-3292) goes as far north as Bar Harbor. From Boston, the bus stops in Portsmouth, NH; Portland, Brunswick, Lewiston, Augusta, Waterville, Bangor, and Bar Harbor.

BY TRAIN

Starting in December 2001, train service to Portland has resumed from Boston's North Station. Two morning trains and two afternoon trains are scheduled for the initial runs, but more may be added depending on the response. The trains will stop in Old Orchard Beach, Saco, and Wells, as well as Portland; tickets and schedule information are available at Amtrack, 800-872-7245 or www.amtrack.com.

BY PLANE

If you are not traveling by car, you most likely will arrive in Maine via plane. There are major airports in Portland, Augusta, and Bangor, all with connecting flights to smaller airports in Rockland and Bar Harbor. Many choose to fly into Boston's Logan Airport, only 1.5 hours to Kittery and 2.5 hours to Portland by car. All of the large airports are served by the major airlines. In addition, there are several small coastal and island airports with independent air services that have connecting flights.

Augusta State Airport—207-626-2306; Continental Connection.
Bangor International Airport—207-947-0384; Business Express, Continental Express, Delta, Northwest, US Airways Express.
Hancock County/Bar Harbor Airport, Trenton (near Bar Harbor)—207-667-7329; Continental Connection.
Knox County Regional Airport, Owls Head (near Rockland)—207-594-4131; Continental Connection.
Portland International Jetport—207-774-7301; Business Express, Continental, Continental Express, Delta, United, US Airways.

GETTING AROUND THE COAST OF MAINE

BY CAR

There are three ways to drive up the coast: the fast way on I-95; the medium-fast way on U.S. Rte. 1; and the slow-and-easy way on smaller state highways and roads that often turn out to be the fastest of all. Which route you take depends on your destination—or how serendipitous you want to be.

The three most-visited spots in Maine and on the coast are: Acadia National Park, L.L. Bean in Freeport, and Old Orchard Beach. Depending on your intentions and schedule, you may wish to see—or avoid—all three.

Acadia is one of the most beautiful parks in the national park system. To get to Acadia, take Rte. 1 or Rte. 1A to Ellsworth. From Ellsworth take Rte. 3 to Bar Harbor. The park is less than a mile from Bar Harbor. Bar Harbor is 211 miles from Kittery, 122 miles from Eastport, and 46 miles from Bangor. The portion of Acadia on the Isle au Haut can be reached by ferry from Stonington. Most of Acadia's five million yearly visitors speed up or down I-95 to Augusta or Bangor before heading coastward along Rte. 3 or Rte. 1A. Once they arrive, they drive the famed Park Loop Road, a 20-mile winding road through the

One of the best ways of exploring coastal waters.

Tom Hindman

35,000-acre park, which culminates at the top of 1,530-foot Cadillac Mountain with views of Blue Hill, Penobscot, and Frenchman Bay. In recent years, the number of vehicles on the loop has been so heavy that there have been traffic jams.

To reach Freeport, most visitors opt for exit 17 or exit 19 off I-95 (the coastal extension that begins as Rte. 295 in South Portland and leads to Topsham before rejoining the Maine Turnpike). The signs from the highway lead directly into Freeport, home of L.L. Bean and a growing community of factory outlets.

To get to Old Orchard Beach, most travelers take exit 5 off I-95, which leads to Rte. 5 and Old Orchard Beach. The town is home to a seven-mile long beach—one of the state's most significant sand beaches and the closest to Canada. During July more than 80 percent of the vacationers in Old Orchard Beach are French Canadian.

Then there is the rest of the coast. A small road sign leading off Rte. 1 on the right reads "Friendship." The whole Penobscot peninsula gets a similar simple sign or two. If you opt to heed one of these signs and turn off—and deciding which one or two to take can be the hard part, since any one could be considered a vacation destination—most likely you will find other visitors, but not as many as in Acadia, Freeport, or Old Orchard Beach. You could also find a place like Jonesport, where fishermen's houses are piled around the waterfront like lobster traps.

The best way to see the area is by car, unless you can get to Acadia National Park without one, and want to stay there, where you can travel on the free Acadia Bus system all over Mount Desert. Given the relatively long distances between towns on the coast be sure to plan carefully before you leave. Many secondary routes that access towns along the coast are narrow, two-lane roads, and they make travel slower than you might expect. For example, it takes a full hour to get from Rte. 1 at Orland to Stonington via Rtes. 175 and 15.

If you want help getting around the coast, and you're a member, check in with AAA. They can map various routes to your particular destination. Their offices on the coast are:

Portland—AAA Maine
425 Marginal Way
207-774-6377
Mailing address:
P.O. Box 3544
Portland, ME 04104
www.aaanne.com

South Portland—AAA Maine
443 Western Ave.
So. Portland, ME 04106
207-775-6211
www.aaane.com

CAR RENTALS

If you are flying into Boston, Portland, Bangor, or Bar Harbor, chances are you will rent an automobile to explore the coast. It is best to call well ahead of your visit to reserve a rental car, particularly during the busier season between Memorial and Labor days.

Alamo Rent A Car: 800-327-9633; www.goalamo.com (1000 Westbrook St., Portland; 207-775-0855). Pick up at the airport.

Avis: 800-831-2847; www.avis.com (Portland Jetport, 207-874-7500; Bangor Airport, 207-947-8383).

Budget: 800-527-0700; www.budget.com (Portland Jetport, 207-774-8663; Bar Harbor Airport, 207-667-1200; Augusta Airport, 207-622-0210; Bangor Airport, 207-945-9429; Rockland Airport, 207-594-0822).

Enterprise: 800-736-8222; www.enterprise.com (Portland Jetport, 207-854-0560; Bangor Airport, 207-990-0745; with other offices in Portland, Saco, Brunswick, Rockland, Lewiston, and Augusta).

Hertz: 800-654-3131; www.hertz.com (Portland Jetport, 207-774-4544; Bar Harbor Airport, 207-667-5017; Bangor Airport, 207-942-5519).

National Car Rental: 800-227-7368; www.nationalcar.com (Portland Jetport, 207-773-0036; Bangor Airport, 207-947-0158; Rockland, 207-594-8424).

COASTAL TOWN ACCESS

Here are approximate distances between selected cities and towns within the state. The time it takes to travel these distances varies widely, depending on time of year, traffic conditions and route traveled. The highway speed limit in Maine is 55 mph in populated areas, 65 mph in rural regions.

From Kittery to:	Miles	From Eastport to:	Miles
Old Orchard Beach	37	Machias	44
Portland	50	Bar Harbor	122
Freeport	66	Belfast	141
Brunswick	76	Camden	160
Augusta	107	Rockland	167

From Kittery to:	Miles	From Eastport to:	Miles
Boothbay Harbor	109	Boothbay Harbor	207
Rockland	131	Brunswick	217
Camden	135	Freeport	227
Belfast	153	Portland	243
Bangor	183	Old Orchard Beach	262
Bar Harbor	211	Kittery	293
Machias	249		

Others:	Miles
Bangor to Bar Harbor	46
Augusta to Rockland	42
Augusta to Belfast	47

BY PLANE

A fast way to get around the coast is by air. Following is a list of air charter services that fly on the coast.

Acadia Air Inc., Bar Harbor Airport; 207-667-5534; www.acadiaair.com.
Maine Aviation Corporation, Portland Jetport; 207-780-1811; www.maineavia
tion.com; info@maineaviation.com.
Maine Instrument Flight, Augusta Airport; 207-338-2970; www.maine-instru
ment.com.

BY FERRY

O ne of the advantages of visiting the coast of Maine is that you have so many opportunities to ride a ferry. Island residents live with their inner clocks set to the ferry schedule, and so will you when you plan to visit one of

The Islesboro Ferry leaves Lincolnville.

the coastal outlands. For information on ferries statewide, write or call the *Maine State Ferry Service,* P.O. Box 645, 517A Main St., Rockland 04841; 207-624-7777. Their Rockland number is 207-596-2202; their web site is www.state .me.us/mdot/opt/ferry/feryinfo.htm. Ferries for Maine's islands are listed in the **Recreation** section of each chapter under **Ferries.**

SHORT CUTS

Bottlenecks are common on the main thoroughfare, Rte. 1, that stretches the entire length of the coast. (I-95 follows the coast only between Kittery and Brunswick.) Rte. 1 in Maine is a two-lane highway, with few exceptions, and is often packed.

Sometimes traffic jams are unavoidable. Freeport is intolerable on a rainy day. Shop, if you can, when the sun shines. Rte. 1 between Kennebunkport and Ogunquit is almost always busy. The Park Loop at Acadia National Park is packed during the summer and empty before Memorial Day and after Labor Day. (The loop closes at the first snowfall and reopens in late spring. Cross-country skiers "own" the loop during the winter.) The bridge over the Sheepscot River at Wiscasset is another trouble spot.

Below are some shortcuts we've found. They are routes that will take you off the beaten track—and most of the time get you back on your way faster. If you don't want to miss the action, take Rte. 1 one way and the shortcut the other. Many of these shortcuts are just as scenic as more heavily trafficked routes.

- To avoid downtown Ogunquit en route to Perkins Cove. As you travel north on Rte. 1, take a right onto Pine Hill Rd. Follow to Shore Rd. and take a left. You'll come out at Perkins Cove.
- To miss the slow-moving traffic on Rte. 1 in Brunswick, continue on I-95 to Rte. 196 (exit 24) and follow south through Topsham to Rte. 1.
- To avoid bottlenecks at the bridge to the east of Bath, as well as the Wiscasset bridge. Take I-95 north to the Gardiner exit. Go east on Rte. 126 until you reach Rte. 32. Follow Rte. 32 south until you reach Rte. 1 in Waldoboro.
- To eliminate the heavily trafficked section of Rte. 1 through Rockland. Take Rte. 90 off Rte. 1 in West Warren. It leads you into Rockport, just south of Camden, and can save you up to 30 minutes on a busy summer day.
- To avoid the long jog in Rte. 1 through Hancock, Sullivan, Gouldsboro, Steuben, and Milbridge. Take Rte. 182, 4 miles east of Ellsworth, to Cherryfield. It is a few miles shorter than Rte. 1 and the Rte. 1A section from Milbridge to Harrington and is faster and much less crowded. It winds through the hills and is one of the most scenic roads in New England.

CHAPTER THREE
Endless Beaches
KITTERY TO KENNEBUNK

A summer day as blissful as they can be.

Most of Maine's just more than million residents live and work in the south of Maine. Why? The sea, the long, flat beaches, the proximity to Boston, the mountains to the west—all make it irresistible. Depending on what direction you're coming from, Maine begins or ends in **Kittery**, Maine's first city, incorporated on Oct. 20, 1647. Ships for the Civil War were built here, so was the nation's first submarine. The shipyard, which is open to the public and sits on Seavey Island in the middle of the Piscataqua River, is actively functioning today.

Kittery's is a retail economy based around factory outlet and discount designer stores. This is the beginning—or end—of a long stretch of what could be called the "shopper's coastline." The oldest residential part of town is in the pretty area called **Kittery Point**, which can be reached by Rte. 103, a winding, wooded state road that intersects with U.S. Rte. 1 and leads on toward Rte. 1A and York.

The Yorks are a group of small villages—**York Village, York Harbor, York Beach**, and **Cape Neddick**—which were among the first areas of the coast to be settled during the 1600s.

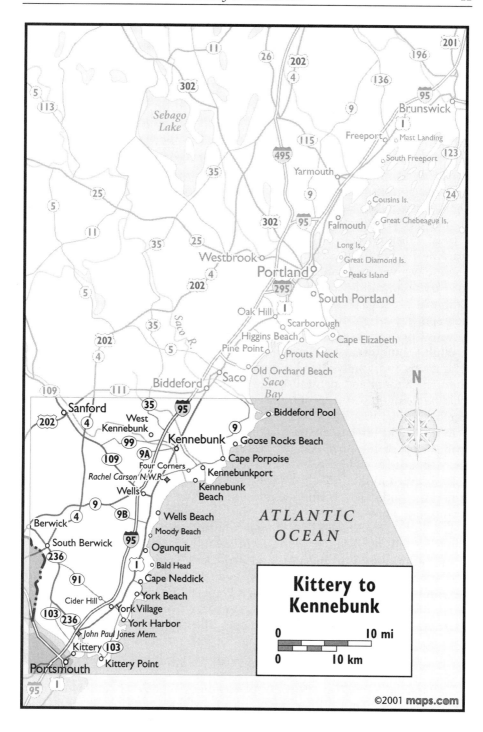

N

Kittery to Kennebunk

0   10 mi

0   10 km

©2001 maps.com

York has a well-preserved historical district. The Old Gaol Museum at the heart of York's "living history district" is the earliest example of stone architecture in the U.S. For most people, though, the Yorks have other charms. Some of the coast's best beaches are right here. Cape Neddick was one of the state's first summer resorts. Today York's coastal routes and shoreline are marked by an eclectic mix of stately homes, antique shops, working lobster boats, and striking stretches of fine white sand.

During the high season in July and August, **Ogunquit** and **Wells** have almost a carnival-like atmosphere and are packed with visitors from New York, Boston, Montreal, and Quebec who come for the cool ocean breezes, good restaurants, healthy cultural calendar—and great beaches. Wells and Ogunquit together have about seven miles of beachfront, roughly the same amount as Old Orchard.

Once a fishing village, Ogunquit, which in Algonquin means "beautiful place by the sea," was discovered by artists during the mid- and late 1800s. These days, you still can see painters with easels perched at the side of the road trying to capture the elusive south coast light as it plays on Bald Head Cliff, which rises a sheer 100 feet from the ocean. This area is a favorite vacation spot for artists of all kinds and for tourists who come to shop quaint Perkins Cove and walk Marginal Way, the mile-long coastal footpath.

While Ogunquit caters to an art-minded crowd, Wells, with a beach rimmed with shops and family-style restaurants, is a favorite stop for travelers with children. Birders and naturalists also flock here to visit the Rachel Carson Wildlife Refuge, 1600 acres of fragile coastal wetlands, a haven for an amazing number of migrating birds during spring and summer.

Kennebunkport has all the makings of a resort town: winding country roads, acres of coastline, stately pines, gracious inns, interesting restaurants, shops, boutiques and galleries, sandy beaches, and the sea.

First settled in the 1620s, the area's early history was peppered with Native American raids. The **Kennebunks** evolved into fishing and shipbuilding towns, and many of the historic captains' mansions are now handsome inns. This area became known as a summer "watering place" in Victorian times, when city folk arrived by train to take in sea air and rusticate.

Kennebunkport is the most often visited. Dock Square, a lively hub of shops and restaurants, is a major draw, as is Ocean Avenue, which snakes past **Cape Arundel** and the Bush estate at Walker's Point. To the south, Kennebunk Beach offers fine sand and a sheltered cove. A short drive north on Rte. 9 to **Cape Porpoise** gives one a glimpse into the past. The Cape is still very much a fishing village, and its harbor is a working one. The waters are so thick with lobster traps, it is almost impossible for pleasure boats to anchor anywhere near shore.

To the west, Kennebunk itself is a period piece. Eighteenth- and nineteenth-century homes offer a primer of architectural styles from Colonial and Greek Revival to Federal and Victorian. Best known is the Wedding Cake House, so

Walker's Point, former President Bush's summer home and once again a president's retreat, when his son President George W. Bush, makes a visit.

Herb Swanson

named because of its icing-like embellishments, a sterling example of Victorian excess. The bell swinging in the steeple of the First Parish Church was cast by Paul Revere and the steeple designed by Christopher Wren.

KITTERY TO KENNEBUNK: LODGING

Kennebunk

SEASONS INN
207-985-6100 or
   800-336-5634.
www.theseasonsinnofthe
   kennebunks.com.
55 York St. (Rte. 1 south),
   Kennebunk 04043.
Open: All year.
Price: Inexpensive to
   Expensive.
Credit Cards: AE, D, MC, V.
Handicap Access: Yes, but
   call ahead during the off-
   season.

Set against a backdrop of pines only minutes away from downtown Kennebunkport, this modest place has more appeal than most motels. During the high season that's particularly appreciated in this town where lodging can be hard to come by and expensive. Wood balconies lend a rustic air to the low-slung brick-and-stucco building, and the 40 rooms are, for the most part, tastefully decorated. Color cable TV, phones, air-conditioning, and continental breakfast are among the perks, and there is an outdoor pool. No pets.

Kennebunkport

CAPE ARUNDEL INN
Innkeeper: Jack Nahil.
207-967-2125.
www.capearundelinn.com.

Set on a hillside with handsome trees and shrubberies, this gray-shingled inn makes the most of its aerie over the Atlantic. The common areas, dining room, and guest rooms (seven at the inn, six at

cai@capearundelinn.com.
P.O. Box 530A, Ocean Ave.,
   Kennebunkport 04046.
Open: Mar.–Jan.
Price: Expensive to Very
   Expensive.
Credit Cards: AE, MC, V.
Handicap Access: Limited.

the motel, one in the carriage house) have dramatic panoramas of the sea. Rooms are decorated in pale tones—cream spreads with dark wood antiques and reproductions. A few of the bathrooms are on the small side, but many have vintage sinks and claw-foot tubs. Country wicker and antiques fill the parlors, while the dining room leans toward Early American. Not so the food, which is modern and inventive. Children in the motel only. No pets. No smoking.

Herb Swanson

The Captain Lord Mansion dresses up for the holidays.

**CAPTAIN LORD
MANSION**
Innkeepers: Bev Davis and
   Rick Litchfield.
207-967-3141.
www.captainlord.com.
innkeeper@captainlord.
   com.
P.O. Box 800,
   Kennebunkport 04046.
Corner of Pleasant and
   Green.

This is one of the coast's great inns. Seven generations of Lords lived in grand style here before it became an inn. Today it is an elegant stopping place in the historic district of this handsome seaside town. There are 16 bedrooms on three floors, all with private bath, 14 with gas fireplaces. Most have king- or queen-sized beds. A suite has been added to the mansion, featuring a grand bath with a double Jacuzzi and its own fireplace. The suite has another gas fireplace in the bedroom and a king-sized canopy bed, and not a little touch of the

Open: All year.
Price: Expensive to Very
Expensive.
Credit Cards: D, MC, V.
Handicap Access: Limited.

sybarite. The inn is filled to the brim with lovely antiques (most from the Federalist period), oriental rugs, and art. The beautifully restored woodwork and staircases are knockouts. A three-course breakfast includes muesli, fresh fruit, and yogurt; homemade muffins, and either French toast, fresh fruit pancakes, quiche, or Belgian waffles. With advance notice, the innkeepers are more than willing to accommodate a guest's special diet. The inn offers guests beach parking passes, beach towels, umbrellas, and mats. Children 12 and older. No pets. Non-smoking.

GREEN HERON INN
Owners: Charles and Carol
Reid.
207-967-3315.
www.greenheroninn.com.
info@greenheroninn.com,
P.O. Box 2578, 126 Ocean
Ave., Kennebunkport
04046.
Open: All year, except
Jan.–early Feb.
Price: Moderate to
Expensive.
Credit Cards: None,
personal checks and
travelers' checks
accepted.
Handicap Access: Yes.

Less than a mile from Dock Square, the Green Heron is a homey stop, just the thing for families. Rooms (there are 10 of them plus a cottage with kitchenette) are cozy with pastel quilts, extra pillows, modern motel-style bathrooms, TV, and air-conditioning. Each sleeps four (there's a double plus a trundle). The inn has many of the comforts of home—local and big city newspapers, books, jigsaw puzzles, cards, and games. An elaborate breakfast is included, with a range of choices from homemade English muffins, buttermilk biscuits, vegetable frittatas, blueberry pancakes to orange French toast and Welsh rarebit. No smoking. Pets allowed but not in the common rooms. Children welcome.

WHITE BARN INN
Innkeeper: Laurence
Bongiorno.
207-967-2321.
www.whitebarninn.com.
innkeeper@whitebarninn.
com.
P.O. Box 560 C, 37 Beach
Ave. (off Rte. 9),
Kennebunkport 04046.
Open: All year.
Price: Expensive to Very
Expensive.
Credit Cards: AE, MC, V.

It's hard to imagine this as a boardinghouse in 1800. It's too grand: lush landscaping, antiques, and English country floral fabrics. Fresh flowers, robes, and comfortable beds are a given in the 25 rooms, all with air-conditioning, telephones, and private baths. Seven junior suites also have fireplaces, sitting areas, marble baths with whirlpools, and TVs. The parlor, with its claret walls, elegant wing chairs, and garden views, is an ideal spot for an aperitif. The inn features an outdoor pool for guest use in the summer months. And the restaurant is arguably the best (and most expensive) in town. Breakfast is included in the room rate, along with afternoon tea (dinner is separate). Special off-season packages with dinner are available. No smoking.

Kittery

INN AT PORTSMOUTH HARBOR
Innkeepers: Kim and Terry O'Mahoney.
207-439-4040.
www.innatportsmouth.com.
6 Water St., Kittery 03904.
Open: All year.
Price: Expensive.
Credit Cards: MC, V.
Handicap Access: Limited.

This carefully renovated brick Victorian is a very civilized place to stay, located just across the New Hampshire border and not far from one of Maine's shopping meccas. The dining room and four of the five well-appointed guest rooms offer travelers excellent views of the Piscataqua River and its boat traffic. All have private baths with lovely restored bathroom fixtures. We recommend breakfast on the patio, with wild Maine blueberry streusel French toast, after blueberry and lemon soup—if the weather's good. No pets, children under 12, or smoking.

Ogunquit

HARTWELL HOUSE
Owners: Jim and Trisha Hartwell.
207-646-7210 or 800-235-8883.
www.hartwellhouse inn.com.
info@hartwellhouseinn.com.
P.O. Box 1937, 312 Shore Rd., Ogunquit 03907.
Open: All year.
Price: Moderate to Expensive.
Credit Cards: D, MC, V.
Handicap Access: Yes.

With 16 rooms in its two houses, Hartwell House is among the largest B&Bs in Ogunquit. Modeled after the English country inns of Europe, it is also one of the most elegant and serves a lovely "European" tea every day at 4:30. The rooms are large, full of light, carefully decorated, and furnished with Early American or English antiques. All are equipped with air-conditioning and have private baths, and many of the rooms have decks, patios or balconies, and views of the water. Several extremely large suites include a kitchen and a living area and are good for families or groups traveling together. Unlike many of the town's inns, the Hartwell has a good bit of property. Its two buildings flank Shore Rd., assuring privacy and plenty of greenery and gardens to enjoy. No TV or telephones in the rooms. No pets or smoking. No children under 14.

THE TRELLIS HOUSE
Innkeepers: Jerry and Pat Houlihan.
207-646-7909.
www.trellishouse.com.
P.O. Box 2229, 2 Beachmere Pl., Ogunquit 03907.
Closed: Jan.

The Trellis House is the sort of place that becomes familiar quickly, where guests feel at home soon after arriving. Originally a summer cottage, the gray-shingled house with large screened porch looks friendly, comfortable, and homey. Rooms are filled with antiques and collectibles. A fireplace in the living room encourages conversa-

Price: Moderate.
Credit Cards: MC, V.

tion and mingling, and there are many private nooks in the house. There are six guest rooms, including a two-room suite, all with private baths. A carriage house that has been renovated to hold four rooms, all with private baths. Three of the rooms feature fireplaces. Best of all, the Trellis House is within walking distance of the village, the beach, Perkins Cove, and Marginal Way. Full breakfast included. Children 14 and older. No smoking.

York

DOCKSIDE GUEST QUARTERS
Innkeepers: Eric and Carol Lusty.
207-363-2868 or 888-860-7428.
www.docksidegq.com.
info@docksidegq.com.
P.O. Box 205, York 03909.
Harris Island Rd. (just off Rte. 103).
Open: All year.
Price: Moderate to Expensive.
Credit Cards: D, MC, V.

Located on a peninsula in York Harbor, this hideaway compound mixes Yankee austerity with renovations and million-dollar views. The Dockside Restaurant is a short walk. People living aboard their boats sometimes move here for the winter. There's a shuffleboard court, croquet, and a sandbox. There are five guest bedrooms in the main house and an elegant white clapboard summer cottage with black shutters. Most have a bath, a porch, and direct access to the level, well-kept lawn. The four cottages are clean and neat. All of the apartments have private baths and private decks.

York Harbor

EDWARDS' HARBORSIDE INN
Innkeeper: Jay Edwards.
207-363-3037 or 800-273-2686.
www.edwardsharborside.com.
P.O. Box 866, York Harbor 03911.
Stage Neck Rd. just off Rte. 1A.
Open: All year.
Price: Inexpensive to Very Expensive.
Credit Cards: MC, V.

Come by boat and tie up at the pier. Take advantage of fishing rods made available to guests. This three-story, turn-of-the-century, sprawling, gabled inn looks like a mass of sails in a brisk wind. Inside, the house is immaculately kept, open, airy, and quiet. Most of the 10 rooms have a view, TV, and air-conditioning. Some have fireplaces; some share baths, others have private baths. All are furnished simply and elegantly. Out front, the well-tended lawn leads to Little Harbor Beach. Breakfast is continental, and a nice feature is afternoon wine and cheese, a great relaxer after a hard day at the beach. Children 10 and older. No pets or smoking.

KITTERY TO KENNEBUNK: DINING

Cape Neddick

CAPE NEDDICK INN
207-363-2899.
Rte. 1, Cape Neddick 03902.
Open: Tues.–Sun., except
    Mar.
Price: Expensive.
Cuisine: Country gourmet.
Serving: D.
Credit Cards: AE, MC, V.
Reservations:
    Recommended.
Handicap Access: Limited.
Special Features: Art
    gallery.

From the outside, the Cape Neddick looks like a typical country inn. Inside, the decor is clever and rather modern with a split-level dining room, abstract sculptures, and expressionistic canvases on the walls. The wood-burning fireplaces make things warm in cold weather. Chef Proprietor Johnathan Pratt changes the menu every two or three weeks; scallop ravioli with lobster sauce and crispy shallots made the right autumn beginning, and there were steamers and seafood chowder, made to demanding specifications, as well. The menu doesn't abandon the traditional things, but improves on them. Poached lobster in vermouth cream or venison stew in dried red currant sauce were delicious entrées, and the bread pudding with caramel sauce completed meals meant for the foraging time of fall.

Eating lobster outside at a picnic table makes it taste better.

Tom Hindman

How to Eat a Lobster (Notes on a paper placemat)

Twist off claw. (Beware spurts of hot juice, and sharp edges on the shell).

Crack each claw with a nutcracker, pliers, knife, hammer or what have you. (Rocks work.)

Separate the tailpiece from the body by arching the back till it cracks. (No mercy.) Bend back and break the flippers off the tail. (There's meat inside if it's a big one.)

Insert a fork where the flippers broke off and push. (Or crack open lengthwise, and pull.)

Unhinge the back from the body. Don't forget that this contains the "tomalley," or liver of the lobster, which turns green when it is cooked and which many people consider the best eating of all. (Others warn about mercury contamination; but it is delicious.)

Open the remaining parts of the body by cracking sideways. There is some good meat in this section. (Especially in the tops of the legs, and especially when it's a big lobster.)

The small claws are excellent eating and may be placed in the mouth and the meat sucked out like sipping cider from a straw. (Well, it's not so easy, but if you slide your teeth up the length of the leg joints, the meat comes out like paste from a tube. Congratulations on your daring, important new skills!)

Kennebunk

CHERIE'S BISTRO AND WINE BAR
207-985-1200.
7 High St., Kennebunk 04043.
Closed: Sun.
Price: Expensive.
Cuisine: Regional.
Serving: D.
Credit Cards: MC, V.
Handicap Access: Yes.

The food in this sleek new restaurant pleases with freshness and rightness; the pine-nut crust on the halibut complimenting the tender pale meat of the fish, as the hazelnut crust did for the more assertive swordfish. The filet mignon could speak lushly for itself, and was suitably paired with delicious, fresh vegetables like sliced carrots and red peppers, and tender new potatoes, roasted and garnished with parsley. The lavender panna cotta was silken, less unctuous than the more common crème brûlée but still rich, a dish of pleasure for any mouth. The Key lime tart with hazelnut crust brought a sour child out of a nightlong funk; it should have been ordered before dinner, but how could I have known that?

Kennebunkport

ALISSON'S
207-967-4841 or
800-667-2896.
5 Dock Square,
Kennebunkport 04043.

Alisson's is a classic burger joint, and jammed in summertime Kennebunkport. There's a butcher block bar where you can wait and watch. The help is affable and on-the-ball. On the menu, it's burgers,

Open: Daily.
Price: Moderate.
Cuisine: American.
Serving: L, D.
Credit Cards: AE, D, DC,
    MC, V.
Handicap Access: Yes.

soup, sandwiches, salads, bar appetizers, fried seafood, and daily dinner specials, as well as a famous giant lobster roll. Some of the names may be too cute, but the burgers make up for it. The French fries and onion rings are good, too. Alisson's also makes a noteworthy cookie monster, good for two, with Tollhouse cookies, ice cream, and chocolate sauce.

Kittery & Kittery Point

**CAP'N SIMEON'S
    GALLEY**
207-439-3655.
Rte. 103, Pepperell Rd.,
    Kittery Point 03905.
Closed: Tues. in winter.
Price: Inexpensive to
    Moderate.
Cuisine: Seafood.
Serving: L, D, SB.
Credit Cards: AE, D, MC, V.
Handicap Access: Yes.
Special Features: Great
    lighthouse view.

This is the perfect place to pop sweet scallops in your mouth or curl up with a nice French fry and gaze out the window at the sea. That's if you can get a window seat. The lobster—usually brought in earlier in the day to the docks below—may require more concentration, but it's worth it. The interior has the feel of an old boat that has been sealed up tight with yearly coats of shellac. There is nothing fancy going on in here with the food, either. The purpose is to see that you're properly filled full of fresh seafood and side orders, and to go on your way. But not before you're ready to leave.

**CHAUNCEY CREEK
    LOBSTER POUND**
207-439-1030.
Chauncey Creek Rd.,
    Kittery Point 03905.
Open: Mothers Day
    weekend–mid-Oct.
Price: Moderate.
Cuisine: Lobster.
Serving: L, D.
Credit Cards: MC, V.
Special Features: Great no-
    frills lobster.

This old-fashioned lobster pond sits against the edge of an embankment rising from a creek. Across the way are thick woods, making this like a nice homey tree house where you can lay waste to a lobster or two. They start serving at 10:30am, and we've known friends to indulge in a late lobster breakfast now and then. The steaming mounds of clams and mussels are succulent and legendary. The service is to the point, probably because they don't indulge in any side dish fanfare here. Bring your own beer or wine—and your own potato salad. Chauncey's is out of the way but well known.

Ogunquit

ARROWS
207-361-1100.
www.arrowsrestaurant.com.
Berwick Rd. (3 miles west of
    village), Ogunquit 03907.

Arrows is famous. It is usually in *Gourmet*'s list of the best restaurants in the country, and it is on any self-respecting Maine gourmet's list as well, although many of the locals might feel obliged to

Closed: Mon. and
  Dec.–Mar.
Price: Very Expensive.
Cuisine: Regional American
  with ethnic accents.
Serving: D.
Credit Cards: CB, MC, V.
Reservations:
  Recommended.
Handicap Access: Limited.

mention, "It's so expensive." At least at Arrows you can see why. Never was there so scrupulous a parking lot attendant, politely requesting I repark my car to achieve a better angle. And it was a wonderful place to wait for my hour-late dinner companion, with the bread person offering a rich foccacia and a sweet potato roll for consolation. I liked the split of Pouilly-Fuissé I ordered, too. We had the tasting menu and the multiple courses were exciting and wonderful, as I had anticipated. The chilled Hudson Valley foie gras tasted as dense and pleasurable as it could be, the house-made pickles thin as fine silk, and tiny, picked outside somewhere in the perfectionist gardens, along with the lettuces that followed, everything exactly right, not a blemish in sight. The service, split among many, was neither overweening nor neglectful; perhaps they take psychology lessons to get it so right. The grilled venison satisfied my hunger for the dark flavor of rare meat, and its accompanying narrow glass full of truffle cream set off sparks in my cerebral cortex. We had small, delicious pieces of cheese and tiny desserts, and good coffee, of course. We were happy.

JACKIE'S TOO
207-646-4444.
59 Perkins Cove, Ogunquit
  03907.
Open: All year.
Price: Inexpensive to
  Moderate.
Cuisine: American.
Serving: L, D in summer;
  L in winter.
Credit Cards: MC, V.
Handicap Access: Yes.

Jackie's Too is known for the generosity with which they pack their lobster rolls, among the least expensive in town, and all the basics that people like are on this menu. In the summer, the best seats are on the deck, within a stone's throw of the rocky cove. The atmosphere is casual and comfortable. In the off-season, you get a spectacular, albeit protected, view of the water.

JONATHAN'S
207-646-4777.
2 Bourne Lane, Ogunquit
  03907.
Closed: Tues. Nov.– Mar.
Price: Moderate to
  Expensive.
Cuisine: New England and
  Continental.
Serving: D.
Credit Cards: AE, D, MC, V.
Reservations:
  Recommended.
Handicap Access: Yes.

Jonathan's offers a raw bar and an extensive menu that leans toward seafood and pasta but also includes dishes like jaeger schnitzel and Tennessee tenderloin of pork. Owner Jonathan West's art collection covers the dining room walls and represents well-known local painters, past and present. You can take in the carefully tended gardens visible through the dining room windows. Jonathan's also provides an old-fashioned bright spot in the local nightlife with a convivial piano bar and weekend sing-alongs.

98 PROVENCE
207-646-9898.
www.98provence.com.
P.O. Box 628, Shore Rd.,
   Ogunquit 03907.
Open: Apr.–first week of
   Dec.
Cuisine: French Provençal.
Serving: D.
Price: Expensive.
Credit Cards: MC, V.
Reservations:
   Recommended.
Handicap Access: Yes

This is the southern Maine secret passage to Provence, the French world of strong, deep flavors and rich, delicious food. The foreign pleasures have drawn diners from New Hampshire and Massachusetts, as well as further north in Maine, who know from word of well-fed mouth how reliable the food is here. The table d'hôte menu offers a fixed-price dinner with appetizer, entrée, and dessert, or you can order à la carte, as we did, starting with boned quail stuffed with fig chutney, and a fricassee of lobster with honey and ginger cream: both delicious, though I need a while longer to agree that lobster tastes better slightly undercooked. Then on to rabbit stewed in red wine with sage buttered pappardelle, the meat tender, the sauce rich and flavorful, and the wide flat noodles al dente, and sea scallops with wild mushroom risotto. The risotto was perfectly made, each grain of rice chewy and dense with flavor; and the slightly undercooked scallops I do now prefer. Nougat glacée came last, frozen dried fruit and nuts in whipped cream, it was a novelty that pleased us. The espresso smelled like heaven and tasted like it could get you there.

York & York Harbor

FLO'S HOTDOGS
Unlisted phone.
Rte. 1, York 03909.
Open: All year.
Price: Inexpensive.
Cuisine: American.
Serving: L.
Credit Cards: None.

It's not the hot dog. It's the sauce, the abuse, the atmosphere, and probably something deeper than that. Just past Pie in the Sky on Rte. 1, this one-story shack with no real sign is the destination of experienced travelers, rich and poor, who come here from all over the country. There's no real parking lot. You just pull over. Inside, not only is there no view, there are no windows, just a few old yellow wooden swivel stools and an order counter. "Here the customer is never right," says Gail, Flo's daughter-in-law. Ah, delicious.

YORK HARBOR INN
207-363-5119 or
   800-343-3869.
www.yorkharborinn.com.
Rte. 1A, York Harbor 03911.
Open: All year.
Price: Moderate to
   Expensive.
Cuisine: American.
Serving: L, D, SB.

This 17th-century white clapboard inn offers broiled scrod, milky clam chowder, a cluster of many small dining rooms, and a partial view of the harbor. Heavy wood beams, low ceilings, creaky wood floors provide a historic sensibility. The menu has grown more elaborate over the years, with delicious possibilities like seared sea scallops served on spinach risotto, a wonderful combina-

Credit Cards: AE, MC, V.
Reservations:
  Recommended.
Handicap Access: Yes.

tion, or classic roast rack of lamb. This is also good place for a dose of classic New England dining, with steamed lobster, crab cakes, and mussels cooked in white wine.

KITTERY TO KENNEBUNK: FOOD PURVEYORS

BAKERIES

Bernard's Bakery (207-646-26698; Shore Rd., Ogunquit). Delicious bread and cake.

Bread & Roses (207-646-4227; 28A Main St., Ogunquit). Fresh pastries and bread baked on the spot.

Cherie's Sweet Treats & Other Eats (207-985-1200; 7 High St., Kennebunk). Peppermint brownies, strawberry-topped cupcakes, and raspberry-walnut tarts compete with the blueberry and strawberry pie in the summertime; the winter selection is sure to be fine.

BREWERIES

Kennebunkport Brewing/Federal Jack's Brew Pub (207-967-4322; 8 Western Ave., Kennebunk). A brew pub and microbrewery at the site of a historic shipyard, and brewer of Shipyard Export Ale. The pub is okay. The beer is better.

CANDY & ICE CREAM

The Goldenrod (207-363-2621; York Beach). A vacation at the beach wouldn't be the same without saltwater taffy. They make it right here and call it "kisses." Watch it being made or grab an ice-cream soda at their old-fashioned soda fountain. Also a full restaurant.

Harbor Candy Shop (207-646-8078; 248 Main St., Ogunquit). European-style chocolates are made and sold here in a very elegant atmosphere. Their marzipan is out of this world.

DELIS & TAKE-OUT

Anthony's Food Shop (207-363-2322; 679 Rte. 1, York). Beer, apples, pizza, but best is a selection of great Green Mountain coffees like Columbian Supremo, served with real cream. If you didn't get a decent cup of coffee for breakfast, stop here.

Hamilton's (207-646-5262; 2 Shore Rd., Ogunquit). Eat-in or take-out available from this deli on the main drag. A favorite breakfast spot for residents.

Old Salt's Pantry (207-967-4966; Dock Sq., Kennebunkport). Don't be fooled by its size. This tiny deli offers a huge take-out menu: sandwiches, subs, burgers, gourmet tidbits, wine, and beer.

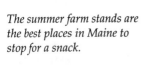

The summer farm stands are the best places in Maine to stop for a snack.

Herb Swanson

FARM STANDS

Pine Tree Gardens (207-646-7545; 411 Post Rd., Wells). Local produce, wine, cheese, and fresh flowers.
Spiller's Farm Stand (207-985-2575; Branch Rd., Rte. 9A, Wells). Farm produce, and pick your own crops (see **Berry & Apple Picking**, below).
Wallingford Farm (207-985-2112; Rte. 1, Kennebunk). From local produce to plants to gifts.
Zack's (Rte. 91, York). Corn, pumpkins, and all the rest, during the growing season.

FAST FOOD

Bob's Clam Hut (207-439-4233; Rte. 1, Kittery). Fried clams, sweet and steaming, are served here year-round. The ultimate in fast finger food.

GOURMET FOOD STORES

Stonewall Kitchen (207-351-2712; 469 U.S. Rte. 1, York and 207-236-8979; 182 Middle St., Portland). Mmmmm. Roasted garlic and onion jam. Ginger-peach tea jam. This award-winning maker of gourmet condiments opened a second store in Portland's Old Port. They've also added a children's line, so now you can get one of their clever peanut butter and jam kits for the little folks back home.

KITTERY TO KENNEBUNK: CULTURE

ARCHITECTURE

Few examples of the structures built by European settlers prior to 1760 remain. Farmhouses, forts, and other early buildings were victims of the ongoing French and Indian Wars, which lasted from 1675 to 1763. One exception is the *Old Stone Gaol* in York, a stone building built in 1653. The old jail house is now a museum and is the oldest stone building still in use in the United States.

The Greek Revival took hold in Maine during the mid-1800s, a time when the coast was experiencing a great influx of wealth from the shipbuilding and shipping trade. Many of the newly wealthy were ships' captains, and their houses, which line the coast, are rich with elegant woodworking and flying staircases. A good example of the Greek Revival is the *Sarah Orne Jewett House* in South Berwick. In Kennebunk, the *Wedding Cake House* is perhaps the state's most conspicuous example of the Gothic. Portland is home to the state's most outstanding example of the Italianate phase of the Gothic Revival.

Guided walking tours detailing Kennebunk's architectural heritage leave from the *Brick Store Museum*; www.brickstore.com; brickstore@cybertours .com. Call 207-985-4802 for information.

GALLERIES

Mast Cove Gallery (207-967-3453; 1 Mast Cove Ln., Kennebunkport). This gallery offers what art critic Gail Glickman calls a "solid introduction to Maine art." 10:30–4 daily, with some seasonal changes.

GARDENS & GARDEN TOURS

Fairy Garden At Kennebunk Free Library (207-985-2173; 112 Main St., Kennebunk). Children's garden includes a touch and sniff section.

Hamilton House (603-436-3205; Vaughan's Ln., S. Berwick). Overlooking the Pisquataqua River, these are some of the most beautiful grounds in Southern Maine. Open June–mid-Oct., dawn to dusk.

St. Anthony Monastery and Shrines (207-967-2011; 28 Beach Ave., Kennebunkport). This tranquil retreat is a turn-of-the-century Tudor mansion purchased by the Lithuanian Franciscans in 1949. The gardens and lawns are beautiful. A wooded walkway follows the Kennebunk River and offers fine views of the well-manicured grounds and the ocean. Grounds are open to the public (guest accommodations are available).

J. David Bohl

Overlooking the Pisquataqua River, the Hamilton House has beautiful grounds and gardens.

GUIDED TOURS

During the summer months, the *Ogunquit Chamber of Commerce* operates a free, unnarrated trolley that covers the town's high spots from Perkins Cove to the west and Footbridge Beach to the east. The four trolleys—all named after garden flowers—operate daily from Memorial Day weekend through Columbus Day.

The *Intown Trolley Company* in Kennebunkport (207-967-3686) has provided old-fashioned narrated tours of the seaport for more than 10 years, including historical notes, stops at the Franciscan monastery, major inns, hotels, and shopping. There is a nominal fee for the service, and the fare is good for the entire day. The Intown Trolley leaves from the bottom of Ocean Ave. near Dock Sq. during July and August, and it is good to line up 15 minutes before scheduled departure.

HISTORIC BUILDINGS & SITES

FORT MCCLARY
207-384-5160.
Rte. 103 (Kittery Point Rd.),
 Kittery Pt. 03905.
Season: May 30–Oct. 1.
Nominal admission.

This 1715 granite fortification saw strategic duty during the Revolutionary War, the War of 1812, the Civil War, and the Spanish-American War. The fort was named for Andrew McClary, a local soldier who died at the Battle of Bunker Hill.

HAMILTON HOUSE
603-436-3205.
www.spnea.org.
Vaughan's Ln., S. Berwick
03908.
Season: June–mid-Oct.;
hourly tours Wed.–Sun.
11–5.
Nominal admission
charged; grounds open
dawn till dusk year
round.

First built for a wealthy merchant during the 18th century, Boston residents Emily Tyson and daughter Elise altered it in 1898 for use as a summer home. The two women, friends of author Sarah Orne Jewett, outfitted it in grand Colonial Revival style. Several of the younger Tyson's period photographs are on view, testament to the civilized coastal summer life they enjoyed. The gardens and grounds are lovely, and many visit to picnic in warm weather or cross-country ski in winter.

**LADY PEPPERELL
HOUSE**
Kittery Pt.
Season: Summer: 1–4.
Admission charged.

The 1760 Georgian home of Sir William Pepperell's widow (Sir William was given a baronetcy for his success at the Battle of Louisburg on Cape Breton) contains period furnishings and several family portraits—including a portrait of Jane Pepperell, the first painting to be associated with Maine, as well as a good collection of fans and dishes.

NOTT HOUSE
207-967-2751.
Maine St., Kennebunkport
04046.
Season: Mid-June–mid-Oct., Tues.–Fri. 1–4.

Also known as "White Columns," this beautiful Greek Revival home dates to 1853. It still retains many of its original features and furnishings including wallpapers, carpets, and furniture.

**OLD YORK HISTORICAL
SOCIETY**
207-363-4974.
www.oldyork.org.
707 York St., Old York
03909.
Season: Mid-June–Sept. 30.
Nominal admission.

A "living history" museum that comprises six buildings, including the Old Gaol (1719), the oldest public building still in use; the Emerson-Wilcox House (1740); the Elizabeth Perkins House (1731); the Jefferds Tavern (1750); the Old Schoolhouse; and the John Hancock Wharf and Warehouse. A good representation of the life and commerce of an 18th-century seaside town. Demonstrations of cooking and maritime crafts; displays of period furniture, china, and glass, and the only complete set of American crewel work bed-hangings in existence (at the Emerson-Wilcox House).

**SARAH ORNE JEWETT
HOUSE**
207-384-5269.
www.spnea.org.
5 Portland St., S. Berwick
03908.

First built in 1718, this mansion was later enlarged and remodeled for civic leader Jonathan Sayward, well known during the Revolution for his Tory sympathies. The owner was wealthy but frugal, and with its small, modest rooms and good, locally made woodwork and furniture, this well-

The house of Sarah Orne Jewett, who wrote The Country of the Pointed Firs, *a book Willa Cather characterized as "A message to the future, a message in a universal language...that even the scythe of Time spares."*

Maine Historic Preservation Commission

Season: June 1–Oct. 15, Wed.–Sun. 11–5; tours on the hour. Nominal admission.

preserved home provides a realistic view of a Mainer's lifestyle during the 18th century. The house also has a good collection of Chippendale and Queen Anne furniture, family portraits, and china brought back as booty from the successful skirmish with the French at Louisburg in 1745. Maintained by the Society for the Preservation of New England Antiquities.

SAYWARD-WHEELER HOUSE
603-436-3205.
www.spnea.org.
79 Barrell Ln. Extension, York Harbor 03911.
Season: June–mid-Oct., Sat., Sun. 11–5; hourly tours.
Admission charged.

It was once the home of Jonathan Sayward, a local merchant who remodeled in the 1760s. Few changes followed, and it has been on show since the 1860s. Original furnishings and family portraits remain.

LIBRARIES

Historical Society of Wells & Ogunquit (207-646-4775; who@dwi.net; Rte. 1, Wells). A collection of manuscripts and genealogies pertaining to the two towns and their early residents.

Kennebunk Free Library (207-985-2173; 112 Main St., Kennebunk).

Ogunquit Memorial Library (207-646-9024; 74 Shore Rd., Ogunquit). Nannie Connarroe built the library in 1897 as a memorial to her late husband George M. Connarroe. It is on the National Register of Historical Places. Open June–Sept., Mon.–Sat. 9–12, 2–5.

Rice Public Library (207-439-1553; www.rice.lib.me.us; 8 Wentworth St., Kittery). Housed in its original 1888 building, the Rice has an extensive collection of Maine books and historical materials on Kittery.

LIGHTHOUSES

The historic, whitewashed lighthouse at *Goat Island* was automated in 1990 as a cost-saving measure by the government. There are 60 lighthouses along the coast of Maine, each with its own legends of shipwrecks, ghosts, drownings, and rescues. Some now serve as museums, private homes, or bed and breakfasts.

You can check out *Cape Neddick Light,* built in 1879, from Sohier Park (follow the signs leading off Rte 1A in York). Stay for a picnic. This is a lovely park with interesting rock formations and good vantages for bird watching.

MUSEUMS

AUTO MUSEUM AT WELLS
207-646-9064.
wellsauto@aol.com.
1181 Post Rd., Wells 04090.
Season: Memorial
Day–mid-Sept.: daily
10–5. Memorial
Day–Columbus Day:
weekends 10–5.
Admission: $4 adults; $2
children 6–12; under 6
free.

Once a private collection, now a nonprofit car-lovers' organization, this museum has a collection of more than 70 restored gas-, steam-, and electric-powered automobiles. Stanley Steamers, Rolls Royces, Fords, and motorcycles, license plates, bicycles, antique toys, and nickelodeons; this is an entertaining look at our motoring past, among other things. Particularly fun are rides in one of the museum's Model Ts.

BRICK STORE MUSEUM
207-985-4802.
www.brickstoremuseum.org.
117 Main St., Kennebunk
04043.
Open except from
Christmas to Mar:
Wed.–Sat. and by appt.
Admission $5 adults, $4.50
seniors, $2 students
under 6 free; discounts
available.

This museum that tells the story of Kennebunk began as a small collection of artifacts on display in the town's old general store. These days it encompasses an entire block and runs changing exhibits highlighting the region's maritime and social history. From June to September, the museum offers guided walking tours pointing out the town's architectural highlights.

KITTERY HISTORICAL AND NAVAL MUSEUM
207-439-3080.
Located near the
intersection of Rte. 1 and

Kittery is Maine's oldest town, and this relatively young museum (1976) commemorates the port's shipbuilding history. There is a 12-foot model of the *Ranger*, John Paul Jones' ship that had its keel laid here. Other exhibits feature the accom-

Rte. 236, next to the Town Office on the Rogers Rd. Extension.
Season: June–mid Oct., Tues.– Sat. 10–4, or by appointment.
Admission: $3 adults; $1.50 kids 7–15; those under 7 free; families of 3 or more, $6 max.

plishments of the naval yard, the first U.S. shipyard and the one responsible for the building of several Civil War ships, as well as the country's first submarine.

OGUNQUIT MUSEUM OF AMERICAN ART
207-646-4909.
183 Shore Rd., Ogunquit 03907.
Season: July 1–Sept. 1: Mon.–Sat. 10:30–5, Sun. 2–5.
Admission: $4 adults; $3 seniors and students; under 12 free.

Built by the painter Henry Strater, the museum houses a good collection of 20th-century American artists who came here to scramble over the rocks, soak up the summer sun and, of course, paint and sculpt. A late director of the Metropolitan Museum of Art described this as a gem, "the most beautiful small museum in the world." A new wing has been added to house special summer shows and selections from the permanent collection. Works on view are by Walt Kuhn, Marsden Hartley, Rockwell Kent, and others.

SEASHORE TROLLEY MUSEUM
207-967-2800.
www.trolleymuseum.org
195 Log Cabin Rd., Kennebunkport 04046.
Season: June–Oct. Daily, 10–5. Tours 11:15, 1:30.
Admission charged.

Back when mass transportation was fashionable, handsome trolleys like the ones on display here carried passengers almost everywhere. This museum has the world's largest and oldest collection—more than 100 vintage cars from Biddeford, Saco, San Francisco, Nagasaki, and Rome. It also operates a two-mile stretch of track for sunset trolley rides and a streetcar workshop where visitors can see a trolley restoration in process. Call or write them for a list of special streetcar events sponsored by the museum throughout the year.

NIGHTLIFE

The Club (207-646-6655; www.clubogunquit.com; 13 Main St., Ogunquit). This is the place to dance on the south coast.

Federal Jack's Brew Pub (207-967-4322; 8 Western Ave., Kennebunk). Live music on the weekend, and the neighborhood brew on tap.

The Front Porch Cafe (207-646-4005; 1 Shore Rd., Ogunquit). Listen to the strains of the piano until the wee hours in this piano bar. There is also a restaurant here.

Mast Cove Gallery (207-967-3453; 1 Mast Cove Lane, Kennebunkport). This gallery hosts jazz and blues concerts every Wednesday night in the summer. Past performers have included Bill Mays, Thomas Snow, James Montgomery, and Bruce Marshall.

SCHOOLS

Landing School of Boat Building and Design (207-985-7976; www.landingschool.org; River Rd., Arundel). Learn how to build your own sailing craft in their September to June program.

SEASONAL EVENTS

Harvestfest (207-363-4422; York). An old-fashioned New England harvest festival with oxcart races, apple bobbing, and a big-time tug of war. The weekend after Columbus Day.

July 4th Weekend Celebration (207-967-0857; Kennebunk and Kennebunkport). Concerts, picnic, silent auction.

Laudholm Trust Nature Crafts Festival (207-646-1555; Wells Reserve at Laudholm Farm, Wells). Juried crafts show by artists and craftspeople. Weekend after Labor Day.

Sandbuilding Contest (207-646-2939; Ogunquit). Late July.

THEATER

Theater in coastal Maine is generally an unpretentious experience. Patrons often arrive in jeans and Bean boots to enjoy Shakespeare, Fugard, Mamet, or Pinter. Call for season schedules, times, and ticket prices.

Hackmatack Playhouse (207-698-1807; www.hackmatack.org; 538 Rte. 9, Berwick). Musicals in the summer.

Ogunquit Playhouse (207-646-5511; www.ogunquitplayhouse.org; Rte. 1, Ogunquit). For more than 66 summers they have presented musicals and comedies with big-name performers. June–Sept.

Shenanigan's Productions (207-646-6825; www.shenanigans.org; P.O. Box 248, Ogunquit 03907). Dinner theater at Jonathan's (see **Dining**) Wed. July–Sept.

Theater Cruises (207-967-4938 or 207-967-5595; Kennebunkport Marina on Ocean Ave., Kennebunkport). Maritime Productions writes, directs, and acts in a two-hour cruise on the ocean, during the months from June to September, recounting "tales of intrigue and horror from our Maritime Past and Present." Not for kids under six, or the squeamish.

KITTERY TO KENNEBUNK: RECREATION

Herb Swanson

Striper fishing in York, with Nubble Light in the distance.

BEACHES

Crescent and Seapoint Beaches; Seapoint Rd., Kittery. Crescent Beach, a 625-yard sand beach and its 550-yard sister beach Seapoint across a small peninsula are nice, but have limited parking.

Drakes Island and Laudholm Beaches; Rte. 1 to Drakes Island Rd., Wells. This is really one beach with two names. It's comparatively quiet here in the height of the summer, even when nearby Moody is jammed. It is 940 yds. with accompanying saltwater farm and nature center; limited parking.

Gooch's Beach; Rte. 9 to Sea Rd., then left onto Beach Ave. past Kennebunk Beach, Kennebunk. The beach of choice for Kennebunkport residents and summer people including surfers, this is a crescent-shaped sand and shingle beach with a rocky point; 1,300 yds.; parking is limited to those with permits, so take the trolley. It's well worth the ride.

Goose Rocks Beach; Rte. 9 to Dyke Rd., then left onto King's Hwy., Kennebunkport. Lovely beach that attracts both swimmers and bird watchers (there's a salt marsh at the southeast end); 3,600 yds.; parking limited.

Kennebunk Beach; Rte. 9 to Sea Rd., then left onto Beach Ave., Kennebunk. Sand and shingle beach popular among families and surfers. It's hard to park here, and illegal if you don't have a sticker; take the trolley instead; 820 yds.

Long Beach; Rte. 1A, York, and Short Sands; Rte. 1A, York Beach. Long Beach, at 2,180 yds., and **Short Sands**, 410 yds., are two of the south coast's most popular beaches. The surfers like the waves. Parents like Short Sands, because it is near the heart of York Beach, so tired young beach bums can easily refuel with a snack. There are lifeguards and rest rooms at both. Parking is limited, so arrive early.

Moody Beach; Rte. 1 to Bourne Rd., then right onto Ocean Ave., Wells. A couple of years ago in a heated courtroom battle, residents tried to cut off public access to the beach. In a blow to the coastal aristocracy, they failed. Moody Beach is 2,750 yds. and surrounded by a honeycomb of summer cottages; facilities nearby; fee for the limited parking.

Ogunquit Beach; Rte. 1 to Beach St., Ogunquit. People love the sand here. It's refined, white and abundant (1,620 yds.). One local newspaper describes this as "very popular with the gay community"; another publication says that it is "near summer art colony." We call it fun. Facilities; fee for parking.

Parsons and Crescent Surf beaches; Rte. 9 to Parson's Beach Rd., Kennebunk. You get to these two pretty beaches along a private way owned by the Parson family. Total is 1,700 yds.; no facilities; limited parking.

Wells Beach; Rte. 1 to Mile Rd., then left onto Atlantic Ave., Wells. Motels and condos line the beach; 4,000 yds.; facilities; fee for parking.

BERRY & APPLE PICKING

Spiller Farms (207-985-2575; store: 207-985-3383; SpillerFarms@Juno. com; Rte. 9A, Wells). Strawberries and raspberries. June 10 to end of season. Apples. Pick-your-own-pumpkins and hay rides offered in the fall.

BICYCLING

Breton's Bike Shop (207-646-4255; www.bretonsbikeshop@cybertours.com; Rte. 9B, Wells).

Cape-Able Bike Shop (207-967-4382; www.capeablebikes.com; 83 Arundel Rd., Kennebunkport).

Wheels and Waves (207-646-5774; www.bikeandsurf.com; 579 Post Rd., Rte. 1, Wells).

BIRD WATCHING

Rachel Carson National Wildlife Refuge (207-646-9226; 321 Port Rd., Wells). This famous refuge includes 5,000 acres of salt marsh, white pine forest, and many, many birds. It is managed by the U. S. Fish and Wildlife Service, which offers limited access to birders and naturalists. Maps and guides to the preserve are available.

Seapoint Beach (Seapoint Rd., Kittery). Good bird watching on a tiny peninsula that sticks out into the Atlantic Ocean, just southwest of Brave Boat Harbor.

Webhannet River Marsh (off Rte. 1, Wells). Good birder's vantage for spotting shore birds and migrating waterfowl.

Wells National Estuarine Research Reserve (207-646-1555; Laudholm Farm Rd., Wells). This reserve has seven miles of trails on estuaries, rivers, and beaches. Wednesday mornings there is bird banding at 8am. Children's programs. Visitor's Center, 10am–4pm, Sun. noon–4pm. Trails, 8am–5pm. Parking fee July and August.

BOATING

CANOEING & SEA KAYAKING

Excursions–Coastal Maine Outfitting Co. (207-363-0181; 1399 Rte. 1, Cape Neddick 03902).

Kittery Rent-All & Sales (207-439-4528; Rte. 1, Kittery). Canoe rentals.

World Within World Sea Kayaking (207-646-0455; www.worldwithin.com; 746 Ocean Ave., Wells).

CHARTER AND RENTALS

Atlantic Explorer (207-967-4050, res., 207-967-4784, info.; www.atlanticexposure.com, www.nonantumresort.com; Nonantum Resort, Kennebunk). An ecology cruise that features a remote underwater video camera and has featured schools of fish, seals, and incensed lobsters: virtual scuba.

Edna (207-967-8809; Schooner Wharf, Kennebunkport). Capt. Richard Woodman is an obliging captain known to perform many ceremonies at sea for his guests aboard his pretty schooner. Two-hour and four-hour crewed sails, two-person minimum; private charters also negotiable.

Riptide Charters (207-363-2536; www.eangler.com; 1 Georgia St., York).

DEEP SEA FISHING BOATS

Bunny Clark (207-646-2214; www.bunnyclark.com; Perkins Cove, Ogunquit). Mid-March–mid-November. Full- and half-day trips as well as 12-hour "fishing marathons."

Ugly Anne (207-646-7202; www.uglyanne.com; Perkins Cove, Ogunquit). April–November. Half-day trips only July–Labor Day. Full-day trips April–July and September–November.

TOUR BOATS

Deborah Ann Whale Watching (207-361-9501; Perkins Cove, Ogunquit).

Finestkind Scenic Cruises (207-646-5227; www.finestkindcruises.com; Perkins Cove, Ogunquit).

Perkins Cove Lobster Tours (207-646-7413 or 207-361-9123; Perkins Cove, Ogunquit).

First Chance Whale Watch (207-967-5507; www.firstchancewhalewatch.com; 4 Western Ave., Lower Village, Kennebunk). Four-hour trips with guaranteed sightings. Sometimes a plane scouts the water first for whales. Shorter scenic trips on the Second Chance from same place.

CROSS-COUNTRY SKIING

Vaughan Woods State Park (207-384-5160; Old Fields Rd. off Rte. 236, South Berwick). 4.5 miles of snow-covered hiking trails that take you by Salmon Falls River and Cow Cove. Two miles are classified "easy," the other four miles are more difficult. Unstaffed.

FAMILY FUN

Fun-O-Rama (207-363-4421; funorama@nh.ultranet.com; 7 Beach, York Beach). Arcade.

Jellystone Park (207-324-7782; Rte. 109, Sanford/Wells). Family camping at Yogi Bear's place! Wacky fun all night long!

York Wild Kingdom (207-363-4911; www.yorkzoo.com; Rte. 1, York). Contained wild animals and an amusement park, summers only.

GOLF

Cape Arundel Golf Club (207-967-3494; Old River Rd., Kennebunkport). 18 holes, 5,869 yds., par 69. Cart and club rental, pro shop, clubhouse, lessons.

Cape Neddick Country Club (207-361-2011; www.capeneddickgolf.com; P.O. Box 2039, Shore Rd., Ogunquit). 18 holes. The course is available on the shoulder seasons occasionally, or if you stay at a hotel that has tee privileges, Like the York Harbor Inn; see web site for others.

Dutch Elm Golf Course (207-282-9850; Brimstone Rd., Arundel). 18 holes, 6,230 yds., par 72. Cart and club rental, pro shop, clubhouse, lessons.

The Ledges Golf Club (207-351-9999; www.ledgesgolf.com; 1 Ledges Drive, York 03909). 18 holes. Cart and club rental, pro shop, clubhouse, lessons.

The Links at Outlook (207-384-GOLF; www.thelinksatoutlook.com; Rte. 4, South Berwick 03908). 18 holes, 6,500 yds., par 71. Cart and club rental, pro shop, clubhouse, lessons.

Webhannet Golf Club (207-967-2061; Kennebunk Beach). 18 holes, 6,136 yds., par 69. Cart rental, pro shop, lessons. Call 24 hours in advance.

HIKING AND WALKING

Marginal Way, Ogunquit. Begin near Rte. 1 in Ogunquit and follow the paved
footpath over cliff and ledges all the way to Perkins Cove. It's about a mile
and is perfect for a morning constitutional or an evening sunset stroll.

Rachel Carson National Wildlife Refuge, Wells. Follow the signs off Rte. 9 to
parking area and trail head. This is another short and pretty walk rich with
coastal flora and fauna. The refuge borders the Wells National Estuarine
Sanctuary, a 16,000-acre preserve.

NATURE PRESERVES

A long with the *Nature Conservancy* and the *Maine Audubon Society*, both
described in the opening overview, several smaller conservation organiza-
tions have established a network of nature preserves that grace the coast like
pearls on a loosely strung necklace. Beginning in the south coast with the
Wells National Estuarine Sanctuary and the *Rachel Carson National Wildlife
Refuge*, these few small preserves are rich with avian and plant life, and they
are fragile havens for bird watchers, ecologists, and the garden variety of
nature lover. Spring, summer, and fall are good times to walk the trails and
observe nature in action. Many of the preserves turn over their trails to cross-
country skiers in the wintertime.

*Laudholm Farm, a working
saltwater farm in Wells.*

Herb Swanson

Laudholm Farm, Wells. Part of the Wells Reserve that also links the Carson
Refuge, this is a saltwater farm that boasts soils more fertile than the richest
Iowa farmland. Visitors can tour buildings and grounds to get a taste of this
endangered agricultural tradition.

Rachel Carson National Wildlife Refuge, Rte. 1, Wells. The naturalist summered on the coast, and during her lifetime she was instrumental in estab-

lishing the national environmental movement with the writing of environmental classics like *Silent Spring* and *The Edge of the Sea*. Her estate was willed to the Sierra Club and the Nature Conservancy. Today, this refuge is a living reminder of her crusade—and a wonderful place to observe nature. The mile-long trail built by volunteers in 1988 is handicap accessible.

Refuge at Brave Boat Harbor, Seapoint Rd., Kittery Point. Small refuge on a tidal inlet with good bird watching and an interesting trail through a salt marsh.

Wells National Estuarine Research Reserve, Rte. 1, Wells. An educational and research facility set on 1,600 acres of coastal marshland and woods with seven miles of nature trails. There are guided nature, birding, sky watch, and wildflower tours in the summer. Admission is free, but there is a nominal fee for guided tours and parking in July and August.

SEASONAL SPORTING EVENTS

Great Inner Tube Race, early August. On the river in Ogunquit. (207-646-2939).

Kite Flying Contest, early Sept. On the beach in Ogunquit (207-646-2939).

Sand Building Contest, mid-July. On the beach in Ogunquit, the time of this contest is governed by the tides (207-646-2939).

SURFING

A surfer and a kayaker ride the waves off Kennebunk Beach.

Herb Swanson

It's a south coast sport. That's where the best waves are, and, in the fine tradition of Moon Doggie and Gidget, that's where the best beaches are. Don't plan on sunbathing when you surf. The truth is that the best surfing is in the fall and winter. Even then surfing here is mostly for beginners. Here are some prime surf apprentice spots.

Gooch's Beach, Kennebunkport. Best surfing is at low- to mid-tide. The steep, thick waves break both right and left.

Moody Beach, Wells. Best waves at high tide. They break close to shore.

Wells Beach, Wells. Surfing best during the incoming tide. The waves break both right and left over sandbars.

York Beach, York Beach. Best waves are at low- to mid-tide, and they break right and left.

TENNIS

Kennebunk (207-985-6890; Parsons Field, Park St.). Two courts, plus four courts at Kennebunk High School.

Ogunquit (207-646-3032; Agamenticus Rd.). Three courts.

Wells (207-646-5826; Wells Recreation Park on 9A or Branch Rd., Wells). Four courts; key needed for the padlock, buy it at the Park or Town Hall.

York Municipal Courts (207-363-1040; Organug Rd.). Two courts at the high school are available; sign-up sheets are posted on the courts.

WHALE WATCH

Deborah Ann Whale Watching (207-361-9501; Perkins Cove, Ogunquit).

First Chance Whale Watch (207-967-5507; 4 Western Ave., Lower Village, Kennebunk). Four-hour trips with guaranteed sightings. Sometimes a plane scouts the water first for whales.

KITTERY TO KENNEBUNK: SHOPPING

ANTIQUES

Antiques on Nine (207-967-0626; 81 Western Ave., Rte. 9, Kennebunk). American and continental furniture, architectural elements, and textiles—even old garden accessories.

The Barn at Cape Neddick (207-363-7315; www.capeneddickantiques.com; Rte. 1, Cape Neddick). Recognized for its selection of American country furniture, accessories, and antiques, decorative arts, garden and architectural elements.

The Farm (207-985-2656; Mildram Rd. off Rte. 1, Wells). Fine English antiques from the 18th and 19th centuries and oriental porcelain. *Yankee* magazine called this one of the best in New England.

Kenneth & Ida Manko (207-646-2595; on Seabreeze, one-half mile off Eldridge

Rd., Moody). An intriguing selection of Americana and folk art, including old weathervanes.

MacDougall-Gionet Antiques Associates (207-646-3531; 2104 Post Rd., Rte. 1, Wells). For close to 50 years, dealers—now there are 60—have gathered in an old barn to show and sell formal and country period antiques.

Riverbank Antiques (207-646-6314; Wells Union Antiques Center, Rte. 1, Wells). Old statuary, antique pots, and other garden stuff. Wall lights, hanging lamps, French, English, and American furniture.

BOOKSTORES

Books Ink (207-646-8393; 15C Shore Rd., Perkins Cove, Ogunquit). Focus on math and history, catering to elementary and high school teachers, as well as general interest books.

Harding's Book Shop (207-646-8785; Rte. 1, Wells). A book collector's paradise with old and rare books, maps, and prints.

Kennebunk Book Port (207-967-3815; www.kbookport.com; 10 Dock Square, Kennebunkport). Books sold in an old rum and molasses warehouse, built in 1775.

Ogunquit Round Table (207-646-2332; 54 Shore Rd., Ogunquit). General bookstore, with something for everyone, open year-round.

CLOTHING

Dock Square Clothiers (207-967-5362; Dock Square, Kennebunkport; and 207-646-8548; Perkins Cove). Classic, natural-fiber clothing for men and women sold at two locations.

The Lazy Daisy (207-641-2820; 19 Shore Rd., Ogunquit). Summer linens, bright colored totes, and cotton sweaters.

GIFTS & SOUVENIRS

Animal Instinct (207-646-6304; www.animalinstinct.com; toys@animalinstinct .com; Main St., Ogunquit). Great stuffed animals, puppets, dolls, and toys for the young and young at heart.

Brass Carousel (207-646-8225; 13 Perkins Cove Rd., Ogunquit). Virginia metal crafts, brass, jewelry, decorative accessories, kites.

Brick Store Museum Shop (207-985-3639; www.brickstoremuseum.org; 105 Main St., Kennebunkport). Antique reproduction toys including a jacks set, rag doll kit, and old-time picture book. The shop also has grown-up gifts.

Compliments (207-967-2269 or 800-248-2269; www.complimentsgallery.com; Dock Square, Kennebunkport). An unusual gallery of outré pottery, mirrors, jewelry, lamps, and objets d'art. They also carry the Kate Libby calendar, a popular poster format calendar done by Maine artists.

Lighthouse Depot (207-646-0608; www.lighthousedepot.com; Rte. 1, Wells). Maine is almost as well known for its lighthouses as for its lobster. Here there are two floors of lighthouse memorabilia ready to go home with you.

Port Canvas (207-967-2717 or 800-333-6788 for the office; www.portcanvas .com; 9 Ocean Ave., Kennebunkport). Canvas suit bags, travel bags, duffels, totes, raincoats in a variety of sizes and colors. Custom orders taken too. Store open May through Dec.; office year-round.

JEWELRY

Swamp John's (207-646-9414; Oar Weed Rd., Perkins Cove, Ogunquit). They've been making and selling jewelry, including rings, earrings, and pins of Maine tourmaline, for more than two decades.

OUTDOOR & SPORTING GOODS

Kittery Trading Post (207-439-2700 or 888-587-6246; www.kitterytradingpost .com; info@kitterytradingpost.com; Rte. 1, Kittery). Just as Freeport's outlets grew up around Bean's, the shopping mecca here seemed to spring from the roots established by this rambling outdoor store full of canoes, sleeping bags, parkas, and pocket knives.

Liquid Dreams Surf Shop (207-641-2545; www.liquiddreamssurf.com; 365 Rte.1, Ogunquit). Surf stuff, skateboards, and clothing. Cold-water wet suits galore. They also rent.

Wheels and Waves (207-646-5774; www.bikeandsurf.com; Rte. 1, Wells). Surfboards.

CHAPTER FOUR
Our City on the Sea
THE PORTLAND REGION
BIDDEFORD TO FREEPORT

Hadlock Field is the place to be on a summer afternoon, watching the Sea Dogs at bat and eating a Sea Dogs biscuit (cookies and ice cream, of course).

Herb Swanson

Call it the "Maine Riviera" for its 7.5-mile sandy beach and its summer population, 60 percent of which is French-speaking Canadian. Or call it the "Coney Island of Maine" for its predominance of asphalt and its honky-tonk, boardwalk atmosphere.

French-speaking Canadians don't care what Old Orchard Beach is called—many consider it the capital of Maine. Since the 1850s, when the Grand Trunk Railroad opened between Montreal and Portland, French Canadians have flocked to Old Orchard Beach and its long, sandy beach—the closest to Montreal and Quebec City.

Everywhere is the sign "Ici on parle français," perhaps because so many year-round residents of Old Orchard and nearby **Biddeford** and **Saco** are of French ancestry. This part of the coast does all it can to make French Canadians feel at home, and there's still a devoted French-speaking following for its lovely beach and 4,000 campsites, 90 motels, 350 cabins, 120 restaurants, and 15 arcades. Restaurants feature bilingual menus. St. Margaret's Catholic Church on Old Orchard St. holds a mass in French every Sunday. Many of the corner stores sell French-language newspapers from back home in Quebec and Montreal.

If there is one city on the coast that is an anomaly, it is **Portland**. Outsiders may not be able to understand this at first. To the rest of Maine, Portland is considered more a suburb of Boston than the state's largest city and home to one-fifth of Maine's approximately one million inhabitants.

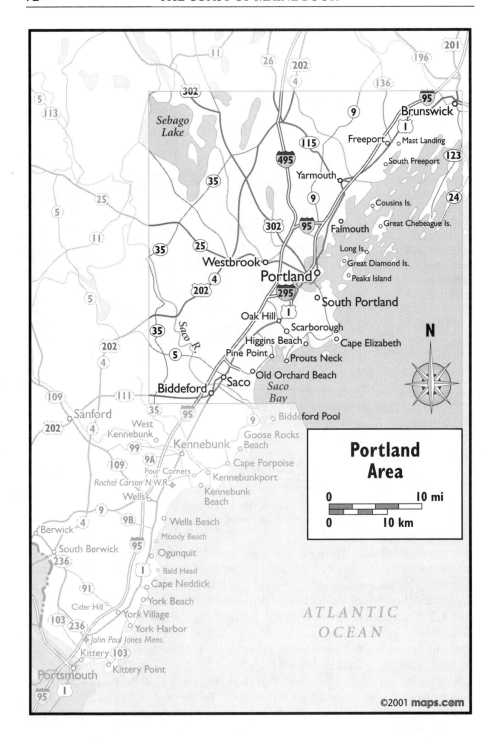

Portland
Area

0 ——————————————— 10 mi

0 ——————————————— 10 km

©2001 maps.com

Maybe that's because of its big-city ways. Boutiques. Ethnic food. Many classy, wonderful restaurants. A full-time, professional symphony orchestra. The I. M. Pei–designed Portland Museum of Art. An international ferry (to Nova Scotia) and an international airport. And, of course, the Old Port, the old waterfront commercial district that has been made over into a mecca for shoppers and business people. A writer for the *New York Times* once described it as the "San Francisco of the East."

The city sits on a moderately hilly peninsula framed by the Fore River to the west, the Presumpscot River to the East, and Casco Bay to the north. With its working waterfront and underneath its big city ways, it is the latest incarnation of a 19th-century seaport.

There are hundreds of islands large and small in Casco Bay (several of which have become bedroom communities for working Portlanders) that are fun to explore, with good swimming, biking, and walking.

A newcomer to **Freeport** will certainly see that this town was built for shopping. Rte. 295 off the Maine Turnpike deposits the traveler on a two-lane road leading right through town. For the most part, the view from the car window is good enough to eye the buttons on a Ralph Lauren shirt or catch the winsome line of a canoe bow at L.L. Bean.

Way back before there were factory outlets, and before there was even an L.L. Bean, this was a favored stopping place for the British navy. His Majesty's ships would berth and pick up the famous Maine white pine the Royal Navy used to make their masts. Even today, two major landmarks commemorate this early trading route—Upper Mast Landing and Lower Mast Landing where the mast pines were collected before being shipped.

Until 1981, there was L.L. Bean and the kind of stores you'd find on Main St. in any small town. Now it is wall-to-wall factory outlets. But the true beauty of Freeport isn't in the great bargains to be found there. It's that the town has retained much of its feel as a New England village and knowing that only two minutes' drive east on Bow St. and you're out in the country. There you get a sense of the way this part of the coast used to be: hilly, green pastures, tidy 18th- and 19th-century farmhouses, country lanes, pines, and firs.

THE PORTLAND REGION: LODGING

Cape Elizabeth

INN BY THE SEA
Innkeeper: Maureen
  McQuade.
207-799-3134 or
  800-888-4287 (out of
  Maine).

This modern-day, gray-shingled inn is a 43-suite complex, each suite featuring Chippendale furniture, TV, and VCR packed away in a cherry armoire, and terry-cloth robes in the closet. Many have ocean views. There are four cottages with rock-

www.innbythesea.com.
40 Bowery Beach Rd. (Rte.
   77), Cape Elizabeth
   04107.
Open: All year.
Price: Expensive to Very
   Expensive.
Credit Cards: AE, D, MC, V.
Handicap Access: Partial.

ing chairs on their porches. Amble down to Crescent Beach on the wooden walkway bordered by rose bushes. There are tennis courts, shuffleboard courts, a swimming pool, and a restaurant—the Audubon, which looks out on Casco Bay. Pets can be accommodated in certain suites with advance warning, and children are welcome. No smoking.

Chebeague Island

CHEBEAGUE INN
Innkeepers: The Bowden
   family.
207-569-2288.
www.chebeagueinn.com.
Box 492, South Rd.,
   Chebeague Island 04017.
Open: May–Sept.
Price: Moderate to
   Expensive.
Credit Cards: D, MC, V.

On a gently sloping hill overlooking Casco Bay, the Chebeague Inn is the sort of old-style seaside hotel that's fast becoming extinct. The 21 rooms—some are on the small side—are simply done in pale tones. Many have ocean views, as does the dining room, which serves breakfast, lunch, and dinner. While there's a public golf course right next door and beaches nearby, more sedentary types will set up camp on the expansive porch with its cane-backed rocking chairs. There's also a comfortable living room with loungers and a stone fireplace should the weather turn chilly. Chebeague Island is a 15-minute ferry ride from Cousin's Island and an hour's ride from Portland, and it's probably the island inn closest to shore.

Freeport & South Freeport

**ATLANTIC SEAL BED &
   BREAKFAST**
Innkeeper: Captain Thomas
   Ring.
207-865-6112 or
   877-ATLSEAL
www.atlanticsealbedand
   breakfast.com.
25 Main St., Box 146, South
   Freeport 04078.
Open: All year.
Price: Expensive to Very
   Expensive.
Credit Cards: AE, MC, V.
Handicap Access: None.

The tiny, picturesque village of South Freeport sits on the water; since it was built in the mid-19th century, so has the Atlantic Seal. Innkeeper and tugboat captain Tom Ring grew up in this old Cape, and generations of his family have gone to sea and returned with furniture, treasures, and seascapes, which fill the house. The four homey rooms have pumpkin pine floors, hand-hooked rugs, beds with homemade quilts, and private baths. One comes with a private whirlpool bath with a private deck, another has a window seat overlooking the harbor and a wood-burning fireplace. Capt. Ring has built a stone walkway down to the inn's dock and a deck overlooking the harbor with four rocking chairs. Breakfast is served on Sunday-best blue Camilla Spode with a silver setting and can include feather-bed eggs or blueberry and apple pancakes. Mountain bikes and a rowboat are available for guests. Tom also offers cruises out to the neighboring islands on the *Atlantic Seal* and the *Arctic Seal* (see **Recreation, Boating,** below). No smoking. No pets. Children welcome.

HARRASEEKET INN
Innkeepers: The Gray
  family.
207-865-9377 or
  800-342-6423 out-of-state.
www.harraseeketinn.com.
162 Main St., Freeport
  04032.
Open: All year.
Price: Expensive to Very
  Expensive.
Credit Cards: AE, CB, D,
  DC, MC, V.
Handicap Access: Yes.

With 84 rooms and suites, a health club and indoor pool, the Harraseeket Inn offers the kind of amenities you would expect to find in most big hotels. Right on the village's main street, this elegant, black-shuttered inn is really a series of connected buildings. The newest was built in 1997; the other two in 1798 and 1850. Many of the rooms have fireplaces, Jacuzzis, steam baths. All have air-conditioning and cable TV and are decorated in tasteful muted florals. The parlor has cushy wing chairs and couches and is accented with gleaming old silver and dark wood antiques. The dining room has a solid wine list, a growing reputation for inventiveness, and a commitment to using local seafood and produce (see **Dining,** below). The tavern is more casual. Breakfast, afternoon tea, and hors d'oeuvres are included in the room rate. Special packages available.

ISAAC RANDALL
  HOUSE
Innkeeper: Cindy Wellito.
207-865-9295 or
  800-865-9295.
www.isaacrandallhouse.
  com.
10 Independence Dr.,
  Freeport 04032.
Open: All year.
Price: Moderate to
  Expensive.
Credit Cards: D, MC, V.
Handicap Access: Very
  limited.

Just down the block from what is now the outlet center of Freeport's shopping district, descendants of Mayflower passengers built this farmhouse; later it was a stop on the Underground Railway and still later a speakeasy during Prohibition. The 10 rooms all have private baths, telephones, and air-conditioning; five have fireplaces. They share an upstairs sitting room with a VCR and a common-area kitchen, stocked with cheese, crackers, and soft drinks. Full breakfast can include homemade granola, pancakes, and raspberry coffee cake. Bring skates in the winter for the pond out back. There's also a caboose which has been converted into guest quarters with a queen-sized bed, two stacked singles, and bath with shower. Pets allowed. No smoking.

Old Orchard Beach

ATLANTIC BIRCHES
  INN
Innkeepers: Kim and Ray
  DeLeo.

This homey inn, set in a 1910 Victorian on one of the town's few tree-lined streets, seems out of place among the strip motels. The Deleos bought the inn in June 2001, and have added antiques and

207-934-5295 or
  888-934-5295.
www.atlanticbirches.com.
20 Portland Ave., Old
  Orchard Beach 04064.
Open: All year.
Price: Moderate.
Credit Cards: AE, D, MC, V.

charm. The inn has two one-bedroom kitchenette apartments and three guest rooms in the cottage, as well as five large bedrooms in the main house, with a guest living room for relaxing. An in-ground pool is welcome, keeping guests cool in hot summer months. Guests can relax on the big porch, read, or watch passersby coming and going from nearby Old Orchard Street, the town's main strip. The rooms have flowered wallpaper, oriental rugs, and lots of antique touches. Continental breakfast included: fresh-baked muffins, fruit salad, cereals, toast and bagels, and juices are served every morning. Children are welcome.

Portland

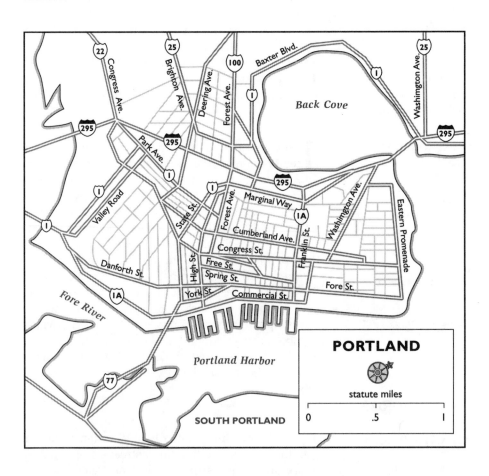

THE DANFORTH
Innkeeper: Barbara
 Hathaway.
207-879-8755 or
 800-991-6557.
www.danforthmaine.com.
danforth@maine.rr.com.
163 Danforth St., Portland
 04102.
Open: All year.
Price: Expensive to Very
 Expensive.
Credit Cards: AE, MC, V.

The Danforth is an 1823 Federal-style brick mansion with polished wood floors, spacious rooms, grand staircases, and 12 fireplaces. The nine guest rooms have been fully restored and furnished with private baths, some with working fireplaces. A townhouse with kitchen facilities, located one block up the street, is available for a long visit. Most rooms have deep white carpeting and follow rich color schemes (cool sea green, navy blue, and gold). A good choice for a family, Rooms No. 5 and 6 are rented together as a suite and share a bath. A full breakfast is included and is available in your room or in the sunroom. Health club passes are available for the guests.

**THE EASTLAND PARK
  HOTEL**
207-775-5411 or
 888-671-8008.
www.eastlandparkhotel
 .com.
157 High St., Portland
 04101.
Open: All year.
Price: Moderate to
 Expensive
Credit Cards: AE, D, DC,
 MC, V.
Handicap Access: Yes.

This old hotel with over 200 rooms has had a checkered existence; and up to the summer of 2001, many of the windows on its wide facade were broken or missing. Yet it was functioning as a hotel. A woman I know who works there said it was a matter of getting the historic preservation committee's approval for new, old windows; at any rate, they are now fixed. The Eastland was bought at a bankruptcy auction by Magma Hospitality Corp., a company that has a reputation for making a silk purse from whatever it chooses, and so far, so good. Several floors have been transformed into luxurious rooms. The tattered flags are now new, the windows clean, the bar on the top, with its good view, looks elegant (but why wasn't the Armangnac on the drinks list available?). Portland appreciates the huge investment; may the travel gods reward them.

INN AT PARKSPRING
Innkeepers: Lionel and
 Elinor Berube.
207-774-1059 or
 800-437-8511.
www.innatparkspring.com.
135 Spring St., Portland
 04102.
Open: All year.
Price: Expensive.
Credit Cards: AE, MC, V.

The ParkSpring was the first of the small, first-rate inns serving Maine's most cosmopolitan city. In a renovated 1835 townhouse on a busy city street, the inn is quiet and private. All six rooms have private baths The walls of the Courtyard room—our favorite—are painted a buttery yellow and a door leads to a city garden where guests may breakfast alone. Otherwise breakfast is at a long table in the sunny breakfast room. The Park-Spring is two blocks from the Portland Museum of

Art and not far from galleries, shops, and the Old Port. Children over 10. No smoking.

INN ON CARLETON
Innkeepers: Phil and Sue
  Cox.
207-775-1910 or
  800-639-1779.
www.innoncarleton.com.
46 Carleton St., Portland
  04102.
Open: All year.
Price: Expensive to Very
  Expensive.
Credit Cards: D, MC, V.

This stately Victorian-style brick townhouse is within walking distance of nearly all of Portland's sights, restaurants, and shopping. There are wide pine floors in several of the tall-ceilinged guest rooms, paintings and pastels by Maine artists on almost every wall, and a gorgeous English garden out back. The service is friendly and accommodations comfortable. There are six guest rooms, all with private baths. A full breakfast—usually homemade waffles, blueberry pancakes with real maple syrup, or quiche—is served in the formal dining room. After dinner in town, stroll along the Western Prom, just down the street. Children ages nine and up. No smoking; no pets, although there are two resident Maine coon cats, named Ben and Jerry.

The Pomegranate, in the middle of an old, established neighborhood of big homes in Portland's West End, has a striking decor and sense of style.

Michael Loomis

**THE POMEGRANATE
INN**
Owner: Isabel Smiles.
207-772-1006 or
  800-356-0408.

Near Portland's Western Prom, this stucco Georgian looks proper from the outside, but step inside and the visitor will be left breathless. Isabel Smiles was an antiques dealer and interior

www.pomegranateinn.com.
49 Neal St., Portland 04102.
Open: All year.
Price: Moderate to Very
   Expensive.
Credit Cards: AE, D, DC,
   MC, V.
Handicap Access: 1 room.

designer before she and her husband turned their efforts to innkeeping. Guest and common rooms feature exuberant hand-painted walls with trompe l'oeil and other imaginative motifs, along with a collection of original paintings, sculpture, and highly unusual antiques. There are eight rooms, each decorated differently and each with a private bath. Four of them have fireplaces. The carriage house has been converted into a separate, private suite with a kitchen for travelers. Below the suite is a garden-side guest room. Breakfast included. No children under 16, no pets.

WEST END INN
Innkeepers: Nicholas and
   Rosa Higgins.
207-772-1377 or
   800-338-1377.
www.westendbb.com.
146 Pine St., Portland 04102.
Open: All year.
Price: Moderate to
   Expensive.
Credit Cards: AE, MC, V.

This small inn in an immaculate 1871 brick townhouse is located on a quiet residential street in Portland's historic West End. There are six tastefully appointed guest rooms, each with its own modern, spacious bathroom and cable TV. A full, hot breakfast is included. The inn is within walking distance of the Western Prom and its views of the Fore River and the White Mountains. It's also a longer walk (or a short drive) to downtown and the city's Old Port. Children seven and older welcome. No smoking, no pets.

Scarborough

BLACK POINT INN
207-883-2500 or
   800-258-0003.
www.blackpointinn.com.
510 Black Point Rd.,
   Scarborough 04074.
Open: All year.
Price: Very Expensive.
Credit Cards: AE, D, MC, V.
Special Features: Outdoor
   pool, heated indoor pool,
   sauna. Children's
   activities. Four golf clubs
   available to guests.

The Black Point Inn is a luxurious place, with breakfast, afternoon tea, and a five-course dinner included in the daily rate. Three miles of beach lie outside, and you can carry a drink from the library bar to the porch and sit on the rockers on a summer evening. A birthday dinner there one year was marked by the disappearance of John F. Kennedy Jr.'s plane near Martha's Vineyard, and the news on the screen in the bar seemed to fit the age and traditions of the hotel, with all the sorrow and history it has passed through. No doubt some of the guests were family friends. It is a stoic, proud place, and the interior decoration is old-fashioned and the best quality.

THE PORTLAND REGION: DINING

Ever since I have been living in and visiting Portland, the city has regaled me with its good food and great restaurants. Several restaurant owners have continued their good work with new, great restaurants, and others have arrived from far away to renew a fading restaurant's joie de vivre, like Rob Evans from the French Laundry on the west coast, now running Hugo's. A dreary day in February can be transformed into Alladin's cave of wonders, when you stare alternately at the snow slamming into the buildings and cars on Commercial Street, from the big windows at Fore Street Restaurant, to the handsome young man slamming his cleaver into the roast loin of pork he's pulled off the fire. The open fires of various restaurants keep us alive during the long winter, when we congregate around them for the survival of our own joy in living.

Biddeford

BUFFLEHEADS
207-284-6000.
122 Hills Beach Rd.,
  Biddeford 04005.
Open: Daily year-round
  except 2 weeks in Nov.
Price: Inexpensive to
  Moderate.
Cuisine: Family seafood.
Serving: L, D.
Credit Cards: MC, V.
Handicap Access: Yes.
Special Features: Deck,
  take-out.

A wonderful, bright, family-style restaurant right on the way to pretty Hills Beach, providing friendly service, generous portions, and Two-fer Tuesdays, when you can get two dinner entrées for the price of one. The lobster pie is to die for. If you're traveling with someone who's not up to seafood, take heart. They have pasta, chicken, duck, and the Buffleburger on the menu, as well. The place is named for a chubby little duck that winters nearby in pretty Biddeford Pool. Ask your waitress for a pair of binoculars so you can see if you can spot one.

Freeport & South Freeport

JAMESON TAVERN
207-865-4196.
115 Main St., Freeport
  04032.
Open: Daily.
Price: Moderate.
Cuisine: American seafood.
Serving: L, D.
Credit Cards: AE, D, DC,
  MC, V.
Reservations: Optional.

The Jameson Tavern has been here practically forever, catering to the masses, most recently shoppers resting up from their L.L. Bean experience. Burgers and sandwiches are served in the Tap Room. The more formal offerings can be found in the pretty, unfrilly dining room. This isn't wildly exciting food: lobster, seafood, quiche, burgers, and sandwiches. But it will fortify you before you head out to the outlets again, and it does offer something for almost everyone. The tavern is a local historical stop, where Maine's founding fathers gathered at the beginning of the 19th century and decided to separate from Massachusetts.

Herb Swanson

The Harraseeket Inn has a Sunday brunch as sumptuous as a feast.

HARRASEEKET INN
207-865-9377 or
  800-342-6423.
162 Main St. (Rte. 1),
  Freeport 04032.
Open: Daily.
Price: Expensive.
Cuisine: Regional
  American.
Serving: B, L, D, SB.
Credit Cards: AE, D, MC, V.
Reservations:
  Recommended.
Handicap Access: Yes.
Special Features: Tableside
  cooking.

The menu here is always good for a surprise or two, and features local produce, fish, and meat well prepared and in interesting combinations. Decor is understated—white linens, fresh flowers, and flickering candles. Menus change weekly with nightly additions. Service is attentive, yet not overbearing. Start with warm crab crespelle topped with cherry tomato corn relish or chilled fennel vichyssoise with lemon crème fraîche. A Caesar salad for two can be made at the table. Main courses run from butter-braised lobster on Yukon gold and chive pancakes to ostrich filet with sweet potato hash. There are also classic dishes like rack of lamb and chateaubriand, carved at your table. There is a good by-the-glass selection of wine and an excellent wine list. Dessert is a must—try the sundae with dense homemade chocolate ice cream and caramel and fudge sauce, apple pie with a scoop of rich vanilla, or the Harraseeket's fresh fruit sorbet. For those who prefer, cheese and fruit are also on the roster.

**HARRASEEKET LUNCH
  & LOBSTER**
207-865-4888.
End of Main St., South
  Freeport 04078.
Open: May–mid-Oct.
Price: Inexpensive to
  Moderate.

Twenty minutes from downtown Portland and 10 from downtown Freeport, this is a favorite getaway, serving lobster on the deck with a protected view of boats, pine-topped islands, and Wolf's Neck. During the height of the season the line is long, and the kitchen can get a little over-

Cuisine: Seafood.
Serving: L, D.
Credit Cards: None.
Handicap Access: Partial.

whelmed, but they always remain cheerful and courteous. Better yet, schedule your visit for anything but the height of the lunch or dinner hour. For those who can make do with just lobster, clams, and corn, there's another window around the side of the shack where there is rarely anyone waiting. All the seafood tastes heavenly, the fries have that nice, dry clean taste, and the corn is worth ordering two ears at a time. The pies are okay; the homemade ice cream is better.

THAI GARDEN
207-865-6005.
491 U.S. Rte. 1, Freeport
  04032.
Open: Daily.
Price: Moderate.
Cuisine: Thai.
Serving: L, D.
Credit Cards: AE, CB, D,
  DC, MC, V.
Handicap Access: Yes.
Special Features: Take-out.

Located in a strip mall on the southern outskirts of Freeport, you come here for the masaman curry and pad Thai. The menu is large and varied with ample vegetarian entrées. If you like Thai food, you can't do much better than this. We have to admit that sometimes we go shopping up the road just so we can enjoy this Thai food.

Old Orchard Beach

JOSEPH'S BY THE SEA
207-934-5044.
55 West Grand Ave., Old
  Orchard Beach 04064.
Closed: Nov.–Mar.
Price: Moderate.
Cuisine: French with
  regional touches.
Serving: weekend B, D.
Credit Cards: AE, MC, V.
Reservations: Suggested.

In a town of snack bars and surf-and-turf joints, go to Joseph's for escargots served with native dulse, a wild mushroom torte, and fettucini Genovese (fresh pasta with artichokes, shiitake mushrooms, spinach, raisins, pine nuts, and lemon basil olive oil). Joseph's is known for its Angel Hair Pasta Maison (made with shrimp, scallops, and fish sautéed in sun-dried tomatoes, garlic, herbs, and cream). There's also a Saco Bay soup—scallops, mussels, and local fish in a bouillabaisse. Most people prefer to eat outside on the screened porch, which overlooks a manicured lawn with gardens, dunes, beach, ocean, islands, and sky.

Portland

BACK BAY GRILL
207-772-8833.
www.backbaygrill.com.
65 Portland St., Portland
  04101.

From grilled asparagus with yellow beets and chèvre to duck liver tortellini, from rare tuna steaks to lobster in white wine sauce, from rhubarb tart to vanilla Bavarian cream, the courses here are delicious. The wine list has a huge number of selec-

Closed: Sun.
Price: Expensive.
Cuisine: Regional American grill.
Serving: D.
Credit Cards: AE, D, DC, MC, V.
Reservations: Recommended.
Handicap Access: Yes.

BELLA CUCINA
207-828-4033.
653 Congress St., Portland 04101.
Closed: Mon.–Tues.
Price: Moderate to Expensive.
Cuisine: New Italian.
Serving: D.
Credit Cards: AE, CB, D, DC, MC, V.
Reservations: Good idea on weekends.
Handicap Access: No.

BOONES FAMOUS RESTAURANT
207-774-5725.
6 Custom House Wharf, Portland 04101.
Open: All year.
Price: Inexpensive to Moderate.
Cuisine: Seafood, American.
Serving: L, D.
Credit Cards: AE, CB, D, DC, MC, V.
Handicap Access: Yes.
Smoking Section.
Reservations: For parties over 6.

CINQUE TERRE
207-347-6154.
6 Wharf St., Portland 04101.
Open: Daily.

tions for particular connoisseurs; and after-dinner samplers of ports or sauternes make adventuring further in wine for novices fun, even if you do have to ask for the menu again to try and identify which is which. You will have the close attention of the waitstaff, who will fill your coffee cup over and over without needing to be beckoned. Find their menus, which change often, on the website.

Jim Ledue has been cooking in Portland for years, starting with the rest of his family at the Good Egg Café, which many of us wish were still around. What, I asked him, makes his vegan mashed potatoes so good? "It's the extra-virgin olive oil," he responded, continuing "We are not going for shock value." What you get here is reliable, delicious, and satisfying. The mixed sea roast of monkfish, swordfish, and scallops gives all the attention to the fresh fish, and with 13 white wines and 12 reds available by the glass, it all comes together just the way a customer likes it. He also offers light meals like a small salmon pasta dish with spinach and garlic to accommodate modest appetites.

We like this place for its atmosphere. The outside deck is a former ferry pier, and a good place to hang out on summer dog days because there's always a salty breeze and a cool harbor view. The menu, plain and simple New England seafood, is better at dinner than at lunch, but the service is more efficient earlier in the day. We have found the haddock a little too buttery for our taste and the pie merely adequate. Maybe this is a good place for limited objectives, like a cold beer with chowder. On a hot day, a cold draught at the open-air bar is sure to make up for any shortcomings.

Inside the brick walls of this old seaport building, you can find yourself, via your taste buds, on the Italian Riviera. Never have I eaten gnocchi like this, handmade, delicate, tender, the way Marcella

Price: Moderate to
  Expensive.
Cuisine: Italian, Ligurian
  Coast.
Serving: D.
Credit Cards: AE, MC, V.
Reservations:
  Recommended.

Hazan insisted they could be. They offer half portions, solving the endless problem of overloaded plates; but a half portion really is small, so be ready to order several courses. It's a delightful necessity. The arugula salad with shaved Parmesan was pristine and fresh, the leaves of arugula large, tender, pungent. Grilled vegetables with goat cheese made a splendid antipasto, followed by a pasta of linguini with clams, garlicky and savoury. Secondi, the meat or fish course, features Tuscan grilled steak, quickly made and enjoyed; the grilled salmon was perfect.

FORE STREET
207-775-2717.
288 Fore St., Portland
  04101.
Open: Nightly.
Price: Expensive.
Serving: D.
Credit Cards: AE, MC, V.
Handicap Access: Yes.
Reservations: Highly
  recommended.

Fore Street sits discreetly at its address with a tiny sign; it never advertises, and yet it is filled every night of the year, even during deep winter snowstorms. The dining room is large and noisy, centered around large, open wood ovens. The menu changes daily, with many items apple-wood smoked or grilled. Lots of the appetizers and salads come from local farms and gardens in season. I can always enjoy the roast pork and the roast quail. Since it's often impossible to get a table, stop in at the small, elegant bar located just to the left as you come in the door. The chairs are comfortable and the martinis exceptionally dry. One appetizer makes a small meal, and two make a perfect dinner. Dessert may be impossible to include if dinner was too ample, but it has left me with pleasant memories, especially the peach tarte tatin and the homemade chocolates.

Lobster and tomato salad could be the focus of attention on a summer evening at Hugo's.

Herb Swanson

HUGO'S
207-774-8538.
www.hugos.net.
88 Middle St., Portland
  04101.
Open: Tues.– Sat., year-
  round.
Cuisine: Artful American.
Price: Expensive.
Credit Cards: AE, MC, V.
Reservations:
  Recommended.

At Hugo's, Mainers learn about local Maine corolla potatoes, seasonal wild mushrooms, and farm-raised venison. But it's never simple, or rather, the venison sings its own song from the middle of a lovely plate of chestnut cream, wilted Swiss chard, and potato "mincemeat" tart, but the chorus makes it memorable. A mackerel tartare was available during the summer mackerel run, when people line the Maine state pier to fish for them, and the pink flesh of the fish was as good as I had ever known. A friend was recollecting her own perfect piece of fish there, "The best piece of fish I ever had." Credit that to Rob Evans's skill at making the sauce and garnish work for the food, instead of a distraction. The portions are modest, so your appetite is never overwhelmed. Let yourself enjoy one of the chef's tasting dinners, for nutrition par excellence.

KATAHDIN
207-774-1740.
106 High St., at the corner
  of Spring, Portland
  04101.
Closed: Sun. dinner and
  Mon.
Cuisine: American.
Price: Inexpensive to
  Expensive.
Serving: D, SB.
Credit Cards: D, MC, V.
Handicap Access: Yes.
Reservations: Not accepted.

We come here all the time, usually to get the Blue Plate Special and its accompanying mound of mashed potatoes. There's a metal mermaid sitting over the entrance and people who know what they're doing in the kitchen, and on any given night, the clientele is a good cross section of Portland, with many regulars. When we're not eating the blue plate special with meat loaf, we like the crab cakes, and we almost always order the fried oysters appetizer, with their crisp cornmeal coating and tender inside.

PEPPER CLUB
207-772-0531.
78 Middle St., Portland
  04101.
Open: Daily.
Price: Inexpensive to
  Moderate.
Serving: D.
Credit Cards: None.
Handicap Access: Limited.
Reservations: No.

Very organic and mostly vegetarian, except for hamburgers and an occasional chicken. The burgers are big, juicy, and made from organic beef. This is Portland's version of southwestern-meets-Los Angeles—lots of huevos rancheros colors painted in jagged angles on the walls, and big black booths. All items are written in multi-colored chalk on the big blackboard and are multi-ethnic in origin. They make a nice pie.

PORT BAKE HOUSE
207-773-2217
205 Commercial St.,
  Portland 04101.
Open: Daily.

This used to be just a lunchtime joint and bakery where the mostly business crowd hunched over a tiny counter and devoured big and tasty sandwiches. They went upscale recently and converted it into a little bistro with an expanded menu

Price: Inexpensive to
　Moderate.
Serving: B, L.
Credit Cards: MC, V.
Handicap Access: Limited.
Reservations: No.
Special Features: Take-out
　and bakery.

STREET & COMPANY
207-775-0887.
33 Wharf St., Portland 04101.
Open: Daily.
Price: Moderate.
Cuisine: Seafood, pasta.
Serving: D.
Credit Cards: AE, MC, V.
Handicap Access: Yes.
Reservations:
　Recommended.
Special Features: Patio
　dining.

WALTER'S CAFE
207-871-9258.
15 Exchange St., Portland
　04101.
Open: Daily.
Price: Moderate.
Cuisine: American bistro.
Serving: L, D.
Credit Cards: AE, MC, V.

Scarborough

**SPURWINK COUNTRY
　KITCHEN**
207-799-1177.
150 Spurwink Rd.,
　Scarborough 04047.
Closed: Mon.; late
　Oct.–mid-Apr.
Price: Inexpensive to
　Moderate.
Cuisine: Family.
Serving: L, D.
Credit Cards: D, MC, V.
Handicap Access: Yes.

full of quiche, some more ambitious entrées, and some of the best soup and sandwiches around. We especially like sipping our soup on the second floor patio. The fish soup, when they have it, is quite good; the view of the harbor is one of the best in town.

Garlic from the open kitchen perfumes the air at this casual, subterranean retreat, which sits on a funky cobblestone alley in Portland's Old Port. Dried flowers, rough wood, and family-sized cans of olive oil and tomatoes give the place an ethnic feel. They serve no red meat here; salmon, swordfish, scallops, and shrimp are constants. There's also a soup of the day and changing specials like tuna Niçoise and sole meuniere. Pastas come with a variety of creative seafood sauces. The wine bar offers one of the best selections in town.

With the exposed brick walls and views into the open kitchen from the downstairs dining room (there are two more small dining rooms upstairs)— you could imagine yourself in almost any urban hot spot. The menu reads like an American melting pot: cool Asian noodle salad; east end pannini; southwest spring rolls; Carolina barbecue. Boring maybe, but we harbor a soft spot for their giant grilled burgers and homemade chips. The service is solidly efficient and the food reliable and satisfying.

The Spurwink is a low-slung beach bungalow in the middle of a coastal salt marsh near some of our favorite beaches. A local favorite, especially among families and the older Cape Elizabeth crowd, they serve simple Down East classics, a few light items, a selection of half sandwich and cup of soup, and daily specials. They also offer an occasional surprise, for instance their black beans and rice, which we like. Beer and wine are available by the glass. All desserts are homemade, and the wild blueberry pie is top-notch. Kids' menu and take-out available.

THE PORTLAND REGION: FOOD PURVEYORS

Abby Zimet, a local journalist, picks out flowers at the Farmers' Market in Deering Oaks Park, Portland.

Herb Swanson

BAKERIES

European Bakery and Tea Room (207-781-3541; 395 Rte. 1, Falmouth). Wonderful hermit cookies, and many cakes, breads, and other pastries.

Isabella's Sticky Buns Café & Bakery (207-865-6635; 2 School St., Freeport). Good coffee, old-fashioned, large sticky buns, chocolate éclairs.

Sophia's (207-879-1869; Middle St., Portland). This bakery on Tommy's Park in the Old Port makes good bread, good cake, and high-end pizza for the lunch crowd.

Standard Baking Company (207-773-2112; 75 Commercial St., Portland). Most people say their baguettes are the best. They make over a dozen kinds of bread, and 10 kinds of pastry, including an extraordinary cinnamon bun, perfect scones, ginger cake, and rich brownies. This is the best bakery in southern Maine, working relentlessly to maintain the highest quality. The revised Rustica loaves are chewy, and the flavor created by the slow rising is superb.

Sugar (207-228-2058; Portland Public Market, Cumberland St., Portland). This offshoot from a restaurant next door called the Commissary makes pignoli cookies that are utterly delicious, plus fruit tartlets perfect for a dinner party.

BREWERIES

There continues to be an explosion of microbreweries in Maine. D.L. Geary, maker of Geary's Pale Ale, one of the very first microbrews made, is still going strong, and he's added a smokey London Porter to the roster. There are so many micros and such an appreciative audience that recently a microbrew (Shipyard Export Ale) sold more beer in Maine than Budweiser. Can you imagine that? If you are looking for a good place to sample the full range of Maine micros, check out The Great Lost Bear in Portland (207-772-0300; 540 Forest Ave.).

Allagash Brewing (207-878-5385; www.allagash.com; 100 Industrial Way, Portland). Tours available.

Casco Bay Brewing (207-797-2020; www.cascobaybrewing.com; 57 Industrial Way). Tours available.

Geary Brewing Company (207-878-2337; 38 Evergreen Dr., Portland). They brew a fine ale here, and if you can't get to the brewery, you can find it at almost any grocery store or gourmet shop in the area. Tours available, Mon.–Fri., call for an appointment.

Gritty McDuff's (207-772-2739; www.grittys.com; 396 Fore St., Portland). This seems like just about everyone's favorite brew pub in New England. They are so popular, they now have a second brew pub (207-865-4321; 183 Lower Main St., Freeport), and they bottle a line of their "best" beers. We like this place, even though we find the brew can be watery.

Shipyard Brewing Company (207-761-0807; www.shipyard.com; 86 Newbury St., Portland). The "sister" brewery to the Kennebunkport Brewing Co. They brew a fine winter ale, Old Thumper Extra Special Ale, and more. Tours available.

CANDY & ICE CREAM

Beal's Old Fashioned Ice Cream (207-828-1335; 12 Moulton St., Portland; and 207-883-1160; 161 Pine Point Rd., Scarborough). Standard flavors run the gamut from vanilla to deep, dark variations on chocolate, and sometimes a surprise, like lemon-mint. It's really good.

Ben & Jerry's Ice Cream (207-865-3407; 83 Main St., Freeport). Big enough to accommodate long lines in all kinds of weather. Sometimes you need ice cream after a long day shopping.

Browns Apiaries (207-829-5994; 239 Greely Rd., Cumberland). They raise bees here and sell the sweet by-products. Honey, strained and with the comb, in half-pound to one-gallon sizes, candles, honey candy, and bee-keeping supplies. Call ahead.

Haven's (207-772-0761; 542 Forest Ave., Portland). All the candy is perfect for Easter bunnies and Valentines customers.

Haven's Factory Store (207-772-1557; 87 County Rd., Westbrook) The candy is made here, and 70 feet of glass windows lets you witness it. Tours are often offered.

Tiger's Ice Cream (207-347-6149; 15 Pleasant St., Portland). Chocolate velvet ice cream is a popular flavor, and the chocolate-lined Tiger cones are unique. Handmade chocolates.

Wilbur's Chocolate Shoppe (207-865-6129; 13 Bow St., Freeport). All-natural chocolate—creams, berry flavors, milk and dark.

DELIS & TAKE-OUT

Aurora Provisions (207-871-9060; 64 Pine St., Portland). Upscale takeout, such as lamb stuffed with goat cheese. We like their macaroni and cheese and chicken pot pies, available frozen, and the Asian noodle salad. Daily roast chickens, rice crispie treats with ganache, fabulous cakes, and cookies.

Federal Spice (207-774-6404; 225 Federal St., Portland). Tasty, low-fat renditions of the ever-popular burrito. We especially like the pumpkin rice. No credit cards.

Granny's Burrito's (207-761-0751; 420 Fore St., Portland). Sit down and enjoy a burrito at the picnic-style tables or grab one to go.

Hattie's Deli (207-282-3435; in Biddeford Pool). Blueberry pie, and a breakfast and lunch place.

West End Grocery (207-874-6426; 133 Spring St., Portland). This little neighborhood deli makes fabulous sandwiches and apple cake.

FAST FOOD & PIZZA

American Pie (207-774-7437; 865 Forest Ave., Portland). Eat in by the open ovens, or take out. The pizza is great, Italian pasta dishes delicious; families fill this place up.

Flatbread Company (207-772-8777; 72 Commerical St., Portland). Another open pizza oven with fine pizza, and here all the ingredients are organic.

Lobster Cooker (207-865-4349; 39 Main St., Freeport). This is fast food the Maine way. Crisp fried haddock sandwiches, fresh fish chowder, and, of course, lobster rolls—served in a cheery, no-nonsense atmosphere.

Mark's (corner of Exchange and Middle Sts., Portland). Dogs and smoked sausages from a little red cart. There's a park next door for you to sit in, if it's warm enough.

Mesa Verde (207-774-6089; 618 Congress St., Portland). Good, straightforward Mexican food.

O'Naturals (207-781-8889; www.onaturals.com; 240 Rte. 1, Falmouth). Fast food with organic and/or healthy ingredients; try the oven baked fries "without the guilt."

Ricetta's (207-775-7400; 29 Western Ave., South Portland, and 207-781-3100, 240 Rte. 1, Falmouth). A lunchtime buffet offers a variety of wood-oven baked pizzas.

Silly's (207-772-360; 40 Washington Ave., Portland). Free delivery of their spicy pizza. Milkshakes and burgers, fish and chips, Asian noodles, Abdullah wrap sandwiches.

FOOD FESTIVALS

Yarmouth Clam Festival (207-846-3984). Third week in July. Every year for almost 30 years, the folks in Yarmouth pay tribute to the clam. They eat lots of fried ones, then they go take a ride on the roller coaster at the midway.

GOURMET FOOD STORES

Micucci's (207-775-1854; 45 India St., Portland). An Italian grocer at the foot of Munjoy Hill, Micucci's has all the fixings for an authentic Italian feast, including fresh mozzarella.

HEALTH FOOD & FARM MARKETS

Portland Green Grocer (207-761-9232; 211 Commercial St., Portland). Terrific fruits and vegetables. Great bakery breads, wines, and an ever-improving selection of cheeses and gourmet deli meats.

Herb Swanson

The Portland Public Market is great for lunch, for putting together a picnic, for a coffee break, or an afternoon bite of cake—as well as for buying groceries.

Portland Public Market (207-228-2000; 25 Preble St., Portland). A bit out of the way , but worth the side trip. More than 20 vendors selling everything from farm fresh produce and organic beef to fresh flowers, buffalo meat, and wine.

Wolf Neck Farm (207-865-4469; Wolf Neck Rd., off Flying Point Rd., Freeport). Lean, delicious all-natural beef and lamb raised on a beautiful saltwater farm run by the state university system. They've been operating for more than 100 years and selling natural beef since 1959; drive down the dirt road to get a slab to thaw out for a seaside barbecue.

THE PORTLAND REGION: CULTURE

During the late 1800s, Winslow Homer painted at Prouts Neck, a 112-acre point of land stretching into the Gulf of Maine south of Portland (his mother was born in Bucksport). You can find examples of his work, plus some Wyeths, Wellivers, and other well-known Maine painters at the Portland Museum of Art.

The most American of poets, Henry Wadsworth Longfellow, was born in Portland in 1807, and he immortalized the town in his poem "My Lost Youth." He and novelist Nathaniel Hawthorne were classmates at Bowdoin College in Brunswick, both graduating in 1825. Author and environmental activist Rachel Carson, who summered on the south coast, found Maine a wonderful laboratory for her study of the environment. She wrote *The Edge of the Sea* here.

ARCHITECTURE

Portland is home to the state's most outstanding example of the Italianate phase of the Gothic Revival. The *Victoria Mansion,* also known as the Morse-Libby House, was built in 1859 and is rich in Italianate detail.

After the Civil War, the coast became a summer playground for wealthy Bostonians and New Yorkers. During the late 1800s they built grand "cottages," summer homes that were the size of small—and sometimes not-so-small—mansions. Boston architect William R. Emerson made a great impact with the cottages he designed for wealthy patrons on Mount Desert Island—rambling wooden shingled buildings with large airy rooms that also incorporated native granite and stone. Portland architect John Calvin Stevens expanded on Emerson's principles and lined streets throughout the state with stately shingled cottages for both summer and year-round residents.

Since the mid-1600s, though, the predominant trend in coastal architecture has been simplicity and practicality. That is still seen in the small lobster and fishing shacks that seem to grow out of the rocks and have changed little during the past 100 years, as well as in the new *Maine Maritime Museum* in Bath, I. M. Pei's *Portland Museum of Art,* and perhaps the most famous home in Maine, the *Olson House* in Cushing, made so by artist Andrew Wyeth in his painting *Christina's World.*

For architecture buffs, there is a state inventory of Maine architecture on file at the architectural archives at Colby College in Waterville. The *Frances W. Peabody Research Library* at Greater Portland Landmarks (207-774-5561; landmarks@maine.rr.com; 165 State St., Portland) is a good place to get a basic education in the region's architectural heritage. The organization offers an excellent walking tour map of the city's historical districts, which include an impressive Victorian residential district with homes of the Italianate, Gothic Revival, Queen Anne, Colonial Revival, and Shingle styles. Throughout the summer, Landmarks offers a series of guided tours of historically and architecturally significant neighborhoods in Portland and the islands of Casco Bay.

GALLERIES

Frost Gully Gallery (207-773-2555; 1159 Rte. 1, Freeport). Drawings, paintings, prints, and sculptures by contemporary Maine artists. Mon.–Fri. 12–5, or by appointment.

Institute of Contemporary Art (207-879-5742; www.meca.edu; Maine College of Art, 522 Congress St., Portland). Work by the faculty of this growing art school, and annual senior thesis shows. They also show challenging international and national art; this is a good place to find out what's on the mind and in the eye of young artists everywhere.

June Fitzpatrick Gallery (207-772-1961; 112 High St., Portland). Tucked in an old house on a busy street, this tiny gallery often offers a fresh alternative to more "established" art hanging on the walls of the Portland Museum of Art (which is up the street and around the corner). Tues.–Sat. 12–5.

Salt Gallery (207-761-0660; www.salt.edu; 110 Exchange St., Portland). Operated by the Salt Center for Documentary Field Studies, this gallery features documentary photographic works by Salt students, alumni, and professional photographers. Mon.–Fri. 11:30–4:30 off-season, longer in season. Call for information.

GARDENS & GARDEN TOURS

There are several annual garden tours on the coast that no self-respecting garden lover would miss. One of those is *Greater Portland Landmarks* (landmark @maine.rr.com) annual house and garden tour, which in early summer gains the tourist entrance to a selection of the city's splendid private gardens (207-774-5561).

Tate House Museum Herb Garden (207-774-6177; www.tatehouse.org; 1270 Westbrook St., Portland). Fifty herbs.

Wadsworth-Longfellow House (207-774-1822; 487 Congress St., Portland). The garden through the gates is a tranquil retreat all summer long.

GUIDED TOURS

ABC Taxi (207-772-8685) in Portland offers a custom tour service. You can book one of their Chrysler taxis for $20 an hour.

Custom Coach of Portland (800-585-3589; www.customcoachandlimo.com) provides personalized tours for groups ranging from one to 50 people. They are based in Portland, but will go anywhere in the state of Maine, 24 hours a day. Custom Coach also will lease a van, limousine, or bus to larger groups.

Greater Portland Landmarks (207-774-5561; www.portlandlandmarks.org) provides downtown walking tours every Fri. and Sat. at 10:30am from July–Columbus Day. Tours meet at 305 Commercial St., Portland and highlight the city's architectural history. The tour guides are lively and the price is right: $8.

Mainely Tours (207-774-0808; www.mainelytours.com) offers 90-minute guided tours of downtown Portland. Guides will point out historical sites while traveling from the city streets to the rocky coast at Portland Head Light. $13 adults, $12 seniors, $7 kids.

HISTORIC BUILDINGS & SITES

ADMIRAL ROBERT E. PEARY HOME
207-624-6080.
Eagle Island, Casco Bay.
Season: June–Labor Day, daily 10–6. Accessible by boat.
Admission charged.

Construction of this handsome summer home began five years before Peary discovered the North Pole. The restored home features many striking design elements, including three quartz and fieldstone fireplaces. There are nature trails and a public pier where ferries, tour boats, and visiting sailors can tie up.

NEAL DOW MEMORIAL
714 Congress St., Portland 04102.
Open: Year-round, Mon.–Fri. 11–4.
No charge.

Neal Dow was a Quaker who was a leader in social reform during the 19th century. The memorial is the home he and his wife, Maria Cornelia Durant Maynard, built in 1829. Dow was an outspoken advocate for temperance, an abolitionist, Civil War general, two-time mayor of Portland, and candidate for the U.S. presidency on the Prohibition Party ticket. His home, now managed by the Maine Women's Christian Temperance Union, is on the National Register of Historical Places and is a Colonial Revival gem.

PORTLAND OBSERVATORY
207-774-5561.
www.portlandlandmarks. org.
138 Congress St., Portland 04101.
Season: Memorial Day–beg. of Oct.

Built in 1807, this is the last remaining signal tower on the eastern seaboard. The architecture is striking with heavy timbers forming a hexagonal shingled tower that narrows at the top and was renovated from top to bottom in 2000–01. The views of Greater Portland and the Casco Bay provide a good orientation for the traveler who has just arrived in town.

VICTORIA MANSION
207-772-4841.
www.victoriamansion.org.
109 Danforth St., Portland 04102.

Also known as the Morse-Libby House, the imposing brownstone Italianate villa built for Ruggles Sylvester Morse seems always ready for a soiree in another world. Morse was a hotelier

Season: May–Oct., Tues.–
Sat. 10–4, Sun. 1–5. Open
by appt. rest of year.
Admission charged.

between 1858 and 1860, and much of this small mansion is packed with lavish Victorian details. Seven hand-carved Italian marble fireplaces and mantels preside over rooms so elaborate they force us to marvel. Christmas in the "Turkish" room (where the gentlemen gathered to smoke) and in the large parlors is a spectacle that draws many visitors every year. Gift shop in the Carriage House.

WADSWORTH-
LONGFELLOW HOUSE
207-774-1822.
www.mainehistory.org
489 Congress St., Portland
04101.
Season: June–Oct., daily
10–5.
Admission charged

This is the boyhood home of poet Henry Wadsworth Longfellow. Built in 1785 by Henry's grandfather, Gen. Peleg Wadsworth, it is the oldest brick house in Portland, and today it contains family artifacts and furnishings dating from 1750 to 1900. Museum store next door at the Historical Society.

LIBRARIES

Dyer Library (207-283-3861; 371 Main St., Saco). Associated with the York Institute Museum, the Dyer is home to genealogical materials, Maine history, city records, and manuscripts of local interest.

Maine Historical Society Library (207-774-1822; www.mainehistory.org; 485 Congress St., Portland). More than 60,000 monographs and serials published after 1497, including the state's most comprehensive collection of historical documents and printed materials.

Portland Public Library (207-871-1700 or 800-649-7697; www.portland library.com; 5 Monument Sq., Portland). One of the largest libraries in the state. The Portland Room houses an excellent Maine collection, including old children's books. Mon., Wed., Fri. 9–6; Tues., Thurs. noon–9; Sat. 9–5.

Salt Documentary Archive (207-761-0660; www.salt.edu; 110 Exchange St., Portland). Collection of photographs and tape-recorded interviews detailing the way of life of people in Maine. Home of *Salt* magazine.

LIGHTHOUSES

Portland Head Light (207-799-2661; Shore Rd., Cape Elizabeth), constructed in 1791 at the order of President George Washington, is the oldest on the East Coast. The lighthouse and quarters were renovated in 1992 and now are home to the Museum at Portland Head Light. The lighthouse and museum adjoin Fort Williams Park, a pretty seaside park complete with ruins of an old fort built in the late 1800s, tennis courts, and a baseball diamond.

Contrary to its name, the *Cape Elizabeth Light at Two Lights State Park* (Two Lights Rd. off Rte. 77, Cape Elizabeth) is only one working lighthouse. In

1824, two lights were built to mark the spot. In 1874, the lighthouses were rebuilt, and only one remains active today.

MUSEUMS

CHILDREN'S MUSEUM OF MAINE
207-828-1234.
www.childrensmuseumof me.org
142 Free St., Portland 04101.
Memorial Day–Labor Day, Mon.–Sat. 10–5, Sun. 12–5; Labor Day–Memorial Day, Tues.–Sat., 10–5, Sun. 12–5.
Admission: $5 children and adults; children under one free.

This museum is in spiffy quarters next door to the Portland Museum of Art and is a hit with kids and parents. Not only are there many "hands-on" exhibits covering the science bases, but the museum also pays homage to commerce and business. Among other entertaining experiences are exhibits that show how a bank, a supermarket, a village, and a farm work. Check out the Camera Obscura at the top, which on clear days offers a bird's eye view of Portland and the islands of Casco Bay.

DESERT OF MAINE
207-865-6962.
www.desertofmaine.com.
95 Desert Rd. (2 miles west of I-95 Exit 19), Freeport, 04032
Season: Early May–mid-Oct., daily 9–6.
Admission charged.

The first chapter in the history of this geologic oddity occurred during the Ice Age, when glaciers deposited sand and minerals. During the late 1700s and early 1800s, a family of farmers came, clearcut the land, grew crops, grazed their animals, and failed to use good farming techniques to prevent erosion of the thin layer of topsoil. What remains is a genuine sand desert smack in the middle of coastal Maine, a favorite local tourist attraction since the mid-1930s. Walking and coach tours available. Gift shop, picnic grounds, and campground on the premises.

PORTLAND MUSEUM OF ART
207-775-6148
www.portlandmuseum.org.
7 Congress Sq., Portland 04101.
Open: Tues., Wed., Sat., Sun. 10–5. Thurs., Fri. 10–9. Also Mon. 10–5 Memorial Day–Columbus Day only.
Admission: $6 adults; $ 5 seniors and students; $1 youths 6–12; children under 6 free.

Maine's oldest public museum resides in an impressive granite and brick structure designed by I. M. Pei. The permanent collection includes a worthwhile selection of American and European art, including paintings by Van Gogh, Picasso, Degas, and many by Winslow Homer (he painted and lived part of the year at Prouts Neck, about 15 minutes from the museum), as well as a significant holding of Colonial and Federal portraits. The museum also is temporary home to visiting exhibitions. On Fridays after 5pm the doors are open free of charge.

SACO MUSEUM
207-282-3031.
www.sacomaine.org.
371 Main St., Saco 04072.
Season: Year round, Tues.,
   Wed., Fri., Sun. 12–4.;
   Thurs. 12–8.
Admission: $4 adults; $2
   under 16 and over 60.
   Free Thurs. 4–8.

This regional history and art museum dates from 1866. It exhibits paintings, textiles, household items, and furnishings from several periods in American history, including Colonial, Federal, and Colonial Revival. The adjoining gallery hosts changing art exhibits, and the library has an excellent Maine history collection.

MUSIC

**CUMBERLAND COUNTY
   CIVIC CENTER**
207-775-3458.
www.theciviccenter.com.
1 Civic Center Sq. (corner
   of Spring and Center
   Sts.), Portland 04101.
Open: Year-round.
Tickets: $6–$35, depending
   on event.

The acoustics aren't great, but that doesn't daunt folks who travel from way Down East and the far northern reaches of the state to hear good music. Folk, rock, heavy metal (plus the occasional circus, ice show or big truck-pulling contest) play here. The Pirates Hockey team does too.

**PCA GREAT
   PERFORMANCES**
207-773-3150 (office);
   207-842-0800 (tickets).
www.pcagreatperformances
   .org
477 Congress St., Portland
   04101.
Season: Sept.–June.
Tickets: $10–$50.

Every year this group books a range of traveling talent from perennial favorites like the Canadian Brass Ensemble or the Flying Karamazov Brothers to world-class performers like Isaac Stern and the New York City Opera Company. Concerts are held at the **Merrill Auditorium.**

**PORTLAND STRING
   QUARTET**
207-761-1522.
22 Monument Sq.,
   Portland.
P.O. Box 11, Portland 04112.
Season: Oct.–Apr.
Tickets: $20 single concert;
   $75 season's pass (4
   concerts). Senior
   discount. Free for those
   21 or younger.

This is one of the few classical quartets to endure a quarter of a century rehearsing, touring, and performing together without a single change in personnel. The result is a mature sound that can take on the most difficult work and play it beautifully. The group's music is an impeccably performed mix of classic and new chamber works commissioned for the group. When this talented quartet isn't traveling the world, they perform at Woodford's Congregational Church.

**PORTLAND SYMPHONY
   ORCHESTRA**
207-842-0800.

Portland is the smallest city in the U.S. to have a full-time symphony orchestra, and local audiences are extremely appreciative. The symphony,

www.portlandsymphony. com. 477 Congress St., Portland 04101. Concerts throughout the year.

under conductor and music director Toshiyuki Shimada, performs the classics and pops most of the year in the **Merrill Auditorium**. During the summer, they take to the outdoors with a series of concerts at various locations around the state.

NIGHTLIFE

The Asylum (207-772-8274; asylum@gate.net; 121 Center St., Portland). Dance club, sports bar, and restaurant. The club features both live bands and DJs playing disco, house & hip-hop, Latino, modern rock, and R&B. Lunch and dinner, 11am–11pm.

Big Easy Blues Club (207-871-8817; 55 Market St., Portland). Maine is hardly blues central, but Thursday through Saturday you'd never know it once you're inside the door here.

The Brunswick (207-934-4873; 39 West Grand Ave., Old Orchard Beach). Music, full restaurant and bar on the beach. Year-round.

The Comedy Connection (207-774-5554; www.mainehumor.com; 6 Custom House Wharf, Portland). A barrelful of laughs at Maine's only full-time professional stand-up comedy club; many of their comedians receive nationwide recognition. A light fare menu and wait service is available before, during, or after the show at the Waterfront Cafe. Reservations welcomed.

The Industry (207-879-0865; 50 Wharf St., Portland). A hopping dance club for those 18 and older. Serves alcohol and is open Friday and Saturday nights.

Mulligans at Millside (207-284-9283; 23 Lincoln St., Biddeford). Pool, darts, bar, and full menu.

SCHOOLS

Acorn School for the Performing Arts (207-761-0617; 496 Congress St., Portland).

L.L. Bean Outdoor Discovery Program (888-552-3261; www.llbean.com/odp; Casco St., Freeport). An interesting series of low-cost lessons that cover everything from cross-country skiing (on weekends beginning in January) and fly-fishing (in spring and summer) to kayaking, and emergency wilderness medicine. Free evening lectures on topics ranging from survival in the Maine woods to making soap, paddling sea kayaks, building fly rods, and more.

SEASONAL EVENTS

Cumberland County Fair (207-829-4182; Cumberland Fairgrounds, Cumberland). Livestock, rides, agricultural and cooking competitions. Mid- to late Sept.

La Kermesse-Franco Americaine Festival (207-282-1567; Biddeford). Food,

Herb Swanson

A ride at the Cumberland County Fair.

entertainment, parade, cultural displays documenting the French-American heritage in southern Maine. Late June.

Portland Chamber Music Festival (800-320-0257; www.pcmf.org; Westbrook College Campus, Portland). Classical and contemporary music in August featuring musicians from symphonies and quartets around the country.

Yarmouth Clam Festival (207-846-3984; www.yarmouthmaine.org/clam.htm; Main St., Yarmouth). Entertainment, crafts, bike race, midway, and of course clams. Mid-July.

THEATER

The Carriage House Theater (207-415-8178; Post Rd., Freeport). For the Love of Theater, a semiprofessional theater group, started up in 2001 and will present plays and musicals.

City Theater (207-282-0849; 205 Main St., Biddeford). Sept.–May.

Freeport Community Players (207-865-6041; Freeport High School, Freeport). Young community theater group that presents three shows annually—in the spring, summer, and winter. Visiting performers welcome to audition.

Portland Stage Company (207-774-0465; 25A Forest Ave., Portland). Solid local company that often brings actors up from Boston and New York for bigger roles. Sept.–May.

THE PORTLAND REGION: RECREATION

AUTO RACING

The chance to see auto racing is rare on the coast. *Beech Ridge Motor Speedway* (207-885-0111, automated race information at 207-885-5800; www.beechridge.com; 70 Holmes Rd., Scarborough) features four divisions of stock car racing on a 1/3 mile track. Starting time April through September is 6:30pm every Saturday evening. Call for times of special events.

BALLOONING

Even if the winds are blowing inland, you are almost assured a good view from the White Mountains to the shore. Spring flights are tricky—and often canceled—due to the changeable Maine weather. September and October tend to be the busiest months because of foliage flights, so be sure to make your reservations early. Experienced balloonists say winter flights are the most spectacular, when the air takes on a crystalline clarity. Dress warmly, though; it will be much colder at an 800-foot altitude than it is on the ground.

If you want to see the south coast by air, you have a few choices. *Balloon Rides* (207-761-8373 or 800-952-2076; www.hotairballoon.com; 17 Freeman St., Portland) boasts of having "Southern Maine's oldest balloon company." Also, call *Hot Fun* (207-799-0193; www.hotfunballoons.com; Cape Elizabeth) and *Balloons Over New England* (800-788-5562; www.balloonsovernewengland .com; Kennebunk).

BASEBALL

Win or lose, the *Portland Sea Dogs*, the Double A affiliate of the Florida Marlins, keep Hadlock Field (207-879-9500; 271 Park Ave., Portland) filled to capacity throughout the season. This is a young team with an exceptionally loyal following, including former President George Bush who often is asked to throw in the first ball. At a game with the New Haven Rangers in August 2001, his wife Barbara threw in the ball, while he stood in as catcher. The Sea Dogs are so popular that getting a ticket to witness Eastern League baseball in one of the 6,500 seats is sometimes difficult. Monday nights are your best bet. We suggest calling well in advance.

BEACHES

The swimming is great at *Ferry Beach*, in Scarborough, where water over a long, shallow sandbar warms up early in the summer and is kept protected by Prouts Neck. *Higgins Beach* in West Scarborough is a beautiful, broad stretch of sand bound by a modest, old-fashioned summer village (there is no boardwalk in sight, and dogs run free after 4pm).

Crescent Beach State Park; Rte. 77, Cape Elizabeth. The *Maine Times* calls this "one of Maine's best family beaches." Sand and stone beach; 1,560 yds.; picnic tables, snack bar, fishing. Entrance fee.

Crescent and Seapoint Beaches; Seapoint Rd., Kittery. Crescent Beach, a 625-yard sand beach and its 550-yard sister beach Seapoint across a small peninsula are nice, but have limited parking.

Ferry and Western Beaches; Rte. 207 to Ferry Rd., Scarborough. Actually three beaches, including two that wrap around a rocky point and lead up to tony Prouts Neck. The tide rips right at the point, and at high tide you can almost reach out and touch the lobster boats in the harbor. You can let your dog run free after 4pm. Total of more than 1,700 yds.; limited parking, for a fee.

Ferry Beach State Park; Rte. 9, Saco. A fine sand beach that stretches more than 4,500 yds. It is part of a 117-acre state park with all the facilities, including picnic tables, toilets, and bathhouse. Fee is charged at gate. Parking.

Fortunes Rocks Beach; Rte. 208, Biddeford. Long sand beach that's great for swimming; 3,740 yds.; parking limited.

Hills Beach; off Rtes. 9 and 208, Biddeford. An excellent, if short, swimming beach, on a 530-yd. sand spit protecting Maine's largest tidal basin. People like to bird watch here (see below). Facilities nearby; parking limited.

Old Orchard and Surfside Beaches; Rte. 9, Old Orchard Beach. Some call this the Canadian Riviera, and more often than not the language spoken here is French. Lovely fine white sand beaches with a total length 3,320 yds. Bathhouse. Fee for parking.

Pine Point and Grand Beaches; Rte. 9, Scarborough. Two fine white sand beaches and sand spit totaling 2,500 yds. Facilities nearby; fee for parking.

Scarborough Beach; Rte. 207, Scarborough. This is a barrier beach with dunes that protect a freshwater marsh. It's so popular among swimmers and surfers that it often fills to overflowing by noon on a hot day; 2,060 yds.; picnic tables, grills, bathhouse, fishing; fee for parking.

Winslow Memorial Park; Rte. 1 onto South Freeport Rd. (at the Big Indian) and follow to Staples Rd., South Freeport. Nestled in the middle of a pretty, immaculate town-run park and camping area, this is another great beach for the family. The small, man-made beach is sheltered although untended by a lifeguard. Picnic tables, playground, rest rooms; entrance fee charged.

BERRY & APPLE PICKING

Jordan's Farm (207-767-3488; 21 Wells Rd., Cape Elizabeth). Strawberries. End of June through August 1. Mon.–Sat. 7am–7pm.

Maxwell's Farm (207-799-3383; off Rte. 77 near Two Lights, Cape Elizabeth). Strawberries. Mid-June–mid-July. Mon.–Sat. 7am–8pm. Closed Sun. Call ahead.

Spiller Farms (207-985-2575; store: 207-985-3383; SpillerFarms@Juno.com; Rte. 9A, Branch Rd., Wells). Strawberries and raspberries. Mid-June to end of season. Apples. Hours fluctuate.

BICYCLING

The *Casco Bay Bicycle Club* has maintained a steady following of all kinds of cyclists. Their information line (207-828-0918) will astound you with choices. Or you can write to them at 84 Gloucester Rd., Cumberland 04121. Otherwise, the best bet for updates on new groups, trails, tours, and races is to call the local bike shop.

Allspeed Bicycles (207-878-8741; www.allspeed.com; 1041 Washington Ave., Portland).

Back Bay Bicycle (207-773-6906; 333 Forest Ave., Portland).

Bicycle Habitat (207-283-2453; 294 Main St., Saco).

Brad's Bike Rental and Repairing (207-766-5631; peaksmerc.com; 115 Island Ave., Peaks Island).

CycleMania (207-774-2933; www.cyclemania1.com; 59 Federal St., Portland).

Haggett's Cycle Shop (207-773-5117; 34 Vannah Ave., Portland).

Joe Jones Ski and Sports (207-885-5635; Joejones.com; 456 Payne Rd., opposite Wal-Mart, Scarborough).

L.L. Bean Bicycle Dept. (207-865-4761; www.llbean.com; Main St., Freeport).

Quinn's Bike Shop (207-284-4632; 140 Elm St., Biddeford). Rentals and repairs.

Rodgers Ski and Sport (207-883-3669; 332 Rte. 1, opposite Scarborough Downs, Scarborough).

BIRD WATCHING

Biddeford Pool (Rte. 208, Biddeford). A one-mile wide tidal basin and broad mud flats at low tide. There is excellent bird watching here, because many species of shore birds stop here en route to northern and southern climes. Open Mon.–Fri., 8–4:30.

Maine Audubon Society (207-781-2330; www.maineaudubon.org; 20 Gilsland Farm Rd. (off Rte. 1), Falmouth). The Gilsland Farm Sanctuary is home to the society. More than 60 acres of salt marsh, fields, and forest serve as a workshop and touring ground for naturalists. There is a great bookstore for naturalists, with the best selection of optics and guides around. Early morning bird walks and the children's discovery room are open to the public. Weekend programs. Mon.–Sat. 9–5; Sun. 1–4 (noon–5 in summer).

Scarborough Marsh Nature Center (207-883-5100 June–Sept., 207-781-2330 Oct.–May; www.maineaudubon.org; smnc@maineaudubon.org; Pine Point Rd., Scarborough). The Maine Audubon Society operates an education center on this 3,000-acre saltwater marsh. They offer guided tours, including full-moon canoe tours, and there's also a self-guided tour (directions in a pamphlet available at the center). You can rent a canoe until 4pm. Art programs and walks are available for kids. In the early morning on Wednesdays, a bird-watching walk is offered. Open daily 9:30am–5:30pm in summer; weekends only between Memorial Day and start of summer season.

BOATING

CANOEING & SEA KAYAKING

L.L. Bean Outdoor Discovery Program (888-552-3261; www.llbean.com/odp; Main St., Freeport). Throughout the summer, the L.L. Bean store staff gives canoe and kayak lessons on a nice, easy stretch of the Royal River in Yarmouth. The academic wing of the outdoor store also hosts an annual Sea Kayak Symposium in July.

Curtis Rindlaub

Kayakers are given careful instruction before launching themselves into the sea, as with this class on Peaks Island run by Maine Island Kayak Company.

Maine Island Kayak Co. (207-766-2373 or 800-796-2373; www.maineisland-kayak.com; 70 Luther St., Peaks Island). Trips and instruction.

Maine Island Trail (207-596-6456; www.mita.org). The waterway is a kind of Appalachian Trail for boaters. It begins with islands in Casco Bay and follows the coast Down East past Machias, a distance of 325 miles.

Scarborough Marsh Nature Center (207-883-5100 June–Sept., 207-781-2330 Oct.–May; www.maineaudubon.org; smnc@maineaudubon.org; Pine Point Rd off Rte. 1, Scarborough). Hourly canoe rentals and self-guided canoe tours of the marsh. Also guided tours, including "full-moon" tours. The center is open 9:30am–5:30pm; last canoe rental at 4pm. Open daily from mid-June until Labor Day, weekends only Memorial Day–mid-June.

CHARTER & RENTALS AND FISHING

Atlantic Seal Cruises (207-865-6112 or 877-ATLSEAL; www.atlanticsealcruises .com; Main St., Box 146, South Freeport). Cruises to Eagle Island, Admiral Perry's house, seven days in the summer, and to Sequin Island, Thursday and Sunday, where the Friends of Sequin will give a guided tour of the Sequin Island Lighthouse with its original Fresnel lens. The lighthouse was built in 1857. (140 foot elevation to lighthouse; you need to be fit to climb the island trail.)

Atlantic Yacht Charters (207-767-3626; South Portland). Four-hour minimum, 12-person maximum, on a 50-foot yacht with a master bedroom suite.

Bay View Cruises (207-761-0496; 184 Commercial St., Portland). Summer cruises, seal watch.

Devil's Den Charter Boat (207-761-4466; DiMillo's Marina, Portland). Tuna, blues, stripers.

Lucky Catch Lobstering (207-233-2026; 170 Commercial St., Portland). Captain Tom takes you out to pull traps, you can learn how to haul, bait, and set them, if you wish. Pants and boots are available.

Old Port Mariner Fleet (207-775-0727 or 800-437-3270; www.marinerfleet.com; Long Wharf, Portland). The *Indian 11*, the *Casablanca*, and the *Odyssey* sail out into the harbor and beyond in search of whales and carry along dinner, music, and fishing gear, depending on the vessel.

Palawan (207-773-2163 or 888-284-PAL1; www.sailpalawan.com; Long Wharf, Portland). Half-day, full-day, and evening trips aboard a gorgeous vintage 58-foot ocean racing sloop.

SAILING LESSONS

Spring Point Sailing School (207-799-3976; www.smtc.net; Southern Maine Technical College, South Portland). Classes for beginning sailors, including private lessons by appointment.

BOWLING

Big 20 Bowling Center (207-883-2131; Rte. 1, Scarborough). 20 candlepin lanes.
Vacationland Bowling Center (207-284-7386; Rte. 1, Saco). 32 candlepin lanes.

CAMPING

Recompense Shores Camp Sites (207-865-9307; Burnett Rd., Freeport). Tent and RV campsites, showers, electrical hookups, and one of the best views in the area. Next door is a state-run organic beef farm.

Winslow Memorial Park (207-865-4198; Staples Point Rd., Freeport). Small, municipally run park with camp and picnic sites and a lovely man-made beach.

CROSS-COUNTRY SKIING

Bradbury Mountain State Park (207-688-4712; six miles west from the Freeport exit of I-95, Pownal). From the top of Bradbury Mountain (460 feet) you can see past L.L. Bean to the ocean. Ten miles of trails; two difficult paths, two intermediate, and four trails for beginners. Trail maps are available at the entrance.

Gilsland Farm (207-781-2330; Gilsland Farm Rd., Falmouth). This is the home of the Maine Audubon Society. Three-and-a-half kilometers of trails through their country backyard. Open dawn to dusk.

Mast Landing Sanctuary (207-781-2330; Upper Mast Landing Rd., Freeport). Also owned and operated by the Maine Audubon Society. Five kilometers of foot trails and canoe ways wind through estuaries, forests, and orchards. Open dawn to dusk.

Valhalla Country Club (207-829-2227; Valhalla Rd., Cumberland). In winter, you can check out the snow conditions right from Interstate 295 at this weekend-only free touring center on a rolling golf course. Peak Performance, a local recreational outfitter, also offers lessons and equipment rentals.

Wolfe's Neck Woods State Park (Wolf Neck Rd., Freeport). This small park is officially closed during the winter, but skiers like to ski the snow-covered walking trails, which wind for about four miles through the woods and follow along the edge of Casco Bay and the Harraseeket River.

FAMILY FUN

There's recreation and then there's recreation. When you get tired of going to the beach, the perfect remedy is a stroll down the boardwalk at *Old Orchard Beach*, where you can get your fortune read, ride the Ferris wheel, and eat more than one man's share of fried things—French fries, fried clams, and fried dough. If you're somewhere else on the coast and looking for family fun, here is some more good stuff, kids.

Aquaboggan Water Park (207-225-2443; Rte. 1, Saco). Can't miss it. Kids love it. Water slides, splash pools for tots, bumper boats, races cars, shuffleboard. A real fun time. June to Labor Day 10am–6pm.

Funtown U.S.A.–Splashtown (207-284-5139 or 800-878-2900; www.funtownsplashtownusa.com; Portland Rd., Saco). Need we say more? Open at 10am in the summer.

Maine Narrow Gauge Railroad Co. & Museum (207-828-0814; www.datamaine .com/mngrr; 58 Fore St., Portland). This train is immensely popular with travelers young and old. A well-preserved two-foot narrow-gauge train follows about 1.5 miles of track on Portland's Eastern Prom. Train rides and tours of the adjacent museum are available seven days a week, mid-May–mid-Oct. and Dec. holidays.

Pirate's Cove Adventure Golf (207-934-5086; www.piratescove.net; 70 First St., Old Orchard Beach). 36 holes. "Explore the wonderful and mysterious hide-out of pirates!" 9am–11pm.

Westerly Winds (207-854-9463; 771 Cumberland St., Westbrook). Pitch n' Putt golf course, driving range, miniature golf, and pitching machines for hardball and softball. Swimming, tennis, and basketball courts. 9-hole golf course.

FERRIES

Casco Bay Lines (207-774-7871; www.cascobaylines.com; Casco Bay Ferry Terminal, Commercial St., Portland). This is the place to take a long boat ride with narrated tours, over five hours to Bailey Island (with time to eat seafood at Cook's Lobster House), three hours for the Mail Boat, one hour to Peaks and back; this last is around $5 and a simple way to get out on the water, any time of the year. Other cruises may be limited to the summer.

Cousins Island to Great Chebeague Island (207-846-3700; Chebeague Transportation Company, Chebeague Island). Year-round service. Parking is available in a lot on Rte. 1, in Cumberland, with shuttle bus service half an hour before the ferry departs Cousins Island.

The Scotia Prince (800-845-4073 or 207-775-5616; www.scotiaprince.com; 468 Commercial St., Portland). This ship takes over 200 cars to Yarmouth, Nova

Fishing from a breakwater.

Herb Swanson

Scotia, every day during the summer. You can go just for the ride, returning on the next day, or take your car across. Gambling starts as soon as you are in international water.

FISHING

L earn from the pros at "fly-fishing school." L.L. Bean's *Outdoor Discovery Program* every year offers intense fly-fishing instruction in addition to frequent free programs about fishing. Call the outdoor school (888-552-3261; www.llbean. com/odp; Casco St., Freeport). (See **Boating charters** for fishing boats).

GOLF

Biddeford-Saco Country Club (207-282-5883; Old Orchard Rd., Saco). 18 holes, 6,200 yds., par 71. Cart and club rental, pro shop, clubhouse, lessons, snack bar.

Dunegrass Golf and Beach Resort (207-934-4513 or 800-521-1029; www.dune grass.com; 200 Wild Dunes Way, Old Orchard Beach). 18 holes, 6,644 yds., par 71, plus a 9-hole, 5,906 yds. par 35. Cart and club rental, pro shop, clubhouse. Restaurant and vacation packages.

Freeport Country Club (207-865-0711; Old County Rd., Freeport). 9 holes, 2,955 yds., par 36. Cart and club rental, pro shop, clubhouse.

Nonesuch River Golf Club (207-883-0007; www.nonesuchgolf.com; 304 Gorham Rd., Scarborough). 18 holes, clubhouse, pro shop.

Pleasant Hill Country Club (207-883-4425; 38 Chamberlain Rd., Scarborough). 9 holes, 2,400 yds., par 34. Cart and club rental, pro shop, clubhouse, snack bar.

Riverside Municipal Courses (207-797-3524 or 207-797-5588; 1158 Riverside St., Portland). Two courses: 18 holes, 6,520 yds., par 72; and 9 holes, 3,152 yds., par 36. Cart and club rental, pro shop, clubhouse, lessons.

Sable Oaks Golf Club (207-775-6257; www.sableoaks.com; 505 Country Club Dr., South Portland). 18 holes, 6,359 yds., par 70. Cart and club rental, clubhouse, pro shop, snack bar, lessons.

South Portland Municipal (207-775-0005; 155 Wescott Rd., South Portland). 9 holes, 2,171 yds., par 33. Cart and club rental, pro shop, snack bar.

Val Halla Golf Course (207-829-2225; Val Halla Rd., Cumberland). 18 holes, 6,200 yds., par 72. Cart and club rental, pro shop, clubhouse, lessons.

Willowdale Golf Club (207-883-9351; 52 Willowdale Rd., Scarborough). 18 holes, 5,980 yds., par 70. Cart and club rental, pro shop, snack bar.

HARNESS RACING

S tandardbreds pulling a two-wheeled sulky and driver compete against each other for your betting pleasure. There's only one harness racing track on the coast of Maine—*Scarborough Downs* (207-883-4331; exit 6 off the Maine Turnpike, Scarborough, just southwest of Portland). It also happens to be the largest of its kind in New England. Races run Wed., Fri., and Sat., 7:30pm, Sun. 2pm, Mar. through beginning of Dec. The season varies; call for schedule.

HEALTH CLUBS

Maine Coast Fitness (207-883-3858; 605 Rte 1., Scarborough). Weights, lifecycles, stair masters, and fitness machines.

The Racquet and Fitness Center (207-775-6188; 2445 Congress St., Portland). Racquetball, tennis, aerobics, weights, fitness machines, lifecycles, spin bikes, and sauna.

Saco Sport and Fitness (207-284-5953; 329 North St., Saco). Pool, sauna, whirlpool, racquetball, aerobics, weights, lifecycles, stair masters, and fitness machines.

YMCA (207-283-0100; Alfred Road Business Park, Biddeford). Aerobics, fitness machines, Bio climbers, Nautilus, rowing machines, lifecycles, pool, and sauna.

YMCA (207-874-1111; 70 Forest Ave., Portland). Pools, sauna, squash, racquetball, aerobics, fitness machines, and basketball gym.

YMCA Casco Bay (207-865-9600; 14 Old South Freeport Rd., Freeport). A new facility with pool, fitness machines, and saunas.

YWCA (207-874-1130; 87 Spring St., Portland). Pool, aerobics, sauna, weights, yoga, water aerobics, and self defense.

HIKING & WALKING

Back Cove, Portland. This 3.5-mile walk around Back Cove in Portland is a popular one on a warm spring or summer evening. What's that smell? Baked beans? That's the B & M Baked Bean factory across the way putting the final touches on a new batch of the sweet beans.

Bradbury Mountain State Park, Pownal. A little north and west of Freeport on Rte. 9, this small state park is a great place to get out of the car and stretch the legs. You'll get a good view of Casco Bay and the White Mountains from the summit of this small, bald mountain.

Wolfe's Neck Woods State Park, Freeport. Just a few miles from the commercial craziness of downtown Freeport, this is truly a cool haven in the spring and summer. The 200-acre state park is on a small peninsula jutting into Casco Bay. The park has four miles of well-marked trails that lead along Casco Bay past Googins Island (where a pair of osprey return from South America to nest every year) through a stand of white pine and along the Harraseeket River.

HORSEBACK RIDING

Bush Brook Stables (207-284-7721; 463 West St., Biddeford). Lessons, boarding, indoor riding arena.
Long Horn Equestrian Center (207-883-6400; 338 Broad Turn Rd., Scarborough). Public trail rides, lessons.

NATURE PRESERVES

East Point Sanctuary, Biddeford Pool. A 30-acre sanctuary on the largest tidal pool in Maine. Two trails ring the water and give views of birds and possibly harbor seals at high tide.
Fore River Sanctuary, Portland. A 76-acre preserve on the Fore River Estuary. This small pocket of nature includes a portion of the old Cumberland and Oxford Canal and Jewel Falls, the city's only waterfall; 2.5 miles of nature trails.
Gilsland Farm, Rte. 1, Falmouth. The headquarters for Maine Audubon sits on 60 acres of salt marsh just minutes from Portland with 2.5 miles of trails. Good walks, great cross-country skiing, and one of the region's best selection of natural history books in the society's gift shop.
Mast Landing Sanctuary, Freeport. Another of the small refuges set aside by Maine Audubon, this one winds through the hills, fields, woods, and salt marshes near busy downtown Freeport. There are self-guided nature walks, and you can tent, camp, and picnic here.
Scarborough Marsh Nature Center, Scarborough. Maine Audubon operates this nature center on the coast's largest saltwater marsh. Self-guided nature walk, as well as several special events and educational programs. You can rent a canoe here, too, to visit marsh animals in their natural habitat. This is a great way to "get into" coastal biology.
Wolfe's Neck Woods State Park, Freeport. This small park is truly one of nature's gems. Well-marked, self-guiding nature trails through coastal woods on Casco Bay and the Harraseeket River. Lovely picnic area. Nominal fee in summer time.

ROCK CLIMBING

In spite of this being the rock-bound coast, rock climbing is not one of the most popular pastimes. Consequently, good rock climbing spots have not yet been well mapped. The coast of Maine offers climbers both challenges and solitude. On the south coast, there are really only two climber's hangouts that we know of: *Fort Williams Park* in Cape Elizabeth just south of Portland and the *Maine Rock Gym* (207-780-6370; www.mainerockgym.com; 127 Marginal Way, Portland). The gym, a gathering place for lithe athletes, has been such a hit that they have built a climbing tower outside.

SEASONAL SPORTING EVENTS

Beach Olympics, mid-August. On the beach in Old Orchard (207-934-2500). Kids and adults enjoy this three-day event to benefit the Maine Special Olympics. Round-robin volleyball, water-balloon races, ice cream eating contests, and more. Live music and entertainment at night.

Peaks Island-to-Portland Swim, early August. Strong-armed swimmers often finish the 2.4 mile swim from Peaks Island beach to East End Beach in Portland in under one hour (contact YMCA, 207-874-1111).

SKATING

The Arena (207-283-0615; Alfred Rd., Industrial Business Park, Biddeford). July 31–April 14. Indoors.

Deering Oaks Park (207-874-8793; State St. and Park Ave., Portland). December–February. Outdoors, and dependent on the weather. The City of Portland plows the ice when it can.

Family Ice Center (207-781-4200; 20 Hat Trick Drive, Falmouth). New inside and outdoor facilities.

Mill Creek Park (207-767-7651; Cottage Rd., South Portland). December–February. Outdoors.

Travis Roy Ice Arena (207-846-2384; Rte. 1, Yarmouth). Indoors. Mid-July to end of March.

Payson Park (207-874-8793; Baxter Blvd., Portland). December–February. Outdoors.

Portland Ice Arena (207-774-8553; 225 Park Ave., Portland). July through April. Indoors.

Yarmouth Community Services Park (207-846-9680; Main St., Yarmouth). Check out the skating nearby on the Royall River, too. December–February. Outdoors.

TENNIS

Biddeford (207-283-0841; Memorial Park, May St.). Three courts with night lights. Also Clifford Park, Pool St., has two courts.

Old Orchard Beach (207-934-2500; www.oldorchardbeachmaine.com; Emerson Cummings Blvd. and First St. near high school). One court; plus three clay courts at Ocean Park and two more at Memorial Park.

Portland (207-874-8793; Deering Oaks Park). Eleven courts, and six more across town at Deering High School; four courts on the Eastern Promenade; four courts at Payson Park on Baxter Blvd.

Portland Athletic Club (207-781-2671; 196 Rte. 1, Falmouth). Six indoor courts, about $34 hr.

Racket and Fitness Center (207-775-6128; 2445 Congress St., Portland). Nine tennis courts, about $30. per hour.

WHALE WATCH

Odyssey Whale Watch (207-775-0727; www.marinerfleet.com; Commercial St., Long Wharf, Portland).

THE PORTLAND REGION: SHOPPING

ANTIQUES

Centervale Farm Antiques (207-883-3443 or 800-896-3443; www.centervale .com; 200 Rte. 1, Scarborough). A huge barn filled with antique furniture.

F.O. Bailey (207-774-1479; 141 Middle St., Portland). Great showroom and a terrific mix of stuff from rustic pottery to highly polished highboys.

Magpie's (207-828-4560; 610 Congress St., Portland). On the second floor, this is the place for unique jewelry, antiques, and hand-braided rugs.

Portland Architectural Salvage (207-780-0634; archsal3@aol.com; 919 Congress St., Portland). We've found many fine things to take home from here, from Tuscan garden ornaments to eight-foot doors for our old Victorian parlor.

Red Wheel Antiques (207-865-6492; 291 Rte. 1, Freeport). We think some of this mix of old dishes, tools, glassware, lamps, military items, and paraphernalia is overpriced. Still, we keep going back to find that occasional bargain.

Auctions on the Coast

If you're looking for antiques or just a Victorian knick-knack to take back to your Aunt Pearl, auctions provide the chance to cut out the middleman and get a feel for the worth of something by competing against professional buyers. Estate auctions are even more fun, because they give you a truer sense of time and place than many historic homes or museums. Most of the auction houses listed below will be glad to put you on their mailing lists. *The Maine Sunday Telegram* and *The Maine Times* often run notices of upcoming auctions in their classified sections. Another source of auction notices, the *Maine Antique Digest* has auction news and an entertaining column of auction gossip complete with photographs.

Auctions by Sutherland (207-829-3063; West Cumberland).
F.O. Bailey Antiquarians (207-774-1479; www.fobailey.com; 141 Middle St., Portland).
Thomaston Place Auction Galleries (800-924-1032; Rte. 1, Thomaston).

BOOKSTORES

Allen Scott Books (207-774-2190; www.abebooks.com; AllenHScott@msn.com; Portland). Mr. Scott works over the internet now, and will find rare and used books for anyone who contacts him via the internet. He buys books as well.

Books Etc. (207-774-0626; 38 Exchange St., Portland and 207-781-3784; 240 Rte. 1, Falmouth). This is one of our favorite Maine bookstores, now with a sister store up the coast. Travelers take note, they have an excellent Maine and travel book selection.

Borders Books and Music (207-775-6110; 430 Gorham Rd., South Portland). A café and a huge selection of magazines, books, and music, open daily.

Carlson & Turner Antiquarian Books (207-773-4200 or 800-540-7323; swilson @maine.rr.com; 241 Congress St., Portland). We love to survey these dimly lit shelves. They give away an annual collectors' calendar, with original art on it, that's a treasure in itself.

Cunningham Books (207-775-2246; Longfellow Square (on Congress St.), Portland). A great used book store and a fine place to browse.

Eartha, *the giant globe at the DeLorme Mapping Company, takes up a lot of space.*

Herb Swanson

DeLorme Mapping Company (207-846-7000; www.delorme.com; 2 DeLorme Drive, Yarmouth). DeLorme charts Maine's wilderness—urban and otherwise—from every possible point of view. They also chart the world, using satellites, computers, and automobile navigation systems. If you love maps, globes, or computers, you'll love this place. Check out Eartha, the world's largest rotating globe. The map store is open every day.

Longfellow Books (207-772-4042; 1 Monument Way, Portland). Good in every department.

The Store at Maine Audubon Society (207-781-2330; www.maineaudubon .org; 20 Gislsand Farm Rd. (off Rte 1), Falmouth). A good collection of books for those interested in natural history.

CLOTHING

Amaryllis (207-772-4439; 41 Exchange St., Portland). Unusual women's clothing, shoes, and hats.

The Dancing Elephant (207-775-7111; 415 Forest Ave., Portland). Great kids' clothes.

Joseph's (207-773-1274; 410 Fore St., Portland). The men's and women's clothing stores are as haut as Maine gets.

Levinsky's (207-774-0972; 516 Congress St., Portland). This is a bargain-hunter's institution among tight-fisted Mainers, so much so the store has been immortalized in the pages of *Down East* magazine. This is a good place to outfit the kids for school.

GIFTS & SOUVENIRS

Abacus American Crafts (207-772-4880; 44 Excange St., Portland). Fine crafts and jewelry.

Dunne Roman (207-780-6456; 428 Fore St., Portland). This store, in an Old Port warehouse, is absolutely gorgeous and the perfect place to find a gift for that eccentrically elegant aunt or friend of yours.

Nestling Duck Gift Shop (207-883-6705; 350 Pine Point Rd., Scarborough). A collection of New England gifts, including candles, stoneware, jewelry, and Maine-made crafts.

Something's Fishy (207-774-7726; 22 Exchange St., Portland). Irresistibly ticky-tacky lobster and lighthouse souvenirs for out-of-town family and friends.

HOME FURNISHINGS

Chaudier Cookware Factory Store (207-865-4448; 124 Main St., Freeport). Made in Prince Edward Island in Canada, this cookware is fabulous, and it can be difficult to find on this side of the border. This is the only Chaudier store in the United States.

Cuddledown of Maine (207-865-1713; 231 Rte. 1 South, Freeport). Their down comforters and pillows have been made right here in Maine for 25 years. Beautiful blankets, sheets, and other home furnishings, with up to 70 percent off catalog prices.

Decorum (207-775-3346; decorum@tiac.com; 231 Commercial St., Portland). Old house fanatics travel for hundreds of miles to find nifty, well-made stuff for the house, including reproduction hardware.

Heritage Lanterns (207-846-3911 or 800-544-6070; www.heritagelanterns.com; 70A Main St., Yarmouth). Handcrafted reproductions of 18th-, 19th-, and early 20th-century lanterns, sconces, chandeliers, and lamps.

Maine Cottage Furniture (207-846-3699; www.mainecottage.com; info@maine cottage.com; Lower Falls Landing, Rte. 88, Yarmouth). Furniture in colors that will appeal to modern day rusticators. Also, lighting, vintage-cloth pillows, linen, and sofas.

JEWELRY

Fibula (207-761-4432; 50 Exchange St., Portland). The showcases here are like the who's who of Maine jewelry making: Werner Reed, P.B. Las, Elizabeth Pryor, Sally Webb, Daniel Gibbings, and the shop's owner, Edie Armstrong, who makes beautiful custom wedding bands, earrings, bracelets, and necklaces at her workbench right in the store.

NAUTICAL EQUIPMENT

Aqua Diving Academy (207-772-4200; www.aquadivingacademy.com; 382 Commercial St., Portland). All the diving equipment you need; and basics like swimsuits, goggles, water shoes, for all sizes of grownups and kids.

POTTERY

Maine Potters Market (207-774-1633; www.mainemade.com; 376 Fore St., Portland). Local potter's cooperative featuring stoneware, porcelain, and earthenware. An interesting mix of traditional to funky one-of-a-kind pieces.

Pottery by Peg & Dick Miller (207-846-4981; 19 Smith St. off Rte. 88, Yarmouth). The Millers fashion their wheel-thrown, slab, shingle, and coil pottery from local materials, including native clay, beach sand, wood ashes, seaweed, clam, and mussel shells. Then they fire it in their own kiln. Their glazes are lead-free, and all of their works are ovenproof and dishwasher safe.

Sawyer Street Studio (207-767-4394; 131 Sawyer St., South Portland). Six potters share this space, making functional stoneware and sculpture like Nancy Nevergole's "Vessel Virgins," voluptuous candlesticks. Call for times and date of the open house.

OUTDOOR & SPORTING GOODS

Eastern Mountain Sports (207-772-3776; www.easternmountainsports.com; Maine Mall., South Portland). Clothing, footwear, and gear for campers and hikers.

L.L. Bean (207-865-4761 or 800-221-4221; www.llbean.com; llbean@llbean.com; Main St., Freeport). The big daddy of all outdoor stores in Maine. The store stays open 24 hours every day of the year. The best time to shop—if you can stay awake—is in the wee hours.

Surplus Store (207-775-0201; 28 Monument Sq. on Congress St., Portland). Before there were Marshalls, Loehman's, and shopping warehouses, surplus stores were the place to buy discounted jeans and old army fatigues. This store has all that, plus a good selection of respectably inexpensive camping and fishing gear.

The L.L. Bean store in Freeport offers test rides in their kayaks.

Herb Swanson

L.L. Bean

The lore that surrounds L.L. Bean is almost as numerous as the items sold in the Maine company's mail-order catalog, but here are some salient Bean facts.

L.L. Bean was born Leon Linwood Bean in 1872, a name he changed soon after the turn of the century to Leon Leonwood.
- He was orphaned in 1884.
- He invented the Maine Hunting Shoe in 1911.
- He sent potential customers his first mailing in 1912, a small circular with an illustration and description of the Maine Hunting Shoe.
- In 1951, he threw out the keys to his famous store, making it one of the first stores in America to stay open 24 hours a day, 365 days a year.
- Since then the store has closed only four times: two Sundays in 1962 before the town fathers granted L.L. Bean dispensation from the state's new blue laws; the day in 1963 when President John F. Kennedy was assassinated; and the day L.L. Bean died in 1967.

CHAPTER FIVE
A Long Reach Into the Sea
BRUNSWICK, BATH
THE HARPSWELLS, THE PHIPPSBURG & GEORGETOWN PENINSULAS

Curtis Rindlaub

The buildings of Sebasco Harbor Resort stretch along the water's edge.

Here begin the many peninsulas that stretch their rocky fingers into the Gulf of Maine, each one ending in a quiet fishing village, an ages-old lighthouse, or a sand beach. For example, just a little to the southeast of Brunswick are the **Harpswells**, skinny stretches of land that reach into Casco Bay and are connected by bridge to the rounded and rocky terrain of **Sebascodegan, Orrs,** and **Bailey Islands**. Making your way to the edge of Mackerel Cove on Bailey Island is only a matter of about 15 miles, but it can seem like time traveling through decades. There's also **Cundy's Harbor** off on its own, a fishing village so heavily populated with photographic subjects that local stores do a brisk business selling film.

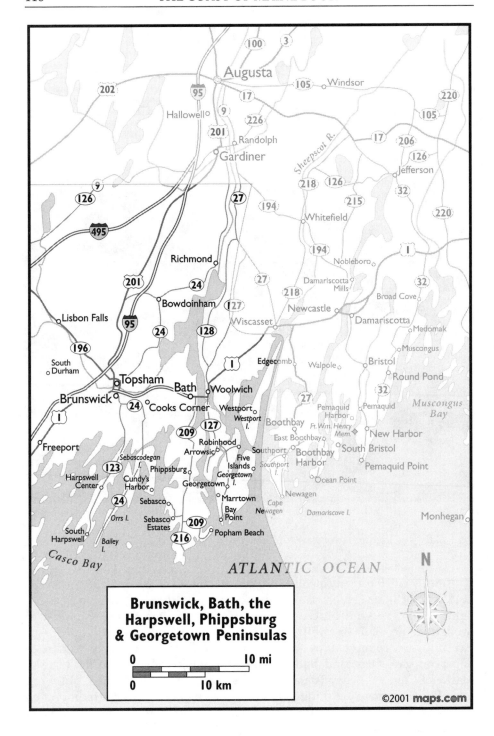

Brunswick, Bath, the
Harpswell, Phippsburg
& Georgetown Peninsulas

0　　　　　　　10 mi

0　　　　　　　10 km

©2001 maps.com

Bowdoin College is the overwhelming presence in **Brunswick**, but there's much more here than just the school, including the Peary-MacMillan Arctic Museum and the Maine State Music Theatre. Harriet Beecher Stowe wrote *Uncle Tom's Cabin* in Brunswick.

Bath is a city of ships and shipbuilding that hugs the shores of the Kennebec, a deep and navigable waterway that feels like the ocean—as if it were capable of handling any vessel large or small. During World War II, Bath built more destroyers than all the shipyards in the entire Japanese empire. Not far from here is the **Phippsburg** peninsula, the home of the first European settlers, and its earliest shipbuilding industry.

Across the Kennebec is **Georgetown Island**, a sprawling network of summer communities and fishing villages with names like **Robinhood, Five Islands, Marrtown,** and **Arrowsic**. Robinhood Cove, which cuts into the island's northeastern side, is often filled with the yachts of summering residents, and Reid State Park at the outermost reaches of the Sheepscot River is a wonderful family park with beautiful beach.

BRUNSWICK TO BATH: LODGING

Bath

INN AT BATH
Innkeeper: Nick Bayard.
207-443-4294.
www.innatbath.com.
innkeeper@innatbath.com.
969 Washington St., Bath
 04530.
Open: All year.
Price: Moderate to
 Expensive.
Credit Cards: AE, D, MC, V.
Handicap Access: One
 room.

Built in 1810 when Bath was a booming shipbuilding town, this handsomely restored Greek Revival home has twin parlors filled with antiques and striking family pieces and a marvelous marble fireplace. There are seven comfortable and roomy guest rooms, all with private bath, TVs, VCRs, airconditioning, and telephones. Several have fireplaces, two with double Jacuzzis next to them and king- or queen-sized beds. Two of the rooms adjoin and can make a suite. This inn is run like a ship, and the rooms are kept immaculate; so the innkeeper asks for no red wine or fruit juice in the rooms, and no removing makeup with the pristine white towels. Whether the guarantee of perfection is worth compliance is your decision. Full breakfast included. Children and pets welcome. No smoking.

Brunswick

**CAPTAIN DANIEL
 STONE INN**
Innkeeper: Louise Holmes.
207-725-9898 or
 877-573-5151.

The Captain Daniel Stone Inn mixes old and new to appealing effect. Capt. Daniel Stone owned the Federal-style home, which has wings that have been added in recent years. Rooms and

www.captaindanielstone
inn.com.
10 Water St., Brunswick
04011.
Off Rte. 1.
Open: All year.
Price: Moderate to Very
Expensive.
Credit Cards: AE, D, DC,
MC, V.
Handicap Access: Yes.

suites have modern conveniences like cable TV, VCRs, and cassette players. Furnishings are period reproductions. Some of the 34 rooms are done in pine, others in mahogany. Several have whirlpool baths and brass beds. The inn also has a popular restaurant, the Narcissa Stone that serves lunch and dinner, in the summer on an outdoor veranda. Light breakfast included.

Harpswell

**CAPTAIN'S WATCH BED
AND BREAKFAST
AND SAIL CHARTER**
Innkeepers: Donna Dillman
and Ken Brigham.
207-725-0979.
926 Cundy's Harbor Rd.,
Harpswell 04079.
Open: Year round; by
reservation only in
winter.
Price: Moderate to
Expensive.
Credit Cards: MC, V.
Handicap Access: Limited.

Perched atop a high bluff, this former Civil War "Union Hotel" affords long views over a small working harbor and beyond to ledge, islands, rivers, and bays. The Captain's Watch is an elegant, unpretentious Greek Revival home decorated with family antiques and collections of old china and quilts. All five bedrooms have private bath and overlook the water or secluded woods. Breakfast included. It would be a lovely adventure to take advantage of Donna and Ken's 37-foot sail charter boat *Symbian*. Ken is a Coast Guard licensed captain and takes guests out for day or overnights. Children 10 and older welcome.

HARPSWELL INN
Innkeepers: Susan and Bill
Menz.
207-833-5509 or
800-843-5509.
www.harpswellinn.com.
108 Lookout Point Rd.,
Harpswell 04079.
Open: All year.
Price: Moderate.
Credit Cards: D, MC, V.
Handicap Access: Partial.

A shipbuilder built this beautiful old home with white clapboards, black shutters, and more windows than anybody would ever want to clean. The downstairs is filled with furniture Susan and Bill Menz have picked up in their travels to China and Europe. There are nine rooms, seven with private baths, and three with fireplaces. There are also three luxury suites, one with a Jacuzzi and two with kitchens. Breakfast in the main house may include quiche, homemade muffins, and French toast. Children over 10 in the main house; children of all ages welcome in the cottages available for rent off the premises of the inn. If you bring a boat with you, there is plenty of parking for trailers, and the inn is right up the road from a public launching ramp into Casco Bay's Middle Bay.

Sebasco Estates

**SEBASCO HARBOR
  RESORT**
Owner: Bob Smith.
207-389-1161 or
  800-225-3819.
www.sebasco.com.
info@sebasco.com.
Rte. 217, Sebasco Estates
  04565.
Off Rte. 209 near
  Phippsburg.
Open: May–Oct.
Price: Moderate to Very
  Expensive.
Credit Cards: AE, D, MC, V.

Sebasco Lodge is a friendly, oddball collection of structures situated on 600 acres at the southeastern tip of the Phippsburg peninsula near Popham Beach State Park. Daily activities center around meals served in the large spit-and-polish dining room, where jackets are suggested but not required. Twice a week, guests move their socializing outdoors, weather permitting. Sunday offers a poolside blueberry pancake breakfast. Tuesday, a weekly lobster picnic. There are plenty of appetite-building activities for guests of all ages: nine holes of golf on a course redesigned in 2001, a saltwater swimming pool, play school for the kids, tennis, shuffleboard, canoeing, lawn bowling, sail and motor boat rental, bingo, and evening dance socials with live music. Clean and comfortable but not luxurious, with wholesome and plentiful meals, recent years have been major renovations. Rates for the modified American plan (breakfast and dinner) available.

Phippsburg

EDGEWATER FARM B&B
Innkeepers: Bill and Carol
  Emerson.
207-389-1322.
www.ewfbb.com.
71 Small Point Rd. (Rte.
  216), Phippsburg 04562.
Open: All year.
Price: Moderate.
Credit Cards: MC, V.
Handicap Access: One
  room.

The Emersons have converted this 1800 farmhouse into a lovely bed and breakfast, and because the owners have green thumbs, the breakfast table often includes bounty from their orchards and organic gardens. The six guest rooms, all with private bath, are comfortable and pretty. This is a good place to stay for bicyclists and kayakers touring the peninsula. There are several great white sand beaches nearby including those at Popham Beach State Park. If you prefer warmer water, however, the B&B has an enclosed swimming pool. No smoking.

Westport Island

**THE SQUIRE TARBOX
  INN**
Innkeepers: Karen and Bill
  Mitman.
207-882-7693.
www.squiretarboxinn.com
1181 Main Rd. (Rte. 144),
  Westport Island, 04578.

Squire Tarbox was a selectman and the town's first postmaster, and he built himself a handsome house you can now enjoy, paying your respects, of course, to the past, as you come and go from the parking lot next to the cemetery. While this handsome, beautifully kept farmhouse inn

Dick Mason

The old Squire Tarbox Inn on Westport Island shows classic Maine farmhouse architecture.

Open: May–Oct.
Price: Moderate to
  Expensive.
Credit Cards: AE, D, MC, V.
Special Features: Goat
  cheese made on
  premises; dairy open
  year-round.

with its pastoral setting may seem charmingly rustic, there is nothing less than polished about the service. The main house has wide colonial floorboards, an interesting mix of antiques, and four guest rooms (two air-conditioned) with private baths and working fireplaces. If you like to be more casual, you can stay in the 1820s barn, from which the Squire's animals were banished long ago. The barn has seven romantically private bedrooms, each with bath, a homey common room, and a wood stove. Breakfast is excellent. The inn no longer serves dinner, but it continues to be a quiet, peaceful place away from the main roads. Beyond hospitality and good food, the primary products here are distinctive goats' milk cheeses, offered as late afternoon snacks—the inn operates in the midst of a working dairy farm complete with its own herd of purebred Nubian goats. Borrow the inn's bikes and pedal off to explore the rolling countryside. No pets—they would disturb the goats; no children under 12.

BRUNSWICK TO BATH: DINING

Bath

KRISTINA'S
207-442-8577.
160 Center St., Bath 04530.
Closed: Jan.
Price: Moderate to
 Expensive.
Cuisine: American eclectic.
Serving: B, L, D, SB.
Credit Cards: D, MC, V.
Special Features: Bakery
 takeout.

Kristina's is consistently on everyone's list of coastal favorites. The upstairs dining room is casual and lounge-like; downstairs is bright, homey, and cheerful with butcher-block tables and potted plants. While it might seem that a breakfast place would be unlikely to make an elegant dinner well, they do. Lunch is a meal of soups, salads, sandwiches, and burgers. Dinner runs from such standards as lamb chops and grilled salmon to more exotic Indian tofu. Try the steamed mussels, garlicky and rich, to start. A light menu includes quiches and burritos. Stop by the bakery case for something good. Their pies are good, and so are their breads and cookies.

Brunswick

HENRY & MARTY
207-721-9141.
61 Main St., Brunswick
 04011.
Open: All year, except
 Sept.; call for schedule.
Price: Moderate.
Cuisine: Healthy gourmet.
Serving: Dinner.
Credit Cards: AE, MC, V.
Handicap access: Yes.
Reservations:
 Recommended.

A lot of us ate here during the Stonecoast Writers' Conference at Bowdoin, and it always served us fresh, delicious food. There are soy "meatballs" for vegans, penne with shrimp and scallops, arugula pizza, or chicken with lemon, capers, and olive oil, for everyone else. I ate every last bit of the blueberry cobbler; cobblers vary with the season. The long room with gold walls has a take-out counter.

RICHARD'S
207-729-9673.
115 Maine St., Brunswick
 04011.
Closed: Sun.
Price: Moderate.
Cuisine: German,
 American.
Serving: L, D.
Credit Cards: AE, D, MC, V.
Reservations:
 Recommended.
Handicap Access: Yes.

Richard's is in town and offers German beers and victuals. The beer roster is prodigious, with numerous offbeat selections, to wash down hearty fare like wiener schnitzel, smoked pork chops, sauerbraten, wursts, potato salad, and sautéed cabbage. An American menu for the unadventurous includes chicken, haddock, and steaks. The interior is brick and wood with high chandeliers, tablecloths, flowers, and candles. The wait staff is particularly good-natured. Tortes and strudels for dessert.

ROSITA'S
207-729-7118.
212 Main St., Brunswick 04011.
Open: Daily.
Price: Inexpensive.
Cuisine: Mexican.
Serving: L, D.
Credit Cards: None.
Handicap Access: Limited.
Special Feature: Huevos rancheros on Sunday.

Every college town needs a Mexican restaurant, and Rosita's is the one nearest Bowdoin College. "Casual" is an understatement here, with beer from a cooler and cafeteria-style service. The folks behind the counter are eager to please, and the place has a friendly feel. All the usual suspects are on the menu: burritos, tostados, nachos, tacos, enchiladas, chili, fajitas, and tamales available in beef, pinto bean, chicken, chorizo, and black beans. Salsas come in hot and mild strengths; the overall firepower of most fixings is quite mild. Sunday breakfasts are unusual, featuring bacon and egg tacos and huevos rancheros.

STAR FISH GRILL
207-725-7828.
100 Pleasant St. (Rte. 1) Brunswick 04011.
Open: Year-round; closed Mon.
Price: Expensive.
Cuisine: Mediterranean and Asian Seafood.
Serving: B, L, D, SB.
Credit Cards: D, MC, V.
Handicap Access: Yes.
Reservations: Recommended.

The bowl of cioppino, a Portuguese fish stew, was all anyone could ask for: full of lobster, swordfish, scallops, and mussels with a spicy tomato Pernod sauce on capelline pasta. Or they can tone down or tune up the fire in the Thai-style mussels and calamari in green curry sauce. The crab cakes come as an appetizer or an entrée. There are clams, swordfish, tuna; many pieces of fish can be had simply broiled or grilled as you like them. You can be certain the fish will be fresh, the cooking skillful, the food delicious, and the wine to drink by the glass or bottle. . . all will be suited perfectly.

Georgetown

FIVE ISLANDS LOBSTER COMPANY
207-371-2990.
www.fiveislandslobster.com.
1447 Five Islands Rd., Georgetown 04548.
Open: Mid-May–Oct., 11am–8pm.
Price: Inexpensive to Moderate.
Cuisine: Seafood in the rough.
Serving: L, D.
Special Features: Outdoor pier dining; BYOB.

The lobster coop of the same name runs Five Islands, so the food doesn't get fresher than this. In addition to lobster, lobster rolls, crab rolls, and crab cakes, daily specials may include steamed mussels and clams, boiled crabs, fried clams or shrimp, pan-seared haddock sandwiches, corn on the cob, and onion rings. Local kids add to the color, taking running dives off the end of the wharf into the icy water; follow them to the ice cream shack after the meal. Avoid the table by the bait shed.

When the shadows lengthen, it's the perfect time to come to the Robinhood Free Meetinghouse for worldly, inspired dinners.

Herb Swanson

THE ROBINHOOD FREE MEETINGHOUSE
207-371-2188.
www.robinhood-
meetinghouse.com.
210 Robinhood Rd.,
Georgetown 04548.
Open: Year-round, fewer
weekdays in winter.
Price: Moderate to
Expensive.
Cuisine: Eclectic.
Serving: D.
Credit Cards: AE, D, MC, V.
Handicap access: Yes.
Reservations:
Recommended.

Congregationalists and Methodists built a meetinghouse in 1855, but now cuisines from all over are meeting each other here. Start in a modified Asian way, with avocado and crab "sushi" in rice paper, then go on to Germany with wiener schnitzel and potato pancakes with lingonberries and sour cream, or to the Caribbean with jerk shrimp and mango, or to Russia with beef stroganoff. Over 30 entrées that move ingredients around like chess pieces make any decision strategic and cunning, but inevitably victorious. The well-known chef Michael Gagne writes, "You are what you do," and he proves to be both meticulous and adventurous.

Sebasco Estates .

THE WATER'S EDGE
207-389-1803.
www.thewatersedgerestaur
ant.com.
75 Black's Landing Rd.,
Sebasco Estates 04565.
Off Rte. 217.
Open: May–Sept.
Price: Inexpensive to
Moderate.
Cuisine: Seafood.
Credit Cards: MC, V.

The Water's Edge is on the peninsula to the east and south of Phippsburg, and getting there takes a fair amount of winding down country roads. You can eat outside when the weather warms up. We were there late in the spring, and inside the former clam depuration shed we found a wood-burning stove to take the chill off. The seafood is fresh from the family's wharf just below. On the day we were there, they had tiny, sweet mahogany clams steamed and served with butter, as well as a fine halibut filet. We finished with bread pudding.

South Harpswell

Herb Swanson

One of Maine's famed peeky-toe crabs.

DOLPHIN MARINA RESTAURANT
207-833-6000.
515 Basin Point (off Rte. 123), South Harpswell 04079.
Open: May 1–Oct. 31.
Price: Inexpensive to Moderate.
Cuisine: Seafood.
Serving: L, D.
Credit Cards: MC, V.
Handicap Access: Yes.

This is where the fishermen come to eat out. They're the ones sitting at the counter with meaty burgers piled with ketchup. You can get burgers in the city. Try the chunky lobster stew. Watch lobster boats or sailboats tie up, or see if the blueberries are ripe in the field. Wash it all down with coffee and a slice of fresh fruit pie in season, and bring a sweater if the wind is blowing, since the boatyard faces into prevailing southwesterlies.

BRUNSWICK TO BATH: FOOD PURVEYORS

BAKERIES

Blue Heron Bakery (207-442-0759; Rte. 1, Woolwich). Everything is vegan; the pies and cookies are delicious. See the sign on Rte. 1, under the trees. The herbal popcorn is perfect.

Kristina's (207-442-8577; 160 Center St., Bath). Pastries and tortes to fuel your way up the coast. They also make great French toast for a sit-down breakfast.

BARBECUE

Beale Street Barbeque and Grill (207-442-9514; 215 Water St., Bath). Try the hickory smoked and grilled ribs.

COOKING SCHOOL

Le Jardin de Cote Cooking School and Restaurant (207-831-8256; Bailey Island). One- to five-day courses in the preparation of basic French dishes like poached salmon and Grand Marnier soufflé.

FAST FOOD

Midcoast Pizza & More (207-443-6631; www.pizzaandmore.com; 737 Washington St., Bath). Casual.

HEALTH FOOD STORES AND FARM MARKETS

Morning Glory Natural Foods (207-729-0546; 60 Maine St., Brunswick. 207-442-8012; 36 Centre St., Bath). Open seven days, these are the places for organic food.

BRUNSWICK TO BATH: CULTURE

A launching at Bath Iron Works, one of Maine's active ship-building centers.

Herb Swanson

CINEMA

Brunswick 10 Cinemas (207-798-3996; Cooks Corner Shopping Center, 19 Granite Rd., Brunswick).
Evening Star Cinema (207-729-5486 or 888-304-5486; Tontine Mall, 149 Main St., Brunswick).

GALLERIES

Chocolate Church Gallery (207-442-8455; chocolatechurch@suscom-maine.net; 798 Washington St., Bath). Part of the lively, regional arts center housed in a grand old church, this gallery features the work of its members and other Maine artists. Tues.–Sat. noon–4.

Icon Contemporary Art (207-725-8157; 19 Mason St., Brunswick). Changing shows of emerging and established Maine and regional contemporary artists. Mon.–Fri. 1–5; Sat. 1–4.

HISTORIC BUILDINGS & SITES

FIRST MEETINGHOUSE
207-833-6336 or
207-833-6322.
Rte. 123, Harpswell Center.
Open: By request only.
No charge.

Constructed in 1757, this is Maine's oldest meetinghouse, and its earliest congregations included what residents called "praying Indians." The building is still in general use as a town office and is an excellent example of early church architecture.

JOSHUA L. CHAMBERLAIN HOUSE
207-729-6606.
www.curtislibrary.com/pejebscot.htm.
226 Main St., Brunswick.
Season: June–Aug.,
Tues.–Sat. 10–4; by appointment during the rest of the year.
Admission: $5 adult, $2.50 children 6–16.

Joshua Chamberlain led a large life, winning a Congressional Medal of Honor in the battle of Gettysburg, accepting the Confederate Army's surrender at the close of the Civil War, becoming governor of Maine (1866–1870) and president of nearby Bowdoin College (1871–1883). He occupied this house (built in 1825) while serving Bowdoin. Several rooms have been restored and are on view, as well as a collection of Chamberlain's Civil War memorabilia.

SKOLFIELD-WHITTIER HOUSE
207-729-6606.
www.curtislibrary.com/pejepscot.htm.
161 Park Row, Brunswick.
Season: June–Aug.,
Tues.–Sat.; tours at 10am, 11:30am, 1pm, and 2:30pm.

Three generations of prominent Brunswickians resided in this handsome 17-room home. They were doctors, mariners, and educators, and the house remains pretty much as it was when the family last lived here in 1925. Maintained by the Brunswick Historical Society.

LIBRARIES

The Bowdoin College Library (207-725-3280; www.library.bowdoin.edu; 3000 College Station, Brunswick 04011). The Bowdoin College Library, refurbished in 2001, makes a haven for quiet reading, and it offers exhibits on its own history and rarities. Mon.–Wed. 10am–1am, Thurs.–Fri. 8:30am–midnight, Sat. 8:30am–11pm.

MUSEUMS

PEARY-MacMILLAN ARCTIC MUSEUM
207-725-3416.
www.bowdoin.edu.
Hubbard Hall, Bowdoin College, Brunswick.
Open: Tues.– Sat. 10–5; Sun. 2–5. Closed holidays. Guided tours available during the academic year; call to schedule.

Bowdoin graduates Admirals Robert E. Peary and Donald B. MacMillan are commemorated here. Peary was the first man to reach the North Pole, on April 6, 1909; MacMillan was Peary's chief assistant. Exhibits include the log and a sledge from the 1909 expedition, plus displays of Inuit art and artifacts from Labrador and Greenland that MacMillan gathered on subsequent expeditions.

BOWDOIN COLLEGE ART MUSEUM
207-725-3275.
Walker Art Building, Bowdoin College, Brunswick.
Open: All year Tues.– Sat. 10–5; Sun. 2–5.
Closed: Mon. and national holidays.
Free.

A beautiful Greek Revival building houses the museum's permanent collections including ancient Mediterranean art and European and American paintings, sculpture, drawings, prints, and photos. Of special interest are the selection of Colonial and Federal portraits and paintings by Winslow Homer, John Sloan, and Rockwell Kent. The museum also regularly features changing art exhibits.

MUSIC

Bowdoin College Summer Music Festival (207-725-3433; www.bowdoin.edu; Bowdoin College, Brunswick). Since 1964 Bowdoin has hosted a summer music school and concert series. More than 200 students study here, and their practicing fills the air during summer nights. Guest teachers from the world's best conservatories, along with other visiting musicians, perform throughout the Music School session.

Seasonal Music

Annual Bluegrass Festival (207-725-6009; www.thomaspointbeach.com; Thomas Point Beach, Brunswick). This Bluegrass music fest is the finale to a long season of camping, music, and fun. Labor Day weekend. Admission: $15–$30, day; $65–$80, weekend (music and accommodations); children under 12 free.

SCHOOLS

Le Jardin de Cote Cooking School and Restaurant (207-831-8256; Bailey Island, Maine). One- to five-day courses in the preparation of basic French dishes like poached salmon and Grand Marnier soufflé.

Shelter Institute (207-442-7938; www.shelterinstitute.com; 873 Rte. 1, Woolwich). Shelter Institute teaches its international student body how to make
their houses energy efficient from the ground up. They sell all energy-related
products and house an incredible home builder's library. Classes year-
round.

SEASONAL EVENTS

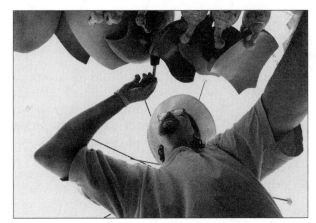

*You can see craftsmen at
work and buy their finished
products at the Maine
Festival.*

Maine Festival (207-772-9012; www.mainearts.org; Thomas Point Beach,
Brunswick). More than 600 artists and craftsmen on site. Folk Arts Village
highlighting music and crafts traditional to Maine, plus bands and perform-
ers from other parts of the country. Early August.
Maine Highland Games (207-364-3063; www.mint.net/bravehrt; Thomas
Point Beach, Brunswick). People of Scottish ancestry show their colors.
Bagpipe bands, highland dancing, food, border-collie demonstrations, and
clan exhibits. Third Saturday in August.

THEATER

Maine State Music Theatre (207-725-8769; www.msmt.org; Pickard Theater,
Bowdoin College, Brunswick). Top-notch musicals with resident professional
talent who for nearly 40 years have belted out great show tunes. June–Aug.
Studio Theater (207-442-7493; Winter St. Center, Bath). Tom and Sherry
Watson stage plays and musicals thoughout the year; call for schedule.
The Theater Project/Young People's Theater (207-729-8584; www.theaterpro
ject.com; 14 School St., Brunswick). More than seven productions a year featuring dramas, contemporaries, and musicals. The Young People's Theater
has classes for school-aged children and community productions involving
both kids and adults. Tickets: $15 adults; $6 kids.

BRUNWICK TO BATH: RECREATION

Kids can come up with a lot of stuff in a tidal stream.

Herb Swanson

BEACHES

Reid State Park; Rte. 127 to Seguinland Rd., Georgetown. A half-mile open barrier spit, this is another great beach. There's a salt marsh, sand dunes, rocky ledges, tidal pools, a bathhouse, picnic tables, fireplaces, and a snack bar. Decent parking. Entrance fee.

BERRY AND APPLE PICKING

Hilltop Raspberry Farm (207-737-4988; Post Rd., Bowdoinham). Raspberries. July 15–Oct. Daily 9–6.
Juniper Edge Strawberries (207-725-6414; 532 Harpswell Rd., Rte. 123, Brunswick). Strawberries. June 15 to end of season. Daily 8:30–5:30.
Prouts Strawberries (207-666-5604; Brown Point Rd., Bowdoinham). Strawberries. Late June–mid-July. 7am–dusk. Closed Sundays.

BICYCLING

Bath Cycle and Ski (207-442-7002; bikeman.com; Rte. 1, Woolwich).
Brunswick Bicycles (207-729-5309; 11 Center St., Brunswick).

BOATING

CANOEING AND SEA KAYAKING

Dragonworks (207-666-8481; RR1, Box 1186, Bowdoinham 04008) Boats, tours, instruction on Merrymeeting Bay.

H2Outfitters (800-20KAYAK; www.h2outfitters.com; P.O. Box 72, Orrs Island 04066). Canoe and kayak instruction for groups or individuals, as well as three-hour guided tours of waters near Bailey and Orrs Islands. Classes offered year-round.

Seaspray Kayaking (888-349-7772; Off Rte. 1, Brunswick). Rent or go on a guided tour. Kids like the Thomas Point Beach Ice Cream Tour.

CHARTERS

Kennebec Jet Boat Adventure Tours (207-442-0092; www.kennebecjetboat .com; 870 Washington St., Bath). From four-hour nature cruises to one-hour excursions.

Herb Swanson

Tranquility accompanies kayakers through the reeds.

M/V Ruth (207-389-1161; www.sebasco.com; Sebasco Harbor Resort, Sebasco Estates). June through Labor Day, explore Eagle Island or go on a pirate cruise.

SAILING LESSONS

Bay Island Yacht Charters and Sailing School (207-596-7550; Bay Island).
Sawyer's Sailing School (207-783-6882 or 800-372-8465; www.boatshow.com/ CaptainBob.html; bobsails25@aolcom; Dolphin Marina, S. Harpswell). One- and three-day instructional cruises aboard a 25-foot sloop.

BOWLING

Columbus Club Bowling Bowl (207-725-5241; 7 Dunlap Rd., Brunswick).
Yankee Lanes of Brunswick (207-725-2963; Bath Rd., Brunswick). 32 tenpin lanes.

CAMPING

Meadowbrook Camping (207-443-4967 or 800-370-2267; www.meadow brookme.com; 33 Meadowbrook Rd., Phippsburg). Heated swimming pool, hot showers, groceries.
Thomas Point Beach (207-725-6009; www.thomaspointbeach.com; off Rte. 24, Cook's Corner, Brunswick). Showers, fireplaces, snack bar, beach with lifeguard

GOLF

Bath Golf Country Club (207-442-8411; Whiskeag Rd., Bath). 18 holes, 6,260 yds., par 70. Cart and club rental, pro shop, clubhouse, lessons.
Brunswick Golf Club (207-725-8224; River Rd., Brunswick). 18 holes, 6,600 yds., par 72. Cart and club rental, pro shop, clubhouse, lessons. On weekends, private until 10am.
Long Shot Golf Center (207-725-6377; 305 Bath Rd., Brunswick). Driving range, lessons, and miniature golf.
North Haven Golf Club (Iron Point Rd., North Haven). 9 holes, 2,060 yds., par 35. Cart and club rental, lessons.

HEALTH CLUBS

The Maine Event (207-729-0129; 126 Main St., Topsham). Pool, aerobics, weights, racquetball, sauna, whirlpool, fitness machines, and lifecycles.
The Maine Pines Raquet & Sport (207-729-8433; 120 Harpswell Rd., Brunswick). Tennis and racquetball, volleyball, yoga, karate, squash, fitness center, childcare.
Women's Fitness Studio (207-729-5544; 21 Standwood, Brunswick). Aerobics, Nautilus, spa services, yoga, childcare.
YMCA (207-443-4112; 26 Summer St., Bath). Aerobics, pool, whirlpool, sauna, racquetball, weights, and basketball gym.

HORSEBACK RIDING

Cherrydale Horse Farm (207-443-6782; Old Brunswick Rd., West Bath). Trails, boarding.

NATURE PRESERVES

Josephine Newman Wildlife Sanctuary, Rte. 127, Georgetown. A 119-acre preserve on the ocean with more than two miles of natural trails. The sanctuary
is bounded on two sides by salt marsh and contains a small pond. Managed
by Maine Audubon.

Robert P. Tristram Coffin Wildflower Sanctuary, Rte. 128, Woolwich. The
New England Wildflower Society owns and operates this 180-acre refuge. It
is home to more than 200 species of flowers, grasses, trees, and other plants.
Nature trails follow the edge of Merrymeeting Bay.

SKATING

Brunswick Parks & Recreation (207-725-6656; on the Mall, Brunswick).
December–March. Outdoors. Free.

TENNIS

Bath (207-443-8360; Congress Ave.). Four courts with night lights.

Brunswick (207-725-6656; Stanwood St. Courts). Five courts with night lights;
bring change.

The Pines of Maine (207-729-8433; 120 Harpswell Rd.). Six indoor courts.

BRUNSWICK TO BATH: SHOPPING

ANTIQUES

Brick Store Antiques (207-443-2790; 143 Front St., Bath). Year-round, seven
days a week.

F. Barrie Freeman (207-442-8452; Quaker Point Farm, West Bath). Old American maps. They also specialize in printed Americana and ephemera.

BOOKSTORES

The Bath Bookshop (207-443-9338; 96 Front St., Bath). Regional books, local
authors, and a good children's book section are featured.

Bookland (207-725-2313; Cook's Corner Shopping Center, Gurnet Rd.,
Brunswick). This is a dependable chain store with a wide selection of books.

Gulf of Maine Bookstore (207-729-5083; 134 Maine St., Brunswick). 22 years
old, this is Maine's best independent, alternative bookstore, featuring a big
poetry section, a large collection of Maine authors and fiction from Maine
Native Americans, gay writers, and others.

Peek-A-Book Cottage (207-833-0007; Harpswell Islands Rd., Bailey Island). April–Dec. 10,000 books from the owners' own collection.

CLOTHING

Wyler Crafts and Clothes (207-729-1321; 150 Maine St., Brunswick). Fashion and crafts in pottery, glass, and wood.

COLLECTIBLES

Native Arts (207-442-8399; www.nativeartsonline.com; Rte. 1, Woolwich). Authentic Native American crafts including Maine basketry and southwestern turquoise jewelry.

CRAFT SUPPLIES

Halcyon Yarn (207-442-7909 or 800-341-0282; www.halcyonyarn.com; service @halcyonyarn.com; 12 School St., Bath). If you knit, spin, or weave or you know someone who does, check this place out.

GIFTS & SOUVENIRS

Village Candle Factory Store (207-729-0800; www.villagecandle.com; 65 Topsham Fair Mall, Topsham). Scented candles.

JEWELRY

Springer's (207-443-2181; 76 Front St., Bath). An old-time Maine jeweler, Springer's sells Maine tourmaline and other fine jewelry.

POTTERY

Georgetown Pottery (207-371-2801; Rte. 127, Box 151, Georgetown). Nine miles from the Bath Bridge, open seven days, year-round; they have a free catalogue.

OUTDOOR & SPORTING GOODS

Kennebec Angler (207-442-8239; 97 Commercial St., Bath). Try demo rods for a day before you splurge on the tackle of your dreams.

CHAPTER SIX
From Crowds to Tranquil Shores
WISCASSET, DAMARISCOTTA
THE BOOTHBAY AND PEMAQUID PENININSULAS

Herb Swanson

The Hallowell Community Band performs on the green in Boothbay Harbor.

Wiscasset lays claim on its sign, on Rte. 1, to being the "prettiest village in Maine." That title is disputable, but the town's location where Rte. 1 crosses the Sheepscot River makes its charm readily visible to anyone traveling up the coast. Adding to Wiscasset's romance are two old schooners lodged haphazardly on the west bank of the river. The *Hesperus* and the *Luther Little* once carried cargo between Boston, Haiti, and Portugal. They were two of thousands of ships that plied the seas until well into the 1920s. Today they are one of the most photographed sites in Maine.

Formerly a trading center, and later a hub of shipbuilding activity, **Boothbay Harbor** today is mostly about boats, activities attached to boats, and people who find the boating way of life appealing. The shady streets of the town, at the tip of a rocky peninsula, are lined with summer-people-minded shops and

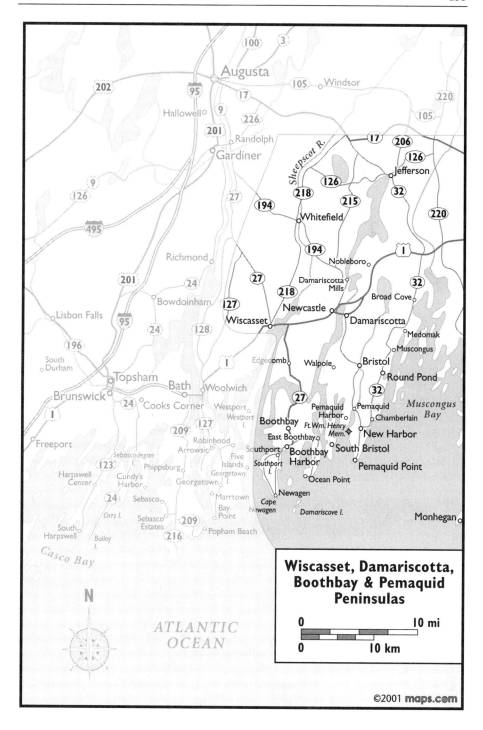

Wiscasset, Damariscotta, Boothbay & Pemaquid Peninsulas

0   10 mi

0   10 km

©2001 maps.com

a wealth of art galleries. The pretty harbor is jam-packed with boats to rent, boats to hire, boats to envy, and boats to drool over and make one consider Captain Kidd's occupation. (The notorious pirate also liked to summer here and reportedly left a buried treasure on nearby **Damariscove Island**. Treasure hunters are still trying to locate the gold coins and jewels.) This is also the port of call for Windjammer Days and the Friendship Sloop Races, two famous Maine boaters' events.

Within half an hour's drive you can see the great boats being built in **East Boothbay**. Nearby are the summer retreats of **Newagen** (on **Southport Island**) to the west and **Ocean Point** to the east.

For centuries Native Americans summer camped here and left behind giant piles of oyster shells, a feat that today is celebrated at the annual **Damariscotta River Oyster Festival**. Not far off Rte. 1, you can still see one of the great shell heaps where the Damariscotta River and the inland Great Salt Bay meet.

Here is another one of those coastal junctures where travelers can push on toward **Rockland** and **Camden** or veer off the main road onto picturesque Rte. 129. This road runs down the Pemaquid peninsula along the river to **South Bristol**, a fishing village, and **Christmas Cove**, a yachting basin so named by Captain John Smith, who anchored here on Christmas Day in 1614. Rte. 130 picks up in the fishing village of **New Harbor**, where Audubon tours of Eastern Egg Rock depart.

The road meanders on through the historic peninsula to **Pemaquid Point**, where there is one of Maine's most stunning lighthouses—**Pemaquid Light**. This spot shows off the Maine coast at its stormy best with the power of the ocean pounding against the rockbound coast. Heading north again, this time on Rte. 32, you can enjoy a good lunch in **Round Pond** and walk around the point where an old quarry sits abandoned. What's left is free for the taking, so everyone has pieces of granite for a marker in their driveway.

WISCASSET TO DAMARISCOTTA: LODGING

Boothbay Harbor

THE GREENLEAF INN
Innkeeper: Jeff Teel.
207-633-7346 or
   888-950-7724.
www.greenleafinn.com.
65 Commercial St.,
   Boothbay Harbor 04538.
Open: All year.
Price: Moderate to
   Expensive.
Credit Cards: AE, D, MC, V.
Handicap Access: Yes.

This bright and airy inn is a nice, quiet refuge with great views in a busy, often honky-tonk town. The 150-year-old white cape is perched on the side of a hill above the bustling harbor just a short walk from the town's galleries, fudge shops, and other tourist town lures. Five comfortable guest rooms have queen-sized beds, cable TV, private baths, and harbor views; there are bicycles and kayaks to borrow. Two guest rooms are on the ground floor. A full breakfast is always offered, and if you're lucky, Jeff might serve his gingerbread waffles or his banana French toast. Breakfast is served inside near the new flagstone fireplace or on the pretty front porch that overlooks Boothbay's bustling harbor. No pets. Children over 12.

SPRUCE POINT INN
Front desk Manager: Nancy
  Bosio-Picket.
207-633-4152 or
  800-553-0289.
www.sprucepointinn.com.
P.O. Box 237, Boothbay
  Harbor 04538.
Open: May–Oct.
Price: Very Expensive.
Credit cards: AE, D, DC,
  MC, V.
Handicap Access: Yes

With championship clay tennis courts, two pools (saltwater and heated freshwater), a fitness center, massage therapy, and children's program, you won't want to leave for any plain old whale watch. The Spruce Point Inn is one of Maine's sprawling resorts: you can rent a cabin or a luxurious suite and have everything taken care of, including your children's summer camp during the day, or their evening meals, in case you want to relax at night after a long bike ride together. Time to enjoy some lobster spring rolls and a rack of lamb without the tedium of negotiations, for either parent or child.

East Boothbay

FIVE GABLES INN
Innkeepers: Mike and Dee
  Kennedy.
207-633-4551 or
  800-451-5048.
www.fivegablesinn.com.
info@fivegablesinn.com.
P.O. Box 335, Murray Hill
  Rd., East Boothbay 04544.
Open: Mid-May–late Oct.
Price: Moderate to
  Expensive.
Credit Cards: MC, V.

This cream-colored inn, perched on a hillside overlooking pretty Linekin Bay near Boothbay Harbor, was restored and renovated in 1989. Airy, uncluttered, and made cozy with country craft accents, the Five Gables is a restful retreat in an otherwise bustling tourist region. All 15 rooms have private baths and water views; five have working fireplaces. Take afternoon tea on the porch overlooking the lush cottage garden. No smoking. Children over 12.

Newagen

**NEWAGEN SEASIDE
INN**
Innkeepers: Scott and
  Corinne Larson.
207-633-5242 or
  800-654-5242.
www.newagenseaside
  inn.com.
P.O. Box 29, Rte. 27 South,
  Newagen 04576.
Open: Mid-May–early Oct.

Pronounced "new wagon," this resort inn sits on 85 acres at the southern tip of Southport Island, six miles from Boothbay Harbor, and retains a '40s look and feel. On inclement days you can hear the foghorn. Most of the 26 rooms have an ocean view; all have private baths (no TV, but telephones are in all rooms), and there are three cottages as well, all refurbished during 2001 and 2002. Daytime, you have a choice of activities—tennis, horseshoes,

Price: Moderate to
  Expensive.
Credit Cards: MC, V.
Handicap Access: Yes.

badminton, volleyball, rowboats, fishing, heated freshwater pool. Almost any good day in season you can hear that quiet, comforting pock pock of the ball being batted back and forth, though now from further away, off the back porch and into a recreational building of its own. The dining room serves breakfast and dinner. Breakfast included; other meals additional.

Newcastle

Herb Swanson

Autumn's harvest is gathered in, and you can expect a lighted fireplace in your suite at The Newcastle Inn.

THE NEWCASTLE INN
Innkeepers: Rebecca and
  Howard Levitan.
207-563-5685 or
  800-832-8669.
www.newcastleinn.com.
60 River Rd., Newcastle
  04553.
Open: All year except Jan.
Price: Expensive to Very
  Expensive.
Credit Cards: AE, MC, V.
Handicap Access: Limited.

This handsome inn and restaurant is just off Rte. 1. The 15 rooms are well appointed and comfortable, all with private bath; seven are in the main house, while six are in the carriage house. There are two upscale rooms with king-sized beds—one room has a fireplace while the other holds a Jacuzzi; another Jacuzzi is in a suite with a queen canopy bed; several of the rooms have views of the Damariscotta River. Nine have fireplaces. The kitchen turns out four-course meals that have won so many fans that the inn now has two dining rooms. The common room, with its stenciled floor, fireplace, and high-backed antique wing chairs, is a great place to relax. There's also a sun porch with comfortable lawn chairs and river views. Children over 12. No smoking. Breakfast included. Cross-country skiing.

New Harbor

THE BRADLEY INN
Innkeepers: Warren and
 Beth Busteed.
207-677-2105 or
 800-942-5560.
www.bradleyinn.com.
3063 Bristol Rd., Pemaquid
 Point, New Harbor
 04554.
Open: All year.
Price: Expensive to Very
 Expensive.
Credit Cards: AE, MC, V.

Built in the late 19th century, the building was "literally gutted" in the late 20th century, brought up to the standards of the modern leisure traveler, and filled with nautical pictures, charts, and huge ship models. There are 16 rooms, all with private bath. There's also a cottage across the croquet court. From the top floor, the cathedral-ceilinged rooms look out onto John's Bay and the gardens. A full breakfast and afternoon tea are included. Dinner, additional, is open to the public. So is the pub, which boasts a granite-topped bar and attracts a mix of guests and local residents. Non-smoking rooms available.

GOSNOLD ARMS
Owners: The Phinney
 Family.
Summer 207-677-3727;
 winter 561-575-9549.
www.gosnold.com.
146 Rte. 32, New Harbor
 04554.
Open: Mid-May–mid-Oct.
Price: Moderate to
 Expensive.
Credit Cards: MC, V.

The Gosnold sits at the entrance to New Harbor, not far from splendid Pemaquid Point and its lovely lighthouse. In its first incarnation this was a saltwater farm. It has also served as a summer boardinghouse for Smith College students (it still has a PLEASE NO MEN PERMITTED UPSTAIRS sign). There are accommodations for 40 to 50 guests (every room has its own bath) spread out among the farmhouse, the three-story barn, and 10 separate cottages. One of the cottages is a former steamboat freight office; another is a steamboat cabin. The dining room seats 80—or you can take your meal on the porch and watch boats pass by. Dinner is real Yankee fare—fresh seafood, beef, and homemade desserts. We haven't eaten here, but with this view, you almost can't lose. Breakfast included, dinner additional. Smoking in the cottages and on the ground floor. Children welcome.

HOTEL PEMAQUID
Owners: Skip and Cindy
 Atwood.
207-677-2312.
3098 Bristol Rd., New
 Harbor 04554.
Season: Mid-May–mid-Oct.
Price: Inexpensive to
 Moderate.

This Victorian inn sits almost at the very end of the Pemaquid Peninsula, not far from the famous lighthouse. The main house is an old-style hotel with 24 rooms; all but four with private bath. The parlors are jam packed with dark period furniture, flowered curtains and upholstery, and an idiosyncratic collection of Victoriana and other "stuff"

Credit Cards: None, but personal and travelers checks are accepted.
Handicap Access: Yes.

—including a check signed by glamour goddess Marilyn Monroe. Our favorite room is the Chauffeur's Quarters, a sunny ground-floor guest room with private bath decorated in not-too-fussy shades of rose. The annex offers a comfortable suite with a kitchen, living room, and cable TV. The hotel also rents four-unit bungalows and operates a five-unit motel with clean, nicely appointed rooms. Cottages can be rented on a weekly basis. Breakfast is not included, although the coffee pot is always on. No smoking.

Wiscasset

SQUIRE TARBOX INN

See under *Westport Island* in the "Lodging" section of Chapter Five, *Brunswick, Bath, the Harpswells, The Phippsburg and Georgetown Peninsulas.*

WISCASSET TO DAMARISCOTTA: DINING

Boothbay Harbor

CHRISTOPHER'S BOATHOUSE
207-633-6565.
25 Union St., Boothbay Harbor 04538.
www.christophersboat house.com
Open: All year.
Price: Expensive to Very Expensive.
Cuisine: International.
Serving: D Thurs.–Sat in winter; D, L in summer only.
Credit Cards: D, MC, V.
Special Features: Wood grill and wine list.

Sitting at a table in Christopher's, with its elegant blond wood interior and solid wine list, you might almost forget that you are in Boothbay Harbor. Let's face it; this town is better known for its activities (shopping, shopping, shopping, and boating) than for fine dining. The menu covers the map with French, Italian, Asian, and Mediterranean accents and, from this continent, a little down-home barbecue. There is also excellent Maine seafood cooked simply and well. Starting with the lobster mango bisque (famous from the *Wall Street Journal*) won't be a mistake; or try the pan-seared Maine peeky-toe crab cakes. Follow with the lobster succotash and we can almost guarantee you won't have room for dessert.

Damariscotta

THE BREAKFAST PLACE
207-563-5434.
Main St., Damariscotta 04543.
Open: All year.
Price: Inexpensive.

Just across and down the street from the historic steeple and clock on St. Andrew's, this morning coffee and baked goods joint also serves a good egg or two. It's been around for ages, serving as a wakeup stop for the local community. Several

Serving: B (7–1), L (11–1).
Credit Cards: No.
Handicap Access: Limited.
Special Features: Bakery.

THE SALT BAY CAFE
207-563-1666.
Main St., Damariscotta
04543.
Open: All year, except Sun.
Price: Inexpensive to
Moderate.
Cuisine: American.
Serving: B, L, D.
Credit Cards AE, MC, V.
Handicap Access: Yes.

East Boothbay

**LOBSTERMAN'S
WHARF**
207-633-3443.
Rte. 96, East Boothbay
04544.
Closed: Mid-Oct.–early
May.
Price: Moderate.
Cuisine: American.
Serving: L, D.
Credit Cards: D, MC, V.
Special Features: Kid-proof
dining; deck with river
view.
Handicap Access: Yes.

Newcastle

THE NEWCASTLE INN
207-563-5685 or
800-832-8669.
60 River Rd., Newcastle
04553.
Open: June 1–Oct. 31,
Tues.–Sun.; Nov.–May,
Fri.–Sat. Closed Jan.
Price: Expensive to Very
Expensive.
Cuisine: Country gourmet.
Serving: D.

years ago, two ambitious transplants from Connecticut bought it; they've raised the level of baking, but kept the hometown decor. Get some of their cheddar cheese biscuits.

The Salt Bay serves typical American food with a polite nod towards light and healthy. Big fat comfortable booths, a little too much carpet, nonthreatening, been-there-forever help. This is *Murder, She Wrote* look-a-like country, and you can imagine Jessica Fletcher and the police chief sitting at the next booth over while the cook lies on the kitchen floor with a knife in his back. You've had this food many times before. It's a good place to come if you're homesick. Pie and bread pudding for dessert.

Wedged between two old shipyards, this family restaurant is fun, with plenty to keep the kids occupied. The long, paneled dining room has the look of an ocean liner; lobster traps, buoys, and paddles hang from walls and ceilings. In fair weather, dine on the deck overlooking the Damariscotta River. Otherwise, take a table in the large dining room. Unlike places that are all gimmicks and no substance, the Wharf has good food and an enthusiastic staff. Savory starters like deep-fried artichokes. Bright salads. And interesting entrées. Occasional disappointments can be avoided by sticking to basics. For dessert, brownie sundaes.

The Newcastle Inn offers one seating each evening. Such regimentation might be off-putting if the food were not so good and the experience enjoyable. The small dining room is lighted by candles and has white linens and fresh flowers. The four-course meal—there's a single set menu each night—is $47.50 (18 percent tip and tax additional). Possibilities include seafood risotto with porcini mushroom broth, roasted haddock with chive cream sauce, or veal tenderloin. Dessert might be

Credit Cards: AE, MC, V.
Reservations: Requested.

an airy chocolate soufflé or mint chocolate chip baked Alaska.

New Harbor

**SHAW'S FISH &
 LOBSTER WHARF**
207-677-2200.
Rte. 32, New Harbor 04554.
Open: May–Oct.
Price: Inexpensive to
 Moderate.
Cuisine: Seafood.
Serving: L, D.
Credit Cards: MC, V.

What a wonderful view. Half the wharf is given over to fishermen and fishing boats, the other half to serving a prodigious supply of seafood, side orders, and pie. Lunch and dinner are self-service, and you can pick your own table, outside, inside, or down on the wharf, where at night there's also an outside bar. From the deck upstairs, you can look down on boats being made ready for the next day's sail. If the young travelers don't want lobster, there's a wide selection of kid's sandwiches and three kinds of cookies at forty cents a pop.

Wiscasset

LE GARAGE
207-882-5409.
15 Water St., Wiscasset
 04578.
Closed: Jan.
Price: Expensive.
Cuisine: New England.
Serving: L, D.
Credit Cards: MC, V.
Reservations:
 Recommended.
Handicap Access: Yes.
Special Features: River view.

Candelabra, cathedral ceilings, and two half-sunk schooners set the scene at this former auto garage right on the river. The effect is dramatic—especially on one of those gray, misty days for which the Maine coast is famous. As atmospheric as Le Garage is, the food is surprisingly down to earth, with starters like ratatouille; savory charbroiled items like chicken, steak, pork chops; fresh seafood; unusual pastas; light salads, and desserts. Homespun desserts include apple crisp, gingerbread, and birdnest meringue.

WISCASSET TO DARAMISCOTTA: FOOD PURVEYORS

CANDY & ICE CREAM

Downeast Candies (207-633-5178; 7 Byway St., Boothbay Harbor). Open from Memorial Day to Columbus Day, they make fudge and toffee in a wide range of flavors.

Orne's Candy Store (207-633-2695; 11 Commercial St., Boothbay Harbor). Old glass-topped counters, saltwater taffy, and countless types of fudge; this could be a movie set. Open Mothers' Day till after Columbus Day, whenever they run out of chocolate.

Round Top Ice Cream (207-563-5307; Bus. Rte. 1, Damariscotta). Since 1924 they've made ice cream at this dairy. Now they also make art and music, but you can still find 52 flavors of the good stuff, 40 flavors of soft serve.

DELIS & TAKE-OUT

Eastside Market and Deli (207-633-4616; 26 Atlantic Ave., Boothbay Harbor). Walk across the long footbridge at the shallow end of this popular harbor to get everything for a picnic lunch.

Treats (207-882-6192; Main St. (Rte. 1), Wiscasset). Using fresh ingredients, they make the best sandwiches in the area, and they're loyal to local farms' produce when in season, organic when available, with delicious pies and baked goods all year round. Wine, cheese, coffee, and tea are also sold here.

FAST FOOD

Brud's Hot Dogs (East Side, Boothbay Harbor). Hot dogs, fast and inexpensive. Since 1948. Sold out of a cart on the east side of town.

GOURMET FOOD STORES

Weatherbird Trading Company (207-563-8993; 72 Courtyard St., Damariscotta). Pâtés, imported beers, and French scents in a 1754 saltbox Cape, sandwiches, and cheese and wine.

FARM MARKETS

Damariscotta Farmers' Market (corner of bus. Rte. 1, Damariscotta). Mid-May–mid-Oct., Fri. mornings.

WISCASSET TO DARAMISCOTTA: CULTURE

AQUARIUMS

Maine Department of Marine Resources Aquarium (207-633-9542; West Boothbay Harbor). A 20-foot touch tank in which you can pet a live (little) shark. Lobster, sea cucumbers, skates, moon snails, and sea stars. Call for a reservation.

CINEMA

Harbor Light Cinema (207-633-3799; Rte. 27 and Rte. 96, Boothbay Harbor). Seasonal.

Lincoln Theater (207-563-3424; off Main Street, Damariscotta). Theater productions as well as first-run films.

Round Top Center for the Arts (207-563-1507; roundtoparts.org; P.O. Box 1316, Business Rte. 1, Damariscotta 04543). This organization sponsors shows of area artists in its Main Gallery, including an annual exhibit of members' work, quilting, and other crafts. Each show is accompanied by a lecture open to the public. Mon.–Fri. 10–4, Sat. noon–4. Also open Sun. 1–4 Apr.–Dec.

GARDENS & GARDEN TOURS

Nickels-Sortwell House (207-882-6218; Main and Federal Sts., Wiscasset). The gardens are being restored to their original 1926 design by the Wiscasset Garden Club. The ships captain's house and gardens are well worth the visit. June–Oct. 15. Admission charged.

HISTORIC BUILDINGS & SITES

BOOTHBAY REGION HISTORICAL SOCIETY
207-633-0820.
Elizabeth Reed House.
www.boothbayhistorical
.org
70 Oak St., Boothbay Harbor.
Season: July–Labor Day,
Wed., Fri., Sat. 10–4; rest
of the year Sat. 10–2.

An excellent collection of period photographs depicting the region's daily activities, including fishing, ice cutting, lumbering, farming, shipping, and shipbuilding. Plus early fishing gear, shipwrights' tools, and navigation instruments.

CASTLE TUCKER
603-436-3205.
www.spnea.org.
Lee and High Sts.,
Wiscasset.
Season: June–Oct. 15, Wed.–
Sun. 11–5; tours on the
hour.
Admission charged.

In 1807 Judge Silas Lee decided to build himself a "great house" on the hill overlooking Wiscasset Harbor, and nothing stopped him, not even his bank account. By the time of his death seven years later he had so heavily mortgaged the house that it became the property of his three neighbors. In 1858 by Capt. Richard Tucker, a third-generation mariner, bought it; the family still owns it. It has original Victorian furniture, kitchen, wallpapers, and a handsome elliptical staircase.

FORT EDGECOMB
Right off Rte. 1 just past
Wiscasset Bridge,
Edgecomb.
Free.

First built in 1808 (to protect the port of Wiscasset) at a vantage point overlooking the Sheepscot River, the restored fort with its octagonal, two-story blockhouse is a great place for a picnic.

FORT WILLIAM HENRY
Pemaquid Peninsula.

The fort changed hands—and names—several times. Fort Pemaquid (1632) was looted by

Season: May–Sept.
   Grounds open year-round.
Admission charged.

pirates; as Fort Charles, it was captured by the French in 1689; Fort William Henry, believed to be New England's first stone fortification, was captured by the Baron de Castine; Fort Frederic was built from the ruins of Fort William Henry in 1729. What you see today is an impressive replica of the fort and the authentic Old Fort House built in 1729. The *Old Burial Ground*, just down the road from here, has graves dating to 1695. Nearby is an archaeological excavation of the Pemaquid settlement established in the 1620s, along with a museum with artifacts from the dig. Many consider this to be one of the prettiest—and most significant—historical spots in Maine.

NICKELS-SORTWELL HOUSE
207-882-6218.
www.spnea.org.
Main and Federal Sts. (Rte. 1), Wiscasset.
Season: June 1–Oct. 15, Wed.–Sun.; tours at 11, 12, 1, 2, 3, 4.
Admission charged.

Built in 1807 for Capt. William Nickels, a shipmaster in the lumber trade, this elegant Federal mansion also did service as a hotel. The furnishings are Colonial Revival style. Don't miss the beautiful elliptical stairway, or the wooden inlay work on the facade of the house. The gardens are being restored to their original 1926 design.

ST. PATRICK'S CHURCH
207-563-3240.
Academy Hill Rd., just off Rte. 1, Newcastle.
Open year-round 9am.–sundown.

The oldest surviving Catholic church in New England, St. Patrick's was dedicated in 1808. The early Federal-style church was designed by architect Nicholas Codd and built from locally fired bricks. The pews and colored glass window date from 1896, but mass has been served continually from the altar since 1808. Be sure to check out the Paul Revere church bell.

LIBRARIES

Skidompha Library (207-563-5513; Main Street, Damariscotta). Good genealogical and local history department.
Southport Memorial Library (207-633-2741; Cape Newagen). Home of one of the largest butterfly collections in the country. Open all year. Tues. & Thurs. 9–11, 1–4, 7–9; Sat.1–4.

LIGHTHOUSES

Pemaquid Lighthouse Park (Lighthouse Rd. off Rte. 130, Pemaquid Point) is a good place to relax for a picnic. The lighthouse was built in 1827, and the keeper's house has been converted to an art gallery and museum featuring exhibits about saltwater fishing.

MUSEUMS

BOOTHBAY RAILWAY VILLAGE
207-633-4727.
www.railwayvillage.org.
Rte. 27, Boothbay.
Season: Mid-June–
Columbus Day, daily
9:30–5.
$7 adults; $3 children.

A quaint New England village and its transportation system (including 60 vehicles) is recreated on eight acres here. There are more than 24 buildings of historical exhibits, including a doll museum. The 1.5 miles of narrow-gauge track and steam locomotive, provide 15-minute rides, carrying you back to a simpler time

MUSICAL WONDERHOUSE
207-882-7163 or
800-336-3725
www.musicalwonderhouse
.com.
18 High St., Wiscasset.
Season: Memorial Day–
mid-Oct., daily 10–5.
Admission: $2 general
admittance fee. One half-
hour presentation $8 .
One-hour guided
presentations: $15 adults;
$14 seniors and children
under 12. Three-hour
guided presentations
available by appointment
only: $30 per person,

For more than 30 years, travelers and music lovers from around the world have made their way here to view Danilo Konvalinka's marvelous collection of restored music boxes and musical instruments. Many are works of art and are capable of playing complicated songs with a wide range of notes. Some date from 1750. There are pocket boxes and floor models, player pianos and other mechanical musical treasures. Konvalinka also buys, sells, and repairs music boxes. Ask about the candlelight concerts.

OLD COUNTY JAIL & MUSEUM
207-882-6817.
www.pchmaine.vs3.net.
Rte. 218, Federal St.,
Wiscasset.
Season: July–Aug.,
Tues.–Sat. 11–4. June and
Sept. weekends
Admission: $2 adults; $1
children.

The jail was built in 1811, has granite walls 41 inches thick, and saw service as recently as 1953. Visitors can peruse prisoners' cells with original graffiti to obtain an unusual view of life in the 19th century. Inside the jailer's house there is a display of early American tools, costumes, artifacts, and changing exhibits about local history.

MUSIC

ROUND TOP CENTER FOR THE ARTS
207-563-1507.
www.roundtoparts.com.
P.O. Box 1316, Bus. Rte. 1,
Damariscotta, 04543.
Open: All year.

The Round Top was once a dairy farm; the cows are long gone, but you can enjoy many flavors of ice cream made here. Today, the farm's main product is music, theater, arts, and crafts, taught and put on display. During warm weather many of their concerts, children's and adults' plays, art and

Tickets: $8–$14 for music and theater events.

crafts shows, lectures, and workshops are staged outside. One of their most anticipated events is the annual Festival Day and Concert on the Lawn in July. This event is fun for everyone, with children's activities and crafts in the morning and orchestra or brass quintet music in the evening. People sprawl out on the lawn with blankets and picnic baskets for a jam-packed day of fun and enjoyment.

NIGHTLIFE

Gray's Wharf (207-633-5629; Pier One, Boothbay Harbor). Open April until October, with entertainment three nights a week throughout the summer. Seafood dining.

SCHOOLS

Watershed Center for the Ceramic Arts (207-882-6075; www.watershedcenterceramicarts.org; 19 Brick Hill Rd., Newcastle). This is a Yaddo for the clay set. Big-time and up-and-coming potters come here. Classes for the general public.

SEASONAL EVENTS

Fall Foliage Festival (207-633-4727; Boothbay Railway Village, Boothbay Harbor). Leaves, music, crafts, food, and fun for the family. Mid-October.

Fishermen's Festival (207-633-2353; Boothbay Harbor). Miss Shrimp Contest, lobster boat races, chowder contest, and other great fisherman things, all to benefit the Fishermen's Memorial Fund. Late April.

Windjammer Days (207-633-2353; Boothbay Harbor). For more than 30 years this windjammer parade has attracted an international crowd. Also antique boat parade, concerts, and exhibitions. Late June.

THEATER

Lincoln Theater (207-563-3424; off Main Street, Damariscotta). Theater productions as well as first-run films.

WISCASSET TO DAMARISCOTTA: RECREATION

AUTO RACING

Wiscasset Raceway (207-589-4780; West Alna Road, Wiscasset). Maine's only high-banked oval, short track, stock car racing is open Saturday nights, April through September.

BEACHES

Pemaquid Beach Park; off Rte. 130, New Harbor. About a half-mile long and backed by dunes. There's a bathhouse, picnic tables, restrooms. Entrance fee.

Popham Beach State Park; Rte. 209, Phippsburg. Not only fine sand, but a fine beach. In fact, one of the finest. More than two miles long; there are picnic tables, rocky outcrops and tide pools, and plenty of parking, which fills up quickly on a hot day. Entrance fee.

BIRD WATCHING

The black-billed cuckoo taps out his hollow message in code. . . .— E. B. White

Hog Island Audubon Camp (Muscongus Bay). Osprey drop in here; so do eagles. Audubon annually sponsors two six-day field ornithology sessions. The *Todd Wildlife Sanctuary* on the island hosts a variety of nesting birds. Workshops include a one-day trip to Matinicus Rock. For more information, call the Audubon Society at 207-781-2330.

Salt Bay (Rtes. 215 and 1 through Damariscotta Mills, Newcastle, and Damariscotta). If you don't want to leave your car, Salt Bay is a good spot. Rte. 215 borders the bay along its southwest edge; Rte. 1 leads along the bay to the east. Birds like to rest and feed in the large shallow bay and its mudflats laid bare at low tide.

BOATING

CANOEING & SEA KAYAKING

Island Hopping (603-466-2721; www.outdoors.org; or write Summer Workshop, P.O. Box 298, Gorham, NH 03581). The Appalachian Mountain Club offers experienced canoeists the chance to spend three days exploring the water routes the Abenaki Indians used as they traveled among the islands of Penobscot Bay.

Old Town Canoe (207-882-9645; U.S. Rte. 1, Wiscasset) Sales and rentals only.

Sea Kayaking on Muscongus Bay (207-529-4SEA; www.seaspiritadventures.com; Rte. 32, Round Pond Village). Guided tours and rentals.

Tidal Transit Ocean Kayaking Co. (207-633-7140; www.kayakboothbay.com; 16 Granary Way, Boothbay Harbor). Instruction and custom trips for sea kayakers. Guided tours.

CHARTERS & RENTALS

Balmy Day Cruises (207-633-2284; www.anchorwatch.com/balmy; Pier 8, Boothbay Harbor). Close to shore to see seals and lighthouses, and further off to try for a whale, you can sail, fish, or visit Monhegan Island on one of these boats.

Muscongus Bay Cruises (207-529-4474; www.midcoast.com/~cruises; 289

Maine Island Trail

The Maine Island Trail Association was founded in 1988. The waterway is a kind of Appalachian Trail for boaters. It begins with islands in Casco Bay and follows the coast Down East past Machias, a distance of 325 miles. The trail includes 77 islands where travelers can put ashore and camp for the night. Thirty are privately owned islands; the rest are owned by the state and governed by the Bureau of Parks and Lands.

"What makes the Maine Island Trail a pleasure is its 'connect the dots' character, the 'dots' being islands. Without access to islands along the way, there would be no trail," wrote kayaker Michael Burke in *Yankee* magazine.

Members have access to prudent use of the islands on the trail—as well as a stewardship handbook and guidebook. Members receive a copy of *The Maine Island Trail Book*, a guidebook packed with charts and information. There are about 2,000 members of MITA, 300 of whom regularly monitor usage and erosion on forays to islands they have "adopted."

For information about the organization, contact the Maine Island Trail Association; 207-596-6456; www.mita.org; P.O. Box C., Rockland, ME 04841.

Keene Neck Road, Bremen 04551) A 32-foot Bristol sloop, a 42-foot lobster boat, and a 36-foot lobster "yacht" are available to take you to the birds' favorite places along the shore.

Salt Water Charters (207-677-6229; www.saltwater-charters.com; Round Pond Harbor) Captain Wallace Leeman can take you to Port Clyde for lunch or just around the bay. Also fishing charters, lobstering, seal watching. Half or full day available

CAMPING

The Ponderosa Campground (207-633-2700; www.littleponderosa.com; Rte. 1, Boothbay 04537). July and August, with swimming, golf, laundry, and hook-ups.

FERRIES

Balmy Days (207-633-2284; www.balmydayscruises.com; PO Box 535, Pier 8, Boothbay Harbor 04538). Captain Bill Campbell offers daily ferry service to Monhegan Island in the summer, weekend service in the off season.

Monhegan Island Ferry (207-677-2026 or 800-2-PUFFIN; www.hardyboat.com; P.O. Box 326. New Harbor 04554). Three days a week Hardy Boat Cruises offers a ferry to Monhegan during the summer; everyone agrees you should reserve a ticket in advance, since the summer crowds can overflow. Also available here are Puffin cruises to Eastern Egg Island (see Puffins, below) and Lighthouse and Seal Watch cruises.

The Maine Photographic Workshops

Monhegan Island is well served by ferries in the summer and attracts students, hikers and birders. (See Maine Photographic Workshops, next chapter).

FISHING

Beach and shore fishing is popular in the fall when sunbathers have left; Popham Beach near where the Kennebec River empties into the Gulf of Maine near Bath is a good spot to try your luck.

If you're a competitive fisherman or you like to be there when the pros weigh their fish, there are two saltwater tournaments held on the coast. *Tuna Tournament & Small Fish Rodeo* usually takes place from July to August. Fair game includes codfish, bluefish, mackerel, and cusk. For more information contact the Boothbay Chamber of Commerce (207-633-2353) or Breakaways Sports Fishing (207-633-6990; breakway@lincoln.midcoast.com; P.O. Box 4, Boothbay Harbor 04538). *The New England Bluefish Open* is held every year during mid-August in the waters near Bath. For more information, contact Eastern Sports Fishing (207-443-8940; ww.gwi.net/~espnbo/; 118 Front St., Bath 04530).

GOLF

Boothbay Region Country Club (207-633-6085; Country Club Rd., Boothbay). 18 holes, 2,668 yds., par 35. Cart and club rental, pro shop, clubhouse.

HEALTH CLUBS

YMCA (207-633-2855; www.brymca.com; Townsend Ave., Boothbay Harbor). Pool, aerobics, weights, racquetball, sauna, and cardiovascular equipment.

HORSEBACK RIDING

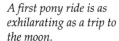

*A first pony ride is as
exhilarating as a trip to
the moon.*

Diana Lynn Doherty

Ledgewood Riding Stable (207-882-6346; 432 Lowell Town Rd., Wiscasset). Trail rides; you must call in advance.

NATURE PRESERVES

Rachel Carson Salt Pond Preserve, Rte. 32, Bristol. Part of the Rachel Carson Sea Coast, the network of protected lands willed to the public by the late naturalist Rachel Carson. A great place to observe marine life from the point of view of a tidal pool. Good views of Muscongus Bay. A map published by the Nature Conservancy (207-729-5181) points out interesting rock formations along the shore.

Whaleback Park, Bus. Rte. 1, near the Great Salt Bay School, Damariscotta. Eight acres along the Damariscotta river have been made accessible, allowing us to see the Glidden Midden in Newcastle, across the water. The midden, Old Norse for waste heap, is a 100-foot long, 20-foot-deep oyster shell heap left from the days when Native Americans lived on this shore and dined off the best oysters in Maine. The Whaleback Midden was even bigger, but in the late 1800s, before the shell's antiquity was protected, it was excavated and crushed to make a feed supplement for chickens; all that is left are the bits of shell you might see underfoot.

PUFFIN WATCHING

Hardy III, **Hardy II Tours** (207-677-2026 or 800-2-PUFFIN; www.hardyboat .com; Rte. 32, New Harbor). The Puffin Watch tours leave from Shaw's Fish and Lobster Wharf in New Harbor, and an Audubon naturalist educates the passengers with lectures, shore bird flash cards, and even extra binoculars.

The captain will circle Eastern Egg Island a few times and will do his best to make sure everyone catches a glimpse of the small, charming puffins who have been reintroduced there.

Pink Lady, **R. Fish and Son** (207-633-3244; www.capnfishmotel.com; Pier 1, Boothbay Harbor).

SEASONAL SPORTING EVENTS

Windjammer Days, late June. Windjammers of all shapes and sizes (contact the Boothbay Harbor Chamber of Commerce, 207-633-2353).

TENNIS

Bath (207-443-8360; Congress Ave.). Four courts with night lights.
Boothbay Harbor (207-633-2855). Two courts.
Damariscotta (207-563-3477; YMCA). Two indoor courts.

WINDJAMMERS

Eastwind (Capts. Herb and Doris Smith; 207-633-6598; www.fishermans wharfinn.com; Fisherman's Wharf, Boothbay Harbor 04538). Two-and-a-half hour cruises to the outer islands and Seal Rocks. June–September.
Sylvina W. Beal (Capt. Steven F. Pagels; 207-288-4585 summer, 207-546-2927 winter; Downeast Windjammer Cruises, P.O. Box 8, Cherryfield 04622). Sails out of Boothbay Harbor for two-hour cruises.

WISCASSET TO DAMARISCOTTA: SHOPPING

Wooden lobster traps are used mostly as souvenirs in these days of metal traps and plastic lines.

Herb Swanson

ANTIQUES

The Ditty Box (207-563-7510; 262 Bristol Rd., Damariscotta). Antiques and collectibles, including old samplers, china, Currier & Ives prints, American country furniture, and early American pressed and glass shelf clocks.

J. Partridge Antiques (207-882-7745; Rte. 1, Edgecomb). You can see the gray barn with the name, Partridge, from Rte. 1. After visiting the Penobscot Marine Museum, in Searsport, come here to start your own Butterworth Collection, perhaps with a small oil of a fleet of sailboats off a coast. Also gorgeous sets of old English chairs.

The Palabra Shop (207-633-4225; 53 Commercial St., Boothbay Harbor). Moses bottles, antique dolls, books, primitives, nautical collectibles, and American jewelry, filling 10 rooms.

The Shady Lady (207-563-6200; Main St., Damariscotta). Old lamps and a big selection of lamp shades to fit them.

BOOKSTORES

Maine Coast Book Shop (207-563-3207; Box 309, Main St., Damariscotta 04543). Penguin novels and coffee-table books, as well as a full selection of paperback and hardcover books. Newly renovated and enlarged, this is a wonderful bookstore.

CLOTHING

Weatherbird (207-563-8993; 72 Courtyard St., Damariscotta). Clothing from natural fibers and comfortable synthetics, classy accessories and jewelry. Also under **Gourmet Food Stores**, so you can treat it like an upscale mall.

COLLECTIBLES

Andersen Studio (207-633-4397 or 800-633-4397; One Andersen Road, East Boothbay). Nature sculpture.

The Maine Country Store (207-882-7757; www.mainecountrystore.com; 2 miles south of Wiscasset on Rte. 1). Fine art reproductions of three generations of Wyeths, and other Maine artists.

CRAFTS

Pemaquid Craft Coop (207-677-2077; 2565 Bristol Rd., New Harbor 04554). Fifteen rooms of handmade crafts, open May through October, weekends till Dec.

FURNITURE

Margonelli Fine Furniture (207-633-3326; 780 River Rd., Edgecomb). Fine handmade furniture.

GIFTS & SOUVENIRS

Enchantments (207-633-4992; www.geocities.com/enchantments; 10 Boothbay House Hill., Boothbay Harbor). Crystals, herbs, incense, and books. Gifts and stuff for the metaphysical crowd.

Granite Hall Store (207-529-5864; 9 Back Shore Rd., Round Pond). An old-fashioned country store in a historic building. Penny candy, antiques, and woolens. Closes after Christmas.

Narragansett Leathers (207-563-5080; Main St., Damariscotta). Leather goods —bags, belts, briefcases—handmade right here.

HOUSEWARES

Village Store & Children's Shop (207-633-2293; Townsend Ave., Boothbay Harbor). Gifts for the home, made here in Maine and elsewhere.

JEWELRY

A Silver Lining (207-633-4103; 17 Townsend Ave., Boothbay Harbor). Blue-berry pendants and other originally designed memories of the Maine coast, cast in sterling, gold, copper, brass, titanium, or gold electroplated.

POTTERY

Edgecomb Potters (207-882-6802; Rte. 27, Edgecomb). Striking and functional pottery for the home. Three stores, including one on School St. in Freeport and another on Exchange St. in Portland's Old Port.

CHAPTER SEVEN
The Great Bay
WESTERN PENOBSCOT BAY
WALDOBORO TO BUCKSPORT

Herb Swanson

The Rockland Breakwater is a fine place to take in the coastal traffic.

Waldoboro was settled by Germans in the mid-18th century, and today is famed for two of the state's culinary landmarks—Moody's Diner and Morse's Sauerkraut. The first five-masted schooner was built here in 1888.

From here, **Friendship** is just a short trip down Rte. 220, which skirts the western shore of the Medomak River. It's hard to believe Friendship exists. Where are the shops, the hotels, the gas stations, restaurants? Here on beautiful, isolated **Hatchet Cove** are a few summer homes, a handful of lobster boats, and a Friendship sloop or two, that famous gaff-rigged working boat now prized by wealthy modern-day sailors. Rte. 97 leads past **Cushing**, another quiet fishing village, made famous by painter Andrew Wyeth.

From **Thomaston**, former home of the state prison (it will be dismantled over the next several years), you can veer off onto Rte. 131, which leads down yet another peninsula filled with history. **Tenant's Harbor** looks simple, but look again. Those are mighty big yachts anchored so casually in the harbor.

Southwest from here is **Port Clyde** (once called Herring Gut), the point of departure for the hour-long boat ride to Monhegan, eleven miles off the coast. Tiny **Monhegan** is besieged with painters: salt breezes sometimes smell of turpentine. The dark forests and dramatic cliffs make the island a hiker's paradise as well.

Once known for its quarried lime rock, **Rockland** now bills itself as the lobster capital of the world. It is the Penobscot Bay region's central working town, and its harbor is filled with lobster boats and commercial fishing boats that regularly fish the waters of the Grand Banks. Rockland is a bustling town that has become gentrified with artists' studios, galleries, and moderately expensive restaurants that clearly aim to serve tourists. Its beautiful art museum, the Farnsworth, has found patrons in its neighbors, the Wyeth family, as well as MBNA, a giant credit card company. Rockland also is a hub of the windjammer trade, and from here ferries regularly travel to **Vinalhaven, Matinicus**, and **North Haven.**

Sitting fifteen miles out in Penobscot Bay, Vinalhaven flourished when granite was quarried here. Today the island has a tenacious year-round population of lobstermen and fishermen and a dedicated coterie of summer residents. To the north is the small and exclusive summer community of **North Haven** on **North Haven Island**. Windjammers and large pleasure boats often anchor in **Pulpit Harbor**.

In striking contrast there is the quiet, tiny island of **Matinicus**. Approximately 100 people make their living here, most of them lobstering and fishing the outer waters of Penobscot Bay. It takes about two hours by ferry to ply the 23 miles of water to the island. Dedicated birders often opt to charter a local boat and keep going another five miles to Matinicus Rock, where nesting puffins can be seen during their breeding season.

Just off Rte. 1 before **Camden** is **Rockport**, a pastoral village where Galloways munch in green meadows and actors, photographers, and boat builders live in mansions by the sea.

The storybook beauty of Camden was captured in the film *Peyton Place*. Today it's considered the shoppers' resting place between Freeport and Bar Harbor; you tend to be resting in traffic there anyway, in the middle of summer. Expensive shops cram the old-fashioned town center. The town is part of a miniature filmmaking boom, and movie stars and movie crews can be seen at work or relaxing over lunch at Camden's restaurants.

This pretty town is a worthwhile destination, although it can be a hard town in which to find a parking space. Space in the harbor is also scarce. Luxury yachts moor next to giant windjammers that ferry passengers on weeklong cruises. When here, be certain to visit Merryspring, a breathtaking public garden, and one of the most famous horticultural sites of New England.

Lincolnville Beach just to the north offers an expansive view of Penobscot Bay. This is also where you catch the ferry to **Islesboro**, the exclusive summer community three miles off shore.

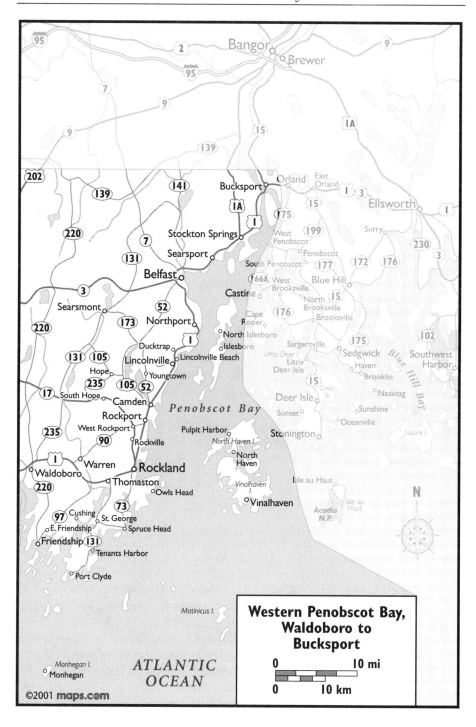

Western Penobscot Bay, Waldoboro to Bucksport

0   10 mi

0   10 km

©2001 maps.com

The towns along this part of the coast, along Rte. 1 without long detours, keep promising to be the next Camden. The fact that each is still waiting to be discovered makes this a wonderful place to visit. Antiques and sea captains' homes abound. Beautiful old houses with ocean views are still more than reasonably priced. There are art galleries, theater groups, and restaurants for big city palates in **Belfast**.

The deepwater port of **Searsport** at the head of Penobscot Bay was once known in ports around the world, and its history is well told at the Penobscot Marine Museum in the middle of town. The grand waterfront houses prove its past wealth; many of them are now converted to inns and bed and breakfasts. Today it considers itself the antique capital of Maine.

WESTERN PENOBSCOT BAY: LODGING

Belfast

BELFAST HARBOR INN
Innkeepers: Michael and Jamie Schnetzer.
207-338-2740 or 800-545-8576.
www.belfastharborinn.com.
stay@belfastharborinn.com.
91 Searsport Ave., Rte. 1, Belfast 04915.
Open: All year.
Price: Moderate to Expensive.
Credit Cards: AE, D, MC, V.
Handicap Access: Very limited.

This inn is just the thing for weary coastal travelers, a two-story motel with a continental breakfast. Large—61 rooms—comfortable, and clean, this is an efficiently run roadside inn just about midway between Belfast and Searsport. Fifty-five of the rooms are non-smoking, and the deck right outside our back door was a great place to convene after a long day. Best of all, the inn sits at the edge of a large expanse of green lawn that leads down to the shore of Penobscot Bay. Ask for a room on the waterside. Dogs are welcome, but should not stay in rooms alone and are charged $10.

Camden

LODGE AT CAMDEN HILLS
Innkeepers: Jack, Linda, and John Burgess.
207-236-8478 or 800-832-7058.
P.O. Box 794, Rte. 1, Camden 04843.
Open: All year.
Price: Moderate to Very Expensive.

The Lodge at Camden Hills offers modern, quiet, clean, efficiently run lodgings to travelers who want a location close to Camden, but away from the traffic and bustle. It is a small, comfortable motel with several efficiency cottages that sit well-separated from each other on a landscaped hillside. Rooms provide the amenities in demand by upscale travelers. Many of the private cottages have their own decks, Jacuzzis, and fireplaces. All of the 20 rooms have private baths, cable TV, air condi-

Credit Cards: AE, D, DC, MC, V.
Handicap Access: Yes.

MAINE STAY INN
Innkeepers: Peter and
   Donny Smith and Diana
   Robson.
207-236-9636.
www.camdenmainestay.com.
innkeeper@camdenmaine
   stay.com.
22 High St. (Rte. 1),
   Camden 04843.
Open: All year.
Price: Moderate to
   Expensive.
Credit Cards: AE, MC, V.

tioning, telephones, and refrigerators. No smoking. Children welcome. No pets.

Intimate, trim, and quiet, this inn is an early 18th-century farmhouse that sits on two acres in the heart of Camden's historic district. Eight bedrooms are in the main house and the attached carriage house; all have modern, private baths. Four guest rooms have fireplaces, one has a wood-burning stove. One is located in a suite complete with a large sitting room and queen-sized bed. Out back there is a majestic four-story barn and gardens filled with over a thousand daffodils. The house is full of things the Smiths have picked up on their travels—including a tonsu, a 300-year-old Samurai warrior's chest. Two parlors with fireplaces have matches on the mantel and wood and paper ready to be burned. Breakfast is cooked on an old Queen Atlantic stove and served on Spode china at a long pine farm table. Usually it's "something eggy one day, something not the next," says Donny. Tea is served in the afternoon. No smoking. Children 12 and older.

Norumbega Inn has a lordly presence.

Herb Swanson

NORUMBEGA
Innkeeper: Kent
   Hammond-Keatinge.
207-236-4646.
www.norumbega.com.
norumbega@acadia.net.
63 High St., Camden 04843.

The Norumbega is a stone castle built about a century ago on a hill by the sea. It is a favorite of honeymooners—perhaps because of its brooding, romantic presence, strong colors, and Victorian antiques. Or maybe it's the kitchen's constant supply of fresh-baked cookies, fresh fruit, and other

Open: All year.
Price: Expensive to Very Expensive.
Credit Cards: AE, D, MC, V.

surprises. Altogether there are 13 guest rooms, including the penthouse. All rooms have private baths, almost all beds are king-sized, and five of the rooms have fireplaces and impressive views. The library suite is just that. Outside there are stately elms and well-kept gardens. For those who love theatrics, the inn hosts "Murder by the Sea," elaborate off-season weekends of role-playing and intrigue. Guess whodunit, and you could win a two-night stay for two. They burn cords and cords of wood, both in the fireplaces in summer and to heat the place in the winter. No smoking.

The Whitehall Inn is the place for old-fashioned relaxation.

Herb Swanson

WHITEHALL INN
Innkeepers: The Dewing family.
207-236-3391 or 800-789-6565.
www.whitehallinnn.com.
P.O. Box 558, 52 High St., Camden 04843.
Open: Late May–mid Oct.
Price: Moderate to Expensive.
Credit Cards: AE, MC, V.

This fine, sprawling old Yankee inn began as a Greek Revival sea captain's home in 1834. It became an inn in 1901 and with many additions has become a favorite coastal retreat. Camden-born poet Edna St. Vincent Millay read her poem "Renascence" to the guests here in 1908. It begins, "All I could see from where I stood/ Was three long mountains and a wood;/ I turned and looked the other way,/ And saw three islands in a bay." They can tell you where to hike to see this view. Between the main inn and two smaller "cottages" across the street, there are 50 guest rooms; 42 with private baths. (All three buildings are on the National Register.) Guest rooms and spacious common areas are quiet, gracious, and comfortable but not deluxe. There are no televisions, but there are books, games, puzzles, a piano, and tennis on the inn's private courts. Tea is served at 4pm. The dining room offers a good wine list and a good menu which changes daily (jackets required). Full breakfast included; dinner additional. Modified American plan available. Children welcome.

Islesboro

DARK HARBOR HOUSE
Inn Manager: Sarah
  Randlett.
207-734-6669.
www.darkharborhouse.
  com.
P.O. Box 185, Main Rd.,
  Islesboro 04848.
Open: Mid-May–mid-Oct.
Price: Expensive to Very
  Expensive.
Credit Cards: MC, V.

This yellow clapboard Georgian mansion built on an Islesboro hillside at the turn of the century has spacious, summer-elegant rooms, and a well-deserved reputation as a restful staging ground from which to explore Islesboro, enclave of the rich and famous. One overheard conversation confirmed this: "Oh, hi, I hear you're building a house—I saw it in *Architectural Digest.*" The inn has 10 guest rooms and two suites; all rooms have private baths and several have balconies. Antiques are everywhere. The service is impeccable. The dining room offers a creative menu. Full breakfast is included; dinner is additional.

Monhegan Island

ISLAND INN
Manager: Krista Lisajus.
207-596-0371.
www.islandinnmonhegan
  .com.
islandinn@ midcoast.com.
Box 128, Monhegan 04852.
Open: May–Oct.
Price: Expensive to Very
  Expensive.
Credit Cards: MC, V.
Handicap Access: No.
Special Features: Private
  bathrooms.

A private bath is a special feature only on a distant island with old-fashioned accommodations. The porch and half of the rooms overlook the harbor and Manana Island; the inn dominates the tiny village. You will have to include the cost of the ferryboat tickets from Boothbay Harbor, New Harbor, or Port Clyde. Still, why not? Here is the quintessential Maine vacation, off on an island far away from the world, hiking on trails through cathedral woods, spying on birds. The restaurant is excellent, and the room price includes breakfast. Children welcome. Two-night minimum stay.

MONHEGAN HOUSE
Innkeepers: Holden and
  Susan Nelson.
207-594-7983 or
  800-599-7983.
www.monheganhouse.com.
Monhegan Island 04852.
Open: Late May–early Oct.
Price: Moderate.
Credit Cards: MC, V.
Handicap Access: No.

Monhegan House harks back to past summers and a different way of life. It has been operated as a guest house since 1870 and has 33 rooms furnished with antiques. Their brochure proudly notes that "All rooms are equipped with electrical power and lights." But while there is plenty of hot water and adequate bath facilities, none of the rooms have private baths. Is it because of this old-fashioned rusticity that this place is a favorite of birders? Children welcome.

TRAILING YEW GUEST HOUSE

Innkeeper: Marian Choiffi.
207-596-0440 or
  800-592-2520.
Monhegan Island 04852.
Open: Mid-May–mid-Oct.
Price: Inexpensive.
Credit Cards: None;
  personal and travelers'
  checks accepted.
Reservations: Required;
  write and send a $25.00
  check to confirm.

Monhegan is an island famous for its simple way of life, its views, and the number of renowned artists who for more than a century have stayed here. The Trailing Yew fits right in, a spartan collection of rustic white clapboard houses clustered around a lawn where guests gather to play horseshoes. The 37 rooms are clean and well-kept. It has the feeling of a well-loved youth hostel, with dirt paths, and a pay phone on the front porch. Minimal electric lighting is provided by generator to most rooms through part of the day and evening; after the generator is turned off, you can read or play cards by oil lamp or candle. Breakfast and a hearty family-style dinner are included with the cost of the room. Children and pets welcome.

Rockland

CAPT. LINDSEY HOUSE INN

Owners: Capts. Ken and
  Ellen Barnes.
207-596-7950 or
  800-523-2145.
www.lindseyhouse.com.
lindsey@midcoast.com.
5 Lindsey St., Rockland
  04841.
Open: All year.
Price: Moderate to
  Expensive.
Credit Cards: AE, D, MC, V.
Handicap Access: Yes.

Stay here if you're off on a windjammer cruise (the owners offer discounts to windjammer passengers) or ferrying to the islands from Rockland Harbor. A mustard-painted 1837 brick house on a quiet side street, this was first a sea captain's home. Today it is an inn, owned by two sea captains, Ellen and Ken Barnes—former theater folk who offer cruises on their schooner *Stephen Taber*. Right next door is the Waterworks, a pub where you can sample the best Maine microbrews on tap. The inn has a pleasant, professional air about it and seems bigger than it is—big enough to give guests plenty of elbow room. There are nine rooms, all decorated with unusual lamps and furnishings collected from around the world in a range of styles.

Beds are big and firm with down comforters and tapestry bedspreads. Every room has a private bath, air-conditioning, television, and telephone. The beautiful private courtyard with gardens is a lovely spot to read—and if you've borrowed one of the library's paperbacks but not finished it, they insist you take it with you. No smoking. Children over 10.

Rockport

THE SAMOSET RESORT

General Manager: Connie
  Russell.
207-594-2511 or

The Samoset is one of the places where Mainers like to stay—possibly because the resort offers so much for a population that tends to be physi-

800-341-1650.
www.samoset.com.
rooms@samoset.com.
220 Warrenton St.,
  Rockport 04856.
Off Rte. 1.
Open: All year.
Price: Moderate to Very
  Expensive.
Credit Cards: AE, D, DC,
  MC, V.
Handicap Access: Yes.

cally active. Ten kilometers of great cross-country skiing in the winter; golf in the summer on an 18-hole course. Tennis, racquetball, indoor and outdoor pools, bicycles, basketball, fitness room with Nautilus, croquet, badminton, volleyball, and horseshoes. How do they fit all this in? The resort sits on an ample 230 waterfront acres. The rooms are modern and comfortable. There is a restaurant on the premises called Marcel's, or you can venture into Rockport, Rockland, or Camden. While everything's deluxe, including the rooms, off-season package deals make it affordable for everyone. Meals additional.

Searsport

**THE WILLIAM & MARY
INN**
Innkeepers: William and
  Mary Sweet.
207-548-2190.
Rte. 1, Searsport 04974.
Open: All year.
Price: Inexpensive to
  Moderate.
Credit Cards: None;
  personal and travelers'
  checks accepted.

In 1774 Capt. Perry Pendleton sailed into town and built a log cabin just across the street from what is now the William & Mary Inn. More than 50 years later, the captain's granddaughter, Prudence, moved into this elegant home on a hill just two miles northeast of Searsport center. Renovations emphasize the architectural features—including the wonderful six-on-six windows. There are three guest rooms with pencil-post beds and reproduction wallpapers; each has its own bathroom tucked into former closets. Breakfast is served in a style befitting this elegant New England home: at the Chippendale table in the dining room.

Tenants Harbor

EAST WIND INN
Innkeeper: Tim Watts.
207-372-6366 or
  800-241-8439.
www.eastwindinn.com.
info@eastwind.com.
P.O. Box 149, Tenants
  Harbor 04860.
Open: Early Apr.–late Nov.
Price: Moderate to Very
  Expensive.
Credit Cards: AE, D, MC, V.

The main house of the East Wind is a former sea captain's home, and most of the rooms in the inn, its downstairs restaurant, and the wide porch offer fine views of Tenants Harbor. Fifteen guest rooms in the main house are filled with antiques and have a spartan Yankee quality; six have private baths. Ten more rooms in the modern "meeting house," all have private baths. There is also a cottage that houses three apartments. All three have kitchens. The restaurant, Windows, serves breakfast and dinner and is a favorite among local residents and business people. Pets are welcome for a fee.

Vinalhaven

THE FOX ISLAND INN
Innkeeper: Gail Reinertsen.
207-863-2122 or in winter
   850-425-5095.
www.bbonline.com/me/
   foxisland.
gailreiner@aol.com.
P.O. Box 451, Carver St.,
   Vinalhaven 04863.
Open: Memorial Day–mid-
   Sept.
Price: Inexpensive to
   Moderate.
Credit Cards: AE, D, MC, V.
Handicap Access: No.

This once was an island home; now it is a small village inn that offers guests comfortable lodging in a homelike setting. There are four lovely, clean, single and double rooms with shared baths and a restored three-room suite with a private bath. Gail serves breakfast and lets guests use the kitchen—a nice option for picnickers and those made hungry by the sea air. There are also bikes for guest use. Children over 10.

The Tidewater Motel looks out over the water in Vinvalhaven.

Curtis Rindlaub

TIDEWATER MOTEL
Innkeepers: Phil and Elaine
   Crossman.
207-863-4618.
www.tidewatermotel.com.
tidewater@ foxislands.net.
P.O. Box 546, Vinalhaven
   04863.
Open: All year.
Price: Moderate.
Credit Cards: MC, V.
Handicap Access: No.

The Tidewater Motel spans Carver Harbor's millrace, with water gushing beneath the motel at every tide. Rooms have water views and decks overlooking the harbor. Innkeeper Phil Crossman is a regular columnist for the Island Institute's newspaper, *The Working Waterfront*, and is considering generating hydropower for the motel from the millrace. Its location in the middle of downtown can be noisy but couldn't be more central, and it is directly across the street from the Harbor Gawker take-out, if you need to do a little eating while you watch the water. Children welcome.

Waldoboro

ROARING LION
Innkeepers: Bill and Robin
 Branigan.
207-832-4038.
995 Main St., Waldoboro
 04572.
Open: All year.
Price: Moderate
Credit Cards: None.

In a town that's world famous for sauerkraut and sausage, this inn is an anomaly. It has built a reputation for accommodating vegetarians and other people on special diets. Built at the turn of the century, this was originally a tourist home. There are four rooms at the inn: one has two queen-sized beds and private bath, the others share a bath and a half bath. Two rooms have double beds, one room has a fireplace. Downstairs there are four tables in the dining room, and every morning they serve fresh coffee cake, muffins, and other homemade breads to their guests, with sides of homemade jams and jellies. Ask for the sourdough pancakes—made from sourdough starter nurtured for more than 17 years. The Branigans are big on gardening, and homegrown flowers are everywhere. No smoking and no pets. Children of all ages are welcome. Breakfast included in room tariff.

WESTERN PENOBSCOT BAY: DINING

Belfast

BLUEBERRY BAY
207-338-9656.
Rte. 1, Belfast 04915.
Open: All year.
Price: Inexpensive.
Cuisine: Home cooking.
Serving: B, L, D.
Credit Cards: MC, V.
Special Features: Pie.
Handicap Access: Yes.

This is a friendly, spanking-clean, family-style restaurant. The breakfast menu offers something for everyone—the Lumberjack for big eaters and "mini" breakfasts for somewhat lighter eaters. At lunch and dinner, you can get boat-fresh seafood grilled, baked, or fried. If you're traveling with picky eaters, try hot dogs, burgers, chicken, or Italian entrées. Finish with the homemade pie. We have a soft spot for the blueberry.

SPRING STREET CAFE
207-338-4603.
www.sringstreetcafe.net.
38 Spring St., Belfast 04915.
Open: All year.
Price: Moderate.
Cuisine: Fusion.
Serving: D.
Credit Cards: MC, V.
Handicap Access: Yes.
Reservations:
 Recommended.

The Sunday tasting menus are a draw, offering the pleasures of several meals in small servings. For instance, starting with cream of tomato, leek, and fennel soup, going on to pork and chicken dumplings or salmon and leek cake, then warm duck salad, and for a "main" course, you could have grilled lamb tenderloin with roasted shallot-Burgundy demi-glace or grilled honey-pepper shrimp with avocado cream. One summer Sunday we finished with the chocolate oblivion torte; no doubt another summer Sunday will be entirely different, and equally good.

Camden

CAPPY'S CHOWDER
HOUSE
207-236-2254.
1 Main St., Camden 04843.
Open: All year. Call for
  winter hours.
Price: Moderate.
Cuisine: American, with an
  emphasis on seafood.
Serving: B, L, D.
Credit Cards: MC, V.
Reservations: Large parties
  only.
Handicap Access: Limited.

THE WATERFRONT
207-236-3747.
40 Bayview St., Camden
  04843.
Open: All year.
Price: Moderate.
Cuisine: American;
  seafood.
Serving: L, D.
Credit Cards: AE, MC, V.
Handicap Access: Yes.
Special Features: View of
  Camden Harbor.

ZADDIK'S PIZZA
207-236-6540.
20 Washington St., Camden
  04843.
Open: All year.
Price: Inexpensive to
  Moderate.
Cuisine: Italian and
  Mediterranean.
Serving: L, D.
Credit Cards: MC, V.
Handicap Access: Yes.

Rockland

AMALFI
207-596-0012.

Cappy's is named after Captain Quinn, born and raised on Penobscot Bay's Eagle Island, and a local waterfront character. Great chowder, good burgers, a good short stack of ribs, and buoyant pancakes (at breakfast). They also are quite competent with locally caught fish. All the food is well-cooked with hearty portions in a cozy atmosphere with plenty of warmth; this is the place to go when the fog is thick. There is an excellent bakery on the lower level. Arrive early before the line forms out into the street.

Camden's harbor may be the most beautiful hereabouts; the Waterfront is the place to watch it from. In summer, the restaurant opens its roomy terrace to salt breezes—all the better to enjoy your lobster and clams by. Seafood is the kitchen's hallmark. Fresh fish, crab cakes, crab pie, linguine with sun-dried tomatoes, and fresh scallops share the menu with steaks and specials like breast of chicken with olive oil and blueberry vinegar. At lunch, sandwiches and salads are teamed with chowders and soups. Crack open a Gritty, dig into a halibut steak, and enjoy the water lapping at the docks.

Zaddik's is probably the closest thing Camden has to a factory. If they're not busy producing, they're standing ready to produce. Zaddik's stresses the freshness of their ingredients . . . no vegetables from Number 10–sized cans. The pizza is actually quite good, although the crust is thick and more chewy than crunchy. The menu offers tastes of the Mediterranean east of Italy, as well as deep into Mexico, including gyros, hummus, quesadillas, etc. There's wide-open space with booths if you prefer to eat in rather than order out. Simplified children's menu.

Amalfi is Rockland's surprise, the Mediterranean on Penobscot Bay. Here you'll find plenty of

421 Main St., Rockland
  04841.
Open: All year.
Price: Expensive.
Cuisine: Mediterranean.
Serving: D.
Credit Cards: MC, V.
Handicap Access: Yes.

THE BROWN BAG
207-596-6372 or
  800-287-6372.
606 Main St., Rockland
  04841.
Open: All year.
Price.: Inexpensive.
Cuisine: Country eclectic.
Serving: B, L.
Credit Cards: MC, V.
Handicap Access: Yes,
  through the back.

olives, olive oil, and garlic in a cozy restaurant. Appetizers include kefta, Turkish meatballs made with beef, lamb, pistachios, and cumin, and a salad of greens with warm Seal Cove goat cheese marinated in balsamic vinegar. The entrées range from tender lamb kabobs to baked haddock with mahoghany clams, and other fish dinners, including paella.

This place specializes in the most important meal of the day, breakfast, and the next most, lunch. They bake daily an edible still life of warm croissants, sticky buns, giant blueberry muffins, and fresh shredded wheat bread toast. Oatmeal, cinnamon swirl French toast, and the excellent omelets are all homemade. Lunch customers line up to place their orders for huevos rancheros, brown bag pockets (scrambled eggs with three cheeses in a whole wheat pita falafel with lemon tahini sauce), a roast beef/boursin sub (the beef is marinated and roasted on the premises), or daily fresh-roasted turkey. Their seasonal pies, cheesecakes, puddings, and cookies are all made from scratch.

Conte's doesn't compromise the flavor of its seafood, or anything else.

Herb Swanson

CONTE'S
No telephone.
Harbor Park, Main St.,
  Rockland 04841.
Open: All year.
Price: Moderate.
Cuisine: Italian seafood.
Serving: D.

First you have to find the place, hiding behind a pile of old traps in an old fish shed on Rockland's waterfront. There won't be a light to guide you at night. Once inside, the restaurant is still elusive, screened from view by the menu, magic-markered on a large scroll of butcher paper hanging from the ceiling. Order here before sitting

Credit Cards: None.
Reservations: Not accepted.
Handicap Access: Yes.

down from the specials of *La Cucina Sfizioza Neapolitana*, the whimsy kitchen. Seafood Alfredo, lobster, calamari, scallops, are served over huge bowls of pasta; paella is a rice dish and steamed lobster is served on its own. Huge salads and loaves of bread cut in chunks are on the tables. Entrées arrive in mixing bowls, each enough for two or three large men. My calamari are lightly cooked and chewy, which I like, but I crave an extra garlic clove or two, and butter. All the spices seem to have gone into my partner's paella, which is dominated by the taste of sausage. Boxes are there so you can pack up your leftovers. Take your cash to the counter to pay up; they do not accept credit cards. "No phone either," the waitress adds, "No reservations, no fryolator, no ketchup, no microwave, no tartar sauce . . . no kidding."

PRIMO
207-596-0770.
2 South Main St. (Rte. 73),
  Rockland 04841.
Open: All year.
Price: Expensive.
Cuisine: Creative
  American.
Serving: D.
Credit Cards: D, MC, V.
Reservations:
  Recommended.

This is the place to be on the Maine coast these days, as fabulous in mid-winter as in the burgeoning days of summer when the building is besieged by gardens and summer visitors. On my trip up and down the coast this place stood out. I wish I could taste right now that grilled striped bass in its Livornese sauce, something that had intrigued me from a concurrent reading of *Kitchen Confidential*, that summer's paperback bestseller about New York restaurants. The sauce is an unctuous combination of black olives, tomatoes, capers, olive oil and garlic, of course; Primo upped the pleasure with an addition of caper berries that I ate like savory cherries off their coarse stems. Yes, they have other dishes, and they all change all the time; grilled sardines will probably return with their season, while lobster bisque might be more of a regular.

The waiter came along with an *amuse bouche* of cantaloupe soup in a shot glass; it was great and I apologized for giving him a hard time. It amused my mouth quite well.

Rockport

**INGRAHAM'S ON
  RICHARDS HILL**
207-236-3227.
www.ingrahams.com.
417 Commercial St. (Rte. 1),
  Rockport 04856.
Open: All year.
Price: Expensive.
Cuisine: American.
Serving: L, D, SB.

The whole family is involved in the success of this newly renovated restaurant, and it's full of mementos: old black-and-white photographs of the owners as kids, and a quilt made by a great-grandmother when she was 11 years old. The "Library" is a bar full of books, and the four pleasant dining rooms are comfortable places to focus on the well-made crab cakes or the Peking Duck that the

Credit Cards: AE, D, MC, V.
Handicap access: Yes.

Ingraham's have figured out to a T without, I would guess, the 10-year apprenticeship normal in Chinese circles. All the fish is delicious, and the oysters Rockefeller start off in the water off of Damariscotta before they meet up with the abundant cheese and bacon.

Searsport

PERIWINKLE'S BAKERY
207-548-9910.
Rte. 1, Searsport 04974.
Season: Closed Jan.
Price: Inexpensive.
Cuisine: Bakery, tea.
Serving: Light lunch.
Credit Cards: None.
Handicap Access: No.

This pretty little bakery and tearoom, tucked into an old white farmhouse right on Rte. 1, is a good place to stop and catch your wind. There are plenty of pecan squares, carrot cakes, pastries, and tarts to sample. They also make good soup, sandwiches on thickly sliced homemade bread, sausage rolls, and a nice delicious, custardy quiche. These folks used to own a bakery in Philadelphia, and Philadelphia's loss is our gain; the husband of the pair comes from England and has converted some of the locals into lovers of English food, like the apple "Victoria slice," and the Cornish pasties.

It is apparent to serious shellfish eaters that in the great evolutionary scheme of things crustaceans developed shells to protect them from knives and forks.

—Calvin Trillin, *Alice, Let's Eat*

Lobsters in the ocean are the color of seaweed and walk along the floor. "A shoe with legs" is how poet Anne Sexton described them. Lobsters are caught by lobstermen who heave a string of box-shaped wooden or vinyl-coated wire traps over the side of their boat. They bait their traps with fish heads and tails and species that don't normally sell well at the fish market. (Somehow it's not surprising to learn that lobsters are carnivores.) With luck, when the lobsterman returns and pulls up the trap, there will be a legal-sized lobster in it. (A waterlogged trap may weigh as much as 70 pounds.) A "keeper" measures at least 3.25 inches and is no more than 5 inches from its eyes to the beginning of the tail. It may or may not weigh a pound or more.

Lobsters in a pot of boiling water turn red. Before the 1800s, lobsters were in such abundance you could simply pick them off the beach, take them home, and cook them. People who could afford it didn't. Lobsters were considered a low-class food. Nineteenth-century prisoners were forced to eat them three times a week, and on Boston's Beacon Hill the servants ate them, although there was a limit to the number they would eat a week.

Finally, in the mid-19th century, fishermen began lobstering by boat, and scarcity produced demand. In this modern age, the Maine fleet lands an annual lobster catch of approximately 30,000 pounds or more.

Vinahaven

THE HAVEN
207-863-4969.
245 Main St., Vinalhaven
  04863.
Closed: Mar.–Apr.
Price: Moderate.
Cuisine: Seafood; exotic
  regional.
Serving: D; call for
  schedule.
Credit Cards: MC, V.
Handicap Access: Yes.
Reservations: Yes, June–Sept.

The menu changes often to incorporate the day's catch, ripening wild berries, or chanterelles harvested from the surrounding spruce woods. Two dining rooms are open in the summer. The back room, by reservation only (and you may need to do this well in advance of a visit), offers a more traditional seafood-restaurant atmosphere. The front room, with no reservation required, is now a favorite place to dine, surrounded by the works of local artists. Haven's has a full bar.

Waldoboro

A slice of delicious cream pie is always available at Moody's Diner.

Herb Swanson

MOODY'S DINER
207-832-7885.
Rte. 1, Waldoboro 04572.
Closed: Fri. and Sat. between
  midnight and 5am.
Price: Inexpensive.
Cuisine: Diner food.
Serving: B, L, D.
Handicap Access: Yes.

Everyone shares counter seats and booths at Moody's: Waldoboroans, summer people, tourists, fishing boat captains, and yacht owners. The corned beef hash is legendary. The cheeseburgers and meat loaf are, too, along with the walnut and cream pies.

PINE CONE CAFE
207-832-6337.
www.pineconecafe.com.
13 Friendship St.,
  Waldoboro 04572.
Open: May–Jan.

Owner and chef Laura Cabot likes to cook locally grown and produced foods, either from her own garden, or from nearby—the crab cakes are made from local crabs, though the capers in the remoulade are from distant Spain. The wine comes

Price: Expensive to Very Expensive.
Cuisine: Regional and seasonal.
Serving: L, D, SB.
Credit Cards: MC, V.
Handicap Access: Yes.
Reservations: Appreciated.

from far away, as well, tasted and put on a list during her winter travels, when the restaurant closes for four months. Trained at La Varenne, a French cooking school in Burgundy, the pleasures of the table are a language she is fluent in, and travelers bend their schedules to enjoy them. The roast asparagus bisque with crème fraîche is rich and delicious, and the daily chowder specials, like a haddock chowder, have the clean, bright taste of the freshest fish. There are vegetarian entrées like wild mushroom ravioli with artichoke cream sauce, as well as barbecued ribs. You can sit in a booth staring into an Eric Hopkins watercolor and feel like you are in orbit, even when the tastes are down to earth.

WESTERN PENOBSCOT BAY: FOOD PURVEYORS

BAKERIES

Borealis Breads (207-832-0655; www.borealisbreads.com; Rte. 1, Waldoboro). 150 acres in northern Maine are planted with organic wheat to supply this wonderful bakery, with stores in Portland, Wells, and Waldoboro. The Portuguese cornmeal bread is chewy and good, the cardamom raisin loaf is delicious toasted and buttered.

The bakery counter at the Frogwater Café is stocked with good things.

Herb Swanson

Frogwater Café and Bakery (207-236-8998; www.frogwatercafe.com; 31 Elm St. (Rte. 1), Camden 04843). The bakery opens daily at 7am, with fresh muffins, white chocolate scones, coffee cake, and Kahlúa cinnamon sticky buns on the weekend. You can also eat lunch and dinner, or a great caesar salad anytime.

Sweet Sensations (207-230-0955; www.mainesweets.com; Rte. 1, Rockport 04856). Raspberry pie and lemon coconut cake, almond macaroons and homemade biscotti—and homemade dog bones for your epicurean dogs.

BREWERIES

Cellardoor Winery (207-763-4478 or 877-899-0196; www.mainewine.com; 367 Youngtown Rd., Lincolnville 04849). Tasting Wed.–Sun. 1–5, in salesroom open May–Oct., afterward by appt. Take a walk in the vineyard to see how the grapes are doing. This is one of the first vineyards in Maine, and it has been releasing wines since 1999.

Sea Dog Brewing (207-236-6863; 43 Mechanic St., Camden). We like their India ale, although we aren't in love with the pub.

CANDY & ICE CREAM

Miss Plum's (207-596-6946; Rte. 1, Rockport). A reporter friend of ours thinks this is the best ice cream on the coast. They also sell sorbet, frozen yogurt, and baked desserts.

DELIS & TAKE-OUT

Camden Deli (207-236-8343; 37 Main St., Camden). New York–style sandwiches, wine and beer, and great desserts.

FAST FOOD

Cod End (207-372-6782; near town landing; Tenants Harbor). From Memorial Day till late June, weekends only, July and August every day, most of September. They serve up fresh, fast seafood, including good lobster rolls and chowder.

Lady Millville Store (207-236-6570; 113 Washington St., Rte. 105, Camden). Fresh dough pizza, subs, burgers, hot dogs, even fast food seafood and chicken.

Wasses (207-594-7472; 2 North Main St., Rockland). *The Washington Post* likes their hot dogs, with chili, cheese, bacon, or sauerkraut.

FOOD FESTIVALS

Bay Festival, Belfast (207-338-5900). Last week in July. This used to be called the Broiler Festival on account of its being a big chicken town. There used to be so much chicken here, you would think twice before visiting. These days, most chickens have moved out of town, but they still celebrate their broilers.

Maine Lobster Festival, Rockland (207-596-0376). First weekend in August. A parade, pageant, and the world's largest lobster cooker. This festival has been famous for more than 45 years.

GOURMET FOOD STORES

Foggy Ridge Gamebird Farm (207-273-2357; 213 Highland Rd., Warren). They raise, dress, and smoke game birds. They also sell live pheasants, partridges, and quails. Call for an appointment.

Great Eastern Mussel Farms (207-372-6317; Long Cove Rd., Tenants Harbor). They've taken the lowly mussel and cultivated it. No tours, but you can buy as fresh a bag of mussels here as is possible to find.

Morse's Sauerkraut (207-832-5569 or 866-832-5569; www.morses@midcoast.com; Rte. 220, Waldoboro). Every once in a while they run a simple ad in the paper that says "Kraut's ready." Maybe eating sauerkraut wouldn't be considered a chore if it were all as good as the fresh stuff made here. Also available are your knockwurst, bratwurst, kielbasa, and the humble dog. Sandwiches available. Since 1918. Seven days a week year-round.

Mystique (207-832-5136; 288 Friendship St., Waldoboro). Open June–Dec. They sell French-style goat cheeses, as well as feta. Goats on the premises.

State of Maine Cheese Company (207-236-8895; www.cheese-me.com; 461 Commercial St., Rockport). Cathe Morrill is responsible for these distinct cheeses: mild and sharp cheddars like Penobscot cheddar and Katahdin cheddar, plain and spiced Monterey cheeses and more, all made from all natural Maine milk. Also jams, wines, candles, all made in Maine.

HEALTH FOOD & FARM MARKETS

Belfast Co-op Store (207-338-2532; 123 High St., Belfast). Whole foods, local produce, fresh bread, and other baked goods.

Belfast Farmers' Market (in back of Reny's plaza). May–Oct., Tues., Fri., Sat. mornings.

Camden Farmers' Market (Colcord Ave., near Union St., Camden). Every Sat. morning, rain or shine.

Fresh Off The Farm (207-236-3260; Rte. 1, Rockport). Native produce, berries, apples and cider in season; natural foods, vitamins, herbs, jams, jellies, maple syrup and candy, pickles, relishes, blueberry syrup, chutney, mustards, dried beans, and local honey year-round.

The Last Stop Poultry Farm (207-273-2809; Rte. 1, Warren). Fresh native broilers and free-range roasting chickens. Fresh native turkeys. Homemade chicken and turkey pot pies.

Rockland Farmers' Market (Public Landing) Mem. Day–end of Oct., Thurs. 9–1.

School House Farm (207-273-2440; Rte. 1, Warren). Daily, late June–Thanksgiving. Their own 24 varieties of apples, six of plums, and four of pears. Fresh vegetables in season. Fresh homemade donuts as well as their renowned cider donuts in the fall.

WESTERN PENOBSCOT BAY: CULTURE

Sculptor Louise Nevelson lived near Rockland for many years. Andrew Wyeth painted his famous canvas *Christina's World* on the site of an old farm near Cushing. In 1991, the Olson family, who owned the three-story farmhouse with gray weathered clapboards, donated the saltwater farm on Hawthorne Point Rd. to the Farnsworth Museum in Rockland. Neil Welliver, whose landscapes hang in the Metropolitan Museum of Art and Museum of Modern Art in Manhattan, has a farm in Lincolnville, northeast of Camden.

Edna St. Vincent Millay was born at 198 Broadway in Rockland (the house, a private residence, still stands) and spent much of her childhood in Camden, the subject of many of her poems.

CINEMA

Bay View Street Cinema (207-236-8722; Bay View St., Camden).
The Colonial Theater (207-338-1930; www.colonialtheater.com; 163 High St., Belfast).
Strand Twin Cinema (207-594-7266; 339 Main St., Rockland).

GALLERIES

Caldbeck Gallery (207-594-5935; 12 Elm St., Rockland). A prestigious gallery showing artists from around the area.
The Center for Maine Contemporary Art (207-236-2875; www.artsmaine.org; Russell Ave., Rockport). Their annual juried art show is a good introduction to new and rising local talent.Tues.–Sat. 10–5 year-round; Sun. 12–5 in summer only. Formerly Maine Coast Artists.
Eric Hopkins Gallery (207-867-2229; www.erichopkins.com; Hopkins Wharf, North Haven). Eric Hopkins' work is most often aerial; his oils and watercolors are swirls of islands and clouds and sky seen from far away. His gallery is a ferry trip from Rockland, or a second ferry trip from Vinalhaven (call Brown's Ferry Service at 867-4621 from the parking lot pay phone; they come over for a small fee).
M.H. Jacobs Gallery (207-338-3324; 50 Main St., Belfast). Traditional representational watercolors and acrylics by artist Marvin Jacobs.

GARDENS & GARDEN TOURS

Since 1947 some wonderful private gardens have been showcased during the *Camden Open House & Garden Tour* on the third Thurs. of July.
Merryspring (Conway Rd. off Rte. 1, on the Camden-Rockport town line). A 66-acre nature park with an herb garden, a lily garden, a 10-acre arboretum,

and more cultivated wonders. Guided tours are available. Open dawn to dusk year-round.

HISTORIC BUILDINGS & SITES

Andre the Seal, honorary Harbormaster of Rockport Harbor, is dead, but his stone image continues to watch over the harbor. Harry Goodridge found Andre when he was a young pup; he raised and trained the seal, who became a local celebrity. The entire state mourned when Andre died in 1986, and his statue is one of the coast's most unusual historic markers. Andre was the subject of the 1994 movie, *Andre the Seal.*

FORT KNOX
207-469-7719.
Rte. 174 off Rte. 1, just east
   of Stockton Springs.
Season: May–Nov.; daily,
   9–sunset.
Admission charged.

Looking west across the Penobscot River from Bucksport, this great granite fort looks like a medieval castle. It was built in 1844 as a defense against the British during the Aroostook War. Today, the fort is the state's most complete historical military structure. Constructed of granite mined from nearby Mount Waldo, it was named for the first U.S. Secretary of War, who was from the territory that eventually became the state of Maine.

Herb Swanson

This mansion, now the General Henry Knox Museum, presides on a hillside just north of Thomaston village.

**GENERAL HENRY KNOX
   MUSEUM**
207-354-8062.
Rtes. 1 and 131, Thomaston.
Season: May 30–mid Oct.;
   Tues.–Sat. 10–4.
Admission charged.

A replica of the 1795 house built by Gen. Henry Knox and his wife, Lucy Flucker. Knox served in President Washington's cabinet as Secretary of War. Guided tours of Montpelier (the name of the mansion) and programs throughout the summer feature guides in authentic Colonial costumes, an antique fashion show, an Independence Day celebration with "Henry Knox," and a silver high tea.

OLD CONWAY HOUSE
207-236-2257.
www.c.house.home.ml.org.
Rte. 1, Camden.
Season: July 1–late Aug.;
  Tues.–Fri. 10–4. May and
  Sept. by appointment.
Admission: $5 adults; $4
  seniors; $1 students 6–18;
  children under 6 free.

The Camden-Rockport Historical Society has restored this old farmhouse, which offers an authentic picture of Maine farm life during the 1700s. There is a blacksmith shop on the premises and a small historical museum.

**OLD GERMAN
  MEETING HOUSE**
Rte. 32, Waldoboro.
Season: June–Aug., daily
  1–4.
Free.

This meetinghouse, which has a spectacular wineglass pulpit and striking, unpainted square-benched pews, was built in 1772 by the German families that settled the town 24 years earlier.

**WALDOBOROUGH
  HISTORICAL SOCIETY**
Rte. 220, just south of Rte. 1,
  Waldoboro.
Season: July and Aug.,
  daily 1–4:30.
Admission free.

There are three buildings here—a schoolhouse, a barn, and a small museum—in addition to an 1819 pound where stray livestock were impounded. The barn houses old toys, period clothing, china, glass, a library, a reconstructed 19th-century kitchen, and a Victorian-style bedroom.

LIBRARIES

Farnsworth Art Museum Library (207-596-6457; farnsworth@midcoast.com; 352 Main St., Rockland). A collection of art reference materials, including books, magazines, and videotapes in a handsome Greek Revival setting. Part of the Farnsworth Art Museum (see **Museums**, below). Call for hours.

Stephen Phillips Memorial Library (207-548-2529; www.penobscotmarine-museum.org; library@penobscotmuseum.org; 5 Church St., Searsport). Part of the Penobscot Marine Museum (see **Museums**, below). Open all year. Call for hours.

LIGHTHOUSES

If you'd like to learn more about lighthouses, visit the *Shore Village Museum* in Rockland (see **Museums**, below). It has one of the largest collections of lighthouse material in the country.

As far as Maine lighthouses go, *Grindle Point Light*, built in 1935, is young. Today the building on Isleboro houses the *Sailor's Memorial Museum*. Open mid-June–Labor Day. Call the Islesboro Town Hall for more information (207-734-2253).

Marshall Point Light (1895) in Port Clyde is home to a collection of lighthouse memorabilia. Open June–Sept., Sat. 10–5, Sun.–Fri. 1–5; May and Oct., Sat.–Sun. 1–5.

A ferry ride away, the keeper's house at *Monhegan Island Light* (1824) is worth a visit because it now serves as a museum that contains exhibits of the island's native plants, wildlife, and Native American artifacts.

Owls Head Light sits on a park called the U.S. Lighthouse Reservation (near Thomaston). The light was built in 1826 and is located at the head of the Saint George Peninsula on West Penobscot Bay. Although Owls Head Light is only 26 feet high, it can be seen from 16 miles at sea.

You can walk on the breakwater 7/8 miles to the *Rockland Lighthouse* (take Rte. 1 north to Waldo Ave. and Samoset Rd.). A favorite fishing spot is at the end of the breakwater under the lighthouse.

MUSEUMS

BELFAST AND MOOSEHEAD LAKE RAILROAD
207-948-5500 or 800-392-5500.
11 Water St. off City Landing, Belfast.
Season: June–mid-Oct., call for schedule.
Admission charged.

The Belfast & Moosehead Lake Railroad (nicknamed "Bull Moose") was founded in 1867 to carry lumber from inland Maine to the coast. That plan was short-circuited only a few years later when B&ML RR decided to hook up with the Maine Central Railroad just 33 miles inland. These days, the line is operated by the City of Belfast, and its mixed freight and passenger runs are shorter. Visitors are invited to ride the rails for ninety-minute or two-hour excursions along the coast several times a day, as it travels between Belfast and Unity. Trains can be chartered for parties and company events.

FARNSWORTH MUSEUM AND WYETH CENTER
207-596-6457.
www.farnsworthmuseum.org.
farnsworth@midcoast.com.
P.O. Box 466, 16 Museum St. (off Rte. 1), Rockland 04841.
Season: Memorial Day–Columbus Day, 9–5. Columbus Day–Memorial Day, Tues.–Sat. 10–5; Sun. 1–5.

The Farnsworth houses one of the best regional collections in the country. The home of this collection is a well-kept complex with the museum, an excellent art library, and the Farnsworth Homestead (1850), a gorgeous Greek Revival home with original high-Victorian furnishing and decor. The focus of the museum's permanent collection is on American art and includes work by the Wyeths, Winslow Homer, John Marin, Fitz Hugh Lane, Edward Hopper, Neil Welliver, and sculptor Louise Nevelson. The Farnsworth Center for the Wyeth Family in Maine includes a renovated Pratt Mem-

The Farnsworth Museum's garden blooms outside in the summer, and in the art on the walls inside all year round.

Herb Swanson

Admission: $9 adults; $8 seniors; $5 students over 18. In winter $8 adults; $7 seniors; $4 students.

orial Church featuring works by Jamie and N.C. Wyeth, and a new wing showing pieces by artist Andrew Wyeth.

FRIENDSHIP MUSEUM
Call the town office for more information: 207-832-7644.
Rte. 220 and Martin's Point Rd., Friendship.
Season: July–Labor Day, Mon.–Sat. 1–4, Sun. 2–4.
Donations welcome.

A one-room brick schoolhouse dedicated to the history of the Friendship sloop.

OWLS HEAD TRANSPORTATION MUSEUM
207-594-4418.
www.ohtm.org.
info@ohtm.org.
P.O. Box 277, Rte. 73, Owls Head 04854.
Season: Apr.–Oct., daily 10–5; Nov.–Mar. daily 10–4.
Admission: $6 adults; $4 children under 12; under 5 free. $16 family. Special events: $7 adults; $5 children under 12. Members: free.

An interesting collection of pioneer aircraft, automobiles, engines, motorcycles, bicycles, and carriages—almost anything that moves. The museum has guided tours of these conveyances, all of which are run from time to time. Some planes and vehicles operated on weekends.

A schooner in high seas by James Butterworth, from the Butterworth Collection at the Penobscot Marine Museum.

Courtesy Penobscot Marine Museum

PENOBSCOT MARINE MUSEUM
207-548-2529.
www.penobscotmarine
museum.org.
museumoffices@penobscot
marinemuseum.org.
P.O. 498, 5 Church St. (off
Rte. 1), Searsport 04974.
Season: Memorial Day–mid-
Oct.: Mon.–Sat. 10–5; Sun.
12–5.
Admission: $8 adults; $6
senior citizens; $3 children
7–15; under 6 free.

In the 19th century, 10 percent of America's deep-water shipmasters lived in Searsport. They brought mementos of the world back to this pretty little town. These nine buildings, restored or converted to individually themed galleries, are a terrific place to spend the day. It is home to one of the largest collections of marine paintings in the state. The Old Town Hall is devoted to the description of the great Down Easters, the square-rigged vessels built in Maine during the late 1800s. The museum sponsors annual events, concerts, lectures, and readings by Maine authors.

SHORE VILLAGE MUSEUM
207-594-0311.
104 Limerock St., Rockland.
Season: June–mid-Oct.,
daily 10–4; by appoint-
ment the rest of the year.
Donations.

This small, lively museum situated on an old Rockland street is crammed to the rafters with an odd and ever growing assortment of historical materials: the world's largest selection of lighthouse paraphernalia; Coast Guard memorabilia; uniforms, weapons, and papers concerning the Maine soldiers who fought in the Civil War; and the Llewella Mills collection of 34 dolls dressed in period costumes from the Middle Ages to the Gay '90s. Kids like it here, where they can ring the captain's bell and touch things.

MUSIC

Harps, dulcimers, brass quintets, jazz quartets—the coast is home to dozens of musical groups and festivals every year. Below we've listed one large organization. There are many more.

BAY CHAMBER CONCERTS
207-236-2823 or 888-707-2770.
www.baychamberconcerts. org.
info@baychamberconcerts. org.
P.O. Box 228, Rockport, ME 05856.
Season: Winter series Sept.–June; summer series July & Aug.
Tickets: Winter $18–$22; Summer $20–$25. Students $5 Winter; $7 Summer.

The summer season includes twice weekly lectures and concerts with the Vermeer Quartet and guest artists. The organization also promotes the music of young performers with five prizes to Maine musicians and its Next Generation program in August. During the winter the group sponsors monthly classical and jazz concerts by world-renowned artists. All concerts take place at the renovated Rockport Opera House.

NIGHTLIFE

The Blue Goose (207-338-3003; Rte. 1, Northport). Contradancing.
Gilbert's Publick House (207-236-4320; Bay View Landing, Camden). Live music and dancing Fri. and Sat. nights. Great microbrewed beer on tap, from Andrew's Brewing in Lincolnville.

SCHOOLS

What is culture, anyhow? We raise the question because this section on schools may suggest an answer. Here you will find schools not only for painters and musicians but also schools for fly fishermen and ocean navigators.

Hurricane Island Outward Bound School (207-594-5548 or 800-341-1744 out-of-state; www.outwardbound.org; Mechanic St., Rockland). Courses lasting 5 to 26 days are offered, as well as semester-long courses in Penobsot Bay, Greenville, and Newry. There are sessions year-round for every age and both sexes; they focus on sailing, rock climbing, dog-sledding, and outdoor problem-solving. Prices are a bit steep. Write Box 429, Rockland 04841.
Maine Coast Art Workshops (207-594-2300; 2 Park St., Rockland 04841). Throughout the summer, five-day workshops with recognized artists are held hereabouts. Sixteen workshops; tuition is about $400.
Maine Photographic Workshops (207-236-8581 or 877-577-7700; www.mework shops.com; Two Central St., Rockport 04856). Photography, cinematography, television production, acting, and other related courses for the aspiring or experienced visual artist. All are taught by established professionals. They operate an excellent gallery on the premises and a good retail store with photographic equipment and accessories.
Penobscot School (207-594-1084; www.languagelearning.org 28 Gay St, Rockland 04841). Ten to 12-week classes in conversational Russian, Japanese,

Spanish, French, Italian, and German and the occasional intensive weekend course—most taught by native speakers. During the summer they teach English as a second language and provide informal cultural events for the community.

SEASONAL EVENTS

Arts & Crafts Festival (207-236-4404; Public Library, Bok Amphitheater, Camden). Crafters from all over show and sell their work. Mid-July and again in October.

Military Aviation Airshow (207-594-4418; Transportation Museum, Owls Head). Fly-bys and demonstrations of armed forces aircraft. Beginning of August is the largest, but smaller ones are held ever other week.

Rockland Maine Lobster Festival (207-596-0376; Public Landing, Rockland). Just about everything to do with lobster, including lots to eat. Early August.

THEATER

Belfast Railroad Maskers (207-338-9668; Maskers Railroad Theatre, Belfast). Wide assortment of comedies and dramas, Feb.–Dec.

Camden Civic Theatre (207-236-2281; Camden Opera House, Rte. 1, Camden). Musicals. Apr.–Nov.

Iron Horse Dinner Theater (207-948-5500 or 800-392-5500; 11 Water St. off City Landing, Belfast). Actually, it's dinner, theater, and a train ride, summer only.

WESTERN PENOBSCOT BAY: RECREATION

BEACHES

Crescent Beach; Crescent Beach Rd., Owl's Head. Popular swimming beach near summer colony. Length, 1,100 yards. Nearby facilities; limited parking.

Lincolnville Beach; Rte. 1, Lincolnville.

Sandy Point Beach; Stockton Springs. About a mile long; there's not much here except beach. No facilities and little parking.

BERRY & APPLE PICKING

Wild blueberries abound in Maine, and more often than not, you'll stumble on a patch if you're out hiking on a mid- to late summer's day. For cultivated strawberries, check out **Spear Farm & Greenhouse** (207-273-3818; Rte. 1, Warren). Call for information.

BICYCLING

Great areas to pedal along the west side of Penobscot Bay include the stretch of *U.S. Rte. 1 between Belfast and Bucksport,* which is littered with old sea captains' homes; the perimeter of *Megunticook Lake,* and on to *Lincolnville.*

BICYCLE SHOPS

Birgfeld's Bicycle Shop (207-548-2916; birgfeld@midcoast.com; 184 East Main St., Searsport) End of Mar.–Oct. Retail bike shop, no rentals, home to Waldo County International Dining and Cycling Society, rides Tues. & Wed. 6pm for dinner, cycling optional.

Browndog Bikes (207-236-6664; 46 Elm St., Rte. 1, Camden). Rents, sells, repairs bikes.

Maine Sport (800-722-0826; www.mainesport.com; Rte. 1, Rockport). Rents, sells, repairs bikes.

Wooden Boats

Pleasure boats and working boats come and go in all shapes and sizes in Maine, but there's something particular about a wooden boat. Museums are devoted to the wooden boat, and a magazine industry flourishes here thanks to wooden boats. There are also schools to help keep the craft of wooden boat building alive. Best of all, you can still look out at the harbor—or practically anyplace else on the coast—and see them in abundance.

In spite of all the extra work wooden boats demand of their owners, many Mainers would not go down to the sea in anything else. They are a living part of the sea. A boat, said someone probably before the invention of fiberglass, is a hole in the water into which you throw money. Nowhere else do people throw money into their wooden boats so willingly as in Maine.

The wooden boat has as important a place in Maine's history as the glacier. The Passamaquoddy Indians cruised the coast in birch bark canoes. The graceful lines of those canoes still live in the famed Old Town canoes made in Bangor. The first wooden ship built in America was constructed in Maine by the colonists of Popham Colony in 1607. It was a 30-ton pinnace called the *Virginia,* and it carried cargo between England and Virginia for 20 years.

At first, Maine boat builders relied on the forests at their back door. As lumber along the south coast became scarce, more boat builders moved Down East to take advantage of cheaper building materials. The industry grew. Soon it seemed like the whole coast was one big shipyard, building good, cheap cargo ships.

The earliest Maine ships were built in the tradition of their British forebears, but by the time of the Revolutionary War, Maine shipwrights had developed their own designs and style of shipbuilding. Speed became important to the merchant marine, and shipbuilders responded with the sleek, fast clipper ship; Maine shipyards built and launched 83 clippers during the mid-1800s. The last of the famous wooden cargo ships built in Maine was a three-masted square-rigger ship called the *Down-*

Easter that was almost as fast as the clipper, but had a deeper, more spacious hull and enabled merchants to haul more with every trip.

Schooners were also built in Maine. Merchants prized them because they were even larger than the clippers and Down-Easters and more economical to operate. Today they operate out of Rockland and Camden serving the tourist trade (See **Windjammers,** below).

The end of the wooden boat as a merchant trading vessel came with the invention of the steamers. Steamships didn't rely on changeable winds and currents. They ran on time, and even the fastest clipper couldn't compete. Ironically, renowned Bath shipbuilder Arthur Sewall built the first steel sailing vessel, *Dirigo I,* in 1894. It weighed more than 2,800 tons.

Maine wooden boat builders took a new tack, building smaller boats for fishermen and pleasure sailors. The style of boat often depends on where it comes from: Peapods come from Penobscot Bay; Quoddy boats from Passamaquoddy Bay; the pretty, gaff-rigged Friendship Sloops from the town of Friendship on Muscongus Bay. There were also punts built to navigate a harbor or any small, calm waterway; dories to ferry people and small loads to and from shore; and pulling boats that were manned by oarsmen who literally hauled large ships that had been becalmed on windless water. Today those same pulling boats are used by Outward Bound students, their courses set on personal development.

For an invigorating taste of Maine's wooden boat heritage, watch the *Friendship Sloop Races,* held every year in late July in Rockland. Sponsored by the Friendship Sloop Society, the sloop races are really a week of wooden boat activities (including three days of racing and events at the *Maine Maritime Museum* in Bath). For more information, contact the Rockland-Thomaston Chamber of Commerce (207-596-0376). Also in Rockland are the spectacular *Schooner Days,* a three-day festival with all the trimmings—food, entertainment, arts, and marine demonstrations—crowned by the Parade of Sail, which features more schooners every year, including the *Stephen Taber,* listed in the National Historic Register.

Windjammer enthusiasts head to Boothbay Harbor in late June for *Windjammer Days.* The festival includes concerts, a boat and a street parade, fireworks, and a chance to tour visiting military vessels. The Boothbay Harbor Chamber of Commerce has all the information (207-633-2353; P.O. Box 356, Boothbay Harbor 04538).

Smart enough to realize that you can't get too much of a good thing, the Rockport-Camden-Lincolnville Chamber of Commerce (207-236-4404) promotes another windjammer fix later in the summer. Pretty Camden Harbor hosts *Windjammer Weekend* every Labor Day weekend, when over two dozen windjammers from ports along the midcoast are on display—including the *Victory Chimes,* which at 170 feet, including the bowsprit, is a tight squeeze in the small harbor and ties up at the waterfront restaurant until Saturday morning.

BOATING

CANOEING & SEA KAYAKING

Belfast Kayak Tours (207-382-6204; hschiller@pocketmail.com; 111 Davis Rd., Freedom). Kayak rentals and tours in the summer, from the Belfast Public Boat Landing. Group discounts.

Belfast Harbor.

Herb Swanson

Island Hopping (603-466-2721; www.outdoors.org; or write Summer Workshop, P.O. Box 298, Gorham, NH 03581). The Appalachian Mountain Club offers experienced canoeists the chance to spend three days exploring the water routes the Abenaki Indians used as they traveled among the islands of Penobscot Bay.

Maine Sport Outdoors School (800-722-0826; www.mainesport.com; Rte. 1, Rockport 04856). Sea kayaking guided tours from two-hour harbor trips to four-day excursions, and all levels of instruction from beginners' clinics to four-day trips. They also rent sea and lake kayaks, canoes, and bicycles (see **Bicycling**).

CRUISING

For the sailboat or motorboat cruiser, the Penobscot Bay region could be considered a paradise, including beautiful fishing villages like Tenants Harbor and quaint, albeit sophisticated, towns such as Camden (a true pleasure sailor's town). Islands make for great side trips. The smallest anchorages are great places to anchor and enjoy a swim on a warm summer day and lobster on the rocks; the largest offer almost all the amenities of the mainland.

CHARTERS & RENTALS

Sailing on the Penobscot Bay (207-852-4800; www.sailbelfast.com; Belfast). Two, three-hour sails off the Belfast Town dock.

Sloop *Surprise* (207-372-6366; www.eastwindinn.com; Tenants Harbor). Capt. Steve Daley sails his Friendship sloop from the East Wind Inn's pier around the islands of Tenants Harbor. Up to six people. Twice daily, May–Oct. Call to confirm information.

SAILING LESSONS

Bay Island Yacht Charters and Sailing School (207-596-7550 or 800-421-2492; www.sailme.com; 117 Tillson Ave., Rockland). Guided tours of the bay as well.

Chance Along Community Sailing Center (207-338-6003; 278 High St., Belfast). Lessons to get around the harbor or down the coast. Rentals from Sunfish to 23-foot boats; half day, full day, or weekly rates.

BOWLING

Candlepin Lodge (207-863-2730; Vinalhaven). Six candlepin lanes.

Oakland Park Bowling Lanes (207-594-7525; Rte. 1, Rockport). Twelve candlepin lanes.

CAMPING

The Rockland area offers dozens of private and public campgrounds, often with great views of the water at campers' prices. Sizes and facilities vary, and the season is short; we recommend calling well ahead for reservations. After Labor Day weekend most campgrounds become lovely, quiet, and wonderfully available.

Camden Hills State Park (207-236-3109; www.state.us.m/doc/prkslnds/reser; two miles off U.S. Rte. 1). Often this lovely campground is full. It's near one of the most popular seacoast towns in Maine, as well as within striking distance for hikers headed up Mount Battie. You should have a reservation to make sure you have a spot during July and August. But you're almost certain to get one the rest of the season if you arrive before 1pm. Showers. Nominal fee. Open May 15–Oct. 15.

FACTORIES

The Bucksport Mill, International Paper Company (207-469-4010; Bucksport). If you start hungering for some industrial wonders, this mill offers tours in the summer for guests 12 and older. The mill manufactures "some of the world's best lightweight coated magazine and catalogue paper." Call for schedule.

FARMS

Kelmscott Farm (207-763-4088 or 800-545-9363; www.kelmscott.org; 12 Van Cycle Rd., Lincolnville). This is a working farm dedicated to preserving ancient breeds of sheep, work ever more valuable with the spread of hoof-and-mouth disease. See Cotswold sheep, Gloucestershire Old Spots pigs, cows, horses, and goats. Wagon rides and a farm store.

FERRIES

The Maine State Ferry Service (207-789-5611; Lincolnville). Ferry to Isleboro. This is near Rte. 1 and offers a clean rest room.

The Maine State Ferry Service (207-596-2202; Rockland). Ferry to Vinalhaven; expect elaborate and long waits for a car. Another service from Rockland goes to Matinicus, over two hours away. And a third goes to North Haven, on the *Captain Neal Burgess*.

Monhegan Boat Line (207-372-8848; www.monheganboat.com; barstow@mongheganboat.com; P.O. Box 238, Port Clyde 04855) Ferry to Monhegan, 60 minutes, reservations recommended.

GOLF

Bucksport Golf Club (207-469-7612; Duckcove Rd., Bucksport). 9 holes, 3,352 yds., par 36. Cart and club rental, pro shop, clubhouse, lessons, snack bar.

Goose River Golf Course (207-236-8488; 50 Park St., Camden). 9 holes, 3,049 yds., par 35. Cart and club rental, pro shop, clubhouse, lessons.

North Haven Golf Club (Iron Point Rd., North Haven). 9 holes, 2,060 yds., par 35. Cart and club rental, lessons.

Northport Golf Club (207-338-2270; Bluff Rd., Northport). 9 holes, 3,047 yds., par 36. Cart and club rental, pro shop, clubhouse, lessons.

Rockland Golf Club (207-594-9322; Old County Rd., Rockland). 18 holes, 6,121 yds., par 70. Cart and club rental, pro shop, clubhouse, lessons.

Samoset Resort (207-594-2511 or 800-341-1650, ext. 511; www.samoset.com; Warrenton St., Rockport). 18 holes, 5,620 yds., par 70. Cart and club rental, pro shop, clubhouse, lessons.

HEALTH CLUBS

Bay Area Fitness (207-338-3567; www.bayareafitnessgym.com; 192 Searsport Ave., Belfast). Fitness machines, weights, aerobics, and lifecycles.

Midcoast Physical Therapy and Fitness Center (207-596-6889; 2 Park Dr., Rockland). Pool, sauna, whirlpool, steambath, Nautilus, weights, fitness machines, lifecycle, stairmasters, and treadmill.

Samoset Resort (207-594-2511 or 800-341-1650; Waldo Ave., Rockport). Pools, hot tubs, sauna, weights, lifecycles, fitness machines, and aerobics.

YMCA (207-236-3375; 50 Chestnut St., Camden). Aerobics, racquetball, weights, pool, sauna, and fitness machines.

HIKING & WALKING

Some of the best hiking on the Maine coast is found near Rockland. Here are some of the more popular hikes and walks.

Bald Rock Mountain, Lincolnville. From the summit, you can see Mount Desert and the Penobscot Bay islands. From Ski Lodge Rd., this is an easy ascent on a well-traveled path to the top. It is a one-half mile walk with an elevation gain of 1,000 feet.

Monhegan Island. Take the Burnt Head trail along the 150-foot cliffs and through cathedral woods—one of the few existing stands of virgin pine in Maine. This is a good day trip. The island has about 17 miles of hiking trails and is ruled by walkers (no vehicles are allowed). Ferries leave for Monhegan from Boothbay Harbor, New Harbor, and Port Clyde.

The stone tower at the top of Mount Battie.

Herb Swanson

Mount Battie, Camden. There aren't many prettier walks than this one. From various lookouts you can see Mount Desert Island, Blue Hill Bay, Camden village, harbor, coast, and Megunticook from the mountain's exposed summit. There's also a stone tower at the top. This walk is even prettier in the fall when the leaves change. A park nature trail joins with a short, steep trail that climbs parallel to the auto toll road. One-mile climb with a 600-foot elevation gain.

Mount Megunticook, Camden. The highest of the Camden Hills, the ridge is ascended by park trails from several directions. The views are more limited on this walk, but there are several good vistas from exposed ledges en route. The Megunticook Trail offers the most direct ascent. It begins near the park entrance and passes a grotto and stream, then rises steeply to Ocean Lookout and panoramic views. Base to Lookout is a one-mile climb with an elevation gain of 1,100 feet.

Mount Megunticook/Mount Battie, Camden. More ambitious walkers can plan to do both hills in one day. The trip begins at the parking lot, continues over Mount Megunticook, across to Mount Battie, and back to the parking area. The total walk is about 4.5 miles, and the top of Mount Battie is a great place for a picnic.

Ragged Mountain, Camden. An easy trail that weaves in and out of the trail and ski lift at Snow Bowl. The elevation gain is about 400 feet, and the trail is about one mile from base to summit.

HORSEBACK RIDING

Hill-N-Dale Farm (207-273-2511; 626 Western Rd., Warren). Lessons, trail rides, indoor arena, day camp, and carousel tack shop.

NATURE PRESERVES

Fernald's Neck Preserve, off Rte. 52, Camden-Lincolnville. Four miles of trails through woods, bog, and along 200-foot cliffs on a 315-acre preserve near Lake Megunticook. Managed by the Nature Conservancy.

Lane's Island Preserve, Vinalhaven. The Nature Conservancy manages a 43-acre refuge here made up of rolling moors and shoreline pounded by rough surf. Trails lead to several beaches. Access is by a stone causeway from Vinalhaven (a car ferry from Rockland services the island of Vinalhaven).

Merryspring (Conway Rd. off Rte. 1, on the Camden-Rockport town line). A private foundation manages this 66-acre nature park. While there are several cultivated gardens, the park also features a 10-acre arboretum and the group's ongoing efforts to preserve native wildflowers.

PUFFIN WATCHING

Mary Donna, **Offshore Passenger & Freight** (207-366-3700; Maine State Ferry Service, Rockland).

SEASONAL SPORTING EVENTS

The Great Schooner Race, early July. Sponsored by the Maine Windjammer Association, this all-day race begins at North Haven and ends in Rockland (contact the Rockland Chamber of Commerce, 207-596-0376).

The Monhegan Island Yacht Race, mid-August.

Owls Head Transportation Rally, early August. Planes, high-wheeled bicycles, and automobiles. More than 300 of them (contact the Owls Head Transportation Museum, 207-594-4418; www.ohtm.org).

Schooner Days, early July (Rockland area Chamber of Commerce, 207-596-0376).

Windjammer Weekend, late August. Parade of sail, fireworks, day sails (contact the Camden Chamber of Commerce, 207-236-4404).

SKATING

Camden Snow Bowl Ski Area (207-236-3438; www.camdensnowbowl.com; Hosmer Pond Rd., Camden). Open December–March. Outdoors. Free.

SKIING

DOWNHILL SKIING

There are not many people who come to the coast to go downhill skiing; the state's biggest ski areas are inland near Bethel and Rangeley. But you can be one of the few to escape the crowds and feel the ocean breezes at the *Camden Snow Bowl* (207-236-3438; www.camdensnowbowl.com; Camden). The vertical drop is about 950 feet; the mountain has 10 trails and is serviced by a double chairlift and two T-bars. Best of all, lift tickets are inexpensive.

CROSS-COUNTRY SKIING

Camp Tanglewood at Camden Hills State Park (207-789-5868; off Rte. 1, Lincolnville). Ten miles of ungroomed trails, graded for entry level to the most skilled skiers. Ask for a map available at the gate. January–March, dawn to dusk.

Samoset Ski Touring Center (207-594-1431; www.samoset.com; P.O. Box 78, Rockport). 4.5 kilometers of groomed trails split evenly between entry level and more difficult.

TENNIS

For a tennis vacation, there are two good resorts: The *Samoset Resort* (207-594-2511 or 800-341-1650; www.samoset.com; Rockport) has both indoor and outdoor courts, so you can play year round; the *Whitehall Inn* (207-236-3391 or 800-789-6565; www.whitehall-inn.com; 52 High St., Camden) is an old-style Yankee resort with tennis courts perched on a hillside above Penobscot Bay.

WINDJAMMERS

Today the only cargo these sea trains carry are tourists. Life on a windjammer was never the cruise it is today. Work for the crew was never optional; private cabins were unheard of for all but the captain; and there were never gourmet meals served at respectable hours.

At 132 feet and capable of carrying 44 passengers, the *Victory Chimes* is the biggest of the windjammer fleet (no wonder many of those passengers hail from Texas). The *Lewis R. French*, built in 1871, is the oldest. *Angelique*, a steel-hulled ketch launched in 1980, is the youngest member of the fleet. That new ships still are being built and the industry is prospering is testament to the enjoyment windjammers provide. The newest windjammers are built true to old ways, only with a few added comforts. In fact, most of the old fleet has been rebuilt or refurbished to serve the cruise business in the style to which its tourists are accustomed. Some of the old ones are still pushed by yawl boats to open water.

Every year near Rockland, home to much of the fleet, there is an annual *Great Schooner Race* in early July. People with timely reservations take part. *WoodenBoat* magazine's annual sail-in during mid-September.

If you aren't lucky enough to visit during one of these events, there are always the cruises. They last from three days in the off-season to six days during the summer. Most windjammer cruises cost between $325–$650. On some windjammers you can take a two-hour ride for less than $20 per person. For more information about the old sailing vessels, you can contact the Maine Windjammer Association, 800-807-9463 or www.midcoast.com/~sailmwa.

American Eagle (Capt. John Foss; 207-594-8007 or 800-648-4544; www.schooner americaneagle.com; schooner@midcoast.com; P.O. Box 482, Rockland 04841).

Angelique (Capts. Mike and Lynne McHenry; 207-785-3020 or 800-282-9989; www.sailangelique.com; windjam@sailangelique.com; Yankee Packet Co., P.O. Box 736, Camden 04843).

Appledore (Captain John McKean; 207-236-8353 or 800-233-PIER; Bayview Landing, Camden 04843). Four two-hour sails daily, late June–mid-Sept. Three two-hour sails daily, mid-Sep.–mid-Oct. Captain McKean mentioned that he takes volunteers for crew when he sets sail for Key West at the end of the season; the intrepid looking for an amazing way to travel south can try out for this in Oct.

Grace Bailey (Owners Ray and Ann Williamson; 207-236-2938 or 888-MWC-SAIL; www.mainewindjammercruises.com; info@mainewindjammercruises .com; Maine Windjammer Cruises, P.O. Box 617, Camden 04843).

Heritage (Capts. Doug and Linda Lee; 207-594-8007, 800-648-4544, or 800-542-5030; www.schoonerheritage.com; schooner@midcoast.com; P.O. Box 482, Rockland 04841).

Isaac H. Evans (Capt. Brenda Walker; 207-594-7956 or 877-238-1325; www. midcoast.com/~evans; evans@midcoast.com; P.O. Box 791, Rockland 04841).

J & E Riggin (Capt. John Finger and Anne Mahle; 207-594-1875 or 800-869-0604; www.riggin.com; info@riggin.com; 136 Holmes St., Rockland 04841).

Lewis R. French (Capt. Dan and Kathy Pease; 800-469-4635; www.midcoast .com/~windjam; windjam@midcoast.com; P.O. Box 992, Camden 04843).

Mary Day (Coastal Cruises, Owners Jen Martin and Barry King; 207-785-5670 or 800-992-2218; www.schoonermaryday.com; captains@schoonermaryday .com; P.O. Box 798, Camden 04843).

Mercantile (Owners Ray and Ann Williamson; 207-236-2938 or 888-MWC-SAIL; www.mainewindjammercruises.com; mwc@midcoast.com; Maine Windjammer Cruises, P.O. Box 617, Camden 04843).

Mistress (Owners Ray and Ann Williamson; 207-236-2938 or 888-MWC-SAIL; www.mainewindjammercruises.com; mwc@midcoast.com; Maine Windjammer Cruises, P.O. Box 617, Camden 04843).

Nathaniel Bowditch (Capt. Gib Philbrick; 207-273-4062 or 800-288-4098; www. midcoast.com/~natbow/; natbow@midcoast.com; P.O. Box 459, Warren 04864).

Olad (Captain Will Gordon; 207-236-2323; www.maineschooners.com; Public

Landing, Downeast Windjammer Packet Co., P.O. Box 432, Camden 04843). 1927 Crosey-built schooner, 57 feet, originally built as a yacht.

Stephen Taber (Capts. Ken and Ellen Barnes; 207-236-3520 or 800-999-7352; www.stephentaber.com; info@stephentaber.com; 70 Elm St., Camden 04843). This is the only windjammer to be listed on the National Landmark Register.

Summertime Cruises Inc. (Capt. Bill Brown; 800-562-8290; www.schoonersummertime.com; info@schoonersummertime.com; 115 South Main St., Rockland, 04841).

Surprise (Capts. Jack and Barbara Moore; 207-236-4687; www.camdenmainesailing.com; surprise@midcoast.com; Drawer H, Camden 04843).

Timberwind (Capt. Rick Miles; 800-759-9250; www.schoonertimber wind.com; info@timberwind.com; P.O. Box 247, Rockport 04856).

Victory Chimes (Capt. Kip Files and Paul DeGaeta; 207-594-0755 or 800-745-5651; www.victorychimes.com; info@victorychimes.com; P.O. Box 1401, Rockland 04841). Three- and six-day cruises on the United State's largest windjammer, built in 1900.

Wendameen (Capt. Neal Parker; 207-594-1751; www.schooneryacht.com; P.O. Box 252, Rockland 04841). One-night cruises on a 67-foot schooner.

WESTERN PENOBSCOT BAY: SHOPPING

Playful lobster sculptures, and an occasional moose, Rockland.

Herb Swanson

ANTIQUES

Though you will find great finds elsewhere, the area from Belfast to Searsport is the most concentrated antique shopping in this area of the coast.

Captain Pinkham's Emporium (207-548-6465; www.sphynx.com/jonesportwood; captt@mint.net; 34 Main St., Searsport). Old tools, furniture, books, paintings. The kind of place where you can make a "find."

Searsport Antique Mall (207-548-2640; Rte. 1, Searsport). Over 70 dealers gather here in the heart of Maine's antique mecca.

Seventy-nine Wistful Vista (207-338-3697; 135 High St., Belfast). Antiques, graphics, and live bait.

Wee Barn Antiques (207-354-6163; 20 Georges St., Thomaston). A fun collection of antique "smalls," glass, furniture, jewelry, and silver.

AUCTIONS

Andrews and Andrews (207-338-1386; 71 Cross St., Northport).

BOOKSTORES

ABCD Books (207-236-3903 or 888-236-3903; www.abcdbooks.com; books@ abcdbooks.com; 23 Bayview St., Camden). Used, rare, and out-of-print books.

BookStacks (207-469-8982, 888-295-0123; 333 Main St., Bucksport). Over 10,000 book titles, 1,000 magazine titles, books on tape, out-of-state newspapers, maps and charts. Swiss chocolate and postcards.

The Fertile Mind Bookshop (207-338-2498; 105 Main St., Belfast). New books and a book and cassette rental collection. Maps, newspapers, cards too.

Owl & Turtle Bookshop (207-236-4769 or 800-876-4769; www.owlandturtle. com; owlturtl@midcoast.com; 8 Bay View St., Camden). They encourage browsing and specialize in children's and nautical books.

The Personal Book Shop (207-354-8058; 144 Main St., Thomaston). Discerning selections.

The Reading Corner (207-596-6651; 408 Main St., Rockland). Great children's department.

CLOTHING

Black Parrot (207-594-9161; 328 Main St., Rockland). Women's clothes in great fabrics and colors.

Coyote Moon (207-338-5659; coyote@acadia.net; 54 Main St., Belfast) Natural fiber clothing and funky gifts.

Star Child (207-594-3335; 481 Main St., Rockland). Wonderful children's clothing, most of it designed by the owner and made around Rockland.

Theo B. Camisole and Company (207-236-0072; 24 Bayview St., Camden). There's nothing like great lingerie, and here is some of the best we've seen. Pretty, lacy things and soft cotton terry robes.

COLLECTIBLES

Ducktrap Bay Trading Co. (207-236-9568 or 800-560-9568; ducktrap@tidewa ter.net; 37 Bayview St., Camden). Decoys, ships' models, carvings, prints, and original art.

Duck Trap Decoys (207-789-5363; www.duck-trap.com; ducktrap@midcoast.com; Duck Trap Rd. off Rte. 1, Lincolnville Beach). Hand-carved decoys by Walt Simmons and over 70 other carvers. Furry animals, too.

Fretz Goldsmiths (207-469-2700 or 877-469-2700; www.fretzgoldsmiths.com; Elm St., Bucksport). Etruscan jewelry techniques inspire their elegant, intricate gold chains.

Ye Olde Coin Shop and Fine Jewelry (207-338-2663; 64 Main St., Belfast). Watches and watch repairs, an engraving sevice, new and estate jewelry.

FURNITURE

William Evans, Cabinetmaker (207-832-4175; 804 Main St., Waldoboro). Reproductions, restorations, and contemporary furniture.

Windsor Chairs (207-789-5188 or 800-789-5188; Rte. 1, Lincolnville). Windsor chairs and other furniture. You can watch them work.

Wooden Screen Door Company (207-832-0519; www.woodenscreendoor.com; 3542 U.S. Rte. 1, Waldoboro). Finely made doors with pine tree or sailboat cut-outs, among others; mortise and tenon joints and Honduras mahogany.

GIFTS & SOUVENIRS

The Leather Bench (207-236-4688; 34 Main St., Camden). Great leather bags, belts, wallets, and clothing.

Maine Gathering and Finest Kind Candies (207-236-9004; www.mainegathering.com; info@mainegathering.com; 21 Main St., Camden). Contemporary and traditional crafts by Maine residents with an extensive selection of Maine Native American baskets and fine candies.

The Right Stuff (207-236-9595; 38 Main St., Camden). A gift and home store crammed with attractive reproductions, period lighting, and cottage-style accessories.

Waldo County Craft Co-op (207-548-6686; Rte. 1, Searsport). Open late May–Mid-Oct, this co-op sells handmade quilts, sweaters, pottery, weaving, woodworking, and more, made by local craftspeople.

HOUSEWARES

Sleepy Hollow Rag Rugs (207-789-5987; Rte. 173 (one mile from Rte. 1), Lincolnville Beach). Watch the weaving here, when the store is open by chance, or call first.

The Store (207-594-9246; 435 Main St., Rockland). Set in the heart of Rockland's old fashioned Main St., this is an upscale kitchen store where you can find whatever essential you need.

Well-Tempered Kitchen (207-563-5762; 122 Atlantic Highway Rte. 1, Waldoboro). You never know when you'll find those perfect custard dishes or that sweet little sauce pot.

NAUTICAL EQUIPMENT

Bohndell Sails (207-236-3549; 198 Commercial St., Rockport). They've been making sails since 1870.

Hamilton Marine (207-548-6302 or 800-639-2715; East Main St., Searsport). Everything you need for your sailboat or motor boat. They ship replacement parts and hardware daily via UPS.

OUTDOOR & SPORTING GOODS

Maine Sport (207-236-7120 or 888-236-8797; www.mainesport.com; Rte. 1 Rockport). Mountain bikes, sea kayaks, canoes, camping gear, backpacks, and fishing equipment for sale and rent. Factory outlet for Moss tents.

POTTERY

Some of the pots at Fireside Pottery basking in the sun.

Herb Swanson

Fireside Pottery (207-273-3767; 1478 Camden Rd., (Rte. 90), Warren). Porcelain with rich blue and green glazes that evoke the water.

St. George Pottery (207-372-6464; Rte. 131, St. George). Nationally recognized Maine potters on exhibit with works for sale.

WOODWORKING TOOLS

Lie-Nielsen Toolworks (800-327-2520; www.lie-nielsen.com; toolwrks@lie-nielsen.com; P.O. Box 9, Rte. 1, Warren 04864). Beautiful woodworking tools made of Manganese Bronze, with blades of high carbon steel; also planes and saws, of a quality not surpassed.

CHAPTER EIGHT
Studios Among the Granite Hills
THE BLUE HILL PENINSULA & DEER ISLE

Herb Swanson

Stonington Harbor.

The gently rolling, boulder-strewn land of this beautiful peninsula and island seems to exert its charm on artists, writers, and craftspeople, with the Haystack Mountain School of Crafts in the southern end only one organized focus among dozens of private studios. As you drive the twisting narrow roads, a small sign will proclaim another potter's home; up a steep driveway you find a studio full of beautiful pottery, with instructions written on a counter if you want to write a check and take some home with you. The potters are elsewhere. Newspaper for wrapping the lovely cups is under the counter. You are on your honor, and your honor is pleased to be trusted.

Castine, at the end of Rte. 175 south of Rte. 1, retains the dignity of streets lined by old elms, having fought off Dutch elm disease with meticulous and unrelenting attention. The walking tour of its old houses has authentic shade as well as original structures. A tour of the Maine Maritime Academy's ship, *State of Maine* can be had whenever the ship is not undergoing maintenance or training new sailors.

Back up Rte. 175, and then south again down the long finger of the peninsula you can reach **Stonington** in an hour and a half and stroll through a gallery

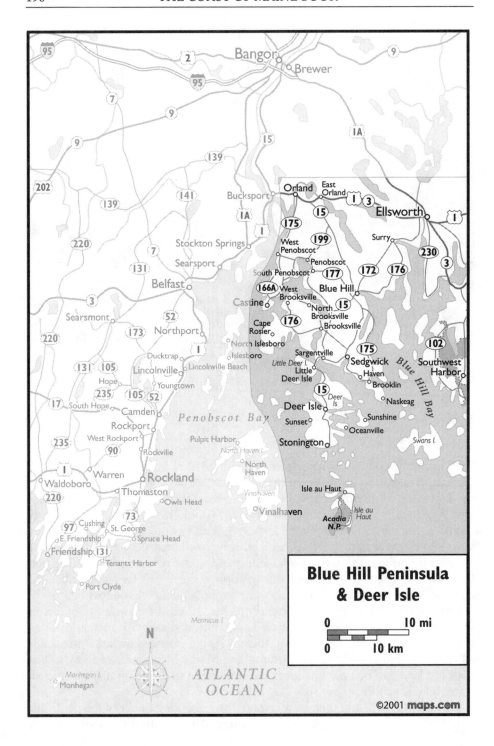

Blue Hill Peninsula & Deer Isle

0   10 mi

0   10 km

©2001 maps.com

showing artists already well known in New York. If the expensive art doesn't interest you, the Granite Museum has a working model of a granite quarry, with little trains hauling stone. The ferry can take you to **Isle au Haut**, where you can spend the night at a lighthouse—as long as you have a reservation.

Blue Hill, with its coop and restaurants and music makes a center for all the winding roads that at the beginning of August are lined with acres of blueberries. To the east is **Cape Rosier,** where Helen and Scott Nearing homesteaded and elaborated a modern version of traditional Yankee self-reliance. To the west is **Brooklin**, where E.B.White summered and where wooden boat building is carried on by his descendents with his perfectionism. To the north are the Blue Hill fairgrounds, busy on Labor Day weekend but not, alas, recently known to display pigs with spider web banners over their stalls, as happened in *Charlotte's Web.* Maybe next year.

BLUE HILL & DEER ISLE AREA: LODGING

Blue Hill

THE BLUE HILL INN
Innkeepers: Mary and Don Hartley.
207-374-2844 or 800-826-7415.
www.bluehillinn.com.
mary@bluehillinn.com.
P.O. Box 403, Union St. (Rte. 177), Blue Hill 04614.
Open: Mid-May–late Oct., with 1 suite available year-round.
Price: Expensive to Very Expensive.
Credit Cards: AE, MC, V.
Handicap Access: Limited.

This place is no newcomer to innkeeping; the lovely old clapboard and brick building framed by stately elms and handsome gardens has been an inn since 1840 (before that it was a private residence). It is, in fact, the oldest continuously operating inn in the state and, like much of the rest of Blue Hill, is listed on the National Register of Historic Places. There are 11 guest rooms, all furnished with period antiques, many with fireplaces. Every one has a private bath; two have ceramic tile floors. The newest suite features a king-sized four-poster bed, cathedral ceiling, raised hearth fireplace, large bathroom, and full kitchen. Full breakfast is included and served year round. Four gourmet wine dinners are served a year.

Brooksville

OAKLAND HOUSE SEASIDE RESORT
Innkeepers: Jim and Sally Littlefield.
800-359-7352.
www.oaklandhouse.com.
jim@oaklandhouse.com.

On 50 acres alongside of Eggemoggin Reach, this enclave of cabins and inns is a world of its own, begun in 1889. The accommodations now include 15 cabins (each in a little stand of trees and most with stone fireplaces), as well as a former summer house, now a 10-bedroom inn reserved for adults, with its own dining room for breakfast.

435 Herrick Rd., Herrick's
 Landing, Brooksville 04617.
Open: May–Oct., with 2
 year-round cottages.
Price: Expensive to Very
 Expensive.
Credit Cards: MC, V.
Handicap Access: No.

Castine

CASTINE INN
Innkeepers: Tom and Amy
 Gutow.
207-326-4365.
www.castineinn.com
relax@castineinn.com.
P.O. Box 41, Main St.,
 Castine 04421.
Open: End of Apr.–end of
 Oct.
Price: Moderate to Very
 Expensive.
Credit Cards: MC, V.
Handicap Access: No.

Dinner is served in the original building, and sum-mer season rates for all accommodations include both breakfast and dinner. This is a wonderful place for families, with hiking trails and beaches, where Thursday nights bring a lobster dinner on the beach, as well as the regular meal in the hand-some dining rooms.

Bright, airy, and welcoming, the Castine Inn offers all a visitor could want by way of lodg-ings in this pretty seaside town—a fine restaurant, harbor views from many of the 20 rooms, and a per-fect location. Perched half way up the main street that ascends from the town's bustling port, the inn is a good example of the many late-Victorian struc-tures that grace this historic area. Relax after a walking tour of the historic town on the lovely front porch among the flowers and rocking chairs, out back in the gardens, in the sitting room with a wood-burning fireplace, or in the sauna. The pub is a good place to have a nightcap and maybe meet a captain from one of the many windjammers that anchor in the bay. Breakfast included; dinner additional, and even guests should make dinner reservations well in advance of a stay. No children under eight. The inn offers showers to visiting yachtsmen and women.

PENTAGOET INN
Innkeepers: Jack Burke and
 Julie VandeGraaf.
207-326-8616 or 800-845-
 1701 (outside Maine).
www.pentagoet.com.
pentagoet@pentagoet.com.
P.O. Box 4, Main St.,
 Castine 04421.
Open: May–Oct.
Price: Moderate to
 Expensive.
Credit Cards: MC, V.
Handicap Access: No.

The Pentagoet, a lovely three-story Victorian with turrets, balconies, and window boxes sur-rounding a porch with rockers, sits right down the street from the water. Its main building and an older colonial structure offer 16 rooms. Pentagoet is Old Breton for "on a hill lined with trees leading to the water," an apt description. Full breakfast is included. Afternoon refreshments are available to guests, iced tea with brownies, for instance, as well as three-speed bicycles. Dinner, which is addi-tional, is very good; reservations recommended in the high season.

Deer Isle

PILGRIM'S INN
Innkeepers: Dan and
 Michele Brown.

There are 12 wide-pine-floored guest rooms in this wonderful 18th-century National Register house, located about 15 minutes' drive from Ston-

Relaxing at the Pilgrim's Inn on Deer Isle.

Herb Swanson

207-348-6615 or
  888-778-7505.
www.pilgrimsinn.com.
innkeeper@pilgrimsinn.
  com.
P.O. Box 69, Main St., Deer
  Isle 04627.
Open: Mid-May–mid-Oct.;
  cottages open all year.
Price: Very Expensive.
Credit Cards: AE, MC, V.

ington. All rooms have private baths, and all are furnished with antiques and Laura Ashley fabrics. There are two parlors where you can read in front of the fire until hors d'oeurves are served as people gather for dinner. "Ginny's," a cozy vintage house adjacent to the inn, has two separate units; each includes a bedroom with queen bed, living room (with a pull-out sofa), cable TV, gas stove, kitchenette, and dining area. "Rugosa Rose," a second two-story guest cottage with bedroom, living room, dining area, kitchenette, gas stove, opened in 2002.

The food is country-inn fare served by well-trained waiters in white jackets. Breakfast may include homemade granola, cheddar omelets, or pancakes. For dinner, first courses have included risotto with nasturtiums, pesto-grilled shrimp, and gazpacho with Maine lobster and fresh chervil. Recent entrées were grilled Stonington scallops with balsamic butter sauce or Deer Isle–raised free-range chickens, cooked with black olives and tomatoes. There is always a vegetarian selection. Breakfast and dinner included in MAP rates, but B&B rates are offered. Children 10 and up are welcome in the main inn, younger children are welcome in the housekeeping units.

Isle au Haut

THE KEEPER'S HOUSE
Innkeepers: Jeff and Judi
  Burke.
207-367-2261.
www.keepershouse.com.
P.O. Box 26, Lighthouse
  Point, Isle au Haut 04645.
Open: May 15–Oct.

Isle au Haut is the best-kept secret of Acadia National Park, and the Keeper's House is a wonderful place to enjoy this national treasure. Guests ride the mail boat from Stonington—the innkeepers ask you to either amuse yourself all day on the island shore and trails or take the later boat. There are five guest rooms, three shared baths, and they

Price: Very Expensive.
Credit Cards: None, but personal and travelers' checks accepted.

are furnished with antiques and comfortable beds with down comforters for cool island evenings. There is no electricity—which makes the candle-lit Keeper's House romantic and cozy. You eat and relax after dinner in candlelight or by the kerosene lantern in the common room. The room rate includes tea, an exquisite dinner cooked by Ms. Burke (bring your own wine and don't expect red meat), as well as a hearty breakfast and a bag lunch to take with you as you explore the island. Be sure to make your reservations early. If you're lucky enough to book your stay in late August, look for the wild blueberries and raspberries that grow in abundance. More than half the island is a national park and full of trails and untouched coastline to explore. Two-night minimum on all weekends. No pets. No smoking.

Sunset

The view from the deck at the Goose Cove Lodge in Sunset.

Herb Swanson

GOOSE COVE LODGE
Innkeepers: Joanne and Dom Parisi.
207-348-2508 or 800-728-1963.
www.goosecovelodge.com.
goosecove@goosecove lodge.com.
P.O. Box 40, Deer Isle, Sunset 04683.
Open: May 15–late Oct.
Price: Expensive to Very Expensive.
Credit Cards: AE, D, MC, V.

On a secluded cove off Penobscot Bay, this is a place for rest, relaxation, and supreme dinners. There are nine private cottages, all off by themselves and all with ocean views. Four attached cottages are near the lodge. The lodge and annex have eight suites, all with private bath. All are simply furnished and complement the surrounding beauty. Dinner may start with crab cakes or warm asparagus salad with crème fraîche, and continue with bouillabaisse of Stonington lobster and mussels with saffron rouille or herb-roasted Island Acres chicken. Golf, tennis, massage, and a small fleet of kayaks are close at hand. The innkeepers also have a huge telescope and an extensive knowledge of the night sky. Activities for children include separate dining with a child-friendly menu and projects that last till 8:30pm, as well as nature hikes at no extra charge, and sailing lessons for a fee.

BLUE HILL & DEER ISLE AREA: DINING

Blue Hill

ARBORVINE RESTAURANT
207-374-2119.
www.arborvine.com.
Main St., Tenney Hill, Blue Hill 04614.
Open: All year; call for winter schedule.
Price: Expensive to Very Expensive.
Cuisine: American eclectic.
Credit Cards: MC, V.
Reservations: Recommended.
Handicap Access: No

John and Beth Hikade have run restaurants for years, and their Firepond, sold and eventually closed, won them a great reputation. Arborvine has been open since July 2000, and their work here has been another success. The various dining rooms in the old Cape Cod–style farm house (with wide-pine floors from the old stands of century pine) are all well appointed, and the gardens are lovely in the summer. You can be sure the garden greens are local in season, and the oysters are from Damariscotta. Medallions of pork with pears and Calvados, or crispy roast duckling are delicious choices, and the fish is chosen according to season and sauced to suit its flavors. Plum Napoleon with orange sabayon and crème caramel are on the dessert menu. The local residents know this place and keep it busy, so a traveler can be assured of good food and service.

JEAN-PAUL'S BISTRO
207-374-5852.
Maine St., Blue Hill 04614.
Open: Summer only.
Price: Moderate.
Cuisine: French.
Serving: L, afternoon tea.
Credit Cards: D, MC, V.
Reservations: Not necessary.
Special Features: Seating on the lawn under umbrellas.

Lunch only, but when you want to leap out of standard American cuisine and savor a traditional *croque monsieur*, there is no better place. This is low-key French, elegant without ostentation. And the pastry draws in an afternoon tea business—sit on the lawn, sip, stare out over the distant water, and philosophize about how wonderful life is.

Brooksville

OAKLAND HOUSE SEASIDE RESORT
800-359-7352.

The four dining rooms of this 100-year-old inn are each dedicated to families with children or to adults only, depending on the residents in the

435 Herrick Rd., Herricks
   Landing Brooksville
   04617.
Open: May–Oct.
Price: Expensive to Very
   Expensive.
Cuisine: American eclectic.
Serving: D.
Credit Cards: None, cash or
   check only.
Reservations:
   Recommended.
Handicap Access: No.

Castine

CASTINE INN
207-326-4365.
P.O. Box 41, Main St.,
   Castine 04421.
Open: May–late Dec.;
   closed Tues.
Price: Expensive.
Cuisine: New England
   regional.
Serving: B, D.
Credit Cards: MC, V.
Reservations:
   Recommended.
Handicap Access: Limited.
Special Features: Porch
   dining in good weather.

DENNETT'S WHARF
207-326-9045.
1 Sea St., Castine 04421.
Open: May–early Oct.
Price: Moderate.
Cuisine: American.
Serving: L, D.
Credit Cards: D, MC, V.
Handicap Access: Yes.

PENTAGOET INN
207-326-8616 or
   800-845-1701.

surrounding cottages. An appetizer might be black sesame-seared sushi-grade tuna or scallops with lobster cream sauce, and entrées have included a double lamp chop with a demi-glace made with raspberries, cherries, and currants, or swordfish with Mediterranean salsa. Prime rib is served every Saturday night. Bourbon pecan pie and strawberry shortcake are sometimes on the list for dessert. This is a handsome inn with understated and authentic elegance.

The restaurant at the Castine Inn is one of the best in Maine. The chef, Tom Gutow, has worked at Park Avenue Bistro, Bouley, and Verbena's in New York. The menu varies with the seasons, depending upon the harvest of local farmers and fishermen. Appetizers range from parsley ravioli filled with wild mushrooms to grilled foie gras or oysters on the half shell. Entrées include lobster with vanilla butter and mango mayonnaise. The dessert list is solid, too: raspberry crème brûlée, Aunt Becky's blueberry kuchen, and assorted sorbets. Service is friendly and efficient. Smoking is permitted only in the pub, where appetizers such as mussel bisque are served. Weather permitting, seating is available on the porch overlooking the handsome gardens.

Dennet's is Castine's waterfront restaurant, serving American surf and turf in a wharf building with boats at the dock. Dollar bills have been stuck to the high, barn-like ceilings, and the waiter says it costs a buck to find out how. The food is as good as the company and about as refined: seafood lasagna, grilled marinated swordfish steak. If standard fare and lots of microbrews are what you are after, this is it. It can get particularly racy when sailors stop by during the regatta season. Great homemade desserts and decent coffee, as well as a kids' menu.

The Passport Pub is in a small parlor hung from floor to ceiling with the owner's collection of

www.pentagoet.com.
pentagoet@ hypernet.com.
P.O. Box 4, Main St.,
  Castine 04421.
Open: May–Oct.
Price: Moderate to
  Expensive.
Cuisine: American.
Serving: D.
Credit Cards: MC, V.
Handicap Access: No.

photographs of historic figures, dominated by a portrait of Lenin and including the famous and the infamous: Castro, Mobutu, Eva Perone, Ghandi, Hiro Hito, Peter Sellers, and Angus King. "It fits well in a town. . . rich with political upheaval and foreign intrigue," Mr. Burke writes in his website: Castine must adore being understood so imaginatively. The food is outstanding. I had incredible mussels marinara, and the meal began with some of the best olives I've ever had, as well as good foccacia. The entrées included lobster pie and Spanish seafood stew, savory and good. I ended with a chocolate tart "on the house," but no guarantees that will always happen, and no, they did not know I was writing this. The service was excellent.

East Orland

DUFFY'S
207-469-1100.
Rte. 1, East Orland 04431.
Open: All year except. Mon.
Price: Inexpensive.
Cuisine: American.
Serving: B, L, D.
Handicap Access: Yes.

Home-style food, muffins the size of softballs, and a clientele that looks like a reunion of Norman Rockwell models. The silverware doesn't match, and the chairs wobble. The motto on the menu says succinctly: "We here at Duffy's are a native-orientated restaurant. We aren't fussy and we're certainly not fancy. If you are, Ellsworth is 12 miles east and Bucksport is 7 miles west." The latest addition to the menu is the peanut-butter pie with chocolate graham cracker crust.

Little Deer Isle

**EATON'S LOBSTER
  POOL**
207-348-2383.
Blastow's Cove, Little Deer
  Isle 04650.
Open: Mother's Day–Oct.
Price: Moderate.
Cuisine: Lobster.
Serving: D.

Eaton's sits on one of those incredibly perfect Maine coves with small islands silhouetted against the horizon at dusk. Indoors or out, bibbed families lay waste to some of Maine's finest: steamed clams, lobster, chowder, French fries, coleslaw, blueberry pie, and coolers of beer (it's BYOB). When we were kids, Eaton's was exactly the same.

Stonington

**THE FISHERMAN'S
  FRIEND**
207-367-2442.
School St., Stonington
  04681.

There's no other place in the world like Stonington, and the Fisherman's Friend is a good place to take it all in. Besides, the food is great, and the fish is certified fresh. Get there early on Friday for

Open: Daily, all year.
Price: Inexpensive.
Cuisine: Seafood, pie.
Serving: L, D.
Credit Cards: D, DC, MC, V.

the all-day fish fry, just $6.50. Don't forget to get a slice of pie; the pie list is longer than the menu. It and all the other desserts are homemade.

And don't expect beer or wine, though you can bring your own with you if you would like. Stonington has been dry since the 1940s, when it had 20 bars and enough quarry men to pack them every night. "The women put a stop to that," our waitress told us, "but we're trying to change that now."

BLUE HILL & DEER ISLE AREA: FOOD PURVEYORS

BAKERIES & CAFES

Bah's Bakehouse (207-326-9510; Water St. behind the Co-op, Castine). Everybody likes to linger over breakfast at this bakery/deli, and then stay on for lunch. Apple-ginger scones, great-looking bread, sweet rolls, and when we were there, tomato-cognac bisque.

Blue Hill Food Coop (207-374-2165; Blue Hill). A small café in the back offers peach-ginger scones and blueberry corn muffins. The store is full of local produce and health food.

Moveable Feasts Delicatessen (207-374-2441; Tenney Hill, Blue Hill). You can get soup, sandwiches, salads, and sweets here Mon.–Fri. 10–3.

Pain de Famille (207-374-3839; Main St., Blue Hill). Baguettes, five-grain bread, levains; cookies and brownies, biscotti, some vegan selections.

Penobscot Bay Provisions (207-367-5177; across from the post office, Main St., Stonington). Patty's baguettes and multigrain bread sell out almost every day; scones and delicious baked goods, and an extensive selection of cheeses that makes some city folk envious.

FARM MARKETS

Blue Hill Farmers' Market (the Beano Building at the Blue Hill Fairgrounds). Sat. mornings May–Oct.

Deer Isle Farmers' Market (Deer Isle Congregational Church parking lot, Rte. 15). May–Oct., Fri. 10am–noon,

Hay's Farm Stand (Rte. 172, Surry Hill, Blue Hill). July–Oct., Mon.–Sat. Certified organic vegetables, strawberries, raspberries, tomatoes, corn, potatoes, and lamb. Also farm sausage, jams, and their homemade Old Goat Soap.

H.O.M.E. (207-469-7961; Rte. 1, Orland). It stands for Homeworkers Organized for More Employment and, in addition to crafts, they sell fresh vegetables in season and storage crops like potatoes and squash. Good selection of locally grown herbs, flour in bulk, grains, and dried fruit.

BLUE HILL & DEER ISLE AREA: CULTURE

Wealthy summer visitors during the early 20th century would arrive here not just for a day or two's stay. They came for months on end. The artists and musicians followed to decorate the walls of their wealthy patrons' summer homes and play concerts for them and their guests. That is why there is such a rich tradition of the arts in this part of the coast. Painters, sculptors, and photographers abound. So do small galleries showing their wares. And almost everywhere in the summer you can hear music.

GALLERIES

Main Street, Stonington, is a place to encounter art in a variety of galleries.

Herb Swanson

Blue Heron Gallery (207-348-6051; Church St., Deer Isle). A barn full of contemporary crafts, including works by faculty members of the nearby Haystack Mountain School with a focus on "functional clay." May–Sept.

Deer Isle Artists Association (second floor, Seamark Bldg., Rte. 15, Deer Isle). Revolving, two-week exhibitions of members' sculptures, paintings, photographs, and drawings. June–Aug.

Larson Fine Art (207-326-8222; corner of Rtes. 175 and 177, South Penobscot). David Larson's studio and gallery exhibits his paintings and sculpture, studies of human conflict and respite.

Leighton Gallery (207-374-5001; Parker Point Rd., Blue Hill). Opening for its 22nd year in late May, critics rave about this gallery owned by sculptor Judith Leighton. It shows her work and that of other well-known sculptors and painters.

Turtle Gallery (207-348-9977; Rte. 15, Deer Isle). Paintings, drawings, prints, sculptures, and contemporary crafts by Maine artists. Nineteen years old in 2002. Memorial Day–Sept.

Watson Gallery (207-367-2900; Main St., Stonington) Two-week shows of New England artists including Jon Imber, Art DiMambro, and Thomas Glover in summer 2001.

HISTORIC BUILDINGS AND SITES

FORT GEORGE AND FORT MADISON
Castine.
Season: Open year-round.

Castine played a major role in the military history of the region, trading hands between the colonists and British during the Revolutionary War and after. Much of that military history is told by these two forts, located at opposite ends of the Castine peninsula. The Brits built Fort George in 1779 and only gave it up to the colonists at the close of the war. Excavation has exposed remnants of the old fort, making this a great place to scramble over the ramparts.

When the British tried to reassume sovereignty over their former colonies during the War of 1812, this small community was one of their staging grounds. Fort Madison, on the other side of this small town from Fort George, was built in 1811 by the U.S. The British captured it in 1814, renamed it Fort Castine, and held the fort and the town until the close of the war one year later. This town-owned park is a good staging ground for a picnic.

THE WILSON MUSEUM
Perkins St., Castine.
Season: Late May–Sept., Tues.–Sun. 2–6.
Admission free.

This is a series of several historic houses and commercial buildings, including a working blacksmith shop, the Hearse House (with 100-year-old summer and winter hearses), and the pre-Revolutionary John Perkins House (admission is charged here). The Wilson is home to a collection of prehistoric artifacts from North and South America, Europe, and Africa that stress man's development of tools from the Paleolithic to the Bronze and Iron ages. It also has a collection of ship models, rocks and minerals, and an 1805 kitchen exhibit.

LIBRARIES

Bagaduce Music Lending Library (207-374-5454; www.hypernet.cm/music lib.html; musiclib@hypernet.com; Rte. 172, Greene's Hill, Blue Hill). A music resource with a collection of more than 700,000 items. Open year-round: Tues., Wed., and Fri. 10–3.

MUSEUMS

DEER ISLE GRANITE MUSEUM
207-367-6331.
Main Street, Stonington.

Everything makes a picture of the days when Stonington and other Maine quarry towns were supplying the big cities with granite for train sta-

Memorial Day–
Labor Day.

tions and city halls. An 8- by 15-foot working model of quarrying operations on Crotch Island has moving derricks, cutting sheds, and waiting ships. Free admission.

STATE OF MAINE
207-326-2420.
Maine Maritime Academy, Castine.
Season: mid-July–late Apr.
Free.

This is the training ship for students at nearby Maine Maritime Academy. When it is in port, you can go aboard for a free tour. Except when the ship is receiving maintenance or training new sailors, tours are on the hour, from 10am to 5pm daily (no tour at 12 noon). Call ahead.

MUSIC

KNEISEL HALL SUMMER MUSIC SCHOOL
207-374-2811.
Pleasant St., Rte. 15, Blue Hill.

Teachers and students perform chamber music concerts Friday evenings and Sunday at 4pm from early July to mid-August.

SURRY OPERA COMPANY
207-667-9551.
Surry.
Season: Call for schedule.

Walter Nowick founded this small, amateur opera company in 1984 with high aims—"to promote beautiful music and work toward peace through people-to-people experiences."

SCHOOLS

Haystack Mountain School of Crafts (207-348-2306; www.haystack-mtn.org; haystack@haystack-mt.org; P.O. Box 518, Deer Isle 04627). One of the foremost craft schools in the country, Haystack offers two- and three-week sessions for artists and crafts persons. Evening lectures by faculty and visiting artists are open to the public. Public tours are offered Wednesdays at 1:00 from June–August.

Maine Environmental Research Institute, Center for Marine Studies (207-374-2135; www.meriresearch.org; P.O. Box 1652, 55 Main St., Blue Hill 04616). This organization, also known as MERI, offers a range of educational programs and cruises for kids of all ages as well as cruises for adults and kids to tour the marine sights of Penobscot Bay. There are courses, lectures, a lending library, gallery, and a store. A visit to the Center is free, and you can put your hands on starfish, crabs, and sea anemones in the Touch Tank while you try to decide which cruise to take. Open all year, Sat. 9–1 in summer.

WoodenBoat School (207-359-4651; www.woodenboat.com; P.O. Box 78, Naskeag Point Rd., Brooklin 04616). Founded by the management at *WoodenBoat* magazine, readers and armchair seafarers come here to live out their dreams.

Each summer the school offers 700 students more than 75 courses on topics like navigation, boat building, and sailing.

SEASONAL EVENTS

Relaxing at the Blue Hill Fair, which has been held every year at summer's end for a century, and provided one setting for Charlotte's Web.

Tom Hindman

Blue Hill Fair (207-374-9976; East Blue Hill). This fair was the inspiration for E.B. White's children's classic *Charlotte's Web*. Labor Day weekend.
Blue Hill Heritage Trust (207-374-5118). Summer walks and talks like "The Geology of the Carter Nature Preserve," and "Lobster Boat Tour of Scenic Waterfront Protection."

THEATER & CINEMA

Cold Comfort Summer Theater (207-326-4311 or 469-3131; several locations throughout Castine). Comedies, dramas, and other summertime fare. Call for more information.
Movies at the Opera House (207-367-2788; Stonington). A summer schedule of movie showings, with occasional live theater productions; call for the schedule.

BLUE HILL & DEER ISLE AREA: RECREATION

BOATING

Eggemoggin Guide Service (207-359-2746; Sedgwick). Captain Pete Douvarjo says his clients caught 19 smallies (smallmouth bass over 5 pounds) in 2000, and average between 15 and 30 a day. Or angle for striped bass, when they are running. He also offers sea duck hunting. One- or two-person limit.
Granite Island Guide Service (207-348-2668; www.graniteislandguides.com; Deer Isle). Sea kayaking, instruction and guided tours with Dana and Anne Douglas.

Maine Environmental Research Institute, Center for Marine Studies (207-374-2135; www.meriresearch.org; 55 Main St., Blue Hill). A visit to the Center is free, and you can put your hands on starfish, crabs, and sea anemones in the Touch Tank while you try to decide which cruise to take, possibly one for the kids on their own to visit an island, or one for both adults and kids to tour the marine sights of Penobscot Bay. There are also courses, lectures, a lending library, gallery, and store. Open year-round, Saturdays 9–1 in summer.

Reversing Falls

Maine with its dramatic tides has several good reversing falls, favorite proving grounds for kayakers and canoeists. What makes reversing falls interesting is the water speed and direction change as the tide changes. The rapids run inland as high tide approaches, and they run out to sea as the tide ebbs. Bagaduce Falls, tumultuous enough to be reserved for experienced kayakers, can also be contemplated from a bordering hillside, and while eating lunch. **Bagaduce Lunch** (326-4729) on Rte. 176 in North Brooksville makes perfect fried haddock, which you can carry out on a tray to a picnic table under a young oak tree. Sandpipers and bald eagles soaring down the river mouth enjoy the noisy falls as much as you.

SAILING LESSONS

WoodenBoat School (207-359-4651; Bernice@woodenboat.com; Brooklin). One- and two-weeklong instructional programs, part of the boat-building school and run by *WoodenBoat* magazine. June–late Sept.

FERRIES

Frenchboro Ferry (207-624-7777, for recorded schedule, 207-244-3254 for more information; Bass Harbor). Frenchboro is on Long Island; a passenger-only ferry that runs only on Friday, the only time a visitor can go to the island and return on the same day.

Isle au Haut Ferry Service and Excursions (207-367-5193; www.isleauhaut .com; Isle au Haut Boat Company Pier, Sea Breeze Ave., Stonington). Seasonal service to Duck Harbor, Isle au Haut's section of Acadia National Park, ferry service to Isle au Haut year-round, changing schedules.

GOLF

Castine Golf Club (207-326-8844; Battle Ave., Castine). 9 holes, 2,977 yds., par 35. Cart and club rentals, pro shop, lessons.

Island Country Club (207-348-2379; Rte. 15A, Sunset). 9 holes, 3,865 yards, par 31. Pull cart and club rental, pro shop, clubhouse, lessons, clay.

HIKING & WALKING

Blue Hill, Blue Hill. A one-mile climb up a Jeep trail. The path leads through open areas and woods. Look for blueberries. (500 feet.)

NATURE PRESERVES

Crockett Cove Woods, Stonington. A 100-acre preserve managed by the Nature Conservancy, this is a good example of an eastern coastal rain forest. It is a great place to visit on a foggy summer day. Self-guided nature trail.

Holbrook Island Sanctuary (207-326-4012; Rte. 176 in West Brooksville). This state wildlife sanctuary of over 1,000 acres was the gift of Anita Harris, who died in 1885, and commanded that her home and the other island buildings be torn down, so the wildlife could flourish. Birds stop here on their migrations. Summer guided tours are offered; one during our stay was a night walk in search of owls.

TENNIS

Island Country Club (207-348-2379; Rte. 15A, Sunset). The well-maintained clay courts here are an aficionado's delight.

BLUE HILL & DEER ISLE AREA: SHOPPING

BOOKSTORES

Blue Hill Books (207-374-5632; 2 Pleasant St., Blue Hill). A healthy selection of books about Maine and New England. Books for children. Fiction for adults.

The Compass Rose (207-326-9366 or 800-698-9366; Main St., Castine). Books and antique prints.

Wayward Books (207-359-2397; Rte. 15, Sargentville). Sybil Pike runs this antiquarian bookstore, filled with used, out-of-print, and "medium-rare" volumes, open May–Dec.

CLOTHING

Water Witch (207-326-4884; Main St., Castine). Jean de Raat sells an amazing selection of hats, dresses, sundresses, and other summer weekend clothes made by local tailors and seamstresses from textiles she's gathered from around the world. Her sundresses may seem a bit pricey, but they are the kind you'll wear again and again.

COLLECTIBLES

Craftsmen display their work at fairs along the coast throughout the year.

Herb Swanson

Belcher's Country Store (207-348-9938; Reach Rd., Deer Isle). They are big on Christmas here, all year round. Antique and collectible tinware, hooked rugs, hand-blown glass, ceramics. Recently the owners opened a baby Belcher's on Water St. in Blue Hill.

Downeast Decoys (207-469-2158; Rte. 1, Orland). Antique and old decoys, as well as new ones carved by Bill Conroy. He will appraise yours, if you ask.

GIFTS & SOUVENIRS

Coastal Designs (207-359-2301; www.songbirdcollectibles.com; Rte. 172 just out of Sedgwick). Songbirds and shorebirds carved and reproduced by Bill Fewell.

Dollhouse Treasures (207-469-7832; Acadia Hwy, Rte. 1, East Orland). This store sells miniatures, dollhouses, and toy replicas. Everything's here for the doll lover, including building materials to make your own dollhouse. Know the building code in your own state.

H.O.M.E. Craft Shop (207-469-7961; Rte. 1, Bucksport). A craft lover's dream, this sprawling store is a cooperative for more than 400 Maine craftspersons—H.O.M.E. stands for "Homeworkers Organized for More Employment." For sale are quilts, toys, jewelry, weaving, pottery, and other handcrafted items, as well as homemade, home-canned goods.

HOME FURNISHINGS

Bruce W. Bulger, Custom Cabinetry and Fine Furniture (207-348-9955; Deer Isle). A beautiful curly maple bed is one of his creations.

Eastman Textiles (207-359-8583; Sargentville). Dye-printed wall hangings, decorative items.

Hand-crafted Furniture by Jeffrey Warner (207-348-2345; Stonington). Meticulous chests of drawers and other furniture.

Harbor Farm (207-348-7737 or 800-342-8003; Rte. 15 just over the causeway, Little Deer Isle). Wrought-iron lamps, European and Maine-made pottery, very cool paving stones (imported from England) for the garden, tiles, drawer pulls, velvet ribbon, and paper plates. Open Mon.–Sat., and summer Sun. afternoons.

Jim Wainright, The Chairman (207-348-2580; Deer Isle). Adirondack and other cedar lawn furniture.

Jutta Graf (207-326-0882; Brooksville). Richly colored, hand-woven cotton rugs.

North Country Textiles (207-374-2715; Main St., Blue Hill, and 207-362-4131; Rte. 175, Penobscot). Home textiles and clothing. The cloth is the thing here, woven by three area designers, and one, Ron King, knits beautiful baby sweaters.

Peninsula Weavers (207-374-2760; Greene's Hill, Blue Hill). From rag rugs to yarn. Weaving classes offered, open year-round.

River Horse Rugs (207-348-2580; weavers@riverhorserugs.net; Deer Isle). Large wool area rugs, unique colors and designs.

Rooster Brother (207-667-8675 or 800-866-0054; 18 W. Main St., next to Union River Bridge, Ellsworth). Cooking equipment and tableware, plus gourmet foods and wine.

Thomas C. Hinchcliffe (207-326-9411; West Sedgwick on Rte. 176). Antiques and reproductions of Windsor chairs using 18th-century joinery, tables made to order.

William Turner, Cabinet Maker (207-367-2749; Stonington). Original, heirloom quality furniture.

POTTERY

Marcia Kola (207-348-5681; Deer Isle). Stoneware and porcelain, cutwork and plain.

Mark Bell Pottery (207-374-5881; two miles south of Blue Hill village on Rte. 176/15). Porcelain vases in stunning rich glazes, modern and classic shapes.

Rackliffe Pottery (207-374-2297 or 888-631-3321; Rte. 172, Ellsworth Rd., Blue Hill). Younger than Rowantrees, but just as famous.

Rowantrees Pottery (207-374-5535; Union St., Blue Hill). Open for 50 years, their glazes, made from locally found minerals, are famous.

Scott Goldberg and Paul Heroux (207-326-9062; North Brooksville). Finely made stoneware with mixed glossy and matt glazing, beautiful forms.

CHAPTER NINE
Where the Mountains Meet the Sea
ELLSWORTH TO HANCOCK &
MOUNT DESERT ISLAND

Sand Beach in Acadia National Park is one of the few sand beaches east of Portland.

Courtesy: State of Maine

If only the French explorer Champlain had known what he had discovered when he first set eyes on **Mount Desert Island** and its rounded mountains almost 400 years ago. Today Mount Desert, which includes **Bar Harbor** and most of **Acadia National Park**, is the most visited place in Maine. Visitors come here to walk the famed carriage trails, built in the early part of this century as a kind of social lifeline connecting the homes of summer residents like the Rockefellers and the Pulitzers. They also drive the 20-mile Park Loop Road along Frenchman's Bay and the road to the top of Cadillac Mountain, where they watch the sun go down from Sunset Point, which has been renamed Blue Hill Overlook by park officials to help reduce overcrowding at dusk. The hike up Cadillac is usually a lovely, lonely climb because so many of the park's visi-

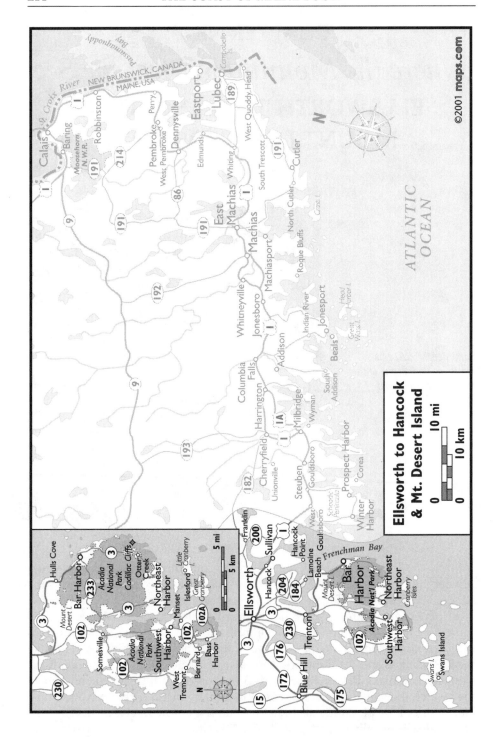

**Ellsworth to Hancock
& Mt. Desert Island**

tors prefer to travel by car. Bar Harbor, a lively, unabashedly tourist town, somehow manages to keep its dignity. Maybe the stately Victorian townhouses lining the streets, many converted to small inns and bed-and-breakfasts, keep check on the proliferating T-shirt and souvenir stores. Maybe the people who get the most out of their visit here only stop mountain climbing, biking, canoeing, and kayaking long enough to grab a bite and a good night's rest. If you like it quieter, there are the civilized charms of tea at the Jordan Pond House in Acadia and the famous Mount Desert gardens bursting in bloom at the height of summer. There also are more secluded island spots like **Northeast Harbor, Hulls Cove, Southwest Harbor** and **Bass Harbor**, and the islands—including **Little Cranberry Island**, the lovely home of the tiny village of **Isleford**. Or do what many Mainers do, and visit in the spring, fall, and winter—when the island is less crowded.

ELLSWORTH TO ACADIA: LODGING

Bar Harbor

INN AT CANOE POINT
Innkeepers: Tom and
   Nancy Cervelli.
207-288-9511.
www.innatcanoepoint.com.
info@innatcanoepoint.com
P.O. Box 216, Eden St., Bar
   Harbor 04609.
Off Rte. 3.
Open: All year.
Price: Moderate to Very
   Expensive.
Credit Cards: D, MC, V.

Closeted away in the garret room of the Inn at Canoe Point on Hull's Cove, one is apt to feel like the heroine of a Brontë novel, but without any of the tragedy. Despite its Tudor trappings and the pounding surf below, the five rooms are stylishly modern. Lots of pillows, sleek subdued fabrics, white walls, and comfortable beds. The master suite has a gas fireplace. In the parlor, the look is polished—dark wood floors, a flickering fireplace, handsome chairs. In summer, a substantial and delicious breakfast is served on the porch: homemade blueberry pancakes, quiches, and muffins. Later in the afternoon, refreshments are served. Set in a wooded area on the edge of a small cove, the inn has a commanding view of Frenchman Bay, and exploring the rocky outcropping is a favored pastime among guests. Though the feeling is remote, Bar Harbor is minutes away. No smoking. No children under 16.

THE LEDGELAWN INN
Owner: Nancy Cloud.
207-288-4596 or
   800-274-5334.
www.ledgelawninn.com.
66 Mount Desert St., Bar
   Harbor 04609.
Open: Early May–mid-Oct.

A short walk from downtown, this large, red-shingled Victorian summer cottage seems as if it were built to accommodate company and lavish parties. All the ornately decorated rooms in the inn and the Carriage House next door provide the proper retreat. Most of the beds are queen-sized, several are kings. Some have whirlpool tubs, sauna,

Price: Moderate to Very
Expensive.
Credit Cards: AE, D, MC, V.
Handicap Access: Some of
the rooms in the Carriage
House.

fireplaces, and sitting areas. All have private baths and mostly original furnishings. The sweeping staircase says come on up, and there are bowls of red apples in the common room. There's a pool out back and a bar in one corner of the living room (open 4pm to midnight). Breakfast buffet for a nominal fee. No smoking. Pets and children are welcome.

**MIRA MONTE INN &
SUITES**
Owner: Marian Burns.
207-288-4263 or
800-553-5109.
www.miramonteinn.com.
Marian@miramonte.com.
69 Mount Desert St., Bar
Harbor 04609.
Open: Early May–late Oct.
Price: Moderate to
Expensive.
Credit Cards: AE, D, MC, V.
Handicap Access: Yes.

A winner of Maine's innkeeper of the year award, Marian Burns has restored this gracious 1865 mansion to its former glory and filled it to the rafters with antiques. There are 13 spacious and elegant rooms, all with private baths, air-conditioning, televisions, and telephones. Nine of the rooms have fireplaces. Two additional suites have double whirlpool baths, queen canopy beds, fireplaces, bay windows with window seats, and cooking units. These suites can be rented for the week during the winter. The grounds are beautifully kept, and the library is a good place to relax after a day scouring the island for fun. Full breakfast is included.

THE TIDES
Owners: Ray and Loretta
Harris.
207-288-4968.
www.barharbortides.com.
info@barharbortides.com.
119 West St., Bar Harbor
04609.
Open: All year.
Price: Very Expensive.
Credit Cards: AE, D, MC, V.
Handicap Access: No.

A fter a year of work, The Tides, a neo-colonial mansion on West Street overlooking Frenchman's Bay, is flourishing as a formal luxury inn. Loretta Harris is a collector of old silver who likes to use her collection to serve her guests, for whom she will do almost anything, for example rising at 5am to make breakfast for an early departure. The departing guests might have had the eggs with herbs or the stuffed French toast with maple sausage that was on the menu that day. The couple that arrived in a Bentley, from Boston, told her The Tides had the best service they had ever encountered in all their world travel. She has poured herself into the decoration of her house, hanging the Czechoslovakian crystal chandelier in the formal dining room, and laying the Turkish carpet in the living room, where wine is served in the afternoon. There is a two-night minimum stay in the height of the summer; young adults 18 or over are welcome. Call about winter stays that include formal dinners made in her magnificent kitchen. On my visit the lawn had been mowed into decorative green brocade.

SUNSET ON WEST
Owners: Nancy and Mel
Johnson.

L ocated in one of the fine large houses along this waterfront street, Sunset is a few doors down

207-288-4242 or
877-406-4242.
www.sunsetonwest.com.
info@sunsetonwest.com.
115 West St., Bar Harbor
04609.
Open: May–Oct.
Price: Expensive to Very
Expensive.
Credit Cards:: MC, V.
Handicap Access: No.

from The Tides and shares its great views of Frenchman's Bay. Delicious breakfasts like baked eggs with Brie or fresh watermelon with marscapone are served on the porch, which overlooks a lawn sloping toward the water. Wine and cheese are served in the early evening. Two rooms with private baths and two suites, one with its own deck above the sea and the other with a fireplace, are fine places to relax after a day hiking or hiking through Acadia National Park. This is a place to relax and enjoy life.

Hancock

LE DOMAINE
Owner: Nicole Purslow.
207-422-3395 or
800-554-8498.
www.ledomaine.com.
nicole@ledomaine.com.
HC77 Box 496, Rte. 1,
Hancock 04640.
Open: Early June–mid-Oct.
Price: Very Expensive.
Credit Cards: AE, D, MC, V.

Le Domaine is less a New England inn and more an auberge. From the small parlor with its wicker and floral settees and tiny bar to the handsome dining room dominated at one end by a huge walk-in fireplace, the inn has the look of a Provençal hideaway. The three rooms and two suites here are decorated accordingly, with good Italian reading lamps, small libraries, crisp new linens, lounge chairs, and lovely fabrics from the south of France. All rooms have private baths, and some have small balconies or terraces. Breakfast is a French-American hybrid—crisp, buttery croissants, homemade granola, yogurt, cream, fresh fruit, and honey from the inn's own hives. The inn's restaurant, with an extensive wine list and excellent cuisine, is included in the **Dining** section. MAP rates are available.

Hancock Point

**CROCKER HOUSE
COUNTRY INN**
Owners: Richard and
Elizabeth Malaby.
207-422-6806 or
877-715-6017.
www.crockerhouse.com.
crocker@acadia.net.
HC 77, Box 171, Hancock
Point 04640.
Open: All year.
Price: Moderate to
Expensive.
Credit Cards: AE, D, MC, V.
Handicap Access: No.

If you want to stay in an area that has a lot in common with older, low-key Maine summers, the Crocker House Inn will do well. After the hectic environment of Rte. 3 south from Ellsworth to Mount Desert, it feels like deliverance, especially after you drive down the calm, quiet five miles on Point Road south from Rte. 1 in Hancock. The furnishings in the 11 rooms are modest but comfortable, and the country setting is a short walk to the ocean. The restaurant downstairs serves dinner as well as breakfast if you want to stay put, and an abundant brunch on Sundays from July to Labor

Day. Four clay tennis courts nearby are another amenity. Moorings can be rented if you like to arrive by sea.

Northeast Harbor

The Asticou Inn overlooks Northeast Harbor from a hill on Mount Desert Island.

Herb Swanson

ASTICOU INN
Manager: Harper Sibley.
207-276-3344 or
  800-258-3373.
www.asticou.com.
asticou@asticou.com.
P.O. Box 337, Northeast
  Harbor 04662.
Open: Mid-May–mid-Oct.
Price: Moderate to Very
  Expensive.
Credit Cards: MC, V.
Handicap Access: Yes.

From the oceanside rooms of this classic old wooden hotel, the water of Northeast Harbor leads out to Sutton Island and the Cranberry Islands. In the foreground are six huge, old arborvitae staring down on some well-tended plots of transient annuals. A pool, a tennis court, a wide porch for breakfast and dinner, other buildings offered for rent as cottages and suites, complete the view. This old-fashioned resort also has chenille bedspreads, antiques in the parlor, and beautiful Chinoiserie paper in the dining room. MAP rates are available, as well as European plan. It seems situated at exactly the right distance away from the towns and near to two wonderful, tranquil gardens: the Asticou Terraces up the hill, and the Asticou Azalea Gardens a few steps down the hill, started by the original owner of the hotel when he bought all the plants from an elegant garden that was to be abandoned. Children are welcome.

GREY ROCK INN
Innkeepers: Janet, Karl, and
  Adam Millet.
207-276-9360.
www.greyrockinn.com.
edencrest@acadia.net.

Breakfast is served in good weather on the porch amid the stone piers, where tables with pink tablecloths sit by fancy wicker chairs. This inn, another former private mansion now earning its keep, has expansive rooms with views from a hill

Rte. 3/198, Northeast
  Harbor 04662.
Open: Mid-May–Oct.
Price: Moderate to Very
  Expensive.
Credit Cards: AE, MC, V.
Handicap Access: No.

above the village of Northeast Harbor. Some have fireplaces. Behind the inn are seven acres of trails, bordered by Acadia National Park; the innkeeper's sons are experienced in hiking the trails and can give you an itinerary tailored to your ambition, as well as answer all the other questions a traveler can come up with. If your ambition is to lay low, enjoy the inn's books and afternoon tea.

THE HARBOURSIDE INN
Owners: The Sweet family.
207-276-3272.
P.O. Box 178, Northeast
  Harbor 04662.
Open: Mid-June–mid-Sept.
Price: Moderate to Very
  Expensive.
Credit Cards: None;
  personal and travelers'
  checks accepted.
Handicap Access: Yes.

Accepting to one guest, this inn has a "monastic quiet" to it. The Sweet family likes it that way. The inn was built in 1888 and retains much old-time character. Rooms are furnished with 19th-century pieces and show distinctive touches, such as Wedgwood-patterned wallpaper, a Wallace Nutting bed, and Gustave Stickly rugs. Each has a private bathroom; most have working fireplaces; some have king- or queen-sized beds; some have kitchenettes; all have telephones. There are three suites with adjoining rooms to accommodate larger families. The inn is a short walk from the village, and the woods behind the inn are honeycombed with hiking trails that extend into Acadia National Park. Breakfasts are simple. No smoking.

MAISON SUISSE
Owner: White family and
  friends.
207-276-5223 or
  800-624-7668.
www.maisonsuisse.com.
maison@acadia.net.
144 Main St., P.O. Box 1090,
  Northeast Harbor 04662.
Open: May–Oct.
Price: Expensive to Very
  Expensive.
Credit Cards: MC, V.
Handicap Access: No.

This shingle-style summer cottage was built over a 100 years ago and designed by Fred Savage. The interior is full of warm, dark wood and fireplaces, with a wide, airy hall. It is right in the middle of the little town of Northeast Harbor, and set back behind gardens from the Main Street. The 10 guest rooms and suites all have baths, TV, and telephones; some have fireplaces; and all are simply furnished and comfortable. One feature of this B&B is the breakfast, to be had at the restaurant across the street anytime between 7 and 11; this (with tip) is included in the room price. Children of any age.

Southwest Harbor

CLAREMONT HOTEL
Owners: The McCue family.
800-244-5036 or
  800-244-5036.
www.theclaremonthotel.com.

This is an incredible turn-of-the-century hotel that has somehow maintained the gentle feeling and pace of days gone by, along with a clientele that knows how to slow down. Jackets are required for dinner, but not ties, and croquet is a major

info@theclaremonthotel
com.
P.O. Box 137, Southwest
Harbor 04679.
Open: Late May–late Oct.
Price: Expensive to Very
Expensive.
Credit Cards: None;
personal checks
accepted.
Handicap Access: Limited.

LINDENWOOD INN
Innkeeper: Esther
Cavagnaro.
207-244-5335 or
800-307-5335.
www.lindenwood.com.
lindenwoodinn@
acadia.net.
118 Clark Point Rd., P.O.
Box 1328, Southwest
Harbor 04679.
Open: All year.
Price: Moderate to
Expensive.
Credit Cards: AE, D, MC, V.
Handicap Access: No.

sport. More modern attractions include the huge granite wharf and float for launching sea-kayaking expeditions or going for a morning swim. The view overlooks the entrance to Somes Sound, the only natural fjord (a modest one) on the Atlantic coast. In the summer the hotel hosts Thursday-night lectures about varied subjects according to the scholars at hand: "Impressionism", for instance, or "America, the New Rome." Jazz and classical music concerts are held as well. People staying elsewhere love to have cocktails at The Boathouse. Children welcome. No smoking.

The Lindenwood has three very private cottages and a piece of the shore. The main house of the inn, located in one of Mount Desert's small, quiet island communities, was a sea captain's home at the turn of the century. The house is flooded with light, while the 16 rooms all have an off-to-themselves feel. Most have harbor views. All have private baths. Some have balconies. There is a heated pool and hot tub for guests to enjoy. There is a restaurant, and breakfast is included for guests staying in the house. No pets. No children under 12 in the inn. Younger children are welcome in suites and cottages.

Swans Island

The Swans Island Ferry leaves Bass Harbor from Mount Desert Island.

Herb Swanson

JEANNIE'S PLACE B&B
Innkeeper: Jeannie Joyce.
207-526-4116.
JRMJoyce@juno.com.
P.O. Box 125, Swans Island
   04685.
35-minute ferry ride from
   Bass Harbor.
Open: All year.
Price: Inexpensive.
Credit Cards: None;
   personal and travelers'
   check accepted.
Handicap Access: No.

T his simple gabled home on Swans Island has three guest rooms that share a single bath—all with double beds. Two rooms overlook Burnt Coat Harbor. The look is plain, homey, and clean, and everyone is treated as part of the family. Your plan needs to include a car ticket for the ferry over, since the B&B is far from the dock and there are no taxis. Jeannie Joyce also rents a housekeeping cottage with a kitchen. It's available for weekly visits or for the night. There's a full breakfast for those who want it that includes homemade bread and muffins, cereal, eggs, and bacon. There is just a chance you might be awakened at 4:30am by a fleet of lobster boats revving up. They also serve dinner, "if need be." No smoking. No alcohol. Children welcome.

ELLSWORTH TO ACADIA: DINING

Acadia National Park

Tea on the lawn at Jordan Pond House in Acadia National Park.

Herb Swanson

JORDAN POND HOUSE
207-276-3316.
www.jordanpond.com.
P.O. Box 24, Bar Harbor
   04605.
Park Loop Rd., Acadia
   National Park.
Closed: Late Oct.–May.

W ith an outdoor patio and a many-windowed dining room, the restaurant makes the most of its location on Jordan Pond. Tea, a repast of meltingly good popovers and raspberry preserves, is served at long tables on the lawn; lunch and dinner can be had on the patio or indoors. So what if the service can be a bit relaxed? Why would you want

Price: Moderate.
Cuisine: American.
Serving: L, D, afternoon tea.
Credit Cards: AE, D, MC, V.
Reservations:
  Recommended.
Handicap Access: Yes.
Special Features: Tea and
  popovers on the lawn.

Bar Harbor

GEORGE'S
207-288-4505.
www.georgesbarharbor.
  com.
fishers@loa.com.
7 Stephens Ln., Bar Harbor
  04609.
Price: Expensive.
Cuisine: Mediterranean
  with ethnic influences.
Serving: D.
Credit Cards: AE, D, MC, V.
Reservations: Suggested.

HAVANA
207-288-2822.
www.havanamaine.com.
info@havanamaine.com.
318 Main St., Bar Harbor
  04609.
Open: Daily in summer, off-
  season Wed.–Sun.
Price: Expensive to Very
  Expensive.
Credit Cards: AE, D, DC,
  MC, V.
Handicap Access: Limited.
Reservations:
  Recommended.

**MAINE STREET
  RESTAURANT**
207-288-3040.
www.mainestreetrestaurant
  .com.

to rush off anyway? Look for lobster roll, curried chicken salad, sandwiches, and quiches at lunch; steaks, chicken, and lots of seafood at dinner.

George's, an excellent restaurant, is behind the First National Bank. The interior is done in rich, soothing colors. Several dining rooms with many windows look out at the canopy of old trees—it's like sitting on the ground floor of a tree house here. With new management in 2000, the menu coaxes customers into trying something new, offering many appetizers with long 10- and 12-dollar lists: shrimp bisque, French feta over broccoli rabe, or crabmeat with artichoke aioli. Grilled swordfish with Mediterranean salsa over couscous or duck breast with rhubarb-ginger sauce are all you can ask for, until the next course, when lemon meringue tartlets vie with the delicious crème brûlée. And then perhaps an eau de vie or a single-malt scotch.

With its rich red walls and deep blue partitions, the bright interior of Havanna clues you in on the spices and rich flavors about to fly into your mouth in the Guyanese Pepper Pot Stew, for instance. Jícama and mango salad is sweet and bright, and might work to lead into coconut-stuffed shrimp or Cuban-style beef tenderloin brochettes. But maybe the shrimp entrée with jalapeños in a lime ginger and coconut sauce is even better. Try the guava mousse for dessert, with the fine coffee.

Local working folks like this place, partly because you can get it to go, partly because of the price, partly because it offers a little bit of everything. In addition to lobster, you can choose from

mainestreet@downeast
.net.
297 Main St., Bar Harbor
04609.
Open: Daily.
Price: Inexpensive to
Moderate.
Cuisine: Family.
Serving: L, D.
Credit Cards: D, MC, V.
Reservations: No.

soups, salads, burgers, vegetarian dishes, as well as the usual choice of side orders, all served in a location that has a comfortable feeling recognizable everywhere.

THE OPERA HOUSE
207-288-3509.
27 Cottage St., Bar Harbor
04609.
Open: May–Oct., Mon.–Fri.
8–11am; internet services
till 9pm every day.
Price: Inexpensive.
Cuisine: American.
Serving: B.
Credit Cards: AE, D, MC, V.
Handicap Access: Limited.

Where else can you listen to opera and eat eggs Benedict or a western omelet that tastes better than any you've ever had, while working or playing on the internet? Only here, where Bruce and April Blair Carlson have reinvented their business at the Opera House. They still have a decor filled with opera memorabilia, the opera music still plays, occasionally a customer will sing, and the piano will be played. But after years of struggling to support the 36-member staff of a full-time restaurant, they now employ four people and have relaxed lives. You take a cinnamon roll and coffee from the central table, write it down on the pad on the table, order whatever you'd like cooked from a waitress, take your list to the cashier and pay up. "Customers love it," April says. There are 16 computers in the back you can work on until 9pm; you can get a beverage but no food after 11am.

**THRUMCAP, CAFÉ AND
WINE BAR**
207-288-3884.
www.thrumcap.com.
123 Cottage St., Bar Harbor
04609.
Open: May–mid-Mar.,
Mon.–Sat.
Price: Expensive.
Cuisine: Contemporary
American, international
influences.
Serving: D.
Credit Cards: MC, V.
Reservations:
Recommended.

A glassed-in wine room in the middle of restaurant, Edwardian period decor, and oriental carpets give the place a big-city look, though the owner, Thomas Marinke, wants to make his new place (in the same spot as his old place, The Porcupine Grill) more casual and friendlier. The lower-priced smaller dishes are the most obvious friendly change. Six dollars for a salad, nine dollars for a house-made pâté or small dish of seafood stew, Italian-style, in tomato broth, and fourteen dollars for grilled salmon with a blue corn crepe and roasted red peppers or a small filet mignon with maytag blue cheese and cabernet-raspberry syrup. You could pair each dish with a wine from the 20 selections offered by the glass, eat like royalty, and feel good about it all. Then leave without feeling overfed, as is so common in almost every restaurant, fine to foul, where portions are sized for fully employed lumberjacks. This is an innovation that deserves success.

Hancock

LE DOMAINE
207-422-3395 or
  800-554-8498.
HC Box 496, Rte 1.,
  Hancock 04640.
Closed: Late Oct.–early
  June.
Price: Expensive.
Cuisine: French.
Serving: D.
Credit Cards: AE, D, MC, V.
Reservations: Suggested.

Here is excellent French country cooking and an encyclopedic wine list (all French with many obscure regional labels) right in the heart of Down East. Everything that comes out of the kitchen is wonderful—dense rich chicken liver pâté (available by mail order), garlicky escargots, rabbit with prunes, quail roasted with garlic and juniper berries. Vegetables (baby string beans and carrots) are from the garden, as are the salad greens. An elegant woman at the next table spent a voluptuous half hour devouring her free-range chicken, cleaning every bone. Desserts include Chestnut Coupe (a vanilla ice cream and chestnut parfait), which was so seductively delicious I was also unable to resist every bite. Bread pudding, mousses, and, in midsummer, a fruit tart with vanilla custard topped by fresh raspberries are other desserts. The luxurious dining room has a Provençal decor with its rich green tablecloths and yellow underclothes. A walk-in fireplace at one end dominates and doubles as a rotisserie. Questioned, a waiter said the copper pots around the huge fireplace were polished every couple of days, as needed; enough information to show how efficiently and even obsessively the inn is run. Service was superb.

Islesford

THE ISLESFORD DOCK
207-244-7494
The Isleford Dock, Isleford
  04646.
Open: Mid-June–Labor
  Day, closed Mon.
Price: Moderate to
  Expensive.
Cuisine: American with a
  Mediterranean influence.
Serving: L, D, SB.
Credit Cards: MC, V.
Reservations:
  Recommended.

For 10 years Dan and Cynthia Lief have run a restaurant on Little Cranberry Island, or Islesford. Don't let the dual names confuse you. You can get there on a ferry from Northeast Harbor or from Southwest Harbor, and see some of the bald hills of Mount Desert that Champlain saw when he pronounced its name. Or eat here as part of the dinner cruise run by the *Sea Princess*, a boat out of Northeast Harbor. Or you could stay on the island, at the B&B (Braided Rugs Inn) if you had reservations. The restaurant alone is worth a trip, and with the quiet island to explore, and a Historical Museum, it could be a lovely day. Food includes kids' favorites like hamburgers and pasta dishes;

On Fridays grown-ups can enjoy Lobster Fisherman's Pie—all the meat in a 1-^{1}/$_4$ lb. lobster with portobello mushrooms and wine sauce. Or try crab cakes or roast chicken from Sunset Acres, an organic farm; everything is made with fresh, organic produce, much of it grown on the island or in Hancock County. The fish and lobsters are local fishermen's catch.

Manset

XYZ RESTAURANT
207-244-5221.
80 Shore Rd., Manset
04656.
Opposite Manset Town
Dock.
Open: Daily, May–Oct.; call
for other hours.
Price: Moderate to
Expensive.
Cuisine: Authentic Regional
Mexican.
Serving: D.
Credit Cards: D, MC, V.
Handicap Access: Yes.
Reservations:
Recommended.

XYZ serves some of the best Mexican food any-where, with a changing menu created from the freshest local ingredients and the most diverse array of chilies. They make an awesome tatemado, a dish from the Colina region: pork loin baked in a sauce of guajillo and ancho chiles, shredded and served with marinated red onions, white rice, and black beans. Be sure to finish with the XYZ pie, cof-fee ice cream in a chocolate cookie crust, with Kahlúa sauce. And wash it all down with their knock-out margaritas. As our waitress said, "You gotta do what you gotta do."

Otter Creek

THE BURNING TREE
207-288-9331.
Rte. 3, Otter Creek
04665.
Open: June–Columbus
Day, closed Tues. till
Sept., then closed Mon.
& Tues.
Price: Moderate.
Cuisine: American with
Caribbean accents.
Serving: D.
Credit Cards: D, MC, V.
Handicap Access: Partial.
Reservations:
Recommended.

The details give away a passion for excellence before you open the sliding front door by the lush tuberose begonias. Gardening is all about the joy of working, and it's someone's passion here. The place was packed on a Monday night at the height of the summer. To me, many of the aging, handsome patrons had the look of actors familiar from late-night movies. Whoever they were, we were all soon absorbed by the real star, the food. Gray sole in a mustard lemon cream sauce with curly endive from the garden out back, or a stack of roasted vegetables on spicy peanut noodles, or gorgeous plates of cioppino, a rich seafood stew with rounds of French bread slathered with saffron aioli—we were all as happy as movie stars ought to be.

Southwest Harbor

PREBLE GRILLE
207-244-3034.
14 Clark Point Rd.,
   Southwest Harbor 04679.
Closed: Sun. & Mon. in the
   off season.
Price: Moderate to
   Expensive.
Cuisine: Mediterranean,
   with American regional
   touches.
Serving: D, SB.
Handicap Access: No.
Reservations: Suggested.

The place to eat in Southwest Harbor, this small, on-the-street spot offers famed crab cakes. Grilled polenta, baked asiago cheese, puttanesca— and a grilled chicken with raspberry chipotle sauce is also served, as well as grilled pork chops glazed with applejack maple syrup and apple chutney. There is a full bar.

SEAWEED CAFE
207-244-0572
146 Seawall Rd. (on way to
   Manset), Southwest
   Harbor 04679.
Open: Most of the year,
   closed Mon. Call for
   winter hours.
Price: Moderate to
   Expensive.
Cuisine: Asian-style dishes
   and Maine seafood.
Credit Cards: MC, V.
Handicap Access: No.
Reservations:
   Recommended.

Was it the small tower of water-rounded stones outside the window, recalling the stone lantern at Asticou Azalea Garden, which had me raking patterns in the smooth mashed potatoes as if they were a Japanese sand garden? It could have been the nigiri sushi I started with, and the wonderful, crunchy seaweed salad. But I forgot everything as I savored the pan-blackened swordfish with citrus buerre blanc, on sesame-sautéed green and new onions. Seared duck breast with crème de cassis could steal all your attention as well. The fresh blueberry and raspberry tart is splendid, and the lemon Shaker pie was full of rich curd and pieces of lemon—tart, sweet, and soul satisfying. The menu here responds to the seasons, offering the best food available. You can bring your own bottle of wine. Sawyer's in Southwest Harbor gives a 10% discount on wine bought to drink at the café.

ELLSWORTH TO ACADIA: FOOD PURVEYORS

BAKERIES, TAKE-OUT DELIS & CAFES

Cottage Street Bakery and Deli (207-288-3010; 59 Cottage St., Bar Harbor). Sit down for a meal or get a sweet to go.

The Deacon Seat (207-244-9229; Clark Point Rd., Southwest Harbor). Breakfast and lunch from 6am to 3pm, daily except Sunday.

Eat-A-Pita (207-244-4344; 326 Main St., Southwest Harbor). Overstuffed pita sandwiches from BLT to curried tofu. Also soups and sweets.

Epi Sub & Pizza (207-288-3507; 8 Cottage St., Bar Harbor). Homemade calzones, pizza, pasta, and other quick stuff like crabmeat rolls and salads.

Little Notch Bread and Café (207-244-3357; 340 Main St., Southwest Harbor). Sourdough bread, sticky buns, and maple apple scones; pizza, pasta, and salads.

Morning Glory Bakery (207-288-3041; 39 Rodick St., Bar Harbor). Onion-walnut-dill and other breads, orange-nut brioche, scones, and sticky buns. Cakes to order.

BREWERIES & WINERIES

Atlantic Brewing (207-288-2337 or 800-475-5417; www.atlanticbrewing.com; 15 Knox Rd., Bar Harbor). Memorial Day to Columbus day, tours daily at 2, 3, and 4; tours include tasting; then on to a tavern and gift shop.

Bar Harbor Brewing (207-288-4592; 31 Otter Creek Dr., Bar Harbor). Tours and tastings July and August, otherwise open by chance. Makes Thunder Hole Ale and Cadillac Mountain Stout, both two-time first-place winners at World Beer Championship, beating Sam Adams and Guinness.

CANDY

Ben & Bill's Chocolate Emporium (207-288-3281 or 800-806-328; 66 Main St., Bar Harbor). If you love candy, this place will fascinate you, with rich handmade chocolates, as well as taffy, marzipan, crystallized ginger, and Heavenly Hash.

FARMERS' MARKETS

Ellsworth Farmers' Market (207-667-9212; 245 Main St. next to Larry's pastry, Ellsworth). Mon. and Thurs., 2–5:30, Sat. 9:30–12:30.

Northeast Harbor Farmers' Market (Wall's Moving and Storage Parking Lot (old High School). Thurs. 9am–12 noon.

GOURMET FOOD STORES

Bar Harbor Jam Company (207-288-9685; 59 Cottage St., Bar Harbor). Wild Maine blueberry jam, relish, syrup, and jelly. Also made-in-Maine specialties and local cookbooks.

Porcupine Island Company (207-288-2965; 4 Cottage St., Bar Harbor). Pickled fiddleheads, jam, chutney, mustard; lots of made-in-Maine food.

ELLSWORTH TO ACADIA: CULTURE

Since the wealthiest people have been coming here for so long, you can be sure pleasure is always at hand; and nowadays it is on offer to any taste. Sports lovers can head to the lumberjack show on Rte. 3 in Trenton for some ax throwing, and music lovers could have heard Musica Petropolitana, a Baroque ensemble from St. Petersburg play violin, cello, flute, and harpsichord. on July 26, 2001. The Arcady Music Festival will bring other distant stars to Mount Desert, while the lumberjacks, another year, might not be from so far away.

FILM

Criterion Theatre (207-288-3441; 35 Cottage St., Bar Harbor). Seasonal, restored to its 1932 Art Deco splendor: movies, live music, and drama.

The Grand (207-667-9500; Main St., Ellsworth). Concerts, stage shows and movies: call for offerings.

Maine Coast Mall Cinemas (207-667-3251; Maine Coast Mall, Rte. 1, Ellsworth).

Reel Pizza Cinerama (207-288-3811; The Village Green, Bar Harbor). Alternative films, pizza, and beer and wine.

GARDENS

Asticou Azalea Gardens (Rte. 3 and 198, Northeast Harbor, Mount Desert Island). Beatrix Farrand's Reef Point gardens were to be abandoned when Charles Savage offered to buy them. Then owner of Asticou Inn, Mr. Savage adhered to the great tradition of Mount Desert philanthropy, using plant materials to create gardens for public enjoyment, an extravagance of color during azalea blooming season in June, and a gorgeous landscape the rest of the year, with emphasis on tranquility. A Japanese sand garden invites contemplation, and the last blossom of a late rhododendron rotates on the quiet stream, during late July. Open 7am–9pm daily.

The Black House (207-667-8671; West Main St., 0.5 mile off Rte. 1, Ellsworth). The formal gardens to the rear of this historic mansion weren't planted until 1903, about 100 years after construction of the house. Following a period of disrepair, Beatrix Farrand worked with the caretakers to reestablish the gardens, formally designed within lilac hedges with annuals and perennials; and now the garden committee keeps it beautiful with new plantings to compliment the old every year.

Thuya Gardens at Asticou Terraces (Rte. 3, Northeast Harbor on Mount Desert Island). A Dawn Redwood with soft, fern fronds for its tiny leaves flourishes by the wishing well; it was brought back from China in the 1950s. A rake artist has been at work on the red, stone dust paths, shaping a raked heart in front of the well, lines and curves everywhere. Pale astilbe at the foot of an old apple tree covered with lichen, a ring of painted Japanese fern at the base of a huge arborvitae: the garden is full of studied beauty. The steep, terraced paths were created by Joseph Henry Curtis, a Boston landscape architect who summered in Northeast Harbor from 1880 to 1928; the formal gardens were designed by Charles Savage. 7–7 daily, July to Labor Day.

The Wild Gardens of Acadia (Rte. 3, Sieur de Monts Spring entrance, Mount Desert Island). Maintained by the Bar Harbor Garden Club, whose volunteers work endless hours to sustain a large collection of native plants. Time spent here before a hike will make you knowledgeable on the trails. Open year-round.

GUIDED TOURS

Bill Sweet, a retired schoolteacher and history buff, was born and raised on Mount Desert Island. He operates the *Sweet William Tour Guide Service* (207-288-5443; 207-548-2190 in winter) in Bar Harbor. Cost for each two-and-one-half hour step-on guide service is $90 per coach. Bill will take you through Bar Harbor and Acadia. Park admission is not included with the fee. It's important to book in advance during July and August.

One of the best ways to see Bar Harbor and Acadia without having to deal with the summer traffic is on *Oli's Trolley* (207-288-9899), a one-hour or two-and-one-half hour ride. The old-fashioned red and green trolley seats 40 and travels the park loop with stops at Cadillac Mountain and Thunder Hole. The guided tour also includes Sieur de Mont Spring, Otter Cliffs, and a running historical narrative of Mount Desert Island from prehistoric times through present day. Two daily tours run from May to mid-October. The summer months are busy, and reservations are encouraged. The bus leaves from downtown Bar Harbor in front of the post office.

To view Acadia by air, *Acadia Air* (207-667-5534; www.acadiaair.com.), which operates out of Bar Harbor Airport in Trenton, offers several scenic flight tours for under $50 per person with a two-person minimum. The shorter, less-expensive flights fly over Acadia, Deer Isle, and Stonington in a Cessna 172. Longer flights go down the coast for views of Castine and Camden harbors. Acadia Air operates scenic flights on demand from mid-May to mid-October. The rest of the year tours can be arranged by appointment.

LIBRARIES

Jesup Memorial Library (207-288-4245; 34 Mount Desert St., Bar Harbor). An interesting collection of historical records of the island's past, including old hotel registers and scrapbooks, some with photos of the island before the 1947 fire. The library is open mid-June–Oct., Mon.–Sat. 1–4 and Wed. 7–9, and by appointment during the winter. Closed holidays.

MUSEUMS

THE DORR MUSEUM OF NATURAL HISTORY, COLLEGE OF THE ATLANTIC
207-288-5015.
College of the Atlantic, 105 Eden St., just north of Bar Harbor.
Season: summer hours, Mon.–Sat. 10–5.
Admission: $3.50 adults; $2.50 seniors; $1.50 teens (13–18); $1 children ages 4–12.

This museum offers an environmental perspective on Mount Desert Island, with interpretive exhibits about more than 50 species of island animals, plants, and trees. Every day at 11am, there is a free program open to all visitors; and the museum hosts weekly evening lectures on topics regarding the native populations of the island, Call for a schedule of events.

ISLESFORD HISTORICAL MUSEUM
207-244-9224.
Islesford or Little Cranberry Island, a 40-minute ferry ride from Northeast Harbor.
Season: June–Labor Day, Tues.–Sat. 10–4.

William Otis Sawtelle began to collect things of historic interest, overwhelmed his own residence with his collection, and opened a museum. I was fascinated by an exhibit that documented the lives of some early settler women, one who raised 12 children on a nearby island, teaching them to read and write as well as feeding them, and spinning, weaving, and clothing them. Others will be drawn in by the shipbuilding history, the Captains who became shipbuilders and made fortunes. The Museum is run by Acadia National Park.

JACKSON LABORATORY
207-288-6051.
www.jax.org.
600 Main St., Bar Harbor.
Season: Mid-June–Sept., Call for hours and dates.
No charge.

The Jackson Laboratory was founded in 1929, and since that time has made a name for itself in the world of mammalian genetic research. Currently the laboratory performs research on such varied human maladies as obesity, cancer, AIDS, allergies, diabetes, reproductive disorders, aging, and transplantation rejection. It also raises more than 2,500 genetically unique laboratory mice and sells them to research scientists around the world. They offer a one-hour lecture and multimedia presentation describing the lab's mission and ongoing research most Wednesdays at 3pm, but occasionally skip a week, so call to confirm.

M.D.I. BIOLOGICAL LABORATORY
207-288-3605.
www.mdibl.org.
Old Bar Harbor Rd., Rte. 3 (northwest of Bar

M.D.I. is a laboratory that conducts research on marine organisms. While most of its work is confined to animals that live in the sea, it has many implications for human health and the environment. Once a week the lab provides the public an

Harbor), Salisbury Cove.
Season: July–Aug., Wed.
only.
No charge.

opportunity to see what goes on here during a lecture, tour, and video presentation.

Fishing the rich waters downeast has been a way of life for centuries; only the boats and the equipment have changed.

State Development Office

MOUNT DESERT ISLAND HISTORICAL SOCIETY
Two locations:
207-276-9323; Sound Schoolhouse, 373 Sound Dr. (Rte. 198), Mount Desert Island; also
207-244-5043; Somesville Museum, Center of Somesville.
Season: June–Oct.;
Tues.–Sat. 10–5.
Admission: $1.00, children free.

Alternating exhibits, parts of the collection of historic tools, machines, tooth-extractors, presented each year for visitors; call for a description. The summer of 2001 was devoted to granite (at the schoolhouse), and the life of the first settlers and their descendants (at the museum).

MOUNT DESERT OCEANARIUM

207-288-5005 (Bar Harbor), 207-244-7330 (Southwest Harbor).
www.acadiainfo.com/oceanarium.
Two locations: Rte. 3, Thomas Bay, Bar Harbor; Clark Point Rd., Southwest Harbor.
Season: Both mid-May–Oct. 9–5.
Admission: $12 adults, $8.95 children.

The two museums are fun stops for any aquatic-minded tourist, particularly the younger ones. At the Maine Lobster Museum in Bar Harbor, a licensed lobster fisherman will take you aboard a real lobster boat and answer your questions about crustaceans (the organization also offers a guided walk through Thomas Bay Marsh). There is a working lobster hatchery on the grounds where you can see between 5,000 and 10,000 tiny lobsters being raised for future release in the Gulf of Maine. The Southwest Harbor Oceanarium, located right next to the Coast Guard base, has 20 tanks filled with resident Maine sea life, a touch tank, and an audio-visual exhibit where you can hear whale songs.

ABBE MUSEUM–BAR HARBOR

207-288-3519.
www.abbemuseum.org.
abbe@midmaine.com.
26 Mount Desert St., P.O. Box 286, Bar Harbor 04609.
Open year-round: Summer, 10–5 daily, till 9 p.m. Thurs–Sat.; Winter, Thurs.–Sun. 10–5.
Admission: $4.50 adults, $2 children 6–15, under 6 free. Discounts for visits to both museums.

The new Abbe Museum, open in October 2001 in Bar Harbor, has more space to show off the artifacts, while more specialized exhibits are shown at Sieur de Monts (see below). During the summer weekends, members of the Micmac, Maleseet, Passamaquoddy, and Penobscot tribes demonstrate Native American arts of basket weaving and jewelry-making, and classes are offered.

ABBE MUSEUM–SIEUR DE MONTS SPRING

207-288-2179.
www.abbemuseum.org.
abbe@midmaine.com.
Rte. 3 near Sieur de Monts Spring, Acadia National Park.
Season: May, June, Sept., Oct., 10–4; July, Aug., 9–5.
Admission: $2 adults; $1 children 6–15, under 6 free. Discounts for visits to both museums.

Set back in the quiet woods by the Wild Gardens, this impressive small museum houses a record of Maine's native inhabitants from 11,000 years ago to now. Stone tools, baskets, musical instruments, and ornaments—some as old as 5,000 years—and a canoe made from a single piece of birch bark are among the items that have been brought together from the Frenchman Bay and Mount Desert Island area. During my visit a sudden wind blew open a door leading into the back, and the Wabanaki woman in charge in the gift shop and I exchanged glances. "A ghost," she said. Dr. Robert Abbe perhaps, who had devoted his life to amassing the Museum's fine collection.

WENDELL GILLEY MUSEUM OF BIRD CARVING
207-244-7555.
www.wendellgilley
museum.org.
gilleymu@acadia.net.
P.O. Box 254, Herrick Rd.
and Main St. (Rte. 102),
Southwest Harbor 04679.
Season: Closes end of Jan.
for the winter. Call for
hours.
Admission: $3.50 adults; $1
children; free to
members.

Wendell Gilley was a plumber until he decided to turn in the wrench and devote himself to his hobby full-time. He carved birds, more than 10,000 of them. Beautiful specimens of airborne nature—wooden eagles, chickadees, ducks, owls, and tiny lyrical songbirds. His birds are in full feather and on view here.

MUSIC

Seasonal Music Events

Annual Bar Harbor Music Festival (212-222-1026; 207-288-5744 after July 1; locations throughout Bar Harbor). This series of classical, jazz, and pops concerts, with an emphasis on young and upcoming talent, celebrated its 35th year in 2001. The Festival has a series of about 13 concerts, three of which offer a buffet dinner. Admission is $15 adults; $10 seniors and students; $18 dinner and music. Season: Early July–early August. Call box office for scheduled times and events.

The Arcady Music Festival (207-288-2141; www.arcady.org; P.O. Box 750, Bar Harbor 04647). Commencing in mid-July and continuing for seven weeks, guest artists perform every Mon., Tues., and Thurs. Call for locations of performances.

Downeast Dulcimer & Harp Festival (207-288-5653; Agamont Park & Congregational Church, Bar Harbor). Song sharing, workshops, and concerts featuring these traditional American instruments. Early July.

Mount Desert Chamber Music Festival (207-276-3988; P.O. Box 862, Northeast Harbor 04662; Mount Desert Island). Tuesday concerts from mid-July–Aug. Since the late '60s the Composers String Quartet, a resident ensemble, has celebrated the works of Haydn, Schumann, Brahms, and Bartók as well as other classical and contemporary composers.

NIGHTLIFE

Carmen Verandah (207-288-2766; www.carmenverandah.com; 119 Main St., Bar Harbor). Located upstairs, this is a place to dance, with different DJ's and some live music. Open nightly in summer.

SCHOOLS

Pierre Monteux School for Conductors and Orchestra Players (207-422-3931; www.monteuxschool.org; P.O. Box 469, Hancock 04640). Named for the conductor who made his home here, this is where one goes to learn to lead in the musical sense. About 20 gifted musicians take part in this two-week summer program. Six concerts are performed at Monteux Hall, off Rte. 1, Hancock.

THEATER

Acadia Repertory Theater (207-244-7260; P.O. Box 106, Mount Desert 04660). Modern comedies and dramas every summer for more than 25 years. Performances at Masonic Hall, Rte. 102, Somesville.
Bar Harbor Theater (93 Cottage St., Bar Harbor). Professional theater with Equity actors. $18 adults, $10 children.

ELLSWORTH TO ACADIA: RECREATION

O f course the great attraction is the landscape, the mountains rising out of the water. Everywhere are features to see and appreciate, caves carved out of the granite by the devouring tides, lakes left by melting glaciers, vistas proffered by trails built by munificent residents. What a pleasure it would be to have a whole summer at hand, and explore everything on foot.

BEACHES

Sand Beach; off Park Loop Rd., near Cadillac Cliffs, Acadia National Park. Possibly more people have driven by this famed pocket beach than any beach in the country. It's on the Loop Rd. There are no facilities. There are so few parking spaces and so many people who want to stop, they sometimes have to close it off during the height of the summer; but take the free bus and you have no problem. If you look closely at the sand you can detect a green tint; this is the only sand in Maine to be composed of more than 50 percent shell fragments, part of which are smashed spiny sea urchin shells. Entrance fee to national park.

BICYCLING

Acadia Bike and Canoe and Coastal Kayaking (207-288-9605; www.acadia fun.com; abckt@acadia.net; bhbike@acadia.net; 48 Cottage St., Bar Harbor).
Acadia Outfitters (207-288-8118; 106 Cottage St., Bar Harbor). Mountain bikes.
Bar Harbor Bicycle Shop (207-288-3886; www.barharborbike.com; bhbike@acadia

Acadia National Park

One of the first National Parks, Acadia was created by the generosity of former Mount Desert residents whose imaginations began, at the turn of the 20th century, to be haunted by the vision of a Mount Desert Island spoiled by overdevelopment and lumbering. In particular, George B. Dorr devoted 43 years of his life to the creation and enlargement of the park, first forming a group that had acquired 6,000 acres of the island by 1913, all through donations from residents, including John D. Rockefeller Jr. The land was offered to the Federal Government. By 1919 President Wilson signed a law creating the park, the first east of the Mississippi, and Dorr became its first superintendent.

The present 35,000 acres are mostly found on Mount Desert Island, but there are outposts on Isle de Haut and Schoodic Peninsula, where bike trails are less crowded than on Mount Desert. Still, Mount Desert Acadia is so huge that even in mid-summer you can find yourself alone on coastal rocks, or at the end of the Wonderland Trail south of Southwest Harbor, or in the stands of old White Pine remaining after the terrible 1947 fire. Fifty-seven miles of carriage roads, designed by Rockefeller, are still reserved for foot traffic, bikes, and horse-drawn carriages (Wildwood Stables near Jordan Pond offers rides and horse rentals), and in the winter the roads are cross-country ski trails.

The roads were built with pink granite and intelligence, but with three million visitors a year, the Park officials are constrained to warn against wash-outs on trails and in the Carriage Roads. Following a period of disrepair, a huge effort has created weekly and seasonal volunteer work parties that do a splendid job in the complicated park. The Friends of Acadia, started in 1986, works with the National Park Service to repair and maintain the trails and roads. The paths' stone culverts and steps, and railings and rungs on steep ascents, are all being rehabilitated and maintained with Friends of Acadia funds and skills training.

Another one of their projects is the wonderful, free, propane-powered bus system called the Island Explorer. Its many different routes free you from your noisome car and allow you to travel from site to site, from the Sieur de Monts Abbe Museum, for instance, to the top of Cadillac Mountain, or to a trail you want to explore—without adding to the traffic or suffering from it. The buses also stop at many hotels and campgrounds, to bring you home or pick you up. It is a little frustrating to drive up Cadillac Mountain with people tailgating you, if you want to move slowly and see where you are, and drivers seem incapable of observing the 25- and 35-mph speed limits anywhere on the Park Loop Rd. It is much better to look out the window of this bus. The buses can transport up to four bicycles each. Since the bus stops at the Hancock County Airport, you could visit Mount Desert without a car, and it could be the best vacation ever.

.net; 141 Cottage St., Bar Harbor). Kids' bikes, strollers and high performance rentals, as well as bikes.

National Park Outdoor Recreation Center (297-288-0007; 1 West St. on the Pier, Bar Harbor). Good parking, and lots of bikes for rent.

Southwest Cycle (207-244-5856; Main St., Southwest Harbor).

BIRD WATCHING

Stanwood Museum and Birdsacre Sanctuary (207-667-8460; Rte. 3, Ellsworth). A 160-acre sanctuary and museum that is the former home of Cordelia Stanwood, a famed ornithologist and nature writer. In the museum there are stuffed birds, eggs, and photos any birder will love.

BOATING

CANOEING AND SEA KAYAKING

Acadia Kayak (207-288-0342; 39 Cottage St., Bar Harbor). Necky Amaruk tandem kayaks.

Acadia Outfitters (207-288-8118; 106 Cottage St., Bar Harbor). Tours, rentals.

Coastal Kayaking Tours (207-288-9605; 48 Cottage St., Bar Harbor). Canoe and kayak rentals. The store also offers sea kayaking tours for coastal waters.

Island Adventures Sea Kayaking (207-288-3886; 137 Cottage St., Bar Harbor). Maine guides, small groups.

Loon Bay Kayak (207-266-8888; at Hwy. 3 Bargain Barn Complex; Barcadia in Bar Harbor). Family tours are a specialty. Second location in Southwest Harbor.

Maine State Sea Kayak Guide Service (207-244-9500 or 877-481-9500; 254 Main St., Southwest Harbor). Small tours, emphasis on natural beauty.

National Park Canoe Rentals (207-244-5854; 1 West St., Bar Harbor). There are 30 canoes available, but reservations in July and August are suggested as all canoes are often rented by 9am. Open daily 8:30-5. Paddles, life jackets, and basic instruction provided.

CHARTERS AND RENTALS

Hinckley Yacht Charters (207-244-5008 or 800-HYC-SAIL; wwwhinckleyyacht. com; hyc@acadia.net; Southwest Harbor). Bareboat sailboat charters to qualified sailors. Thirty boats available from 32 to 50 feet. Reservations suggested.

Mansell Boat Rental (207-244-5625; www.mansellboatrentals.com; mansell@ downeast.net; Shore Rd., Manset). Day sailors and powerboats rented by the day. Sailing lessons.

Masako Queen Deep Sea Fishing Co. (207-244-5385; www.acadia.net/swhtr coc/masako; Beal's Lobster Pier, Southwest Harbor). Occasional whale sighting while fishing for bluefish, mackerel, whatever is running.

M/N Sea Hawk (207-288-2373; Bar Harbor Inn Pier). Two trips daily, deep-sea fishing.

CRUISES

Acadian Whale Adventures (207-288-9800 or 877-237-3610; www.whalesad ventures.com; Golden Anchor Pier, 55 West St., Bar Harbor).

Dive-in Theater (207-288-3483; Bar Harbor Inn pier). "Diver Ed" goes below

Summertime on Mount Desert Island offers an abundance of narrated cruises, with destinations from seals and whales to dinner on an island.

Diana Lynn Doherty

with a camera and a basket. You watch him find ocean creatures, catch them, and then examine them when he brings them back to the surface.

Frenchman Bay Nature Cruise (207-288-2386 or 800-508-1499; www.atlantis whale.com; 1 West St., Bar Harbor). Two-hour cruise to Egg Rock Light-house. Also whale watch cruises on a jet-powered catamaran.

Great Harbor Tours, Ltd (207-244-9160 or 207-460-5200; Southwest Boat in Southwest Harbor). Nature tour or dinner cruise on the *Elizabeth T*, includes a meal at the Isleford Dock restaurant or picnic on Isleford (Little Cranberry Island).

Lobster Fishing and Seal Watch Cruise (207-288-3322; www.whalesrus.com; Bar Harbor Whale Watch Company, 1 West St., Bar Harbor). Watch crew haul traps, examine sea cucumbers, starfish, urchins.

Sea Princess Cruises (207-276-5352; Town Pier, Northeast Harbor). Seals, osprey, eagles, narrated tours, dinner tour to Islesford (Little Cranberry Island).

Somes Sound Lobster Tour (207-276-5352; Town Pier, Northeast Harbor). After the lobster is hauled in, it's cooked on the boat in seawater and served to the passengers

Whale Watcher Inc. (207-288-3322 or 800-508-1499; www.atlantiswhale.com; 1 West St., Bar Harbor).

BOWLING

Eastward Bowling Lanes (207-667-9228; Eastwood Plaza, Ellsworth). 12 candlepin lanes.

CAMPING

Acadia National Park. There are two campsites in the national park. The larger of the two, Blackwoods, is located off Rte. 3, five miles south of Bar Harbor;

www.nps.gov. Call Mistix 800-365-2267 for reservations. Call well in advance. Seawall, the other camp, is on Rte. 102A, four miles south of Southwest Harbor. Seawall sites are first come first serve. Both have attractive, wooded sites, and most amenities during the season (electrical hookups excluded; showers and a camp store are within half a mile). Blackwoods is open all year. Seawall is open between Memorial Day and the end of September. Campsites are easier to come by during the off-season.

Lamoine State Park (207-667-4778; off Rte. 1 on Rte. 184, Lamoine). This is one of the best-kept secrets for campers visiting Acadia during the high season. While sites in the national park are crammed, there are usually available waterside spots in this pretty little campground with 61 sites, as well as great views of Cadillac Mountain and Mount Desert Island. There's a lovely pebble beach nearby, too.

CROQUET

Croquet. The game that makes mergers and acquisitions look like sandbox play. If you don't believe it, go watch the annual *Claremont Croquet Classic*, played during early August on the lawns of the Claremont Hotel (207-244-5036; Southwest Harbor). You're invited.

CROSS-COUNTRY SKIING

There are more than 40 miles of well-marked cross-country ski trails in Acadia National Park on Mount Desert Island.

Roy Zalesky

Acadia National Park (207-288-3338; www.nps.gov/acad; Mount Desert Island). Fifty-seven miles of well-marked carriage roads and trails. A trail map can be had from park headquarters on Rte. 233. Wilderness facility.

FAMILY FUN

Odyssey Park (207-667-5841; Bar Harbor Rd., Trenton). Bumper boats, go-carts, mini go-carts. 10am–8pm, summer season.

Pirate's Cove Adventure Golf (207-288-2133; Rte. 3 near Hulls Cove, Mount Desert Island). 36 holes of miniature golf. 9am–11pm, June–mid-Sept.

Vokes Golf (207-667-9519; Bar Harbor Rd., Rte. 3, Trenton). Driving range and miniature golf.

FERRIES

Beal and Bunker (207-244-3575; Cranberry Isles, leaves from pier at Northeast Harbor). Over 50 years at work ferrying the residents and visitors to the Cranberry Islands, Big and Little, also called Islesford. Call for schedule.

Bar Harbor Ferry (207-288-2984; www.barharborferry.com; Bar Harbor Inn Pier, Bar Harbor). Three trips to Winter Harbor on Schoodic peninsula, daily in summer.

The Cat (207-288-3395 or 888-249-7245, Bay Ferries Bar Harbor Terminal, Bar Harbor). America's fastest international car ferry goes to Yarmouth, Nova Scotia, 2-³/₄ hours.

Cranberry Cove Ferry (207-244-5882; Harbor Ave., Southwest Harbor). Daily trips to Big and Little Cranberry Islands. Call for schedule.

Maine State Ferry Service (207-244-3254; P.O. Box 114, Bass Harbor). Service to Swans Island daily, year-round.

GLIDERS

Island Soaring (207-667-7627; Hancock County-Bar Harbor Airport, Trenton). Soar over Mount Desert Island and Acadia National Park. Closed Tuesdays.

GOLF

The 18-hole Kebo Valley Club in Bar Harbor, built in 1892, has the distinction of being the oldest operating golf grounds in America. The first golf courses in Maine were built along the coast at the turn of the century, just as the game was beginning to take hold in this country.

Bar Harbor Golf Course (207-667-7505; Rtes. 3 & 204, Trenton). 18 holes, 6,667 yds., par 71. Cart and club rental, pro shop, clubhouse, lessons.

Causeway Club (207-244-7220; Fernald Point Rd., Southwest Harbor). 9 holes, 4,718 yds., par 65. Cart and club rentals, pro shop, lessons.

Kebo Valley Club (207-288-3000; Eagle Lake Rd., Bar Harbor). 18 holes, 6,102 yds., par 70. Cart and club rental, pro shop, clubhouse, lessons.

Northeast Harbor Golf Club (207-276-5335; Sargent Drive, Northeast Harbor). 18 holes, 5,430 yds., par 69. Cart and club rentals, pro shop, lessons. But in 2001 the Board of Trustees closed this course to the public in August, opening it again after Labor Day: Check first.

White Birches Golf Course (207-667-3621; www.wbirches.com; Rte 1., Ellsworth). 18 holes, 2,800 yds., par 34. Cart and club rental, pro shop, snack bar.

HEALTH CLUBS

YMCA (207-288-3511; 21 Park St., Bar Harbor). Aerobics, weights, fitness machines, Nautilus, pool, rowing machines, Nordic track, toning classes, and indoor running track. $8.00 day fee for adults.

NATURE PRESERVES

Indian Point-Blagden Preserve, Mount Desert Island. One of the few forested portions of Mount Desert Island that survived the disastrous 1947 fire, this 110-acre preserve is managed by the Nature Conservancy. Pick up a map and guide from the caretaker and explore the intertwined trails leading through spruce, fir, and cedar forests, and along the water. Seals like to sun on nearby islands.

Ship Harbor Nature Trail, Rte. 102A, Mount Desert Island. Thirteen stations describe the geology, flora, and fauna of the island along a 1.4-mile trail. This is a good, self-guided trail for the family. The trail is named for the famous 1739 shipwreck of the *Grand Design* from Ireland.

The Wild Gardens of Acadia (Rte. 3, Sieur de Monts Spring entrance, Mount Desert Island). Maintained by the Bar Harbor Garden Club, this is an exquisite collection of plants native to Mount Desert Island, and a great place to go before a hike so the plants you encounter will be identifiable.

TENNIS

Atlantic Oaks (207-288-5801; Rte. 3, Bar Harbor). Four courts. Night lights. $6 per hour.

WINDJAMMERS

Margaret Todd (207-288-4585; www.downeastwindjammer.com; Bar Harbor Inn Pier, Bar Harbor). 151 foot four-masted schooner, three trips a day, $27.50. Designed by her owner, Captain Steve Pagels.

There are no trees in the way on top of the bald mountains of Mount Desert Island.

Herb Swanson

Hiking in Acadia National Park

There are eight climbing peaks in Acadia National Park on Mount Desert Island. All of them are relatively easy. The tallest and most often climbed is Cadillac, probably because most people choose to climb Cadillac in their cars. On foot, it's less crowded, and many of the best sites come before or after you make it to the top. Below we list favorite hikes in the park. You can get trail information at the park entrance.

Cadillac Mountain, Mount Desert Island. This is a gradual climb that belies the fact that it is the highest peak on the coast. From the park loop road it is about 3.5 miles, with a 1,200-foot elevation gain. Make it a round trip, and you have a strenuous hike on a steep trail.

Dorr Mountain, Mount Desert Island. Stone steps and metal ladders, on the Ladder Trail (difficult), or less steeply, the South Ridge Trail, lead directly up this mountain passing through woods. There are some great views of Frenchman Bay and Cadillac Mountain from its ledges. Base to summit, this is a 1.5-mile walk with a 1,200-foot elevation gain.

Flying Mountain, Southeast Harbor. Short, brisk climb through pleasant woods to a plateau and outlook, with great views of Somes Sound and Cadillac. (Possible loop, descending via Valley Cove; slippery in spring.) Fernald Cove to overlook, 0.5 mile; elevation gain 200 feet. (Loop, 1.25 miles.)

Gorham Mountain, Mount Desert Island. This is a great hike for amateur geologists. Combined with a side trip to Cadillac Cliffs, you will walk among overhangs, arches, and caves. From the summit, you can see many of the park highlights, including the Beehive, Sand Beach, Great Head, Otter Cliffs, and The Bowl. If you want to continue on, a trail leads along the ridge to Champlain Mountain. This is a one-mile hike to the summit, with a 500-foot elevation gain.

Pemetic Mountain, Mount Desert Island. This is one of the best hikes on the coast and perhaps the very best on the island. It lets you warm up on a nice, easy stretch, then gets tougher as the trail gets steeper. It passes through what some call a "storybook forest" to great views of Mount Desert's hills and the nearby islands and ocean. The climb begins at Bubble Pond and continues for one mile with an elevation gain of 1,000 feet. You can make this walk into a 3.75-mile loop by following the trail down to Jordan Pond, then the carriage trail back to Bubble Pond.

Penobscot and Sargent Mountains, Mount Desert Island. This is a wonderfully varied walk with excellent views of Cadillac and the island panorama. It begins tough with a somewhat difficult ascent up Jordan Cliffs, but the rest is relatively easy. After the cliffs, follow the trail from the summit of Penobscot about 1.5 miles past a pretty lake to Sargent, the island's second highest mountain. The climb is about 1,200 feet from Jordan Pond to the top of Sargent.

ELLSWORTH TO ACADIA: SHOPPING

Shoes, paper, lumber, and seafood still comprise much of the industrial and commercial base for the state. Yet since the days the "rusticators" discovered Bar Harbor and summer resorts began to sprout up along the coast and inland, much of the state's economy has focused on catering to seasonal residents and tourists. Shops and roadside stands sell everything from paintings, artwork, and nautical gear to T-shirts, balsam sachets, blueberry pottery, and lobster magnets—everything to remind the visitor that they have been here.

ANTIQUES

Antique Wicker, E.L. Higgins (207-244-3984; Just off Rte. 102, Bernard). 1870 to 1930 wicker, and other antiques.
Southwest Harbor Antiques and Collectibles (207-266-1812; 270 Main St., Southwest Harbor). Open Memorial Day to Columbus Day.

BOOKSTORES

Port in a Storm Bookstore (207-244-4114 or 800-694-4114; www.acadia.net/port bks; 1111 Main St., Somesville). This is a wonderful local bookstore and a great place to spend an afternoon getting your bearings. Open year-round; check their schedule for talks and signings. They also have a very entertaining biennial newsletter, a good music selection, and amiable Tate, the store dog.
Sherman's Book Store (207-288-3161; 56 Main St., Bar Harbor). Books, gifts, and souvenirs. Also hiking and road maps of Acadia National Park.

CLOTHING

The Grasshopper Shop (207-667-5816; 124 Main St., Ellsworth). Unusual, interesting, and comfortable women's clothing. They also have a shop in Camden. Open mid-May–mid-Oct.
Holmes Store (207-276-3273; 114 Main St., Northeast Harbor). Wool and cashmere sweaters, foul-weather gear, Sperry topsiders for boat people.

COLLECTIBLES

Nancy Neale Typecraft (207-244-5192 or 800-927-7469; www.woodtype.com; Steamboat Wharf Rd. off Rte. 102, Bernard). The largest selection of antique wood type in the country. In addition, Ms. Neal creates what she calls "framed assemblages"—type collages—for anniversaries, birthdays, and other events. Open by chance or appointment.

GIFTS & SOUVENIRS

Island Artisans (207-288-4214; www.islandartisans.com; 99 Main St., Bar Harbor, and 207-276-4045; 119 Main St., Northeast Harbor). Beautiful things, both practical and decorative, made by Mt. Desert Island craftspeople and other Maine artisans. Pieces include a large collection of Wabanaki baskets and birchbark work.

HOME FURNISHINGS

Lunaform (207-422-0923; www.lunaform.com; Sullivan) Huge garden planters and urns in classic shapes, made of weather-defying concrete with steel reinforcement. The studio is down a narrow dirt road, with good signs.

Rooster Brother (207-667-8675 or 800-866-0054; www.roosterbrother.com; 29 Main St., next to Union River Bridge, Ellsworth). Speciality cookware and tableware, plus gourmet foods, coffees, and wine.

Susanne Grosjean's Hand-woven Rugs (207-565-2282; www.hogbay.com; 245 Hog Bay Rd., Franklin). Wool flat-weave rugs made from handspun wool, dyed with plant dyes. She grows her own madder and indigo, ancient dye plants, and weaves contemporary, abstract designs.

Swans Island Blanket (888-526-9526; www.atlanticblanket.com; Swans Island). John and Carolyn Crace and a small group of island weavers make blankets from the wool of the local sheep; they make dyes from orange shavings and cochineal shells, among other things. The blankets are hand-woven on shuttle looms, and feel as luxurious as this description would suggest. Sheep are on site, if you can visit the island (see **Ferries**) in the summer from 2 to 5, Monday–Friday. Or you can call ahead anytime, to arrange a visit. Blankets are from $315 to over $1,000.

POTTERY

Gull Rock Pottery (207-422-3990; 325 Eastside Rd., Hancock). Torj and Kurt Wray create wheel-thrown pottery decorated with birds, fish, and scenes from nature.

Hog Bay Pottery (207-565-2282; www.hogbay.com; 245 Hog Bay Rd., Franklin). Functional stoneware, with herons, wild geese, and loons inspiring designs, by Charlie Grosjean.

Islesford Pottery (207-244-5686; Islesford Dock, Islesford, Little Cranberry Island, summer only). Porcelain and stoneware, functional pottery, layered, watery and stone-like glazes, by Marion Baker.

OUTDOOR AND SPORTING GOODS

Cadillac Mountain Sports (207-667-7819; 32 High St., Ellsworth and 207-288-4532; 26 Cottage St., Bar Harbor). One of the best selections of sports footwear in the area, including more than 100 types of hiking boots. The stuff you need for rock and ice climbing and cross-country and telemark skiing. Open seven days a week throughout the year, and until 11pm during the summer in Bar Harbor, 8pm in Ellsworth.

L.L. Bean Factory Store (207-667-7753; 120 High St., Rte. 1, Ellsworth). Brighter and more airy than their Freeport bargain basement, this store often has one-of-a-kind bargains on tents, bicycles, canoes, and sleeping bags, as well as outdoor clothing. Kayaks from Old Town and Perception that are seconds (varnish or other superficial defects), with good discounts.

Only in Maine

During the Civil War one Maine paper manufacturer ran out of cotton rags from which to make his paper. As legend goes, he began importing the cotton wrapping from Egyptian mummies to use in his factory. Today, Maine entrepreneurs are equally as resourceful when making their livings, if not as ghoulish. Here is one of the area's most unusual producers of one-of-a-kind products.

Bar Harbor Weathervanes (207-667-3868 or 800-255-5025; www.barharborweather vanes.com; Rte. 3, Trenton). For centuries weathervanes in the shape of boats and animals have been used by sailors and farmers to tell which way the wind blew. This store serves that tradition with hand wrought copper, brass, or cast aluminum weathervanes in shapes from a heron to a vulture to a basset hound. You can also buy a whole cupola.

CHAPTER TEN
Blueberry Barrens and the First Sunrise
SCHOODIC & NORTH

The first naval battle of the American Revolution was fought near Machias.

Roy Zalesky

Just east of Mount Desert is the Schoodic Peninsula, the tip of which is part of Acadia National Park, a smaller, wilder version of the main portion of the park. The rest of the peninsula is characterized by an anything-goes feeling. Lobstermen rub elbows with the sons of captains of industry and movie stars. Army personnel venture about, caring for a secretive military installation on the point. Year-round residents like to tell the story of one neighbor who bought a whole fleet of little wooden sailboats and every year rounded up family and acquaintances to compete in friendly regattas.

For the majority of coastal Maine visitors, the world ends at Bar Harbor. Washington County, which extends up to the Canadian border, is thought to be poor, flat, and endless. It's not. In fact, it has a beauty all its own, stark as a blueberry barren, religious, pure. Some people love it the best. It's a great place to explore, scramble over the rocks of the rocky coast, search for rare bald eagles and puffins, or just get away from the hubbub of points south.

Everything up here is out in the open, exposed to the elements, in a landscape composed by the wind and the cold. In **Jonesport**, a hilly fishing village, weather-beaten clapboard and shingled houses huddle together as if to draw comfort from one another. There's also **Dennysville**, tucked into the countryside on the Dennys River where stately Georgian homes rise up from the rolling landscape and make this look more like the manor-strewn countryside of England than Down East.

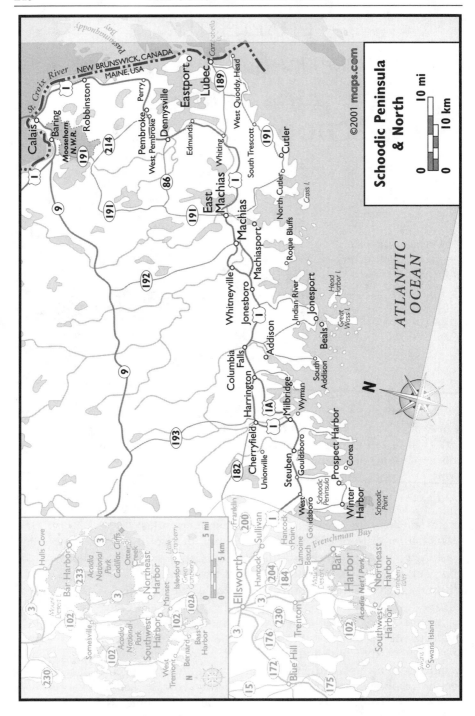

Schoodic Peninsula & North

©2001 maps.com

ATLANTIC OCEAN

Machias, which is Passamaquoddy for "bad little falls," is the most businesslike of towns. It's a get-em-in-get-em-out place where waitresses wait on busloads of people headed out of town almost as quickly as they drive in, no questions asked. Settled by the English in 1633, this was a favorite repair and refueling spot for pirates in the late 17th century. For those American history students who thought the Revolution was a unanimous undertaking by all colonists, think again. Prosperous lumbermen, who understood quite well that England was their best customer, argued for a long while about whether or not to support the revolt. They did, and a few months later nearby **Machiasport** was the site of the first naval battle of the Revolutionary War. Stalwart Mainers, you'll be glad to know, won the skirmish, captured the British armed schooner *Margaretta*, and inspired leaders in Philadelphia to establish a navy.

Lubec sits on a narrow strip of land that juts into Cobscook Bay and is a quiet town with tree-lined streets and wonderful views of the bay. Just down the road is West Quoddy Head, the easternmost point of land in the United States and site of a beautiful state park and a lighthouse that is enshrouded by fog 59 days of the year. Lubec is also the only auto route (via bridge) to Campobello Island, the summer home of President Franklin D. Roosevelt. To get there, you have to go through customs—Campobello is within Canadian territory—although the presidential landmark is operated jointly by the U.S. and Canadian governments. The island is also a bird watcher's haven, part of the famous Quoddy Loop that extends through northeastern Maine and southeastern Nova Scotia.

Eastport has been described as a city of dreamers, and there are ample examples of the city's saga of boom-and-bust. During the early 1800s, when trade between the United States and England was embargoed, Eastport gloried as a smuggler's port. It was certainly far enough Down East to escape diligent enforcers.

Fishing was, and remains today, the city's main industry. Cod, pollock, haddock, halibut, and herring once flourished in the cold offshore waters, but during the past 25 years have dwindled. During the late 1800s to mid-1900s, sardines were big business, and canneries lined the waterfront (sardines are actually small herrings). During the 1980s, the bay's sweeping tides and deep coastal waters were discovered to be ideal for farming salmon in offshore pens. Now, every year the town celebrates the domesticated Atlantic salmon with a festival in early September. To the outsider this hillside town, with very few gift shops and art galleries, has an almost deserted feel. The A&P was empty on my visit, the block that faces the incoming traveler was empty, as was the next handsome old brick place on the left. The police station is the best-looking downtown building, its white, elaborate crown molding freshly painted and the brick in good repair; so this isn't exactly the wild west.

The empty sidewalks can seem strange. A little girl selling homemade beach-glass magnets from a card table on Main Street was its friendliest face. A Bar Harbor man joked about Eastport's Empty Building Festival.

That might be exactly what you're looking for, if you are the kind of traveler who finds the crowded summer sidewalks of Ogunquit, Boothbay, and Bar Harbor a form of torture.

SCHOODIC & NORTH: LODGING

Corea

BLACK DUCK INN ON COREA HARBOR
Owners: Barry Canner and Robert Travers.
207-963-2689.
www.blackduck.com.
bduck@acadia.net.
P.O. Box 39, Crowley Point Rd., Corea 04624-0039.
Open: Apr.–mid-Nov.
Price: Moderate to Expensive.
Credit Cards: AE, D, MC, V.
Handicap Access: No.

Corea seems so far away, and what a wonderful thing that can be. As you drive east on Rte. 195, the landscape grows rugged, the tips of the spruce and tamarack are bent away from the northeast in obedience to the prevailing wind. The land itself seems to have lost its skin, but that was no doubt the fault of an ancient glacier that scraped it all away and left the rock exposed. Barry Canner and Robert Travers still manage to garden around their charming house and studio, giving a welcome look to their front door. Relaxed, pleasant rooms and lots of handsome furniture are perfect for a retreat. Local art hangs on the walls, including a landscape by lobsterman Harvey Crowley.

Breakfast minimizes butterfat without any sacrifice of flavor, with orange-glazed French toast, or cranberry and apple muffins. Two dogs and one cat are in residence, as well as a chainsaw fish sculpture by Arthur Smith of Steuben. The harbor is peaceful and beautiful, and 10 acres behind the house offer trails for walking. Under one- and over seven-year-old children are welcome.

Machias

RIVERSIDE INN & RESTAURANT
Owners: Carol and Tom Paul.
207-255-4134.
www.riversideinn-maine.com.
riversideinn@maineline.net.
P.O. Box 373, Rte. 1, East Machias 04630.
Open: All year.
Price: Moderate.
Credit Cards: AE, MC, V.

The inn is a pretty 1820 Cape-style sea captain's home overlooking the East Machias River, and is set in well-maintained gardens. There are three guest rooms, each with private bath. Two are in the main house, while the third is in a neighboring carriage house. The carriage house also offers a suite with living room, kitchen, and its own deck overlooking the river. The Pauls owned an antiques store in Newport, Rhode Island, and furnished the small but elegantly appointed main house rooms with antique furniture and old linens. The prix-fixe dinner here Friday and Saturday nights, friends tell us, is one of the best and tastiest bargains way Down East (BYOB). Breakfast included; dinner, by reservation, is additional. No children under 12.

Eastport

TODD HOUSE
Owner: Ruth McInnis.
207-853-2328.
1 Capen Ave., Todd's Head,
    Eastport 04631.
Open: All year.
Price: Inexpensive to
    Moderate.
Credit Cards: MC, V.
Handicap Access: Yes.

After a career in Portland, Ruth McInnis returned home to Eastport where she bought and restored this classic Cape farmhouse (on the National Register of Historic Places). It was built during the Revolutionary War on the shore of Passamaquoddy Bay. The owner, a storehouse of local history, will gladly take you on a tour and has opened up her library of Maine, Revolutionary War, and Civil War history books. The six rooms vary greatly in feel: one has a working fireplace; several are packed with carefully chosen antiques and brimming with historical significance; two are strictly modern with queen-sized beds, cable TV, private modern baths, and kitchenettes. A simple but ample breakfast is served in the common room: cranberry muffins, fancy breads, cereal, and some very welcome fresh fruit. Ms. McInnis might also be willing to sell a few of the Wabanaki baskets she's accumulated over the years. Children and pets are welcome. No smoking.

WESTON HOUSE
Owners: Jett and John
    Peterson.
207-853-2907 or
    800-853-2907.
26 Boynton St., Eastport
    04631.
Open: All year.
Price: Moderate.
Credit Cards: None.

The Weston House is a civilized place. The formal parlor, with comfortable sofas and wing chairs, odd lamps, and a dish of pistachios on the coffee table, is the perfect place to curl up with a book. There's also a cheerful back room for watching TV. Breakfast is a gourmet affair: pancakes with apricot syrup, fresh-baked breads, popovers, or whatever else Jett Peterson—a prodigious cook—fancies (Mrs. Peterson will also pack box lunches and make dinner on request). A handsome garden offers a gazebo with a bench for contemplation. Five comfortable guest rooms are furnished with handsome antiques, floral fabrics, and oriental rugs; some have fireplaces and four-poster beds as well.

Jonesport

**RASPBERRY SHORE BED
& BREAKFAST**
Innkeepers: Nan and
    Timothy Ellis.
207-497-2463.
www.jonesportmaine.com.
skitech@midmaine.com.
Rte. 187, P.O. Box 409,
    Jonesport 04649.

Out of the way in the out-of-the-way fishing village of Jonesport, this small Victorian home offers access to a working way of life that not many people get to see anymore. You hear the lobstermen heading out into the bay and can sit in lawn chairs for morning coffee and afternoon meditation. The gardens here are lovingly tended, the rooms filled with antiques and beautifully appointed. Breakfast

Open: All year.
Price: Moderate.
Credit Cards: None.

includes homemade breads, bacon, fresh fruit, yogurt, and sometimes "heart-attack eggs," eggs cooked with six cheeses. Kayaks and bikes are available for rent.

Lubec

THE HOME PORT INN
Owners: Dave and
  Suzannah Gale.
207-733-2077 or
  800-457-2077.
www.homeportinn.com.
theinn@homeportinn.com.
45 Main St., P.O. Box 50,
  Lubec 04652.
Open: Mid-June–mid-Oct.
Price: Moderate.
Credit cards: AE, D, MC, V.
Handicap Access: No.

The Home Port Inn has established itself as a place to eat dinner, and that is particularly welcome in a neck of the woods without a lot of good restaurants. Its seven rooms each have a private bath, and some have a view across part of the Bay of Fundy toward Eastport. A large downstairs room is open to guests for an afternoon cup of tea. On my visit the delicious smell of raspberry pie baking in the kitchen filled the house, enough to lure me in for dinner and lodging anytime. "Well-behaved children" are welcome.

**PEACOCK HOUSE BED
& BREAKFAST INN**
Innkeepers: Dennis and Sue
  Baker.
207-733-2403 or
  888-305-0036.
www.peacockhouse.com.
27 Summer St., Lubec
  04652.
Open: May–end Oct.
Price: Moderate.
Credit Cards: MC, V.
Handicap Access: Yes.

Built in 1860, this modest white clapboard house sits on a quiet corner. Step over the threshold and find yourself at a crossroads where Texas meets New England. The bed and breakfast is named for five generations of the Peacock family who once lived there. Two Southerners—Chet and Veda Childs—converted it to a lodging house. A sumptuous full breakfast is served family-style, with orange French toast the house speciality. Five small to large rooms, all with private baths, are decorated with a mix of comfortable modern and reproduction furniture. The smallest, the Captain's Cabin, is a cozy single. The largest, the Margaret Chase Smith, is named after the Maine senator and has cable TV. No pets. Children over seven. No smoking.

Machias

**MICMAC FARM
  GUESTHOUSES**
Owner: Bonnie Dunn.
207-255-3008.
www.micmacfarm.com.
Rte. 92, Machiasport
  04655.
Open: July–late Oct.
Price: Inexpensive.

These are plain cabins, though nicely appointed; what makes them so delightful is the setting. From your tiny deck you look out through a birch stand to the Micmac River, and all you can hear is the wind rustling the leaves, while the light glitters according to the tides on the water. One room is available in the main house, an 18th-century farmhouse built by a potter seeking a safe haven from

Credit Cards: MC, V.
Handicap Access: No

the Revolutionary War. The large room has its own view of the river, as well as a TV and a whirlpool tub. The house is charming, the quiet more so.

Prospect Harbor

OCEANSIDE MEADOWS INN
Innkeepers: Sonja Sundaram and Ben Walter.
207-963-5557.
www.oceaninn.com.
oceaninn@oceaninn.com.
Box 90, Rte. 195, Corea Rd., Prospect Harbor 04669.
Open: May–Nov.; by reservation the rest of the year.
Price: Moderate.
Credit Cards: AE, DC, MC, V.
Handicap Access: Yes.

Set on the Schoodic Peninsula near the farthest reaches of Acadia National Park, this 19th-century sea captain's home is still one of the best bargains on the coast. Spacious, immaculate, and quiet, all the rooms have a private bath. A separate old stagecoach inn at the head of the bay has seven rooms, also all with private baths, two rooms for receptions, and a full country kitchen. It's perfect for large families and longer-term guests. Family reunions are popular here. The main house sits on a beautiful 200-acre preserve just yards away from a lovely private cove and sand beach. The landscape has been thoughtfully incorporated into the experience of a visit, with trails through the woods and paths through the dune grass maintained to conserve and help the environment. The sound of the surf is a great lullaby. Well-behaved children and amiable dogs are welcome. Breakfast and tea included. No smoking.

West Gouldsboro

SUNSET HOUSE BED & BREAKFAST
Owners: Kathy and Carl Johnson.
207-963-7156 or 800-233-7156.
www.sunsethousebnb.com.
lodging@sunset housebnb.com.
Rte. 186, West Gouldsboro 04607.
Open: All year.
Price: Moderate to Expensive.
Credit Cards: AE, D, MC, V.

This bed-and-breakfast offers ocean views from the front bedrooms and views of a freshwater pond and an old millstream from the rear bedrooms. Six rooms, three with private bath, are small and cozy. A full kitchen on the third floor can combine with three bedrooms to become a suite. Breakfasts are fortifying: French toast from fresh homebaked bread; sourdough waffles; fresh herbed goat cheese omelets. Book your winter stay in advance, and you may be asked to stay for a home-style dinner cooked by Carl, who was named Maine's Chef of the Year in 1994 by the American Culinary Federation. No pets are allowed; there is one cat in residence. The Johnson family keeps goats, and guests are invited to the morning milking. No smoking. Bikers take note: the Sunset House is located near the 27-mile bike trail through the Acadia region.

SCHOODIC & NORTH: DINING

Columbia

PERRY'S SEAFOOD
207-483-2045.
Rte. 1, Columbia 04623.
Open: All year except 2
  weeks at Christmas.
Price: Moderate.
Cuisine: American
  roadhouse.
Serving: B, L, D.
Credit Cards: All.
Handicap Access: In the
  rear.
Special Features: Smoking
  & non-smoking rooms.

Perry's Seafood is a straightforward eatery on the east side of Rte. 1, where vacationers re-order the fried onion rings and scallop stew they remember from last year, and business people hold their lunch meetings. It's fast, friendly, fresh, generous, and clean. Puddings and pies, even the fillings, are made from scratch by the owner. No false notes here except for the butter. It's not real, but the whipped cream is, and they're probably open to persuasion on the butter.

Eastport

**THE EASTPORT
  CANNERY
  RESTAURANT**
207-853-9669.
167 Water St., Eastport
  04631.
Open: May–Sept., closed
  Mon.
Price: Inexpensive to
  Moderate.
Cuisine: Seafood, family-
  style.
Serving: D.
Credit Cards: MC, V.
Handicap Access: Yes.
Reservations: Not
  necessary.

The Cannery, by the ferry dock in Eastport, has a view over international water. Once a sardine packing plant, it became a popular seafood restaurant, then fell into disuse. Now it is renovated, and another owner has opened another Cannery restaurant.

With the restaurant half-full the two waitresses cannot keep up. They need help. After 20 minutes go by, my waitress brings me a beer. It's a bad night, and things are going wrong, but I am in place till the end. The salad is half mesclun and half iceberg lettuce. The dressing is so full of vinegar it makes me cough. Dinner arrives an hour after I arrived: grilled local salmon (raised in a pen), corn on the cob, French fries. The salmon is well done, and I have lost the habit of eating it that way. The corn is over-cooked. The French fries are wonderful. I make myself content, biting one after another; they are hot, crisp, and delicious.

LA SARDINA LOCA
207-853-2739.
28 Water St., Eastport
  04631.
Open: All year, closed
  Tues..
Price: Inexpensive.

There are not a whole lot of restaurants in this small border town. But that didn't stop the Maggiani's from deciding Eastport was missing a good Mexican restaurant. Touted as the "Eastern-most Mexican restaurant and bar in the U.S.A.,"

Cuisine: Mexican.
Credit Cards: MC, V.
Serving: D.
Handicap Access: Partial.

this brightly colored, friendly, successful establishment has been providing tacos, enchiladas, burritos, and "especials" to the locals for years. If you're uncomfortable being easternmost, or your nose detects cigarette smoke, they also have an extensive "to go" menu.

WACO DINER
207-853-4046.
Bank Sq., Eastport 04631.
Open: Daily.
Price: Inexpensive.
Cuisine: American diner.
Serving: B, L, D.
Handicap Access: Limited.

It's tempting to mispronounce the name of this place, but just try it and a dozen people will correct you. Wack-o is the right way to say it, and the name is suitable for this quirky little spot. Lunch counter standards—clam chowder, corned beef hash, grilled frankfurters, fish and chips, and all sorts of pies—make up the bulk of the menu, but there are some surprises: scallop stew, tuna noodle casserole, fried clam rolls, homemade English muffin toast, and Grapenut pudding. Best of all, the place looks as if it's been around for eons, with worn vinyl stools, old-timey booths, and counters all crammed in a space the size of a postage stamp. Service may be a little surly, but that only adds to the charm.

Jonesport

SEAFARER'S WIFE
207-497-2365.
120 Main St., Jonesport 04649.
Open: All year.
Price: Inexpensive to Moderate.
Cuisine: American, Seafood.
Serving: L, D.
Credit Cards: MC, V.

Two restaurants in one, there's the Seafarer's side and the Old Salt side. The latter is favored by the locals and those who want a quick veal Parmesan sandwich or, of course, fish. The Seafarer's Wife requires reservations for its higher-end fare. Baked stuffed lobster tails, scallops in cream sauce, and, simply, chicken with stuffing. BYOB. We had a bottle in the car, so it worked. If you're curious about the other, there's only a door separating the two restaurants. Whichever you choose, all the fish is fresh from the shores of Great Wass.

Lubec

THE HOME PORT INN
207-733-2077 or
    800-457-2077.
www.homeportinn.com.
45 Main St., P.O. Box 50,
    Lubec 04652.
Open: Mid-June–mid-Oct.
Price: Moderate.
Cuisine: American.

Try the fresh lobster pie made with butter and sherry; or seafood casserole made with scallops, haddock, and shrimp if you've had enough lobster, or perhaps the baked scallops. Two possibilities are on the menu for a vegetarian, and that is another recommendation in an area without a lot of variety: vegetable curry with rice and freshly sautéed vegetables, also served on rice. The smell

Serving: D.
Credit Cards: AE, D, MC, V.
Handicap Access: No.
Reservations: Requested.

of that raspberry pie is still obsessing me down through these pages, but there is blueberry pie, too, in season.

Machias

THE ARTIST'S CAFE
207-255-8900.
3 Hill St., Rte. 1, Machias
  04654.
Closed: Sun. & Mon.
Price: Expensive.
Cuisine: American
  Seasonal.
Serving: L, D; call for
  winter hours.
Credit Cards: MC, V.
Handicap Access: No.
Reservations: Requested.

The big hardware store has five-gallon blueberry buckets for sale, and hay is lying flat on the fields around Machias, drying in the late July sun. The paintings by the chef of the Artist's Café, oil abstractions, are crazy quilts of summer color, cobalt and saffron and lime. The sliced duck breast lined up on the plate like small round dominos has cubed mango shaped in crosses on a four-leaf clover of cucumber, with a flourish of a daylily petal. The rice is bisected with a wedge of avocado. It is art that I delight in consuming, the Arborio rice deeply flavored in a risotto of wild mushroom, orange, and broth. Others in the restaurant are feeding each other bites of corn tortilla layered with ricotta or crab cakes. Rich chocolate cake? Lemon sherbet with fruit? The gingerbread made with fresh ginger and topped with whipped cream made another piece of art, the rich cream draped like a 50s flip over the side of the cake.

**BLUE BIRD RANCH
  FAMILY RESTAURANT**
207-255-3351.
3 East Main St., Rte. 1, just
  north of Machias 04654.
Open: Daily, all year.
Price: Inexpensive.
Cuisine: American family.
Serving: B, L, D.
Credit Cards: AE, D, MC, V.
Handicap Access: Yes.
Reservations: Unnecessary.

Your children can draw while you recharge on the coffee and fresh raspberry cream pie. Whether you want breakfast, lunch, or dinner, the friendly people here will bring you something good. The waitress was enthusiastic about the offerings and recommended garlic shrimp with angel hair pasta, salmon Caesar salad, or spinach manicotti. Locals think highly of this place. You can get a cocktail and also any kind of the fried fish standard in most Maine roadside restaurants here, and this is where I would go if that was what I wanted.

HELEN'S RESTAURANT
207-255-8423.
Rte. 1, Machias 04654.
Open: All year.
Price: Moderate.
Cuisine: American.
Serving: B, L, D.
Credit Cards: AE, D, MC, V.
Handicap Access: Yes.

As the tour buses in the parking lot suggest, Helen's is very good at hooking hungry travelers. For them it's faster to do it than think about it. All fried foods are cooked in cholesterol-free oil, which means you can then go ahead and get your dose from one of their fine cream pies. The strawberry pie is famous. When my waitress at Helen's would not recommend anything on the menu, we had a rib-sticking pork sandwich with homemade mashed potatoes and gravy because Helen's makes you feel that way. That feeling stuck all the way to Eastport. There's good parking, and a metal bedpan with dried flower arrangement hangs in the women's room.

Steuben

Herb Swanson

Alva Lowe's bean fence, at the Kitchen Garden Restaurant in Steuben, where the food grows just outside the door.

THE KITCHEN GARDEN RESTAURANT
207-546-2708.
kitchengarden@acadia.net.
335 Village Rd., Steuben 04680.
Open: July & Aug., Wed.–Sun.
Price: Very Expensive.

Jesse King and Alva Lowe have made a beautiful home in Steuben, and during the summer gardening season they share the abundance with their restaurant. The stone steps with cushions of mossy thyme charm you as you step inside the simple white cape set above and below their expansive gardens. Summer residents come back every year they have the opportunity.

Cuisine: Seasonal Creative
  American.
Serving: D, at 7pm.
Credit Cards: None, cash or
  check only.
Handicap Access: No.
Reservations: Required.

Alva Lowe has woven birch saplings into a gorgeous support for green beans, but the evening I met him the blueberries were taking up his attention. The menus change with the crops and feature organic produce and free-range chicken, transformed into Alva's Jamaican Jerk chicken (with 24-hour notice) during the week of my visit. The meal is prix fixe ($35 in 2001) and includes an appetizer, perhaps crab cakes, a soup, a salad, and a choice from entrées like broiled beef tenderloin, baked haddock in lemon shallot sauce, or a sweet pepper and leek tart.

Winter Harbor

CHASE'S
207-963-7171.
Rte. 186, Winter Harbor
  04693.
Open: Daily.
Price: Moderate.
Cuisine: American; New
  England diner.
Serving: B, L, D.
Credit Cards: AE, CB, D,
  DC, MC, V.
Handicap Access: Yes.

Chase's is Maine's answer to the diner: chowder, burgers, sandwiches, and broiled and fried seafood served in a no-nonsense, no-frills setting. The lights are bright and the chairs worn, but the food is right on the mark and the help on their toes. When was the last time you saw waiters carrying three plates on an arm? Among the better picks: broiled fresh haddock, fried clams, chowder, and specials like a fried flounder basket. Bread pudding or pie for dessert. Afterwards, take a spin out to Schoodic Point and work it all off by climbing along the rocks.

**FISHERMAN'S INN
  RESTAURANT**
207-963-5585.
www.oceaninn.com/
  fishermansinn.
7 Newman St., Winter
  Harbor 04693.
Open: May–early Dec.
Price: Inexpensive to
  Moderate.
Cuisine: Seafood.
Serving: D.
Credit Cards: AE, D, MC, V.
Handicap Access: Yes.

The lighthouse border on the wallpaper is the most elaborate element in this plain and accommodating restaurant. The salad came from Darthia Farm, an organic farm in Gouldsboro; the fine desserts, Indian Pudding, maple crème brûlée, and the seasonal, warm blueberry pie, exactly right at the end of July, are made by a local baker for the restaurant.

Lobsters come from the Winter Harbor Coop down the road, where the rest of the fish arrives as well. They make lobster pie, lobster out of the shell, and baked lobster as well as lobster bisque with sherry or a big lobster salad on a crisp roll for lunch.

SCHOODIC & NORTH: FOOD PURVEYORS

BAKERIES & CAFES

Cinqueterre Farm (207-726-4766; www.downeastonline.com/cinqueterre.shtml; RR1, Box 264, Ox Cove Rd., Pembroke). Since 1998, Les Prickett has baked baguettes, multigrain and raisin breads, and Gloria Christie has baked pies, at this farm down a side road off Rte. 1. They also make jams, pickles, and delicious pecan tartlets, as well as apple tarte tatin. Order a pie before the weekend to pick it up Friday. The raspberry jam is very good.

Mama's Boy Bakery & Café (207-963-2365; Winter Harbor). Breakfast features omelets, lunch with cold salads and sandwiches, delicious coffee to enjoy on the porch on the water. Jams and preserves, as well as blueberry or cranberry-apple pies.

CANDY & ICE CREAM

Katie's on the Cove (207-454-8446; www.katiesonthecove.com; Box 237, Rte. 1, Mill Cove, Robbinston). Hand-dipped chocolates made from old and well-loved Passamaquoddy Bay candy makers recipes. The "Maine Bear Paws" (maple caramel and pecans dipped in chocolate) honor the University of Maine's women's basketball team. Delicious chocolate-dipped marzipan, crystallized ginger, and more.

FAST FOOD

The Crossroads (207-726-5053; Rte. 1, Pembroke). Located at the site of an old iron works, this little carryout attached to a roadside motel serves the best lobster roll around.

Tall Barney's (207-497-2403; www.hollyeats.com/TallBarneys.htm; Main St., Jonesport). The dining room has year-round white Christmas lights and crepe paper garlands, and there is a testosterone choir at a diagonal table by the front door; all combining to make the right atmosphere for the seasonal smelt dinner, the perfectly fine crab salad roll, or the chicken burger.

GOURMET FOOD STORES

M. Look's Canning Company (800-962-6258; www.amlook.com.; HC 74 Box 165, Whiting; Rte. 191 S. from East Machias). Canned clam chowder, lobster bisque and salmon chowder, clams, lobster meat, and more.

J. W. Raye & Co. (207-853-4451; www.rayesmustard.com; Rte. 190, Eastport). They've been making mustard here since 1903, first for the sardine canning industry that used to flourish here, now for the mass market. Visit their gift shop or get a tour and learn how they make the stuff at the Mustard Museum. Grainy, exotic, and smooth yellow mustards, as well as other stuff.

Herb Swanson

Salmon pens on Cobscook Bay near Eastport; Jim's Smoked Salmon features the locally raised fish.

Jim's Smoked Salmon (207-853-4831; 37 Washington St., Eastport). Jim Blankman smokes Atlantic salmon raised on farms in Cobscook Bay. He will also wrap your salmon gift in a beautifully crafted wood box that he builds himself. Smoked mussels and rainbow and steelhead trout.

Maine Wild Blueberry Company (207-255-8364; 50 Elm St., Machias). The biggest wild blueberry business in the world. Buy frozen, canned, and dried blueberries right from the factory. They call the dried ones "wild chews." They taste like very sweet blueberries and have the consistency of raisins.

HEALTH FOOD & FARM MARKETS

Cross Road Farm Stand (Off Rte. 187 at Indian River Crossroad, Jonesport). Organic isn't a fad here. They've been farming that way for more than 20 years and are certified. More than 200 types of vegetables, 15 kinds of potatoes, unusual salad greens, squashes, and onions.

Darthia Farm (207-963-2770; West Bay Rd., Rte. 186, Gouldsboro). A selection of organic fruits, vegetables, and herbs, as well as homemade jams, vinegars, pesto, yogurt, herb cheeses, and fresh butter. Mon.–Fri. 8–6, Sat. 8–12, June though September. Tours and horse-drawn rides; ask for schedule.

Good Earth Organic Market (207-255-3065; 80 Main St. (Rte. 1), Machias). Open daily, with a large selection of organic produce, fresh-baked bread, and organic foods.

Johnson Farm (207-853-2910; Rte. 1, Perry). Strawberries, potatoes, vegetables.
Machias Farmers' Market (207-638-2664; The Dike, on Rte. 1 just north of the village, Machias). Saturday 8–noon.

WINERIES

Bartlett Maine Estate Winery (207-546-2408; RR 1, Box 598, Gouldsboro). It is a lot of fun to drive off of Rte. 1 and pull up to the winery in the woods for a free tasting. I liked the dry Blueberry Oak served in tiny cups. Mead (a honey wine), apple wine, and wines of pear, blueberry, blackberry, and raspberry, of varying degrees of dry and sweet are made and can sometimes be tasted here. Robert and Kathe Bartlett have been making their fruit wines since 1983. Open Memorial Day–Columbus Day, Mon.–Sat., 10–5, other times by appointment.

FOOD FESTIVALS

Annual Winter Harbor Lobster Festival (207-963-7638 or 800-231-3008 out-of-state; www.acadia-schoodic.org). Mid-August. Almost as famous as Rockland's Lobster Festival. The lobster boat races are a main attraction.
Machias Wild Blueberry Festival (Centre St. Congregational Church, sponsor, 207-255-6665). Scheduled for August 16 and 17, 2002, this mid-August festival includes a pie-eating contest, a one-mile run, and lots of children's activities. Their 2001 brochure states that the festival was begun "To show our thanks to God for the continuing harvest of luscious and nutritious berries that have improved the economic and physical health of all of us for more than a hundred years..."
Salmon Festival (207-853-4644; Eastport). All you can eat, tours of the salmon pens from the water and codfish relays. Early September.

SCHOODIC & NORTH: CULTURE

FILM

The Milbridge Theatre (207-546-2038; Main St., Milbridge).

GALLERIES

The Crow Tracks Woodcarving Gallery (207-853-2336; www.crowtracks.com; 11 Water St., Eastport). Carved birds.
Eastport Gallery and the Center (207-853-4166 or 207-853-4133; www.eastport gallery.com; 69 Water St., Eastport). Sculpture, painting, and other media by almost two dozen regional artists. The Arts Center has a series of concerts, as well as a theater company. Open mid-June–mid-September.

HISTORIC BUILDINGS & SITES

BURNHAM TAVERN
207-255-4432.
Main St., Machias 04654.
Season: Mid-June–Labor
  Day, Mon.–Fri. 9–5;
  winter by appointment.
Admission: $2 adults; 25¢
  kids.

Revolutionary War aficionados will appreciate the importance of this 1770 gambrel-roofed tavern, the oldest building in the U.S. east of the Penobscot River. Local leaders met and planned the first naval battle of the war here, in which Machias patriots aboard the schooner *Unity* captured the British schooner *Margaretta*. The building served as a hospital during the war and a meeting place for local Masons.

RUGGLES HOUSE
207-483-4637.
www.exploremaine.com/~
  ruggles.
RR1 Box 120, Columbia
  Falls 04623.
Just off Main St. (Rte. 1).
Season: June–mid-Oct.,
  weekdays 9:30–4:30; Sun.
  11–4:30.

Judge Thomas Ruggles did it all: he was a lumber dealer, a storeowner, the local postmaster, captain of the local militia, and a judge of the Court of Sessions. His house, designed by Massachusetts's architect Aaron Sherman and built in 1818, befits a man of his many talents and high standing in society. The "flying" staircase is a marvel. So is the hand-carved woodwork, which took an English woodworker three years to complete.

LIGHTHOUSES

The light at West Quoddy Head, the easternmost lighthouse in the United States.

Herb Swanson

West Quoddy Head Light Built in 1807, the boldly striped light at West Quoddy Head in Lubec sits at the easternmost point in the U.S.

MUSEUMS

ROOSEVELT CAMPOBELLO INTERNATIONAL PARK
Mail: P.O. Box 129, Lubec 04652.
Campobello Island, New Brunswick.
Season: Late May–Columbus Day; Natural Area year-round.
Free.

The island summer home of former U.S. President Franklin D. Roosevelt is just a stone's throw from Lubec. Although on Canadian soil, the historic site is maintained jointly by the U.S. and Canada; the only auto route to the island is via the international bridge at Lubec (a ferry provides access on the Canadian side). The house has been restored and contains many of the Roosevelt family's original furnishings.

WAPONAHKI MUSEUM AND RESOURCE CENTER
207-853-4001.
Pleasant Point Indian Reservation, P.O. Box 295, Perry 04667.
Season: Mon.–Fri., 9–11, 1–3 year-round.
Donations.

The Passamaquoddy Indians were among the tribes that once inhabited Maine shores during the summer, but after Europeans settled the coast, their numbers diminished. In 1822 there were 379 Passamaquoddy; today there are more than 2,000. This museum offers a glimpse of their rich culture through the implements they fashioned from nature —graceful birch bark canoes, handsome ash baskets, snowshoes, clothing, and arrowheads. Also on exhibit are photographs that document life on the reservation in the past and present. The museum is a repository for a growing collection of books, tapes, dictionaries, and reference books, all of which serve to preserve the Passamaquoddy language. Classes in the tribe's new written language are taught here.

MUSIC

OCEANSIDE MEADOWS INSTITUTE FOR THE ARTS AND SCIENCES
207-963-5557.
www. oceaninn.org.
P.O. Box 90, Corea Rd., Prospect Harbor 04669.
Season: Thursdays June–July.
Tickets: $10 in advance, $12 at the door.

The restored 1820s barn on the inn property is the concert hall for classical guitar, jazz trios, Baroque violin, harp, string quartets, and opera, as well as science lectures and astronomy seminars.

MACHIAS BAY CHAMBER CONCERTS
207-255-3889.
P.O. Box 332, Machias 04654.
Season: July–early Aug.
Tickets: $8 adults; $5 students; under 12 free.

This group has brought classical chamber music to Machias for almost a quarter of a century. Many of the same instrumental groups that play in Rockport's Bay Chamber series play here in the Machias Congregational Church, which is known for its excellent acoustics. The series of six concerts begins on the first Tuesday evening after July 4.

MACHIAS FOLK FESTIVAL
207-255-1384.
9 O'Brien Ave., Machias 04654.
Season: August, 3rd Weekend
Tickets: $15 or more depending on sponsors.

Featuring fine traditional folk music, with performers from Maine and Nashville and elsewhere. Vassar Clements has been there for every year since 1999 for this annual festival. He played at a big contradance at a grange in Lubec in 2001 and will probably be a part of the contradances in the future.

SUMMERKEYS
6 Bayview St., Lubec 04652.
Season: Wed. evenings in summer.
Free.

The Mary Potterton Memorial Piano Concerts, featuring Summerkeys faculty and guest artists.

SEASONAL EVENTS

Down River Theater Company (207-255-4244; Old Catholic Church, Rte. 1A, Whitneyville). Musical theater from *South Pacific* to *Chicago*. Summer.

Eastport Arts Center (207-853-4133; Dana and Water Sts., P.O. Box 153, Eastport 04631). The Center is comprised of three groups: Stage East, a theater company producing three shows a year ranging from Neil Simon's *Rumors* to Charles Dickens's *A Christmas Carol*; the Eastport Gallery featuring art work in a variety of media; and the Concert Series with at least five concerts a summer.

A ceremonial dance at the annual celebration in Perry; a chance for visitors to witness the new and old customs of the Passamaquoddy.

Tom Hindman

The Gathering, Passamaquoddy Tribe (207-853-4001; Pleasant Point Reservation, Rte. 190, Perry). Traditional dances, crafts, lighting the sacred fire. Mid-August.

July 4 and Old Home Days (207-853-4644; Eastport). Every year this small fishing town of 2,000 quadruples in size when everyone who has ever lived here comes to celebrate the easternmost Fourth of July in the country. Great parade. Make sure to make your lodging reservations early. July 1–4.

SCHOODIC & NORTH: RECREATION

BEACHES

Jasper Beach; off Starboard Rd., Bucks Harbor. This beach is made up entirely of polished pebbles. It's beautiful, even if it makes for difficult swimming.

Roque Bluffs Beach; Roque Bluffs Rd. off Rte. 1, Roque Bluffs. There's also Simpson Pond next door for freshwater swimming, a playground, picnic tables, grills, a bathhouse, bathrooms, and parking. Sand and shingle beach; 910 yds.

BIRD WATCHING

Some of the best birding in Maine—some may even say the best in New England—is in Washington County. Southern birders will head well-bundled in winter for a shore lookout like *Quoddy Head* to see flying murres, kittiwakes and other alcids, a swimming harlequin duck, or a king eider. Or they may hope to see a northern three-toed woodpecker in the spruce forests along the rocky northeastern shore, the year-round habitat of gray jays, northern ravens, and boreal chickadees.

The quiet beaches near the Canadian border are wonderful places to see the fall migration of shore birds. One birder we've heard of spotted 100 species in one day in *Dennysville* on the Dennys River. The *Lubec* and *Eastport* flats host an enormous number and variety of traveling sanderlings, sandpipers, knots, willets, and other beach feeders. Ducks of many species abound, and eagles are regularly sighted. The *Petit Manan National Wildlife Refuge* in Milbridge is an excellent perch for dedicated birders. The 1,841-acre preserve includes Bois Bubert, Petit Manan and Nash islands and is said to be one of the best spots in the state to view the whimbrel, a small European curlew. There are nature trails on the mainland. The islands (with the exception of the northern end of Bois Bubert) are open to the public and can be reached by private boat. *Seal Island* near Machias has pathways and blinds set up for birders and is worth a special trip in June. You can land for a few hours but not stay overnight.

BOAT CRUISES, BOAT RENTALS, PUFFIN WATCHING

Bold Coast Charter Company (Capt. Andrew Patterson; 207-259-4484; www. boldcoast.com; P.O. Box 364, Cutler 04626) Tours on the *Barbara Frost* to Machias Seal Island to see the puffins.

Norton Puffin Tours (Capt. Barna Norton; 207-497-5933; www.mainebirding .net/puffin/norton; RR1 Box 990, Jonesport 04649). Journeys to Machias Seal Island to see thousands of puffins.

Jonesport Boats and Bikes (207-497-2210; P.O. Box 439, Jonesport 04649; Main St.,behind Raspberry Shores B&B). Kayak and bicycle rentals.

Robertson Seatours (Capt. James Robertson; 207-546-3883; www.robertsonsea tours.com; RR1 Box 202F, Cherryfield 04622). Small cruises from Millbridge Marina on a classic lobster boat; islands, lighthouses, osprey, loons, herons.

Seafarer (Butch Huntley; 207-733-5584; seafarer@nemaine.com; 9 High St., Lubec 04652).

Sunrise County Canoe and Kayak (207-454-7708; 5A Water St., Machias 04654; seasonal office on Rte. 1 by Helen's). Sea kayak guides, trips, and rentals.

Our Family Moved Here in 1760

Captain Barna B. Norton will tell you and everyone else that the Treaty of Paris, signed in 1783, finalizing the boundaries of the United States after the American Revolution, awarded Machias Seal Island to the United States. How Canada got to maintain the lighthouse on it is another story. And so is Captain Barna's conviction that Machias Seal Island is his family's property, which he contends is proven in 1983 U. S. State Department documents.

In the spring of 2001 Canada threatened boat tour operators like Captain Barna Norton with a refusal to grant visits to the island, saying the landing platform had become too dangerous. After much enjoyable controversy Canada, in Norton's words, capitulated, although it charged money for a landing permit, annoying the local Captains who nevertheless paid.

No one does seem to care quite as much about this island as Captain Barna Norton; he leaves from Jonesport about 7am, to see the 2,500 puffins that were never hunted to extinction here, as they were further south. Also on the island are Razorbill Auks, Arctic Terns, and Common Murres. The trip is two hours, with less than three hours on the island walking from blind to blind to observe the birds in their nests. Bring a bag lunch.

CAMPING

Cobscook Bay State Park (207-726-4412; six miles south of U.S. Rte. 1 at Dennysville). This jewel of a campground has 106 camping sites. Most are for tents, and many have water views. There are even showers (unusual in a Maine state campground). The 864-acre park has picnic benches, hiking, and cross-country ski trails (see below). Mid-May–mid-October.

McLellan Park (Wyman Rd., Milbridge). Washington County operates this family recreational area. Camping, picnicking facilities, and hiking trails.

CROSS-COUNTRY SKIING

Cobscook Bay State Park (207-726-4412 for snow and trail conditions; off Rte. 1, Edmunds). Six miles of roads through woods with terrific views of the bay.

Moosehorn National Wildlife Refuge (207-454-3521; Baring). Fifty miles of service roads closed to automobiles in the winter. Moderate to difficult.

FERRIES

East Coast Ferries (506-747-2159; www.eastcoastferries.com; Eastport Ferry Dock). Eastport to Deer Island and Deer Island to Campobello, July–September.

GOLF

Great Cove Golf Course (207-434-7200; off Rte. 1 in Jonesboro, Roque Bluffs). 9 holes, 1,694 yds., par 30. Cart and club rental, snack bar, clubhouse.
Grindstone Neck Golf Course (207-963-7760; Grindstone Ave., Winter Harbor). 9 holes, 3,095 yds., par 36. Cart and club rentals, pro shop, lessons.
Herring Cove Provincial Park (Campobello Island) 9 holes. May to mid-October.

HIKING & WALKING

West Quoddy Head State Park, south of Lubec. This is the easternmost point of the United States, an elemental and majestic beginning. A two-mile trail outlines the 100-ft. cliffs and Carrying Place Cove. Several miles out, you can see Grand Manan, looking like a giant humpback whale. The trails also include a bog walk.

At the Bog at West Quoddy Head State Park

The bird croak was unfamiliar as I stepped out of the boreal forest of West Quoddy Head Park and on to the boardwalk that made a loop in the bog. A knowledgeable couple further on showed me its source: a raven, in the tip of a spruce bordering the bog. She would be looking for that tiny mouse or vole that had crossed the path ahead of me a minute earlier, for her lunch. But what was lying at my feet now drew me down and away from the sky. Pitcher plants, with their elegant deep red lips and veined, vase-shaped bodies, lay in wait for the no-see-em's nestled in the sphagnum moss and crowberry. The dewdrop plants stood lower with their frilled, tiny spatulate leaves, rimmed with hairs with apparent drops of dew on them, making a trap for passing insects, digesting them and feeding the plants with nutrients unavailable in the acid bog. The low tamaracks and black spruce, 80 years old and only six feet tall, broke the low landscape of the bog, a round hollow in the midst of silent woods layered with moss, dead trees, bunch berry, fern, and Dutchman's Pipe. Nature was the groundskeeper here, with no philanthropist needed, except to insure the people keep off. One footprint sinks deeply, scarring the fragile, soft surface, and remains for two years before the slowly creeping plants can heal it over. Stay on the boardwalk.

NATURE PRESERVES

Great Wass Island Preserve, Rte. 187, Beals Island, reached by a bridge from Jonesport, and a later right-hand turn at the T. Almost 1,600 acres of land with two wooded trails through spruce and fir forests edging a long, narrow cove. Magnificent views of the ocean and eastern islands. Two trails through the preserve offer long or short hikes, through a forest full of Jack pine to a granite shore and back by a bog with baked apple berry plants and dragon's mouth orchid. Hikes from 1.5 to 4.5 hours. Managed by the Nature Conservancy.

Petit Manan National Wildlife Refuge, South from Rte. 1 on Pigeon Hill Rd., Steuben. A pleasant trail leads 1.5 miles through a wild blueberry barren and woods to a rugged shoreline, another trail leads to the other side of Petit Manan Point. During fall migration over 4000 ducks make a visit; black ducks, green-winged teals, and mallards feed on the wild rice before taking off for another flight south. Many other birds can be sighted here. Part of a 1,841-acre refuge that includes Petit Manan Peninsula, Petit Manan, and Nash islands, and part of Bois Bubert Island. The islands—except for the northern end of Bois Bubert—are open to the public and can be reached by private boat.

RUNNING

Runner Magazine readers voted the **Schoodic 10K Road Race** on the Schoodic Peninsula as one of the five best in the country. The terrain is relatively flat, the scenery is beautiful, the air and the light clear.

SEASONAL SPORTING EVENTS

The World's Fastest Lobsterboat Races, early July. Takes place near Moosabec Reach (contact the Jonesport 4th of July Committee, P.O. Box 106, Jonesport 04649; 207-497-2804).

WHALE WATCH

Whales are frequent summer visitors off the coast of Maine, but they are not often this close.

Tom Hindman

Capt. Butch Huntley (207-733-5584; seafarer@nmaine.com; 9 High St., Lubec). If he can't make it, he'll tell you who can. Butch also does puffin trips.

Cline Marine Whale Watching (800-567-5880; www.clinemarine.com; 9 Richardson Rd., Deer Island, NB from Deer Island and Campobello, on the Canadian side in New Brunswick). Whale sightings are guaranteed and have included finback, humpback, minke, and right whales.

Whale Watching Excursions (207-853-4303; Harris Point Rd., Eastport). The 56-foot *Janna Marie* is captained by Butch Harris and leaves Eastport at 1:30 daily. She passes the Old Sow whirlpool—at 50 feet across, the largest tidal whirlpool in the Northern Hemisphere. It is mesmerizing at the change of tides.

SCHOODIC & NORTH: SHOPPING

COLLECTIBLES

The chain saw sculptures are always changing in Arthur and Marie Smith's front yard in Steuben.

Marie Smith

Chain Saw Sculptures (207-546-3462; 232 Rogers Point Rd., Steuben 04680). Arthur Smith does the carving with his chain saw, making eagles, fish, bear, boats; Marie Smith, his wife, paints them. Their work is wonderful, charming, fun; they also make baskets, and when I stopped in, one of their children had just sold his first root club carved with designs. They are part Wabanaki and entirely creative.

Darthia Farm (207-963-7771 or 800-285-6234); Box 520, West Bay Rd., Gouldsboro 04607; 1.7 miles off Rte. 1 on Rte. 186). Cindy Thayer would be happy to sign one of her novels for you, either the well-made *Strong for Potatoes*, with its insight into basket weaving and self-discovery, or her more recent *A Certain Slant of Light*, with its vivid descriptions of a hermit on the coast, sheep-sheering, and avoiding people. Hand-spun yarns and hand-knit items

Salmon Aquaculture

Salmon has not been cheaper for years, ringing up at $4.99 per lb. for steaks at Harbor Fish on Customhouse Wharf, in Portland, during January 2002. You have to pay twice as much for the wild salmon shipped here from the Pacific Coast. No Maine wild salmon may be sold commercially, as it is listed as an Endangered Species, and hard to find. The modest price of the farm-raised fish is the consequence of the 2,000,000 metric tons of farmed salmon that now swim into the world markets every year. Some of them came from Downeast Maine, or used to.

Salmon aquaculture is popular in Eastport and Lubec, around Cobscook Bay, where twenty-foot tides sweep in and out, dispersing the tons of nitrogen from fish waste and uneaten feed into the ocean. These by-products can kill off the sea floor life beneath and near fish pens in coastal waters with lower tides. Lobsters do not live in turbulent Cobscook Bay, so lobstermen are not in conflict with fish farmers here. Jobs are scarce, the land is undeveloped, and the people welcome this industry, for the most part. But Robert Peacock, who heads a multi-national fish processing company, fears for his Lubec business processing the salmon, then shipping filets fresh and frozen. The entire farmed salmon population amounting to some two and half million fish was killed off in the winter of 2001–2 to stop the spread of Infectious Salmon Anemia. Peacock believes the anemia was brought into the bay by Canadian boats, from Canadian salmon farms. He said that Norwegian rules quarantine fish farms that have a case of anemia, and no boats are allowed in or out.

The State Department of Marine Resources hopes that fallow time for the waters around the pens will clean the virus out, and plans that the fish be reintroduced afterward.

Further south, requests for 30 leased acres of coastal water for aquaculture are being fought with a passion. The island of Little Scott, which happens to be the site of Robert McCloskey's *Time of Wonder*, would be a near neighbor of a Blue Hill area fish farm owned by a Norwegian company if a lease application were approved. Petitions in Little Deer Isle for increasing the regulation of salmon aquaculture have received almost 100% support, and lobstermen and fishermen agree as much as summer people. The lower tides (3–4 feet compared to 20), the rich lobster fishery, and the more developed coastline all work against the introduction of salmon aquaculture around Blue Hill, and south.

"God bless the people of Eastport," said Jane McCloskey (a daughter of Robert McCloskey), now working in public relations for the East Penobscot Bay Environmental Alliance. "We don't have any quarrel with them." She regrets reports that have cast this as a class issue, and said that one solution would be to zone the coast according to its very different tides and development.

by other local craftspeople. Seasonal organic produce from this saltwater farm. Mon.–Fri. 8–6, Sat. 8–12, June–Sept.

Nelson Decoys Down East Gallery (207-497-5572; School St., Jonesport 04649) Mon.–Sat. or by appointment, the Downeast Gallery specializes in wood carvings of songbirds and shorebirds.

J.E.B. Baskets (207-733-2434; HCR 74, Box 4390, Whiting 04691; on Rte. 189 on the way to Campobello, just off Rte. 1). J. E. Bronson and her mother make handsome baskets. They are not Native American; maybe the land they live on made them learn to be good at this. Open year-round.

Skicin Arts and Crafts (207-853-2840; P.O. Box 295, Perry 04667; Pleasant Point on Rte. 190). Open daily, this is the basket-weaving store in the Indian Point Reservation, with more reasonable prices than you can find at fancier stores in Bar Harbor, although the work is still expensive. And why not? It is beautiful, finely made decorative basketry, made in traditional styles, by Wabanaki men and women. Joseph Nicholas, who can tell you the weavers' histories, runs the store; he started the Waponahki Museum across the street.

The Quoddy Wigwam (207-853-4812; Rte. 1 and Shore Rd., Perry 04667). Kirsten Shorey has a moccasin factory nearby, and you can buy beautiful soft shoes in this store that are based on native moccasins, some lined with soft deerskin. Some Wabanaki crafts here, as well—baskets and bead work.

The Sow's Ear (207-255-4066; 7 Water St., Machias 04654). An engaging collection of clothing, books, toys, and gifts

U. S. Bells (207-963-7184; www.usbells.com; P.O. Box 73, Prospect Harbor 04669; Rte. 186). Sculptor Richard Fisher 's bronze and brass bells are sold around the world. They're in all shapes, all sizes, and for all purposes—including wind chimes and doorbells. Also beautiful handmade quilts. Open Apr.–Oct., Mon.–Fri. 9–4:30, Sat. 9–2.

West Quoddy Gifts (207-733-2457 or 877-974-4384; www.westquoddygifts .com; RR 2 Box 1470, on the lighthouse road, Lubec 04652) If you need a Puffin card deck or lighthouse pen with a whale floating down its length, go here. April–Oct.

POTTERY

Columbia Falls Pottery (207-483-4075 or 800-235-2512; www.columbiafallspot tery.com; Main St., P.O. Box 235, Columbia Falls 04623). Tour the studio or just browse through their collection of majolica and terra cotta pottery, painted with patterns called Lupin, Iris, and Sailboat. Baskets, candles, and paintings by Maine artists and crafts people.

Connie's Clay of Fundy (207-255-4574 or 888-255-8131; www.clayoffundy.com; Rte. 1, East Machias 04630). Connie Harter-Bagley makes high-fire functional pottery with bold blue and white and purple glazes, as well as Raku ware in more abstract shapes.

Dog Island Pottery (207-853-4775; 220 Water St., Eastport 04631). Functional and decorative stoneware handcrafted by the shop's owner, Barbara Smith.

CHAPTER ELEVEN
Practical Matters
INFORMATION

A Maine coast salt-water farm.

Herb Swanson

This chapter is meant to be a modest encyclopedia of useful information about the coast of Maine. Visitors can refer to it when planning trips to the coast and when on vacation here. It covers the following topics:

AMBULANCE / FIRE / POLICE

E xcept as listed below, dial 911 for emergencies.

Town	*Fire*	*Police*	*Ambulance*
Blue Hill	207-374-2435	207-667-7575	207-374-9900
Castine	207-326-4322	207-667-7575	207-374-9900
Ellsworth	207-667-2525	207-667-2133	207-667-3200
Stonington	207-367-2655	207-667-7575	207-348-2300
Winter Harbor	207-963-2222	207-667-7575	207-667-3200

AREA CODE / TOWN GOVERNMENT & ZIP CODES

AREA CODE

M aine's area code is 207.

TOWN GOVERNMENT

There are more than 250 cities, towns, villages and "plantations" from Kittery to Eastport. There are 16 counties in Maine and eight that line the coast. From west to east, they are: York, Cumberland, Sagadahoc, Lincoln, Knox, Waldo, Hancock, and Washington.

Cities have their own charters and city councils. In Maine you don't have to be big to be a city; if you're big, there's nothing to prevent you from being a town. There are 2,000 city people in Eastport and 10 times that number of townspeople in Brunswick.

Although more towns are electing officials and hiring professionals to govern and manage their communities, the annual town meeting predominates. At a town meeting, usually held in March, every resident who shows up has as much pull as the person sitting or standing next to her.

In addition to towns and cities, Maine has 33 plantations—a holdover from the time when the region was part of the Massachusetts Bay Colony. Originally intended to be temporary forms of government, many of Maine's plantations, such as Monhegan and Matinicus islands, have annual meetings, do not have home rule powers, and are incorporated by county commissioners.

Of course, Maine had a thriving democracy long before European settlers arrived. Today, two Native American reservations, at Old Town near Bangor and Perry outside of Eastport, are self-governed nations and exist outside of U.S. federal jurisdiction.

For information about specific coastal plantations, towns, and cities, contact the following town hall offices.

ZIP CODES

Town	*Telephone*	*Zip Code*
Bar Harbor	207-288-4098	04609
Bath	207-443-8330	04530
Belfast	207-338-3370	04915
Blue Hill	207-374-2281	04614
Boothbay Harbor	207-633-2144	04538
Brunswick	207-725-6659	04011
Camden	207-236-3353	04843
Castine	207-326-4502	04421
Damariscotta	207-563-5168	04543
Eastport	207-853-2300	04631
Ellsworth	207-667-2563	04605
Freeport	207-865-4743	04032
Jonesport	207-497-5926	04649
Kennebunkport	207-967-4243	04046
Kittery	207-439-0452	03904
Lubec	207-733-2341	04652
Machias	207-255-6621	04654
Newcastle	207-563-3441	04553
Ogunquit	207-646-5139	03907
Old Orchard Beach	207-934-5714	04064
Portland	207-874-8300	04101, 04102, 04103, 04112
Rockland	207-594-8431	04841
Stonington	207-367-2351	04681
Thomaston	207-354-6107	04861
Waldoboro	207-832-5369	04572
Winter Harbor	207-963-2235	04693
Wiscasset	207-882-8205	04578

BANKS

Bank	*Phone*	*Cash Machine Networks*
Bangor Savings Bank	800-432-1591	NYCE, Plus, Visa
Bar Harbor Banking & Trust	800-924-7787	Plus, NYCE, Visa

Bank	*Phone*	*Cash Machine Networks*
Camden National Bank	800-860-8821	Yankee 24, Plus, NYCE
First National Bank of Damariscotta	800-564-3195	Plus, Scott 24-Hour, Yankee24, NYCE, MasterCard/Visa
Fleet Bank	800-841-4000	Cirrus, NYCE, Yankee24, MasterCard/Visa
Key Bank	800-635-2265	NYCE, Cirrus, MAC, Maestro, Armed Forces, Star Bank
Peoples Heritage Bank	800-295-7400	NYCE, Plus, The Exchange, TX

BIBLIOGRAPHY

BOOKS YOU CAN BUY

AUTOBIOGRAPHY, BIOGRAPHY & REMINISCENCE

Arlen, Alice. *She Took to the Woods.* Rockport, ME: Down East Books, 2000. $16.95. A biography and selected writings of Louise Dickinson Rich, a woman whose writing makes early Maine come alive.

Coomer, Joe. *Sailing in a Spoonful of Water.* New York: Picador USA. $13. Coomer, a resident of Eliot, Maine, writes of the revival of his vintage craft *Yonder*, while reflecting on how his life journeys have drawn him to the water.

Heinrich, Bernd. *A Year in the Maine Woods.* Cambridge, MA: Perseus Books, 1994. $17. A man with a pet raven contemplates the details, on the ground and in the sky, of the countryside of Maine.

Nearing, Helen and Scott. *The Good Life: Helen and Scott Nearing's Sixty Years of Self-Sufficient Living.* New York: Schocken Books, 1989. $14. The homesteading classic.

Small, Constance. *The Lighthouse Keeper's Wife.* Orono, ME: University of Maine Press, 1999. 226 pp., photos, $14.95. Constance Small and her husband Elson tended a Maine island lighthouse for 28 years, and this is her wry tale of that life.

Tatelbaum, Linda. *Carrying Water as a Way of Life.* Appleton, ME: About Time

Press, 1997. 117 pp., $9.95. A series of feisty essays chronicling the author and her husband's quest to head back-to-the-land.

Thoreau, Henry David. *The Maine Woods.* New York: Penguin Books, first copyright 1864. $13.95. With an introduction by the fascinating essayist, Edward Hoagland, this is the classic essay about Maine's backwoods.

FICTION

Landesman, Peter. *The Raven.* New York: Penguin Books. 356 pp., $11.95. Based on the true story of a mysterious disappearance of a pleasure boat, *The Raven,* and its 36 passengers off the coast of Maine.

Maine Speaks. Maine: Maine Writers and Publishers Alliance. 464 pp., $19.95. An anthology of works by writers whose lives have been touched by Maine. E.B. White, Tim Sample, Ruth Moore, Steven King, and more.

McCloskey, Robert. *Blueberries for Sal.* New York: The Viking Press, 1948. 55 pp., illus., $5.99.

———. *One Morning in Maine.* New York: The Viking Press, 1952. 64 pp., illus. $5.99. Two of the best books about Maine to read, for adults as well as children.

Phippen, Sanford, Charles G. Waugh, and Martin Greenberg, eds. *The Best Maine Stories.* Camden, ME: Down East Books, 1986. 320 pp., $12.95. Short stories set in Maine written by some of America's most famous authors from Henry James to Caroline Chute.

Rich, Louise Dickinson. *We Took To the Woods.* Camden, ME: Down East Books, Renewed 1972. $12.95. About going to live alone in a cabin in Maine, her dream come true.

Thayer, Cynthia. *Strong for Potatoes.* New York: St. Martin's Griffin, 1998. $12.95. Blue Willoughby is a girl growing up in down east Maine, with the vital help of her Passamaquoddy grandfather. Cynthia Thayer also weaves and farms at Darthia Farm (see index). Her latest book is *A Certain Slant of Light,* and includes vivid descriptions of sheep farming and living on the land of the coast.

HISTORY

Carson, Rachel. *The Edge of the Sea.* New York: Houghton Mifflin, 1998. Natural history from a brilliant writer.

Judd, Richard W. *Common Lands, Common People.* Cambridge: Harvard University Press. 335 pp., $19.95. The history of conservation ethics in northern New England.

Kress, Stephen, and Pete Salmansohn. *The Project Puffin Book; How We Brought Puffins Back to Egg Rock.* Gardiner, ME: Tilbury House, 1998. $7.95. This inspiring book for children describes the reintroduction of birds once hunted almost to extinction in Maine. Look for a new book by the same authors in September 2002, about saving bird populations around the world.

Kurlandsky, Mark. *Cod.* New York: Penguin Books. 276 pp., $13. Spanning thousands of years and four continents, this book is a biography of the fish that changed the world and was a staple of the Maine fishery for centuries.

Rich, Louise Dickinson. *The Coast of Maine.* Camden, ME: Down East Books, 1993. 400 pp., index, illus., photos. $16.95. A wonderfully rambling history of the coast from the Ice Age to the mid-1970s, punctuated with the author's idiosyncratic interpretations of historical facts.

Rolde, Neil. *The Interrupted Forest; A History of Maine's Wildlands.* Gardiner, ME: Tilbury House, 2001. $20. An ecological history that describes human intervention along with other natural cataclysms of the past.

PHOTOGRAPHIC AND PAINTING STUDIES

Riper, Frank Van. *Down East Maine; A World Apart.* Camden, Maine: Down East Books, 1998. $29.95. Photographs of clamming, lobsterman, as well as schoolteachers, oxen at a fair; portraits of worlds slipping away, and just arriving.

RECREATION

Edwardsen, Elizabeth. *Longstreet Highroad Guide to the Maine Coast.* Marietta, GA: Longstreet Press, 1999. $18.95. Lists parks, preserves, birds and animals with a wonderful eye for the nature of Maine's coast.

Getchell, Dave, and Kate Cronin. *The Maine Island Trail Book.* Rockland, ME: Maine Island Trail Association, 1991. The Maine Island Trail Association publishes this guidebook packed with charts and information only for its members (basic membership if $45.00). For information write to: Maine Island Trail Association, P.O. Box C, Rockland, ME 04841, or call 207-596-6456.

Gibbs, David, and Sarah Hale. *Mountain Bike! Maine.* Birmingham, AL: Menasaha Ridge Press, 1998. $15.95. Hale and Gibbs detail 78 great rides, many of them within 10 miles of the coast.

Isaac, Jeff, and Peter Goth. *The Outward Bound Wilderness First-Aid Handbook.* Lyons & Burford, 1991. 252 pp., index, illus., $14.95. A must-have for anyone discovering the coast by kayak, canoe, sailboat, foot or bike.

Taft, Hank, and Jan, and Curtis Rindlaub. *A Cruising Guide to the Maine Coast.* Peaks Island, Maine: Diamond Pass Publishing 2002. This is the bible for boaters in Maine waters, updated.

Peirson, Elizabeth C., and Jan Erik Peirson. *A Birder's Guide to Maine.* Camden: Down East Books, 1996. 400 pp., illus., $23.95. This is the book birders will want at their side to distinguish teals from mergansers.

Rindlaub, Curtis. *The Maine Coast Guide for Small Boats; Casco Bay.* Peaks Island, ME: Diamond Bay Publishing, 2000. Public access for small boats up and down Casco Bay, outfitters, restaurants, campgrounds, with nautical charts.

Venn, Tamsin. *Sea Kayaking Along The New England Coast.* Boston: Appalachian Mountain Club, 1990. 240 pp., maps, photos, $14.95.

BOOKS YOU CAN BORROW

*The Chase Emerson
Memorial Library in
Deer Isle.*

Herb Swanson

Brault, Gerard. *The French-Canadian Heritage in New England.* Hanover and London: University Press of New England, and Kingston and Montreal: McGill-Queen's University Press, 1986. 264 pp., index, illus.

Caldwell, Bill. *Maine Coast.* Portland: Guy Gannet Publishing Co., 1988. 398 pp. Two collections of a journalist's rambling monologues about the people he has met and places he has visited.

Caldwell, Erskine. *Midsummer Passion and Other Tales of Maine Cussedness.* Camden, ME: Yankee Books. 192 pp. Fifteen short stories Erskine Caldwell wrote while living in Maine.

Carson, Rachel. *The Edge of the Sea.* New York: Houghton Mifflin Company, 1955. The famous naturalist and ecologist's essays on the coast. If you like this, you'll enjoy her other books, *The Sea Around Us* and *Silent Spring.*

Coffin, Robert Tristam. *Saltwater Farm.* New York: Macmillan, 1939. 114 pp., illus. Poetry by the premier poet and prose writer of Maine's middle coast.

Conkling, Philip. *Islands in Time.* Camden, ME: Down East Books, 1981. 222 pp., illus. Former Outward Bound naturalist, now head of the Island Institute, provides a lyrical history of Maine's coastal islands from an ecologist's point of view.

Doty, C. Stewart, ed. *The First Franco-Americans. New England Life Histories from the Federal Writers Project, 1938-1939.* Orono, ME: University of Maine Press, 1985. 163 pp., photos. Collected interviews of first-generation immigrants from Acadia and Quebec.

Eckstorm, Fannie Hardy. *Indian Place Names of the Penobscot Valley and the Maine Coast.* Orono, ME: University of Maine Press, 1978. An interesting journey through Maine by way of Penobscot Indian language and legend.

Federal Writers' Project of the Works Progress Administration, State of Maine.

Maine: A Guide 'Downeast.' Boston: Houghton Mifflin Co., 1937. 458 pp., index, illus., photos. Try to get hold of this thick volume or the revised version, which was published in 1970 by Dorris Isaacson and the Maine Historical Society. It is a thorough account of all Maine: its history, natural wonders, and recreation.

Jewett, Sarah Orne. *The Country of the Pointed Firs.* Boston and New York: Houghton Mifflin Company, 1929. 306 pp.

Leeker, Robert, and Kathleen R. Brown, eds. *An Anthology of Maine Literature.* Orono, ME: University of Maine Press, 1982. 260 pp. A collection of works by native and out-of-state writers, including Nathaniel Hawthorne, Henry David Thoreau, Harriet Beecher Stowe, Sarah Orne Jewett, and Kenneth Roberts.

Monegain, Bernie. *Coastal Islands: A Guide to Exploring Main's Offshore Isles.* Freeport, ME: DeLorme Mapping Company, 1988. 48 pp., index, maps, photos, $4.95.

————. *Natural Sites: A Guide to Maine's Natural Phenomena.* Freeport, ME: Delorme Mapping Company, 1988. 48 pp., index, maps, photos.

Pierson, Elizabeth Cary and Jan Erik Pierson. *The Birders Guide to the Coast of Maine.* Camden, ME: Down East Books. Birds that nest and visit, summer and winter, on the coast and its islands.

Shain, Charles, and Samuella Shain. *The Maine Reader.* New York: Houghton Mifflin Company, 1991. Illus. Four hundred years of Maine through the eyes of explorers, writers, painters, and photographers.

Williamson, William D. *History of the State of Maine (2 vols.) 1602-1820, 1832.* An overview of Maine's history and geography before it became a state.

Willis, William, ed. *Journals of Rev. Thomas Smith and Rev. Samuel Deane, 1849.* The author of this book was a Portland minister whose record of daily life during the Revolutionary War is interesting in its thoroughness.

CLIMATE, WEATHER & WHAT TO WEAR

Maine seasons go by their own timetable. Spring bulbs will often bloom as late as mid-June. Summer generally remains temperate throughout July and August. Cool days of autumn frequently extend well past the foliage's fall, and although it has been known to snow up to 70 inches in one winter, harsh northern winter winds are usually softened by warmer ocean temperatures.

The state's climate is governed by the "prevailing westerlies," the belt of eastward-moving air that encircles the globe at the middle latitudes. The westerlies and warm ocean currents ensure that prolonged hot and cold spells are rare, although coastal weather—with the added moisture from the ocean—can be extremely changeable. Fogs frequently descend upon the coast, and are a reason why Maine mariners are famed the world over for their navigational skills. There are an average of 59 foggy days every year at Quoddy Head Light near Lubec.

> ### What to Wear in Maine
>
> *Rainy days are tough on pedestrians, but I grew up in Maine, so I have no qualms about wearing really dorky clothes when it rains.*
>
> —Al Daimon, Maine's "walking" newsman,
> quoted in *Casco Bay Weekly*
>
> *As I write this, I am wearing heavy long underwear, wind pants, three layers of insulation under a water-resistant jacket, wool socks, a wool hat and fingerless gloves. I look ridiculous, especially since it is now early June. But I'm on a small boat, and it is wicked cold out here.*
>
> —Jeff Isaac, Maine sailor

Knowing how to dress for coastal weather requires understanding the relationship between wind, water, and land. The effects of the ocean can significantly moderate the weather on the islands and for a few miles inland, depending on the direction of the wind. Water off the coast is part of an upwelling of the Labrador Current that has its origin under the polar ice cap. Although the water has traveled hundreds of miles to get here, it still feels like icebergs. The air—or wind—passing over coastal waters is cooled and humidified before it arrives ashore.

On a typical sunny summer day, warm air rises over the mainland and the cool and dense air over the ocean is drawn in to replace it. This produces the summer southwesterly sea breeze. Temperatures along the immediate coast and islands will reflect that of the ocean, which only reaches 60 degrees by late summer, air temperatures range from 60 to 90 degrees, with the warmest temperatures around 80, in mid- to late July. Approaching the coast on a hot day you can feel the air temperature drop 10 or 15 degrees, and often a thick fog will roll in.

If you're headed for the shore, carry a jacket and a pair of long pants, no matter what the TV weather personality says. This is especially true if you're boarding a boat. Unless a frontal passage or storm system is expected, you can leave your foul-weather gear in the trunk.

Clothes should be loose and comfortable for scrambling over rocks and through spruce and raspberry bushes. Garments should be versatile enough to handle rapid changes in temperature. Shorts are fine for strolling or trail hiking during the day when it's warm. If you're going any distance, bring wind pants for protection against the sea breeze and bugs. Summer nights are almost always cool. A medium-weight sweater will get plenty of use. If you cannot bring all of them, choose wool or fleece over cotton. Those fabrics will keep moisture away from your skin, and therefore keep you warmer.

Lightweight hiking shoes are also a good idea. Maine is really just a very thin layer of topsoil over a very thick layer of coarse-grained granite. Since you don't want to damage the soil layer, most of your walking will be on the rocks. The soft soles of sandals and sneakers are quickly worn smooth by avid hikers.

One of the most useful items is a pair of knee-high rubber boots. The tide range in Maine runs from eight to 20 feet, exposing thousands of tidal pools and clam flats for exploring. A good pair of "worm boots" can make your whole trip. Add a cozy pair or two of socks, and they're great for snow, too.

Never mind what the calendar says, fall can begin on the coast during the third week of August. By this time, summer has lost its grip. Increasingly frequent cold fronts bring the prevailing winds to the west and northwest. With the wind off the land, temperatures reflect the cooling mass of the North American continent. Frosts and freezing temperatures can occur from October to May, although Portland experiences only 132 freezing days every year and is usually only four degrees cooler than Boston. The coast receives about 46 inches of precipitation annually. Of that precipitation, it snows only 15 or 20 days, and there are only 10 to 20 thunderstorms every year.

For fall and winter travel in coastal Maine, bring everything from shorts to winter gear, and expect to change often. Good foul-weather gear is essential unless you plan to spend a lot of time indoors. When an approaching winter storm swings the wind to the south or east, the breeze brings relative warmth. Wind off the water can melt the snow out from under your cross-country skis as fast as it fell. The day can seem downright balmy, until the next front sends the temperature plummeting. Precipitation can alternate quickly between rain and snow as the conflicting land and ocean air masses meet.

Spring on the coast can be a real tease. The ocean is very reluctant to warm up. This creates a drastic difference between inland and coastal temperatures and an even more drastic difference between your expectations and reality. You pull out your bathing suit, head for the beach and find that the water is still 43 degrees. The key is to expect it. Remember your fall and winter wardrobe? Bring it. If the wind is off the water, you'll need it. Away from the shore, or with a shore breeze, you can lie around with as little on as at a summer picnic. It all depends on the wind.

People who enjoy reading about the weather will want to look for The Weather Report column in the weekly newspaper *Maine Times*. The rambling weather and natural life accounts are gathered from residents who regularly observe the great outdoors from their windows onto the harbor or field. People from all places along the coast and inland give colorful reports of "flaming

---

Fogs in Maine

E. B. White gave us one of the best descriptions of a Maine fog in his 1948 *Atlantic Monthly* essay titled "Death of Pig."

We had been having an unseasonable spell of weather—hot, close days, with the fog shutting in every night, scaling for a few hours in midday, then creeping back again at dark, drifting in first over the trees on the point, then suddenly blowing across the fields, blotting out the world and taking possession of houses, men, and animals.

swamp maples" or a jack-in-the-pulpit discovered while out looking for mushrooms or pulling up the boat.

For frequently updated coastal and marine weather information, call the National Weather Service, 207-688-3210.

HANDICAPPED SERVICES

A lmost all state and national parks in Maine provide access and facilities for the physically impaired. Most motels and hotels also have rooms easily accessible to the handicapped, although many historic buildings and inns have either not yet complied with or are exempt from the Americans with Disabilities Act. We have tried to provide information on individual restaurants, inns, and bed-and-breakfast establishments that are accessible in the reviews listed the four coastal regions. To confirm, please call ahead.

To find out more about tourist facilities for the handicapped, contact the *Maine Tourism Association*, 207-623-0363 in state and 800-533-9595 out-of-state; P.O. Box 2300, Hallowell, ME 04347.

HOSPITALS

BAR HARBOR: Mount Desert Island Hospital 10 Wayman Ln., Bar Harbor 04609; 207-288-5081. Emergency Room open 24 hours.

BATH: Bath Health Care Center 1356 Washington St., Bath 04530; 207-443-5524; Care for non-life-threatening illness, 8am–8pm.

BELFAST: Waldo County General Hospital 118 Northport Ave., Belfast 04915; 207-338-2500.Emergency Room open 24 hours.

BIDDEFORD: Southern Maine Medical Center 1 Medical Center Dr., Biddeford 04005; 207-283-7000; Emergency Room open 24 hours.

BLUE HILL: Blue Hill Memorial Hospital Water St., Blue Hill 04614; 207-374-2836. Emergency Room open 24 hours.

BOOTHBAY HARBOR: St. Andrews Hospital 3 St. Andrews Ln., Boothbay Harbor 04538; 207-633-2121; Emergency Room open 24 hours.

BRUNSWICK: Parkview Hospital 329 Maine St., Brunswick 04011; 207-729-1641; Emergency Room open 24 hours.

DAMARISCOTTA: Miles Memorial Hospital, 35 Miles St., Damariscotta 04543; 207-563-1234; Emergency Room open 24 hours. Also a walk-in clinic from 8-8

ELLSWORTH: Maine Coast Memorial Hospital 50 Union St., Ellsworth 04605; 207-667-5311. Emergency Room open 24 hours.

MACHIAS: **Down East Community Hospital** Upper Court St., Machias 04654; 207-255-3356; Emergency Room open 24 hours.

PORTLAND: **Maine Medical Center, Brighton Campus** 335 Brighton Ave., Portland 04102; 207-879-8000; 9–9 walk-in clinic.

PORTLAND: **Maine Medical Center** 22 Bramhall St., Portland 04102; 207-871-0111; Emergency Room open 24 hours.

PORTLAND: **Mercy Hospital** 144 State St., Portland 04101; 207-879-3000; Emergency Room open 24 hours.

ROCKPORT: **Penobscot Bay Medical Center** 6 Glen Cove, Rockport 04856 ; 207-596-8000; Emergency Room open 24 hours.

YORK: **York Hospital** 15 Hospital Dr., York 03909; 207-363-4321; Emergency Room open 24 hours.

LATE NIGHT FOOD AND FUEL

The coffee pot is always on all night at the service desk at L.L. Bean, the famous store that remains open 24 hours every day, including Christmas and Thanksgiving. If you need more than coffee—say fuel for your car or your body—here is a short list of notable late-night or all-night stores, restaurants, and gas stations.

CAMDEN: **Cappy's Chowder House** (food), 207-236-2254, 1 Main St., Camden. Daily 11am–10pm, but closed Wed. in the winter).

KITTERY: **Howell's Auto Truck Stop** (food and fuel), 207-439-2466, Rte. 1 bypass, Kittery. Open 24 hours. Restaurant closes during the night, but the pumps and store remain open.

PORTLAND: **Cumberland Farms** (food market and fuel), 207-780-8032, 801 Washington Ave., Portland. Open 24 hours.

PORTLAND: **Denny's Restaurants** (food), 207-774-1886, 1101 Congress Ave., Portland (Congress St. exit off Rte. 295). Open 24 hours.

WISCASSET: **Red's Eats** (food), 207-882-6128, Rte. 1, Wiscasset. Open summer only.

MEDIA

Tr. [Trooper] Joseph Tibbets investigated a burglary at a private camp in Twp. 24. The only item stolen was a hand-operated well pump, however, a chain saw was used to gain entrance through the door.

—*The Downeast Coastal Press*, Sept. 16, 1991

The news business on the coast of Maine is dominated by two major newspaper companies, which publish the *Bangor Daily News* to the north and the *Portland Press Herald* and *Maine Sunday Telegram* to the south. To really learn about the area is to read about it through the eyes of the people who live and work here. For that reason, we recommend reading one of the several flourishing weeklies published on the coast.

Down East, based in Camden, is the granddaddy of Maine magazines, but during the past decade dozens of younger magazines have sprung up, from *Ocean Navigator*, rumored to have been Walter Cronkite's favorite magazine, to *WoodenBoat, National Fisherman* and *Coastal Fisheries News*. Many of these reflect the mariners' lifestyle. Then there are specialty magazines and newspapers like *Maine Antique Digest*, a thick tabloid packed with articles on art, antiques, and Americana, where to get it, and if you missed it, what it went for. *The Maine Times* (800-439-8866, P.O. Box 2129, Bangor, ME 04402-2129) is a great place to look for coastal summer rentals—despite its moving inland from Topsham. It's also a good source for those interested in Maine's liberal agenda. Following is a roundup of the media you will find on the coast.

NEWSPAPERS

BAR HARBOR: *The Bar Harbor Times,* 800-479-3312, www.courierpub.com; P.O. Box 68, 76 Cottage St., Bar Harbor 04609; weekly.

BATH: *Coastal Journal,* 800-649-6241; www.coastaljournal.com; 99 Commercial St., P.O. Box 575, Bath 04530.

BELFAST: *The Republican Journal,* 207-338-3333, www.courier.com; Box 327, High St., Belfast 04915; prjmail@agate.net; weekly. *Waldo Independent,* 207-338-5100, 107 Church St., Belfast 04915; weekly.

BIDDEFORD: *Journal Tribune,* 888-429-1535; www.journaltribune.com; P.O. Box 627, Biddeford 04005; daily. Known as a photographer's paper, and a pleasant place to do serious journalism.

BLUE HILL: *The Weekly Packet,* 207-374-2341, Main St., Blue Hill 04614; weekly.

BOOTHBAY HARBOR: *The Boothbay Register,* 207-633-4620; boothbayregis ter.maine.com; 95 Townsend Ave., P.O. Box 357, Boothbay Harbor 04538; weekly.

BRUNSWICK: *Brunswick Times Record,* 800-734-6397; www. timesrecord.com; Industry Rd., Brunswick 04011.

CAMDEN: *The Camden Herald,* 207-236-8511; www.courierpub.com; Box 248, Camden 04843; weekly.

CASTINE: *Castine Patriot,* 207-326-9300, P.O. Box 205, Castine 04421; weekly.

DAMARISCOTTA: *Lincoln County News,* 207-563-3171, Box 36, Damariscotta 04543; lcn@lincoln. midcoast.com; weekly. *The Lincoln County Weekly;* 207-563-5006, www.courier.com; lcwmail@courierpub.com; P.O. Box 1287, Damariscotta 04543.

EASTPORT: *The Quoddy Tides,* 207-853-4806, 123 Water St., Eastport 04631.

ELLSWORTH: *The Ellsworth American,* 207-667-2576; www.ellsworthamerican .com; 30 Water St., P.O. Box 509, Ellsworth 04605; weekly. One of America's truly great small-town papers. *The Ellsworth Weekly,* 207-667-5514, www.-courierpub.com; P.O. Box 1122, Ellsworth 04605.

KENNEBUNK: *York County Coast Star,* 207-485-2961; www.seacoastonline .com; P.O. Box 979, Kennebunk 04043; weekly. Founded in 1877; several reporters for this aggressive tabloid have gone on to work for the Boston Globe and other big papers.

MACHIAS: *Machias Valley News Observer,* 207-255-6561, P.O. Box 357, Machias 04654; weekly

PORTLAND: *Casco Bay Weekly,* 800-286-6601; www.cascobayweekly.com; 561A Congress St., Portland 04102; free weekly. Great for entertainment news and the skinny on the state's largest city. A worthy alternative to the big daily. *Portland Press Herald/Maine Sunday Telegram,* 800-894-0031; www.portland.com; P.O. Box 11350, Portland 04104. The state's biggest daily.

ROCKLAND: *The Courier-Gazette,* 207-594-4401; www.courierpub.com; 1 Park Dr., P.O. Box 249, Rockland 04841; published Tuesday, Thursday and Saturday.

STONINGTON: *Island Ad-Vantages,* 207-367-2200, P.O. Box 36, Stonington 04681; weekly.

YORK: *The York Weekly,* 207-363-4343; www.seacoastonline.com; 17 Woodbridge Rd., P.O. Box 7, York 03909.

MAGAZINES

Down East Magazine, 800-766-1670, Box 679, Camden 04843; www.down east.com. Bills itself as the magazine of Maine; two-thirds of their 85,000 readership live out of state.

FlyRod & Reel, 800-766-1670; www.flyrod reel.com P.O. Box 370, Camden 04843.

Golf Course News, 207-846-0600; www.golfcoursenews.com; 106 Lafayette St., Yarmouth 04096. Trade tabloid for the greens crowd.

Gourmet News, 207-846-0600; www.gourmetnews.com; 106 Lafayette St., Yarmouth 04096. Trade magazine for the fancy food industry.

Maine Antique Digest, 207-832-4888; www.maineantiquedigest.com; 911 Main St., P.O. Box 1429, Waldoboro 04752.

Maine Boats and Harbors, 207-236-8622; www.maineboats.com; 21 Elm St., P.O. Box 758, Camden 04843.

National Fisherman, 207-842-5608; www.nationalfisherman.com; 121 Free St., Portland 04101. A color glossy founded in 1903, they cover commercial fishing and boat building, as well as other marine-related stories.

Ocean Navigator, 207-772-2466; navigatorpublishing@compuserve.com; 18 Danforth St., Portland 04101.

Salt Magazine, 207-761-0660; www.salt.edu; 110 Exchange St., Portland 04101. Journalistic interviews and studies of the "real people of Maine"; great photos.

WoodenBoat, 207-359-4651; www.wooden boat.com; P.O. Box 78, Brooklin 04616. Beautiful to look at. Covers the design, building, care, preservation, and use of wooden boats, whether commercial or pleasure, old or new, sail, or power.

RADIO

WALZ-FM 95.3; 888-855-2992; Machias; Classic hits.

WBACH-FM, 207-967-0993, 106.3; Kennebunk; Classical.

WBLM-FM 102.9; 207-774-6364; Portland; Album-oriented rock, classic rock.

WBYA-FM 105.5; 207-594-1450; Islesboro; Big band swing and jazz.

WCYY-FM 92.9; 207-774-6364; Portland; New rock.

WERU-FM 89.9; 207-469-6600; East Orland; Diverse music from A to Z, good stuff.

WGAN-AM 560; 207-774-4561; Portland; Talk, Imus, news, sports.

WHOM-FM 94.9; 207-774-6364; Portland; Easy listening.

WJBQ-FM 97.9; 207-774-6364; Portland.

WJTO-AM 730; 207-443-6671; Bath, ABC; Oldies.

WKSQ-FM 94.5; 207-667-7573; Ellsworth; Adult contemporary, light/soft rock.

WLKE-FM 99 207-667-7573; Ellsworth; Country.

WMCM-FM 103.3 207-594-1450; Rockland; Real Country.

WMEA-FM 90.1; 800-884-1717; Portland; Maine Public radio.

WMED-FM 89.7; 800-884-1717; Calais; Maine Public Radio

WMEH FM 90.9; 800-884-1717; Bangor; Maine Public Radio

WMEP-FM 90.5; 800-884-1717; Camden; Maine Public Radio

WMGX-FM 93.1, 207-774-4561; Contemporary and classic hits.

WMPG-FM 90.9 and 104.1; 207-780-4424; Portland; Full service, eclectic.

WPOR-AM 101.9; 207-774-4561; Portland; Country.

WMEM-FM 106.1; 800-884-1717; Presque Isle; Maine Public Radio

WQDY-FM 92.7; 888-855-2992; Calais; Classic Hits.

WQEZ-FM 104.7 Kennebunk Light Rock

WQSS-FM 102.5; 207-594-1450; Camden; Rock with a hard edge.

WRED-FM 96; 888-700-9560; Saco; eclectic.

WRKD-AM 1450; 207-594-1450; Rockland; Talk, news, sports.

WTHT-FM 107.5; 207-797-0780; Portland; Country.

WWMJ-FM 95.7; 800-640-4941; Ellsworth; Oldies.

WYNZ-FM 100.9; 207-774-4561; South Portland; Oldies.

WZAN-AM 970; 207-774-4561; Portland; News and talk.

TELEVISION

Maine Public Television Channel 10; 207-783-9101, Lewiston, PBS.
UPN Channel 35; 207-772-3535, Portland, UPN
WCSH-TV Channel 6; 207-828-6666, Portland, NBC.
WGME-TV Channel 13; 207-797-9330, Portland, CBS.
WMTW-TV Channel 8; 207-775-1800, Portland and Auburn, ABC.
WPXT-TV Channel 51; 207-774-0051, Portland, Fox.

REAL ESTATE

If, after visiting the coast, you decide you want to own a piece of it, you can write to the *MaineReal Estate Commission*, 35 State House Station, Augusta 04333 (207-624-8515) for a list of real estate agents in the areas you like. The fee is $30. That office also can provide names of agents who handle seasonal rentals in coastal areas.

Also, good references for those looking to rent or own along the coast are the *Maine Times* and *Down East* magazine. During late spring, the *Maine Times* publishes a special summer vacation guide with classifieds for rental properties. The supplement is usually available all summer at newsstands throughout the state. *Down East* runs a monthly real estate classified section as well. See "Media," above, for further information about these publications.

ROAD SERVICE

Portland

AAA Maine www.aaanne.com; 425 Marginal Way, 04104; Mon.–Fri. 8:30–6, Sat. 9–1. 207-780-6800 or 800-482-7497.

South Portland

AAA Maine www.aaanne.com; 443 Western Ave., 04106; Mon.–Fri. 9–6, Sat. 9–1. 207-775-6211 or 800-336-6211.

TOURIST INFORMATION

There are several publicly funded information centers and state agencies that provide visitor information. In addition, most chambers of commerce will gladly send packets of information to people planning a stay in their area. Here is an abbreviated list of agencies and chambers for coastal Maine.

FISHING AND HUNTING REGULATIONS

Dept. of Inland Fisheries and Wildlife 207-287-8000; www.state.me.us/ifw; webmaster_isw@state.me.us; 284 State St., Augusta 04333;.

VISITOR INFORMATION and CHAMBERS OF COMMERCE

Acadia National Park Headquarters 207-288-3338; www.nps.gov/acad; P.O. Box 177, Bar Harbor 04609.

Convention and Visitors Bureau of the Greater Portland Visitor Information Center 207-772-5800; www.visitportland.com;cbb@cybertours.com; 305 Commercial St., Portland 04101

Freeport Merchants Association 207-865-1212; www.freeportusa.com; chamber@freeportusa.com; P.O. Box 452, Freeport 04032.

Kittery Information Center (Maine Tourism Association) 207-439-1319; www.mainetourism.com; I-95 and Rte. 1, P.O. Box 396, Kittery 03904.

Kittery Outlet Association 888-KITTERY, www.thekitteryoutlets.com.

Maine Tourism Association 207-623-0363; 800-533-9595 out-of-state and Canada; www.mainetourism.com; metainfo@mainetourism.com; P.O. Box 2300, Hallowell 04347.

Mt. Desert Region 207-276-5040; P.O. Box 675, Northeast Harbor, 04662.

Portland's Downtown District 207-772-6828; www.portlandregion.com; 94 Free St.,. Portland 04101.

Bar Harbor Chamber of Commerce 207-288-5103; www.barhaborinfo.com; visitors@barharborinfo.com; P.O. Box 158, Bar Harbor 04609.

Blue Hill Chamber of Commerce 207-374-3242; P.O. Box 520, Blue Hill 04614.

Bath-Brunswick Area Chamber of Commerce 207-725-8797; www.midcoast maine.com; chamber@midcoastmaine.com; 59 Pleasant St., Brunswick 04011.

Belfast Area Chamber of Commerce 207-338-5900; www.belfastmaine.org; info@belfastmaine.org; P.O. Box 58, Belfast 04915.

Boothbay Harbor Region Chamber of Commerce 207-633-2353; www.booth bayharbor.com; seamaine@boothbayharbor.com; P.O. Box 356, Boothbay Harbor 04539.

Camden-Rockport-Lincolnville Chamber of Commerce 207-236-4404; www. camden me.org; chamber@camdenme.org; P.O. Box 919, Camden 04843.

Damariscotta Region Chamber of Commerce 207-563-8340; www.drcc.org/; info@damariscottaregion.com; P.O. Box 13, Damariscotta 04543.

Deer Isle-Stonington Chamber of Commerce, 207-348-6124; www.deerisle maine.com; P.O. Box 469, Stonington 04681.

Eastport Area Chamber of Commerce 207-853-4644; www.nemaine.com/east portcc; eastportcc@nemaine.com; P.O. Box 254, Eastport 04631

Ellsworth Area Chamber of Commerce 207-667-2617; www.ellsworthcham ber.org; P.O. Box 267, Ellsworth 04605.

Kennebunk-Kennebunkport Chamber of Commerce 207-967-0857; www.visit thekennebunks.com; P.O. Box 740, Kennebunk 04043.

Machias Bay Area Chamber of Commerce 207-255-4402; www.nemaine.com /mbacc; P.O. Box 606, Machias 04654.

Ogunquit Chamber of Commerce 207-646-2939; www.ogunquit.org; P.O. Box 2289, Ogunquit 03907.

Old Orchard Beach Chamber of Commerce; 800-365-9386; www.oldorchard beachmaine. com; info@oldorchardbeachmaine.com; P.O. Box 600, Old Orchard Beach 04064.

Portland's Chamber of Commerce; 207-772-2811.

Rockland/Thomaston Area Chamber of Commerce 207-596-0376; www.mid coast.com/~rtacc; E-mail, rtacc@midcoast.com; P.O. Box 508, Rockland 04841.

Wells Chamber of Commerce 207-646-2451; www.wellschamber.org; wellscham ber@wellschamber.org; P.O. Box 356, Rte. 1, Wells, ME 04090.

Yarmouth Information Center 207-846-0833; U.S. Rte. 1/Exit 17, I-95, P.O. Box 1057, Yarmouth 04096.

York Chamber of Commerce; 207-363-4422; www.yorkme.org; york@gwi.net; 1 Stonewall Lane, York 03909.

Herb Swanson

A view of Jordan Pond in Acadia National Park on Mount Desert Island.

IF TIME IS SHORT

If I had money but little time, I would reserve the Ship Merchant Suite at The Captain Lord Inn in Kennebunkport (207-967-3141, www.captainlord.com), for a night in the fall, when the gas fireplace by the bathtub would make a pleasant heat. I would check in and bathe and then drive down to Ogunquit for dinner at 98 Provence (207-646-9898, www.98 provence.com), where another fireplace, burning wood, greets you on a cold night, just inside the front door, and where the bustle and smells are redolent with good food and civilized pleasure. The handsome waiter would have an accented speech about delicious specials, and I might have to ask him to repeat himself; but perhaps this time I would choose the table d'hôte menu, and good red wine, and enjoy the sense that I had all the time in the world, and that Provence was the place to be when winter was blowing the leaves around on the ground.

If I wanted a less extravagant room rate, I would stay at The Eastland Park Hotel (207-775-5411, www.eastlandparkhotel.com), where four million dollars have swept away the old and rebirthed the original elegance of a city hotel. I would leave the hotel, which sits on the top of a hill, walk down Congress Street to Exchange Street to visit the shops, browse in Books, Etc., drink coffee at Arabica on Free Street, and then walk down Middle Street to Hugo's, (207-774-8538, hugos.net), where I would have made a reservation when I made arrangements for the hotel room. What I may have saved on the room rate would work nicely to splurge on the Chef's tasting menu, which I would also have chosen when I made the reservation. In fact, why not choose the night to visit Portland based on the schedule you can find on the web, for elaborate dinners featuring wines from The Clown, just down the street from Hugo's? I wonder what they would choose to serve alongside the "fish sandwich" made of crispy loup de mer on toasted brioche, with caper remoulade? Or with the oyster shooter with celery juice and chile oil? Another night there is venison osso buco ravioli with root vegetables and juniper berries.

And the next morning I would visit Standard Bakery (207-773-2112, 75 Commercial Street, Portland) for the best morning buns this side of paradise. I would also try to get tickets for next spring and summer games of the Portland Sea Dogs (207-879-9500; Hadlock Field, Park St., Portland), because I'd be feeling like I loved this town and wanted to come back when the weather warmed up.

Now it is summer, and I want an experience of the coast in all its natural beauty; then my destination must be, as it is for so many, Acadia National Park (207-288-3338; Mount Desert Island). Perhaps because this park is the destination of so many visitors, the people of Mount Desert Island have worked hard to make it sustain them; and I would gladly leave my car keys at home, fly directly to Bar Harbor Airport, and take the **Island Bus System** directly to my bed and breakfast, **Sunset on West** (207-288-4242, www.sun setonwest.com, 115 West Street, Bar Harbor 04609). Nancy and Mel Johnson have the maps and answer all the questions, as well as make a delicious breakfast I can eat on their porch, in a house that was one of Bar Harbor's "cottages" and might give me, if I stoke my imagination, the feeling of being a summer visitor a century ago. However I do prefer my own world, troubled though it is, where as a woman I can travel alone. I would go in the morning to **The New Abbe Museum**, 207-288-3519, www.abbemuseum.org, 26 Mount Desert Street, Bar Harbor), and see what the curators have put together, but I would not neglect the old **Abbe Museum**, at Sieur de Monts Spring. If I could I would try to visit both during the Native American Festival, in the beginning of July, to see some of the new basket weaving and other work of Passamaquoddy and Penobscot Native Americans.

Dinner would take me to Mexico, because **The XYZ Restaurant** (207-244-5221, Shore Road, opposite Manset Town dock) has the best Mexican food most people have ever tasted. I would have had the requisite lobster roll at the airport, and gone on a long walk though the Acadia National Park woods, perhaps down the Wonderland Trail. I would be ready for tatemado, a dish from the Colina region: pork loin baked in a sauce of guajillo and ancho chiles. Chiles and garlic grow well in the Maine climate, if only for a short time, and I love them.

Index

LODGING BY PRICE CODE

Price Codes:

Inexpensive:	**Up to $65**
Moderate:	**$65 to $125**
Expensive:	**$125 to $180**
Very Expensive:	**$180 and up**

KITTERY TO KENNEBUNK

Inexpensive–Expensive
Seasons Inn, 43

Inexpensive–Very Expensive
Edwards' Harborside Inn, 47

Moderate
The Trellis House, 46

Moderate–Expensive
Dockside Guest Quarters, 47
Green Heron Inn, 45
Hartwell House, 46

Expensive
Inn at Portsmouth Harbor, 46

Expensive–Very Expensive
Cape Arundel Inn, 43
Captain Lord Mansion, 44
White Barn Inn, 45

PORTLAND REGION

Moderate
Atlantic Birches Inn, 75

Moderate–Expensive
Chebeague Inn, 74
The Eastland Park Hotel, 77
Isaac Randall House, 75
West End Inn, 79

Moderate–Very Expensive
The Pomegranate Inn, 78

RESTAURANTS BY PRICE CODE

Inexpensive	Up to $10
Moderate	$10–$20
Expensive	$20–$30
Very Expensive	$30 or more

RESTAURANTS BY CUISINE

About the Author

Emma English

Nancy English writes essays for *Yankee* Magazine and *After the Sun* Magazine, and freelance articles for *Portland Monthly* She is at work on a novel about raising children in New York City. She lives in Portland, Maine, and loves its many wonderful restaurants and all the beautiful islands a ferry ride away in Casco Bay.